Deviance & Respectability

Deviance & Respectability

The Social Construction of Moral Meanings

Edited by

Jack D. Douglas

Basic Books, Inc., Publishers   *New York / London*

© 1970 by Basic Books, Inc.
Library of Congress Catalog Card Number: 71-103090
Cloth: SBN 465-01638-3
Paper: SBN 465-01637-5
Manufactured in the United States of America
Second Printing

The Authors

DONALD W. BALL lectures in sociology at the University of Victoria, British Columbia. He is interested principally in psychological sociology and deviant behavior, and specifically in the relationship between situational contexts and the selves and identities they provide.

ALAN F. BLUM, whose work is in sociological theory, is Assistant Professor of Sociology, New York University.

ALEXANDER DAVID BLUMENSTIEL, an Assistant Professor, teaches in Boston University's Department of Sociology and Anthropology. His fields of concentration include the sociology of knowledge, the sociology of relational processes, and ethnomethodology.

PAUL CAMPANIS, a research sociologist at Polaroid Corporation in Cambridge, Massachusetts, has taught sociology at Syracuse University. Organizations, industry, and sociological theory are his major scholarly interests.

NORMAN K. DENZIN, Assistant Professor of Sociology at the University of California, Berkeley, works in the field of symbolic interactionism. The author of *The Substance of Sociological Theory and Method: An Interactionist Interpretation,* he also co-edited *The Mental Patient: Studies in the Sociology of Deviance.*

JACK D. DOUGLAS, who wrote *The Social Meanings of Suicide,* is Associate Professor of Sociology at the University of California, San Diego. Sociological theory and deviance and social problems constitute his primary scholarly interests.

JAMES M. HENSLIN, an Assistant Professor of Sociology at Southern Illinois University in Edwardsville, considers social theory, deviance, and the family his chief scholarly interests.

JERRY JACOBS, chiefly interested in deviant behavior, sociological theory, and medical sociology, is Assistant Professor of Sociology at the University of California, Riverside. He is author of *The Search for Help: A Study of the Retarded Child in the Community.*

STANFORD M. LYMAN, co-editor of *A Sociology of the Absurd,* is Associate Professor of Sociology at the University of Nevada, Reno. Race relations and sociological theory are his major scholarly interests.

PETER MCHUGH's primary area of scholarship is social interaction. He teaches sociology at the City University of New York and has published *Defining the Situation: The Organization of Meaning in Social Interaction.*

Marvin B. Scott, Associate Professor of Sociology at Sonoma State College, Sonoma, California, centers his studies on sociological theory and deviance and social problems. He wrote *The Racing Game.*

Robert A. Scott, who works in the areas of sociological theory and deviance, is the author of *The Making of Blind Men* and is Assistant Professor of Sociology, Princeton University.

Ronald J. Silvers is Assistant Professor of Sociology, University of British Columbia, Vancouver. He is principally interested in the sociology of knowledge and in contemporary mass movements.

Gideon Sjoberg, Professor of Sociology at the City University of New York, is primarily interested in the area of urban sociology and theory, including the pre-industrial city.

Ted R. Vaughan considers the sociology of intellectual life his primary scholarly interest. He is Associate Professor, Department of Sociology, University of Missouri.

Martin S. Weinberg, co-editor of *Deviance: The Interactionist Perspective,* is Associate Professor of Sociology, Indiana University, Bloomington, and Senior Sociologist at the university's Institute for Sex Research. The sociology of deviance and the interpretation of social experience are his primary areas of investigation.

Preface

Man is necessarily a social animal. Without society, man cannot exist; without society, he cannot fulfill himself. He is born with a need for other human beings and cannot live without them. Yet social order, the precondition of social existence, cannot be a natural outcome of man's few instinctual drives and behavior patterns.

Human social order is necessarily problematic. Since we must have social order to exist, but cannot achieve it by simply living naturally, it becomes a crucial problem of our existence which we must solve if we are to exist at all. While not all human beings are aware of this existential problem and might inadvertently make the solution of the problem impossible if they were, it is always necessary for some individuals to be aware of the problem and to succeed in solving it for everyone, if we are to continue existing.

Man is also necessarily a symbolic animal, for it is only his capacity to create and work with symbols which he takes in some way to be real that allows him to solve the necessary problem of social order. Being unable to rely on shared instincts (or shared imprintings) to co-ordinate his interactions with his fellows, man must substitute a shared universe of (symbolic) meanings to achieve that co-ordination.

Shared rules are the most crucial social meanings involved in constructing social order. Throughout human experience thus far, shared rules have proven to be a necessary ingredient in constructing any social order that was not merely transitory. Only shared rules, which are essentially prescriptions and proscriptions of typical actions in typical everyday situations supported by various internal commitments and external sanctions, have proven capable thus far of producing the degree of ordering of interactions which human beings have found necessary for existence and for the good life.

While there are now important changes taking place, moral rules have been the most important rules in constructing social order in Western societies. Even governmental and organizational legal rules, which have been growing rapidly in importance in this respect for centuries, have normally been ultimately based on commonly shared

moral rules. Ethical rules, which now appear to be destined for as-
cendancy in the not distant future, are still dominated by moral rules.

Since sociology, like any scientific discipline, has from its begin-
nings been inspired by the problems of human society which its practitioners have felt to be crucial for our own existence, it is easy to see
why sociologists have always considered the problem of social order
to be their one fundamental problem. And, given the crucial importance of moral rules in constructing social order in our Western societies, it is also easy to see why Western sociologists have taken social
morality and its violations, which they have called "deviance" for the
last decade or so, to be a second crucial problem, the solution to
which they considered essential to solving the problem of social order.
As a result, the sociology of deviance has formed much of the core,
the foundation, of sociology.

It is to be expected, then, that any significant attempts to reconstruct fundamental sociological theory will take as a crucial part of
their task the thorough re-examination of the nature of moral meanings and their relations to the construction of social order. This is a
primary reason why the sociology of deviance has for some years been
the most creative and turbulent area of sociological theory.

The recent developments in the theory of deviance have been of
crucial importance in developing the new theoretical perspective on
man and society, the phenomenological or existential perspective. The
traditional perspective of sociological theory, the structural or structural-functional perspective, has implicitly assumed that moral rules are
social absolutes (nonproblematic), external to the individuals. Social
order is viewed as the result of shared socialization practices, stemming
primarily from shared moral rules producing shared ("doubly contingent") patterns of action that, taken together, constitute order in the
social world. The evolving perspective, for which there are several contending names, sees moral rules as problematic and requiring situa-
tioned constructions ("interpretations") for any concrete use ("application") in everyday life. Social order is seen, not as the outcome of
(absolute) forces external to the individuals, but, rather, as the result
of purposeful constructions of social order, in which the problematic
moral meanings are used as one part of the symbolic resources needed
thus far to construct order successfully in our society. The structural
perspective sees man as the product of social order: essence is before
existence. The evolving existential perspective sees social order as one
possibility of man's purposeful actions—one which is aided by, but by
no means necessitated by, the prior existence of social order.

The chapters in this book share in various ways the basic ideas of this evolving perspective. They are all concerned with the problems involved in the social construction of moral meanings and the uses of these constructed moral meanings in constructing social order for some group. All of them, then, are directed at what we see to be the fundamental problems of the theoretical foundations of sociology, the fundamental explanation of human social order.

Since I have tried to develop the basic ideas of this whole perspective clearly and systematically in the first chapter, "Deviance and Respectability: The Social Construction of Moral Meanings," there is no need to go into further details about it here. The other chapters in Part I provide excellent detailed treatments of major aspects of this theoretical perspective. Parts II and III consist of more detailed empirical studies of the theoretical problems dealt with more abstractly in Part I. I believe that in almost all cases the relations between the various chapters and the general (orderly) development of the argument throughout the book will be clear to the readers.

This book has been a co-operative effort in every way. The authors have contributed enthusiastically and, to my biased eye, brilliantly to the project. Without exception they have co-operated willingly in providing the inevitable revisions—those painful bits of self-surgery. As will be apparent, my own thought has profited greatly from their creative efforts. I only hope they feel they have benefited equally from their involvement in this creative venture—and that the readers will benefit most of all.

Jack D. Douglas

La Jolla, California
January, 1970

Contents

Part I

The Social Construction of Moral Meanings

1

Deviance and Respectability: The Social Construction of Moral Meanings

Jack D. Douglas

Of one thing we may be sure. If inquiries are to have any substantial basis, if they are not to be wholly up in the air, the theorist must take his departure from the problems which men actually meet in their own conduct. He may define and refine these; he may divide and systematize; he may abstract the problems from their concrete contexts in individual lives; he may classify them when he has detached them; but if he gets away from them he is talking about something which his own brain has invented, not about moral realities.

John Dewey and James Tufts, Ethics.

Deviance and respectability are necessarily linked together: each necessarily implies the other; each is a necessary condition for the existence of the other. This is by no means simply a matter of abstract and arbitrary definitions given to the terms by sociologists. Deviance and respectability are necessarily linked together in the social meanings of the terms as used by the members of our society in their everyday lives: when we observe and analyze the moral communications in our everyday lives we find that the social meanings of either deviance (immorality) or respectability (morality) can be adequately under-

3

stood only if reference, whether implicit or explicit, is made to the other, its opposite.

As some Christian theologians have argued over the centuries, without evil there would be no good, without Satan no God. The existence of Satan and his evil has not only been as necessary to Western man's way of thinking as God and his good but has at the same time been a necessary condition for adequately understanding the nature of God and his good. (This necessary relationship was, in fact, commonly expressed by the popular definition of evil as the absence of good or of good as the absence of evil.) To Western man being, certainly its moral aspect, is dualistic,[1] and many of the problems of his existence are concerned with working out the relations between this dual and oppositional nature of reality.

In the same way, in our everyday lives morality and immorality, respectability and disreputability, the otherworldly and the this-worldly, the sacred and the secular—each term necessarily implies the existence of its opposite and, consequently, depends on its opposite for its own meaning and, above all, for much of the force it exerts on our lives. Why should there be this necessary dependency between moral opposites?

For one thing, it seems likely that Plato was right in arguing that there are certain fundamental categories of existence that necessarily imply their opposites; or, rather, he would have been right at least in arguing that this is a basic premise of Western thought. As he saw, for Western man life necessarily implies death; death necessarily implies life; and each is wholly meaningful only because of the existence of its opposite. In the same way, he argued that truth and falsehood necessarily imply each other.

While it may be valuable for some purposes to try to explain the existence of this necessary and oppositional dualism, for our purposes here it is sufficient merely to note its existence, its taken-for-granted character in everyday moral communications, and then to proceed to analyze it and its consequences.

The most general consequence of this necessary linkage in social meanings between good and evil is that we will always have evil at the same time that—and precisely because—we have good. Going further, we should even expect that the more intense the belief in good, or the striving for it, the more intense will be the belief in evil, or the attacks on good. An age of saints, then, will also necessarily be an age of satans or demons, and vice versa. An individual striving for goodness will to the same degree be striving against evil, and vice versa.

We can see, then, just why it is that we always have "deviants" and "criminals" with us, why it is that immorality and crime seem such necessary parts of society. Durkheim was certainly right in arguing that immorality and crime are a necessary part of society, but he failed to see how fundamental this necessity is.[2] While it is certainly true, as John Adams and many other men who have helped to construct governments have long argued, that the (official) dramatization of evil-doing and its punishment serve to strengthen "good" behavior, it is far more important to see that the "good" behavior cannot exist unless there is also its opposite, the "evil" behavior. It is for this reason that immorality in its many forms is a necessary and inevitable part of our social reality. As long as our basic categories, our fundamental criteria for evaluating existence, are relativistic in this way, we will have evil, immorality, disreputability, and crime. And there is no indication at all that our basic categories are getting less relativistic. If we do eradicate our present evils, we will simply construct new ones. What really happens is that we eradicate some of our presently worse evils and then we readapt our comparisons: what used to be lesser evils are now the worse evils. (Anyone who objectively observes the current anguish in American society over our "terrible" social problems and immorality could hardly doubt the obvious truth of this statement: what used to be the lesser social problems are now the worse social problems.)

In addition, the comparisons or contrasts between good and evil are not simply linear comparisons—comparisons between better and worse. While it is true that there are social categories to designate many degrees of good and evil, and any comparison can be made in terms of better or worse, it is also true that any comparison between good and evil is at the same time a categorical or absolute comparison. That is, anything that is immoral is subject to the categorical distinction between good and evil. It is this categorical distinction which lies behind the dichotomizing of the social world into morally disjunct categories—right side of the tracks versus wrong side of the tracks, criminal versus noncriminal, stigmatized versus nonstigmatized, respectable versus disreputable, evil versus good, black versus white, and so on. The necessary opposition makes the deviant and criminal necessary, and the categorical contrast makes him into a necessarily different type of being. And, at the same time that good necessarily implies its opposite of evil (and vice versa), good necessarily implies a categorical contrast; if there is a good type, there must be an evil type.

Constructing the Moral Meanings of the Self
in American Society

The general consequence for each individual of the necessary comparisons between morality and immorality is that he must be concerned in all situations with his moral worth relative to the moral worth of other individuals. Except insofar as his self is socially identified with the selves of other individuals, as is true in all intimate relations, such as family relations, each individual gains in moral worth to the extent that others lose in moral worth, and vice versa. (To this extent, at least, moral evaluations constitute a "zero-sum game.") In fact, of course, one can be considered to be moral or respectable only if there are others, not identified with oneself, who are considered to be immoral or disreputable.

At the same time, each individual is constructing an image of himself as a moral (and normal) member of society that is plausible to himself and to significant others, primarily because this plausible image is the fundamental condition (or ground) for carrying on everyday social interaction.[3] To the extent, then, that each individual does want to construct this moral image of himself, he is necessarily committed to a competitive struggle to morally upgrade himself and morally downgrade others (not identified with himself). Since the necessary and opposite linkage between morality and immorality gives upgrading the self and downgrading others an equivalent effect in constructing a moral image of the self (to the extent the image is plausible), either upgrading the self or downgrading others may be employed, but one or the other moral tactic must be used.

We can see, then, why individuals choose to construct images of deviants and criminals and why they try to devise public (official) means for stigmatizing individuals as deviants and criminals. The more effective any individual or group of individuals is in getting the categories of deviance and crime imputed to others, the more effective he is in getting the categories of morality and law-abiding citizen imputed to himself. Others must be degraded if he is to be upgraded.

In American society this necessity of morally degrading others in order to upgrade the self has been greatly accentuated by the intense competitive struggle for social status. The various categories of social status, especially those concerning success and failure, have themselves become morally meaningful categories. While careful analyses of the moral meanings of status categories have yet to be done, it is apparent that the categorical status of poor (and, even more, that of lower class) has as one of its (abstract) meanings that of being immoral, at least to the large middle-class groups. On the other hand, being well off, successful, and so on, means (in the abstract) being virtuous to these same groups.[4] As a result of these moral meanings of status, the intense economic competition in our society has accentuated the need to degrade others in order to upgrade oneself. In fact, since general moral comparisons and status comparisons parallel each other (from best to worst on one scale paralleling best to worst on the other), and since both types of comparisons are relativistic in the same way, degrading and upgrading in terms of one set of comparisons can be made to stand partially for the other set of comparisons. For example, the rich can be presumed to be more virtuous, in general, so the laws and law enforcement directed at them can be the administrative civil laws, and sentences can be light (judges say they have "good prospects"), whereas the laws and law enforcement directed at the poor must be the "moralistic" criminal laws, and the sentences harsh (they have "poor—or bad—prospects"). Again, the very means of saying that someone is both poor and virtuous—that is, "poor *but* virtuous" —involves the presumption that one must normally (in the abstract) expect the poor to be wicked, since this "but" implies a contradiction of normal expectation.

At the same time, the emphases on equality and individual competition have weakened widespread identifications with groups, except with ethnic and racial groups, so that we have nearly a war of all against all in the struggle to upgrade the self and downgrade others. Where we have had common group identities, as in the cases of ethnic and racial identities, these membership categories have been invested with important moral-and-status meanings, so they have simply added to the general need to degrade others. This has been especially true in the case of the dichotomy made between white and colored (Indian, Mexican, Asian, and Negro), which has involved an almost complete parallel between the rankings of categories of color (caste), status, and morality. It is especially because of this nearly total correspondence that the colored groups have been such plausible targets for social degradation and have served so well the common need to degrade others in order to upgrade the self. (It is a common observation that the attempts to degrade those of color are most intense among the lower-class whites, who would be hardest pressed to find other individuals who can be *plausibly* degraded by them.) The once dominant ideas called racism simply served the purposes of such *degradation work* and of legitimizing this degradation ("keeping them in their place").

This confluence of forces producing degradation work and upgrading work has produced the strong tendency toward moralism so often noted in American society. It has also produced the strong support for official moralism, or the use of official agencies to stigmatize individuals, while at the same time helping to produce a great separation between *public morality* (or the publicly supported morality) and private morality (or the morality one adheres to in his private life).[5] If individuals were actually committed to the morality they publicly espouse, as structural-functionalists have generally assumed in sociology, we would probably not find this great separation between public life and private life. But this separation is just what we would expect to find, because it would show the social actors to be quite consistent from their own point of view, if they are partially using the public morality to degrade others, while hoping to be able to avoid such degradation themselves.

Since degrading others and upgrading the self are results of the nature of our social moral meanings and of our status and membership competition, we can expect them to go on as long as our moral meanings are the same, and they will be augmented as long as we have our struggles for status and membership. This means that if we do away with present forms of degradation, we will come up with others, unless the nature of morality (and of status and membership) changes. There is, however, evidence that the nature of morality is changing.

The Nature of Morality and Responsibility

Sociologists have generally preferred not to deal directly with morality and immorality or with the many related phenomena of everyday life—good and evil, respectability and disreputability, innocence and guilt, wicked, tarnished, angelic, and the like. Instead, they have followed the positivist practice of substituting phenomena of their own construction for those of common-sense, everyday life and then studying their own ad hoc phenomena as if these constituted "reality." They have done this in part to avoid the complexities and "biases" of common-sense terms, but the study of their ad hoc reality has simply created another level of complexity: since they have still wanted their studies to be ultimately related to everyday life, they have had to shift back and forth between their ad hoc phenomena and the everyday phenomena, constructing post hoc systems of translating devices and other devices.

The sociologists have generally substituted "values" for the common-sense term of "morality." They have then proceeded to construct many hundreds of confusing and sterile ad hoc definitions of values. In the process they have made things ever more complex and have proved unable to tell us much of value about the important matters of morality and immorality or the many related phenomena.

Philosophers, theologians, moralists, and many others have been more directly concerned with analyzing the everyday phenomena of morality for several thousand years. But they have normally been primarily concerned with discovering what is "really" moral and immoral, rather than with the scientific task of analyzing the properties of the everyday phenomena of morality and immorality. However, in the past fifty years or so the philosophers, and the others in turn, have become increasingly concerned with analyzing the language of morality. These linguistic philosophers, especially those who have taken seriously Wittgenstein's edict that the meaning of language is provided by its use, have had an increasing effect on sociologists' analyses of rules and meanings in general, as can be seen in Blum's analysis of the social meanings of "insanity." [6] Sociologists are now beginning to do the vast amount of research that will be required to determine, through the study of social usage, the meanings of morality—and rules in general— in everyday life. Until we have systematic participant-observer studies of moral meanings (in use), we shall be forced to make use of our current strategy, that is, making extensive use of our own common-sense experience to analyze everyday moral meanings, but tempering this by the use of whatever good participant-observer information we can obtain.

The basic problem with the ordinary approaches to the analysis of the meanings of morality is that they concentrate almost exclusively on disembodied moral statements, assuming that it will be possible eventually to produce a set of rules which can be used to generate all acceptable moral statements which members of society might make and that this kind of analysis provides the meanings of morality. But this kind of covert behaviorism violates the most basic principle of any analysis of social meanings and actions, the principle of the contextual determination of meaning: the concrete meaning of anything (rule, statement, and so forth) is adequately given to members only when its concrete or situated context is provided.[7] The linguist does, indeed, give careful consideration to the contextual effects to be found in conversations themselves. As Moermann has said, "One prominent feature

of conversations is that their participants orient to the sequential placement of the utterances which compose them. The situated intelligibility
which an utterance has for participants frequently depends upon the
particular ways in which they tie that utterance to particular preceding
ones." [8] But this approach still treats language as disembodied both
from the rest of subjective or phenomenal experience and from the
social situation in which the conversation occurs. Because these contexts are even very generally the determinants, for the members, of
both what is said and the meanings of what is said, as we can see in
such analyses (as Penzin's analysis of intimate relations [9]), this linguistic approach will not provide an adequate analysis of social meanings
and actions in everyday life. (They are, however, a necessary part of
such analyses of everyday life.)

Maurice Mandelbaum's phenomenological analysis of morals has
gone somewhat beyond the strictly linguistic approach by analyzing
the fundamental meanings of morals in the everyday experience of
members of society,[10] though he has remained at the philosophical
level, rather than making use of systematic observations and descriptions of moral arguments. As Mandelbaum sees it, there have been
three crucial dimensions of meaning involved in moral communications. First of all, moral experience has been seen by members of society as *external* to themselves, as *given* to them, rather than created
by them. Morality, then, is independent of the will of man and has, indeed, normally been seen as given by God (or by nature) to man.
Second, morality has been seen as necessary, so that there is no escap-
ing it by denying it or hiding from it. Even if one were sincerely as-
tounded to discover that he had done something immoral, he would
still be immoral for having done it—and would suffer divine punishment for it. These first two dimensions are actually general properties
of the absolutist world view which has almost completely dominated
Western thought until recently. This absolutist world view sees social
meanings in general (beliefs, ideas, truth, values, and so on) as part
of some necessary being that is timeless, eternal, external, and independent of man and to which man is necessarily subject.[11] Third, and
most distinctively, moral experience involves a feeling of "appropriateness."

There are a number of basic problems involved in this analysis of
moral experience. The most important problem is the seeming circu-
larity of the feeling of appropriateness. What meaning can one give to
appropriateness that is not already apparent in morality so that appropriateness provides a better understanding of morality? Appropriateness appears to be simply a more general term of which morality is

one form or type of appropriateness, so that morality may help us to better understand appropriateness, but it is very hard to see how the opposite can be true. The attempt to better understand morality in terms of appropriateness is actually an indication of how basic and irreducible the experience of morality is. It is so basic that it can hardly be defined in terms of other, more basic terms. Rather, it must be the basis for defining other terms and must remain largely undefinable except by the ostensive definition of pointing out to a fellow member of society that one means by moral experience the kind of feeling he has in such and such a situation (such as the contemplation of incest).

Another basic problem with this approach, and one which is intimately related to the first, is that it focuses on intrasubjective experience; that is, it deals with the experience of morality in the abstract or independently of concrete situations in which morals are used. Rather than being independent of social situations, a point of view which was fostered by the absolutist world view, concrete moral experience is necessarily intersubjective. That is, any concrete experience of morality necessarily involves the idea of actual or potential social response of approval or disapproval. (This is the idea behind the insight that calling something good, right, moral, or the like, simply means that one approves.) Even the saint in the desert struggling to purge his soul of evil is implicitly treating morality as an experience necessarily involving social response: to him something is moral or immoral because God has decreed it (it is good because God has decreed it, rather than God decreeing it because it is good), and he seeks to be moral by submitting to that decree. (It should be noted, however, that the ideas of God and of the good have been so interlocked that Western theologians have argued for centuries over whether God decrees the good because it is good or it is good because God decrees it, while agreeing that God is the good and so on. Because of the relationship of identity, or near identity, it seemed plausible to argue it either way; yet the combatants, like most combatants, could rarely take such a theoretic stance.)

We must, then, shift the focus of our analyses of moral experience. Rather than attempting to analyze moral experience in the abstract, or independently of its social context, we must always focus on the everyday uses of morality, both through linguistic statements and by other forms of communication, found in social interaction. When we shift our focus in this way we become concerned with somewhat different questions than those which have been of primary moment to Mandelbaum and other phenomenologists concerned with intrasubjective experience. Most importantly, we become concerned primarily with the conditions under which the members of society consider any concrete thing to be moral or immoral (approvable or disapprovable).

Sociologists first turned to this approach in considering the labeling processes [12] or categorization processes by which members of society imputed categories of morality and immorality to individuals. This early approach was a crucial break with the traditional structural approach, which took for granted the common-sense assumption that certain things are necessarily (homogeneously, unchangingly, and nonproblematically) considered immoral by the members of society.[13] Labeling theory argued, on the contrary, that the categorization of something or someone is an independent variable, so that it is problematic. The initial emphasis of the labeling theorists was on the effects of different labels on people, but it was a short jump to considering the social determinants of labeling processes.

But labeling theorists never came to see the problems involved in the application of categories. Most importantly, they never saw the need to determine the conditions under which one category would be applied rather than another. What Blum has argued about mental illness holds equally for meaningful categories in general: " 'Labelling theorists' . . . do not describe the labelling process, but rather, affirm that the process exists and use this as grounds for attacking traditional conceptions of mental illness." [14] What is needed to begin with is the microscopic analysis of the social uses of the categories to determine the general properties of such uses. Blum's analysis of the social uses of the categories of mental illness is one of the few attempts to do this and clearly shows the fundamental importance of the situational (social) contextual determination of the meanings of such categories for the members of society.

When we then analyze the specific conditions under which members of society consider someone (or his actions) to be moral or immoral, as Peter McHugh does in Chapter 3,[15] we find that the fundamental problem is that of determining the conditions of responsibility: under what conditions is an individual considered by members of our society to be (morally) responsible or (morally) unresponsible for a given event? We find in concrete situations that an individual is considered to be responsible for his actions if and only if (1) he has intended to commit those actions and knows the rules relevant to them (they have what McHugh calls theoreticity) and (2) he chose to commit those actions freely, without external restraint (they have conventionality). Actions can be considered to be moral or immoral, then, only to the degree that they are seen to be other than they might have been and done with the knowledge that they are moral or immoral.

The most important conclusion from this argument is that situational determinations of morality and immorality in our society are necessarily problematic. Since it is a necessary condition of morality and immorality that the actions performed might have been otherwise, there are necessarily grounds for argument with oneself and with others over the question of morality: if the actions had to be performed, if he had no arguable choice to make, then he could not possibly be (morally) responsible. As McHugh has put it, "Moral rules not only permit but create and require the possibility of argument, denial, and disconfirmation." [16] This is true as well because intention (and, to a lesser extent, all internal or subjective states) is necessarily problematic. This is true primarily because our common-sense epistemology (or theory of knowledge) considers all events not immediately sense-perceivable to be less certain (and less real).[17]

Given this necessarily problematic nature of moral meanings in our society, we must also conclude that there will necessarily be situational conflicts within and/or between individuals concerning any moral question. We are led, then, to conclude that, contrary to the assumptions of structural-functional and systems theories of society, conflicts over morality and immorality will necessarily occur even when individuals do share the same morals.

But it must also be apparent that social order is possible only if there are means either to resolve such necessary conflicts on other than moral grounds or to bridge them (contain their effects). In our society we find that many devices have been created and used to do both. We find that intention (and other internal states) is objectified by various rule-of-thumb procedures by which we agree to act as if we had objective knowledge of intention. We find, especially, that certain external, antecedent states are treated as if they stand for (are identical with) the internal states, so we have only to observe the external situation to "know" what was intended, what motives were operative, and so on. (In a very important way our positivistic behavioral sciences have simply sought to meet this common-sense need for nonsubjective or objective knowledge about people.)

Even more importantly, this necessary gap makes the use of power essential to the maintenance of social order in our society. The traditional (structural) idea of sociologists has been that there is some level of sharedness of morals sufficient to produce reciprocal (or "doubly contingent") patternings of action in such a way that social order will be created and maintained (if not constituted by that patterning). In this view "authority" (or power exercised in accord with the shared values) is sometimes considered to be necessary (or most efficient) in "maintaining" the actions patterned by the shared morality (that is, to limit "deviance"). If, however, situated moral experience is necessarily problematic, then, regardless of the degree of sharedness of morals, there will always be moral disagreement and there will always be imputations of "deviance" (or immorality). We are led, then, to a totally different conclusion concerning the use of power: the use of power, independently of the necessarily different and conflicting moral experiences of the individuals involved, is necessary to maintain social order in our society.[18]

There is, of course, at least one commonly understood alternative to such use of power, though it really seems to be merely a major strategy of such a-moral exercise of power. This is *mystification*. Men of power normally use various strategies of mystification to construct the appearance of common moral experience to bridge the necessary gap. This is especially apparent in the realm of legal and judicial decision making, in which power and mystification are combined in complex ways to provide a general sense of justice in spite of the fact that some of the participants inevitably feel a sense of injustice. God, tradition, reason, democracy, nationalism, and symbols of power and justice of many kinds (black robes, showing deference to the judges, scales, gavels, flags, and the rest) are interposed to bridge the inevitable gap: the inevitable sense of injustice is checked by trust that God and other higher powers will enforce a greater right, by the belief that wrongs in this immediate situation are outweighed by rights in the greater social context, and by the fears of one's own impotence in the face of the awe-inspiring symbols of power.

The management of such devices of mystification in order to construct social order in a concrete situation is merely one instance of the general social use of moral meanings to help in constructing social order. This will become clearer as we investigate further the nature of the social construction of moral meanings.

The Social Construction of Moral Meanings

A crucial element of the traditional absolutist world view dominant in Western societies has been the taken-for-granted assumption that morals (right and wrong, morality and immorality, and so on) are not only necessary and external to man but also obvious to individuals in any situation: what is morally right and wrong in any situation has been assumed to be completely nonproblematic. As a result, moral decision making has been seen as almost entirely automatic. It was seen as simply the result of applying the given morals to the given situation. There was, as we have already seen, a necessary element of choice; but this choice was thought to be entirely restricted to the choice between doing right and doing wrong. There was no choice concerning what was right or wrong and no choice concerning right or wrong in what ways or to what degrees. All of this was given by the iron necessity of God's will, or Being, or nature, or some other absolute.

Until recently, sociologists have almost universally shared this assumption and have taken it for granted in their studies of society in general. This assumption became basic to the whole structural point of view, which many sociologists came to see as the sociological point of view.[19] It led sociologists to concentrate almost entirely on questions concerning the rates of deviance, the exact nature of which they assumed to be obvious and provided very nicely by official information, and the causes of such deviance, since it seemed very difficult to understand why anyone would do wrong things. Concentration on these problems led to the almost exclusive development of the Durkheimian theory of social rates as the way to study and explain social actions, especially "immoral" or "deviant" actions.

As we have already noted, when we actually observe everyday social activities we find that the members of our society do not, in fact, find it easy to agree on what is right and wrong, moral and immoral, in concrete situations. In accord with the assumption that morals are nonproblematic, they do tend (or have traditionally tended) to assume that morals are obvious, but only in the abstract, independently of any concrete situation in which the individual is actually involved. This assumption of an absolute morality has some real advantages to the individual in many everyday situations, especially insofar as it provides a nonproblematic legitimacy, as he sees it, for his own ideas and actions. This, presumably, is a major reason why it has been so resistant to change (until recently) in spite of the fact that in concrete situations individuals normally become embroiled in many arguments over what is right and wrong for the situation at hand. In fact, in many, perhaps most, forms of everyday activity there would appear to be more instances of disagreement than agreement over questions of right and wrong for the immediate purposes at hand, though most of these disagreements are not readily observable because the individuals involved do not choose to argue openly about them. (This should be especially apparent in any situations involving authority relations. Subordinates generally disagree with superordinates about many concrete questions of morality, but generally in silence. This is a major device for protecting one's self-esteem and self-confidence.)

In most of our concrete everyday situations we do seek to achieve some working agreements about moral questions (and other questions) with the other members involved. Only the existence of such agreements makes it possible to get on with our lives, since the infinite possibilities of action in any situation would prevent our ever getting beyond the first situation if we had to negotiate every detail (or more than a relatively few details) of our interactions. But, on the other hand, the ever-changing nature and complexity of reality and the necessary conflicts over moral questions make it necessary for us to negotiate with the other members only a working agreement, that is, an agreement on how to proceed to achieve our purposes at hand for this situation as it is now defined, rather than seeking to negotiate some final solutions which we could then absolutize (or make independent of persons, purposes, and situations).

These working agreements are achieved only through processes of social construction: the members involved must intentionally construct for themselves concrete moral (and/or other) meanings for the purposes at hand in this situation and they must at the same time do so in such a way as to construct a situated social order (that is, effective agreement). If they fail in their constructive work, the purposes at hand will simply not be achieved and the members will have to seek out a new situation and start over if they want to achieve those purposes.

In some sense, of course, every momentary situation is a new situation and every interaction can only be carried out to achieve our purposes by negotiating the right agreements. In this sense, every activity is new and must be constructed. But this *eternal-flux theory* of human action, possibly useful for some purposes, is quite useless for explaining most of our actions. Just as most of our bodily functions must be performed unconsciously or subconsciously and in predetermined, set ways because their complexity would make it impossible for conscious activity to control them adequately, so most of our socially symbolic or meaningful activity must be performed subconsciously and most of our social interaction must be based on prior agreements if we are to get it done at all. This is why common socialization in common meanings is to some degree essential to the creation and maintenance of any common body of social interaction. But, on the other hand, the abstract meanings which we learn through such socialization could never possibly be adequate for carrying on the immensely complex activities of any society, particularly one so complex and pluralistic as ours. Such abstract meanings, especially as found in the language and a few crucial areas of experience, such as the procedural rules by which the members of society agree on how they are going to reach decisions, provide only the shared symbolic resources which the members of society must draw upon in constructing working meanings for any given situation. When the members face any new situation, or a situation for which they do not have what they see as an adequate (or adequately nonproblematic) working agreement on its meanings, they must decide which of these symbolic resources are relevant to the present concrete situation, and they must then purposefully construct an agreement about the appropriate set of meanings for that situation. As Schutz [20] and many others have argued before, we decide upon this relevancy of symbolic resources and do our meaningful constructions primarily in terms of typifications. We first attempt to construct a typification of the situation: What kind of situation are we facing? What other situations is it like? What are the generic categories covering such situations? It is crucial to find the type(s) of situation faced because it is only such typification which allows us to draw upon previously established working agreements for the purpose of constructing our present working agreement. If we could not draw upon such pre-established working agreements at all, we would potentially be faced with an infinite amount of work in testing out the infinite possibilities. It is, of course, not at all clear just how we do go about deciding on these typifications, but it seems very likely that our typifications of moral experience are done primarily by a process of analogizing. In the case of legal decision making this is actually quite clear. New types of legal decisions are arrived at by deciding first of all which previous cases are most analogous to the present one. As Vaughan and Sjoberg argue in Chapter 6, one can see this process of analogizing at work in the attempts of the Israeli judges to decide under what laws and precedents Eichmann should be tried.[21] There is, of course, a necessary gap, a categorical gap, between such a previous definition of a situation and the newly constructed definition; and the process of analogizing does not really allow one to eliminate this gap. As we should already expect, it allows only (imperfect) bridging of the necessary gap. It does seem, however, to involve a minimizing of the gap as well. A method of least differences seems to be integral to this analogizing process: the smaller the differences of the typifications (or categorical definitions) of the situations, the more analogous and, thence, the more acceptable the newly constructed definition. One, therefore, is not free to construct just any meaning for the new situation. The logic of moral decision making itself involves an important constraint.

But this has a fundamentally important implication: morals alone cannot provide an adequate definition of the situation and, thence, of the appropriate actions. Not only must one define the situation independently, which is an obvious consideration, but one must construct a moral definition for any situation partially on extramoral considerations at some point (all situations are seen as "new" at some time). In this case it is the analogizing process of the so-called logic of morality that varies independently of morals themselves. But there is an even more important way in which moral meanings appear to be originally determined by extramoral considerations.

When one is constructing a new moral meaning for a new situation, even if one uses a method of least differences in analogizing between this and previously defined situations, it seems obvious that there will be many alternative analogous meanings that would be equally acceptable to members of society if considered on this ground alone. (Is this not obvious from a consideration of the inevitable arguments even among judges, such as the justices of the U.S. Supreme Court, who have the greatest possible knowledge of precedents—or previous moral definitions of analogous situations—and of legal reasoning?) Since no method of least differences could solve this dilemma, there must be another factor determining the construction of moral meanings actually made and then agreed upon. This factor appears to be none other than the purposes at hand of the participants, which thus becomes a crucial extramoral determinant of the construction of moral meanings. At this point, of course, it should also be apparent that one very generally gets conflicts among the participants over the purposes they have at hand. And here, once again, is where mystification and power become essential in producing working agreements on the moral meanings to be accepted for use in the concrete situation.

There is, however, an additional kind of moral consideration that serves as something of a guide to the directions which situated constructions of moral meanings "should" take. In addition to abstract typifications (like "be courageous") and pre-established situational typifications which can serve as moral analogues (such as "the Marines at Wake did not flinch before impossible odds"), there are certain deep moral meanings which serve as guides or general contexts for situational constructions. These deep moral meanings, like deep linguistic structures,[22] are generally background meanings; that is, not generally part of the conscious thoughts (or purposeful constructions) of individuals, but forming the frame that delimits much of the conscious thought involved in purposeful constructions. In American society, for example, these deep moral meanings are normally referred to as a sense of fair play, a sense of decency, a feeling of being right, being for the underdog, being a nice guy, and so on. Any member of American society would find it very difficult to define exactly what the concrete (situational) meanings of these might be; yet he would probably be able to tell when they are relevant to a given situation—he could "recognize" the instances of them—and he would have "feelings" related to them that something concrete is right or wrong. (This is done in the same way that members have "feelings" that a grammatical construction is right or wrong without being able to give any specific justification for that point of view.)

Once such working moral (and other) meanings are agreed upon for a given situation, they become relatively nonproblematic and very generally become background meanings for that situation. The participants now take them for granted in interacting with any other member of that situation (one who can be assumed to know such things), so that an outsider, such as a sociological researcher, finds it very difficult even to "make them observable" so that he can learn about them. William Henry has pointed out, for example, that hospital staff at work in an emergency room very often do not have to exchange verbal cues about the work and at times even appear to be doing the repair work "without thinking about it." [23] They have established work routines that enable them to accomplish the task adequately for their purposes at hand. Only when it is no longer accomplished adequately for their purposes at hand do they come to see the meanings as problematic ("we've got a problem") and then seek to reconstruct the relevant meanings. The same is generally true of moral meanings, so that we have various degrees of routinized (nonproblematic) moral meanings. For example, the moral meanings of public nudity have normally been highly routinized in American society. Only recently have they been successfully challenged by those (moral provocateurs) seeking to reconstruct the meanings of situations so that they are first seen as problematic and are then routinized in a different way.

Moral meanings that become highly routinized may even be progressively *absolutized* or *objectified;* [24] that is, made independent of situations, persons, and purposes at hand. These, of course, are the meanings I have previously referred to as abstract meanings, and they are used as symbolic resources. As long as these moral meanings are dealt with only in the abstract, independently of situated social involvements, they may have all the characteristics of Berger and Luckmann's "objectivations." Most importantly, since the individuals who are socialized to accept them as the morals did not themselves create them and are not aware that human beings did create them, they tend to see these morals as not only given, independent, and necessary (absolute) but as thinglike or as objects not subject to individual interpretation. A general result of this has been that individuals in our society have normally had to construct situational interpretations of morals while acting as if they were not doing so.

Situated Constructions of Moral Meanings

In a society in which there is a dominant conception of morality as absolute and as the only appropriate determinant of action, there will inevitably be a fundamental difference between public morality and private morality.[25] And, as a result of this necessary difference between public and private morality, the situated constructions of moral meanings (that is, the concrete interpretations of abstract morals) will be treated by the members maintaining that situated actions as if they are identical (or "indexical" [26]) with the abstract moral meanings.

Life is immensely too complex, too uncertain, too conflictful, and too changing for any set of abstract and predetermined rules to specify activities that will have results seen as adequate by the individual actors. Life itself would soon end if one tried to live in that way. Any rules actually to be applied to life must, therefore, be changeable and adaptable to meet the contingencies of living. Yet this is completely contrary to the absolutist conception of morality and its relation to living. The absolutist insists on subjugating life to the absolute rules.

For whatever reason, it is clear that the Western societies became firmly committed to an absolutist world view, and certainly an absolutist conception of morality, many centuries ago. While this absolutism has waxed and waned, it has always remained dominant and has been very strong in certain societies since its great resurgence in the Protestant Reformation. There are now very serious challenges to this absolutism, and there is clear evidence of changes taking place in the social conceptions of morality (see below), but the absolutist conception remains dominant. As long as this is true, any overt disagreement or challenge of *the* absolute morality will be seen as immoral by most members of society.

In addition, because most members of our society see this absolute morality as a homogeneous unit in which each part is necessary to all others, and because they believe that this absolute morality is *the* fundamental determinant of whatever happens in society, they firmly believe that immorality causes social disorder (or disintegration) and, indeed, that for many purposes immorality can be treated as merely an instance of (or identical with) social disorder. (The sociological theories of disorganization and deviance, especially those of the Durkheimian school and the Chicago ecological school, were firmly grounded in this common-sense theory and show the same confusion over whether there is a causal or an identity relation between factors of disorganization and immorality. Factors of disorganization, anomie, and the like, are both defined in terms of immorality and used to explain this immorality.) As long as these beliefs exist, a disagreement or challenge to any part of the absolute morality—and certainly a challenge to the absolutism of morality itself—will be seen as a threat to social order and, thence, to the very existence of society. A challenge to the absolute morality, then, is seen not only as immoral but as legitimate reason for the greatest anxiety.

Both of these factors, the social responses of anxiety-induced repression and charges of immorality, make it very unwise for members of our society to challenge the absolute morality. Today there is a third factor that makes it even more costly to challenge the official morality. In the past one hundred years American society, like other Western societies, has increasingly become an officially controlled society.[27] The control of thought and behavior seen as immoral, abnormal, and threatening has been increasingly turned over to numerous kinds of official experts of control. The official organizations of control and the laws governing them were largely founded at a time when the absolute morality was even more dominant than it is today, and they were unequivocally entrusted with enforcing that absolute morality and legally given wide discretion to do so. These official organizations have objectified the absolute morality for the whole society: they have become a largely independent force external to the great majority of individuals in society and exercising power over them in matters of morality, normalcy, and social order. (If Durkheim had seen that it is in this sense that morality is external and thinglike to individuals, as well as in the sense that they *think* of it as absolute, hence external to themselves, he would not have fallen into the fallacy of concretizing "society" and, thereby, perpetrating so much nonsense about society's being a level of existence separate from that of individuals.) These official organizations of control then transmit the absolute morality from one generation of officials to another through their training practices and by promoting those most zealous in upholding the absolute morality. The officials then become the protectors of the absolute (official) morality, even to the extent of educating (or propagandizing) the public about the needs for the absolute morality and, thereby, advancing their own interests.[28]

An individual who is seen as not acting in accord with the absolute morality—or, even more, one seen to be challenging that absolute morality and, therefore, threatening the foundations of social order—becomes subject both to condemnation by any segment of the public that wants to attack him (for whatever reason) and, more importantly, to (public) stigmatization by official control agents. We have a situation, then, in which any challenge to the absolute morality can lead to official stigmatization, including arrest and imprisonment (or commitment), regardless of the amount of private support one might actually have among the general public. Even if a majority of the population agrees (privately) with the challenge—or rejection—of the absolute morality, it will normally be impossible for an individual to show this to be the case, since anyone who (publicly) challenges that absolute morality will be subject to the same stigmatization. It is for this reason that we get the public obeisance to and celebration of the absolute morality. When we remember as well that life, especially the complex, rapidly changing lives in our pluralistic and international technological society, cannot actually be lived in terms of that (abstract absolute morality, we see that there will necessarily develop a split between one's professed (public) reasons for doing something and one's actual (private) reasons for doing it, but that this difference between public and private justifications will in almost all cases be denied and hidden by rhetorical interpretations of the absolute morality for the situation at hand intended to make the interpretation appear to others to fit the (abstract) absolute morality. This is to say that there are, indeed, conflicts (as defined by the members involved) between the absolute morality and the situated interpretations and that the situated interpretations are in significant part (purposeful) rhetorical constructions intended either to prevent moral attacks or to win any moral attacks that might occur. These rhetorical constructions of moral meanings, then, are a crucial element in what Goffman and others analyze as self-presentation (and group presentation).

As the split between the public morality and private morality becomes greater, due, presumably, to greater changes and complexities of living adequately, we get the highly purposeful form of self-presentation known as public relations, and, in a very real sense, everyone, or everyone who sees how to be successful, becomes his own public-relations man. In a society in which the changes in living are making this split ever greater and more recognizable, such as in Machiavelli's

Renaissance Italy and our own society, there is a proliferation of common-sense thought concerning the strategies of self-management (for example, how to win friends and influence people). At the same time, in a society such as ours, in which there are such great dangers from disclosure of the truth, resulting from the enforcement activity of the official control agencies, this growing recognition of the split between the (public) fronts and what individuals can be seen to say and do in private leads to a growing sense of hypocrisy and attacks on dishonesty from those who are committed to the absolute morality or wish to profit by appearing to be so committed. In American society it is mainly the young and the isolated rural communities who have lived almost entirely in simple societies, such as the family, in which there is more of a feeling of fit between the public and private who become so alienated from and angry at the hypocritical modern world.

While it should be apparent that this social constructionist theory of morality and social actions constitutes an immensely more complex view of their relations and of the nature of social order in our society than that proposed by the traditional structural theories, which assumed the absolutist perspective, it should not be concluded that anything goes, that all talk of morality is merely sham, and so on. Certainly we must consider this to be a serious possibility, but the evidence does not yet seem to indicate this to be true. At the same time, while it now seems clear that the situatedness of moral meanings (which we shall soon discuss further) makes it far more possible to "get away with anything" than has traditionally been assumed by the simplistic structural theories, the evidence from this argument does not yet support the conclusion that "anything goes."

First of all, the necessary involvement of social response (or of anticipated social response) in any moral experience, which we have discussed earlier, does not mean that moral experience and social response or social use are identical in all situations in our society. This might appear to be a legitimate conclusion from carrying the social response theories, such as C. Wright Mills's argument concerning the "situated vocabulary of motives," to their logical conclusion.[29] Mills's argument was essentially that the anticipation of acceptance or rejection by others was a, if not *the*, basic determinant of the morally meaningful motives an individual would give to his actions, and the possibilities of constructing plausible imputations of this sort, then, became basic determinants of what one would do. Mills's whole argument actually rests on the implicit assumption that at some point there are shared morals which determine social response, simply because it is the existence of such shared morals which is, presumably, determining the acceptability or nonacceptability of the morally meaningful motives imputed to one's actions. If there were no such ultimately shared morals, or something to serve the same function (which is an important consideration), social response would be indeterminate (if not random), so one might as well impute any motive he wished, and actions would be disordered.

The shared abstract moral meanings do appear to set some very broad social limits on what can be justified in any situation in several important ways. First of all, they are socially defined as a necessary part of the symbolic resources that must be used in constructing any justification or any account [30] of one's activities. Most importantly, there are included in this the morally sanctioned rules of reasoning (and of normalcy) which one must be seen to be acting in accord with in constructing any account of one's actions. It is these rules, whether consciously used (foreground) or implicitly assumed (background), which, for example, determine the process of analogizing involved in the moral reasoning by which one moves to a social construction of the moral meanings of a new situation, and it is this that is so crucial in preventing any random leap to a totally new (utopian) definition.

What does appear to happen, however, is that individuals and groups move through progressive situated interpretations of moral meanings. Since all of us live in rapidly changing environments, we all frequently face what we see as new problems and new situations with new meanings for us and demanding new solutions. Through a progressive sequence of such situated interpretations the difference between the public and private morality will grow greater (unless the society in general is moving in the same direction), but the degree to which the individuals involved recognize any such difference must depend on their degree of involvement with an openness to observation by the outside (public). The more private or intimate relations are within the situation, the more they are cut off or secret from public observation, the greater the difference that will develop and the greater their tolerance for this difference. Indeed, in highly intimate relations these differences from the recognized (and accepted for public purposes) public morality may be highly prized and celebrated—and breaches of public morality may be used to demonstrate and increase the feeling of intimacy. This, for example, is what Norman Denzin has found in the highly intimate or private relations of the family,[31] and self-revelations of one's private morality and deviations from the public morality are very generally used to help construct the ethos of intimacy which has been analyzed by Alexander Blumenstiel.[32]

Individuals and groups who, for any reason, have developed what is potentially seen in terms of the absolute morality as a highly immoral form of behavior will tend to make their behavior situated in two ways. First of all, they will seek to justify their behavior by presenting it as an appropriate interpretation of the absolute morality for their situation. Second, they will seek to cut it off—situate it—from the rest of social experience, especially from public experience; and success in keeping it a secret may actually be a fundamental justification for allowing it to continue: it's all right as long as it is not subject to view by the public, the innocent strangers who might be tempted by it were they to know of it and thereby endanger the dominance of the public morality, which would in turn endanger the very foundations of social order. We can, in fact, see this whole process at work in Weinberg's analysis of nudism.[33]

Over long periods of time various groups have succeeded in situating the abstract morality with respect to their own activities so that they are allowed to do what would normally (or under *any* other conditions) be considered to be violations of the abstract morality. These activities are of the nature of moral exceptions (and are direct analogues to the exceptions found so essential centuries ago to making Roman law work adequately in non-Roman Europe). But, even as exceptions, they have always been justified in terms of the absolute morality by arguing that they are actually in the service of the absolute morality—they are only apparent or surface violations. But the appearances have always been of crucial importance (since all appearances are also "real"), so these moral exceptions are always situated as well by hiding or isolating them from public view, thereby making them partially a form of private morality made accountable to the public (absolute) morality.

Professional groups are especially likely to develop such moral exceptions. The way in which the medical profession has over centuries developed the profound exceptions to the sacredness of the body and the privacy of the sex organs is especially informative. But other groups have succeeded as well in constructing such situated moral exceptions. Silvers' study of the construction of an amoral definition of themselves by artists, justified in terms of its necessity for artistic creativity, which is highly valued in society, is an excellent example of this.[34]

As Western society, and American society above all, has become ever more complex in the last century, it has come increasingly to be made up of such groups with their own highly situated (private) moralities to whom the absolute morality has increasingly been seen as an

external force which one must simply manage effectively in constructing moral appearances that will be acceptable for public purposes. As
I have previously argued,[35] this is one important way in which American society has become increasingly pluralistic, so that we have
moved ever further from the simple state of a social system, if, indeed, it makes any sense to argue that American society ever was in
such a state. This society is now far more of the nature of a social conglomerate made up of largely independent groups which are tied together by certain generally shared, abstract goals (health, prosperity,
and security). In this social conglomerate the traditional absolute morality has increasingly become used only for public purposes, as already noted, and has a decreasing effect on what the powerful groups
do in private. In the public arena this absolute morality now serves
mainly as a public celebration of community (we are all Americans, all
Christians—or Judeo-Christians, and so on) and as a primary means
of maintaining the myth of the social system (that is, the myth of the
dominant absolute morality), by which there probably is an important
slowing of the recognition that the absolute morality is no longer a
primary determinant (presumably through individual consciences) of
what people do in private. And, as I have also argued, even this effect
in public situations has continued only because of the power of the official organizations of control.

Toward a New Ethics

Yet even the power of the officials has not been sufficient to prevent
the spreading recognition that there is no longer an absolute morality
to which we can all turn for solutions to any moral questions that
might arise in our everyday lives, confidently taking it for granted that
all others must do so as well (because all consciences are predetermined by the one universal moral good—God) and will necessarily arrive (in their hearts, at least) at the one necessary answer—an answer
which will be enforced with infinite power for all time—and beyond,
to the unimaginable unlimits of eternity. In this very important sense,
while it would certainly be false to say with the radical theologians
that "God is dead," it seems very true to say that God is dying. There
is a spreading recognition that morality is not absolute, but situational; not obvious, but problematic; and not unchanging, but changing very rapidly. There is, as well, a growing feeling that moral experience is not what it once was, so that the very term *morality* hardly

communicates the right meaning and must be replaced with some new term, perhaps *ethics*.[36]

The failure of the officials to prevent this growing awareness, and their having to be content (or discontent) with merely slowing (or controlling) it, has probably been due more to the growth of free speech than anything else. Free speech has, of course, traditionally been subject to control work by officials just like most other spheres of everyday life, especially public life. But the ancient pluralism of Anglo-Saxon society, which long ago produced the ethos of individual freedoms "guaranteed" by government officials, and the American emphasis on the free speech guarantee, have been important in keeping speech relatively freer from official control than actions. (The distinction between mere talk and deeds has been of crucial importance in this whole process.) The growing importance of science in our society, with its fundamental emphasis on free enquiry and free communication, has increased the demands for free speech. Most importantly, the growth of the psychological and social sciences has led to increasing revelations of secret (often supposedly unconscious) thoughts and deeds. The effects of this, especially of the so-called Freudian revolution, have been profound. Today it is easy for (non-fundamentalist) people to talk publicly about private matters which involve profound challenges to the absolute morality—matters which were probably very difficult to talk about in greatest privacy two generations ago. While it is still potentially very costly to admit private violations of the absolute morality through such talks, the effects of this growing free speech on our social conceptions of morality have been profound.

Most importantly, it has become increasingly clear to individuals that they are not alone in their thoughts and actions and that other individuals and groups have very different private moral feelings from their own. This has produced a growing recognition of the insincerity of public moral pronouncements, coupled with the rage for authenticity or sincerity in personal relations (getting behind what are now seen as fronts) and of the actually problematic nature of moral experience. Increasingly it is recognized that moral decisions are not, and cannot be, taken for granted, but rather must be purposefully constructed by the individuals for the purposes at hand. Increasingly it is recognized that moral experience is not imposed on man from outside, but rather is created by man out of his experience in everyday life (his existence) for use in his situations. Increasingly it is recognized that this situational nature of morality (or ethics: rules of interaction) and of action means that individuals are never solely responsible for their own actions, but rather that responsibility must be seen as interactional, as partly individual and partly social. And, last, it is increasingly recognized that this understanding of the existential (or problematic and situational) nature of moral experience and action poses profound problems for social order.

It is not at all clear to members of our society, including the social scientists, where these growing changes are taking us or whether it will be possible for us to maintain social order, while maintaining and building our individual freedoms, in a society in which most of the members do not think of the social rules as absolutes founded in the very nature of being. Whether these new understandings of the human condition will serve to free us from ancient bonds, or will drive us to create a new tyranny to suppress a war of all against all resulting from a sense of libertinage, of freedom from personal responsibility and accountability, will be determined only by the creative efforts that lie ahead. But surely the understandings of moral experience and social order provided by sociologists will be of crucial importance in deciding the success or failure of those creative efforts.

NOTES

1. This necessary dualism has very likely been the basis for the continual appeal of Manichaeism in the Western societies.
2. See E. Durkheim, *Rules of Sociological Method,* ed. G. Catlin (Glencoe: The Free Press, 1950), especially pp. 65–73.
3. This explains why individuals co-operate to prevent embarrassment, flooding out, and the like. See E. Goffman, *The Presentation of Self in Everyday Life* (Garden City, N.Y.: Doubleday, 1959).
4. But it must be remembered here that all moral considerations are contingent on the imputation of intention. See below.
5. See Jack D. Douglas, "Deviance in a Pluralistic Society," in E. A. Tiryakian and John McKinney, eds., *Perspectives on Sociological Theory* (New York: Appleton-Century-Crofts, 1969).
6. See Alan F. Blum, "The Sociology of Mental Illness," Chapter 2 in this volume.
7. For a treatment of the principle of the (situated) contextual determination of meanings, see Jack D. Douglas, *The Social Meanings of Suicide* (Princeton: Princeton University Press, 1967), pp. 235–254.
8. M. Moermann, "Analysis of Lue Conversation: Providing Accounts, Finding Breaches and Taking Sides," Working Paper No. 12 (Berkeley, Calif.: Language-Behavior Research Laboratory, 1968), p. 13.

9. See Norman K. Denzin, "Rules of Conduct and the Study of Deviant Behavior," Chapter 5 in this volume.

10. See Maurice Mandelbaum, *The Phenomenology of Moral Experience* (New York: The Free Press, 1955).

11. For a discussion of absolutism, see my essay on, "The Impact of the Social Sciences," in Jack D. Douglas, ed., *The Impact of the Social Sciences* (New York: Appleton-Century-Crofts, 1969).

12. See especially Edwin M. Lemert, *Human Deviance, Social Problems, and Social Control* (Englewood Cliffs: Prentice-Hall, 1967); and Howard S. Becker, *Outsiders: Studies in the Sociology of Deviance* (New York: The Free Press, 1963).

13. For a detailed criticism of the structural theories of deviance, see Douglas, "Deviance in a Pluralistic Society."

14. See Blum, *op. cit.*

15. Peter McHugh, "A Common-Sense Conception of Deviance," Chapter 3 in this volume.

16. *Ibid.*

17. For discussions of this, see Jack D. Douglas, "The Relevance of Sociology," in Jack D. Douglas, ed., *The Relevance of Sociology* (New York: Appleton-Century-Crofts, 1969); and Jack D. Douglas, "Crime and Justice in American Society," in Jack D. Douglas, ed., *Crime and Justice in American Society* (New York: Bobbs-Merrill, 1970).

18. See Douglas, "Deviance in a Pluralistic Society."

19. *Ibid.*

20. See A. Schutz, *The Collected Papers,* 3 vols. (The Hague: Nijhoff, 1963). But Schutz did not see such construction work as problematic.

21. See Ted R. Vaughan and Gideon Sjoberg, "The Social Construction of Legal Doctrine: The Case of Adolf Eichmann," Chapter 6 in this volume.

22. See Aaron Cicourel, *Method and Measurement in Sociology* (New York: The Free Press, 1964).

23. This is taken from a personal communication with William Henry.

24. For the discussion of "objectivation," see Peter Berger and Thomas Luckmann, *The Social Construction of Reality* (Garden City, N.Y.: Doubleday, 1966).

25. See the discussion of public versus private in Douglas, "Deviance in a Pluralistic Society"; and in Jack D. Douglas, *Deviance and Social Order* (New York: The Free Press, 1970).

26. On "indexicality," see Harold Garfinkel, *Studies in Ethnomethodology* (Englewood Cliffs: Prentice-Hall, 1967).

27. See Douglas, "Crime and Justice in American Society."

28. See the treatment of the origins of the Marijuana Stamp Tax Act in Becker, *op. cit.*

29. C. Wright Mills, "Situated Actions and Vocabularies of Motive," *American Sociological Review,* V (1940), 904–913.

30. See Marvin B. Scott and Stanford M. Lyman, "Accounts, Deviance, and Social Order," Chapter 4 in this volume.

31. See Denzin, *op. cit.*

32. See Alexander David Blumenstiel, "An Ethos of Intimacy: Constructing and Using a Situational Morality," Chapter 14 in this volume.

33. See Martin S. Weinberg, "The Nudist Management of Respectability: Strategy for, and Consequences of, the Construction of a Situated Morality," Chapter 12 in this volume.

34. See Ronald J. Silvers, "The Modern Artist's Asociability: Constructing a Situated Moral Revolution," Chapter 13 in this volume.

35. See Douglas, "Deviance in a Pluralistic Society."

36. For a discussion of the "new ethics," see Douglas, "Crime and Justice in American Society." For an example of this, see Joseph Fletcher, *Situation Ethics: The New Morality* (Philadelphia: Westminster, 1966).

2

The Sociology of Mental Illness

Alan F. Blum

This chapter seeks to display by example and argument a set of perspectives for conceiving of mental illness and for describing it as a socially organized process. The body of literature in the field is ignored,[1] and a way of thinking stimulated by the work of Wittgenstein [2] and the ordinary language philosophers is presented.

Part I presents the parameters of Wittgenstein's approach to description and discusses the import for sociological analysis; Parts II, III, and IV provide actual instances of programmatic illustrations of work conducted under the auspices of such a conception of sociologizing.

I

The important questions that have preoccupied sociologists studying mental illness (and, throughout this chapter—by implication, deviance) have been directed toward issues of prevalence and incidence: How much is there? How does it originate? Both of these questions presuppose *some* solution to one that is fundamentally prior: What is mental illness? Where do we look for the meaning of these terms? How do we go about defining mental illness or anything—from the perspective of a sociologist? To begin to appreciate the depth of this problem, we must understand how to see the world as a sociologist.[3]

As members of society, we "know" that mental illness exists, or more exactly, we know that the naming of mental illness exists. However, within the context of the natural attitude we do not inquire into the possibility of such a phenomenon; rather, we accept the appearance and existence of objects, events, and behavior as givens without inquiring into their possibility; that is, how they manage to be given. In a word, as members of society, we have a practical interest in objects and events, and we accept their givenness.

As sociologists, however, we pretend to challenge the existence of the world in this sense: while we know that mental illness exists in that members name under the auspices of these words in standard, stable, and typical ways, we still raise the question of how mental illness (its regular, standard, stable, and typical usage) could possibly exist.[4] We might then say that all sociological inquiry begins by posing some version of the social order problem: given the standard, stable, and regular production of an event, how is this production possible?[5]

In this respect, we do not intend to raise the question of what factors cause mental illness in the sense of independent variables, or antecedent conditions such as urbanism, industrialization, and so forth. We are not interested in explaining mental illness in this way, but rather in merely describing how it is possible. This means that we are concerned to describe the organized conditions of living together, the forms of life which make the very conception of mental illness possible.[6]

In stating that we have to answer the question, "What is mental illness?" by describing how such a conception is possible, we are saying that a sociological phenomenon is defined in terms of its production. That is, it is defined in terms of the methods and procedures which members employ to make the phenomenon describable.

From the point of view of the natural attitude or of common-sense thought, "What is mental illness?" is answered by invoking some correspondence theory of meaning; that is, by naming certain properties of the world to which the words mental illness purportedly refer or which they reflect or name or picture.[7]

Thus, mental illness is supposed to name or picture or refer to some behavior: to answer "What is mental illness?" we point to or list some set of behaviors which the concept (mental illness) evokes. Since all sociological definition depends on such a correspondence theory of naming, let us examine it.

First note that when we intend to define some concept only and exclusively in terms of behavior, we often act as if the definition refers only to behavior and to nothing beyond it; that is, we ignore the fact that we draw upon a body of knowledge extrinsic to the behavior to apply the definition. Imagine teaching a child the meaning of mental illness. If we should lead this child down the streets adjacent to Columbia University, we would soon encounter a small, elderly woman who regularly rants and raves inside telephone booths and whom everyone in the community recognizes as mentally ill.[8] Wearing a threadbare coat and carrying a tattered copy of the *New York Times,* she regularly screams from within the phone booth to no one in particular.

Suppose we show the child this woman while pointing to her and informing him that this behavior, "what she is doing now," is mental illness. The first problem, of course, would pertain to the issue of ostensive definition: Are we pointing to the act of screaming, or to her carrying a newspaper, or to the type of coat she wears, or at her presence in a phone booth? What is the "that" in "that is mental illness"? This is no small problem, and Wittgenstein has shown us why such definitions are not in themselves adequate; but let us proceed.[9]

Suppose we tell the child that such behavior as just described is mental illness. Then we escort him through the streets of New York, and together we discover other cases of persons "carrying on like that." On each occasion, the child points and exclaims, "That is mental illness." Has the child learned the meaning of mental illness?

Suppose we encounter another lady carrying on in exactly the same way,[10] and in response to the child's designation we have to say, "No, that is not mental illness because do you see that smashed car on the street? She has just been in an accident . . . and those two bodies lying there are her husband and child. So, this is not mental illness because she is shocked, bereaved, and hysterical. These are all extenuating circumstances." In other words, we inform him that while the behavior might look like mental illness, there are certain features of the scene that make this an unreasonable designation. The fact that we knew what to look for, and what to draw upon in the scene, means that we have moved beyond our definition to employ common-sense knowledge. That is, we had to make sense out of the scene to decide the applicability of the terms.[11] Could the child have done this? Not unless he learned the forms of life, the common culture in which we are so immersed. The reason he could not use the concept efficiently is that he does not yet know these forms of life (he is not yet fully socialized).[12]

The child will eventually learn what we mean by the phrase "lost his balance," or perhaps we should say, she will learn how to use it; that will happen when she also learns how we use forms like "lost his way" and "lost his chance" and "lost his turn" and "lost his sense of humor." Wittgenstein says, "To imagine a form of language is to imagine a form of life." And we could, accordingly, say that the child is not ready to learn certain forms because she as yet lacks the forms of life in which those forms of language have a use, have a natural function. The extent to which we share or understand forms of life, share and know, for example, what it is to take turns, or take chances, or know that some things we have lost we cannot look for but can nevertheless sometimes find or recover; share the sense of what is fun and what loss feels like, and take comfort from the same things and take confidence or offense in similar ways. That we do more or less share such forms rests upon nothing deeper: nothing insures what we will, and there is no foundation, logical or philosophical, which explains the fact that we do, which provides the real form of which our lives, and language, are distortions.[13]

Could the child possibly be taught these forms of life by having a little rule book that would summarize all such extenuating circumstances so that he would not make any more mistakes? This is not likely, since such contingencies will tend to refer to private states of the persons producing the mentally ill behavior (grief, shock) and such private states become accessible only through an inspection of their observable manifestations (the so-called mentally ill behavior). Thus, to define mental illness in this way is to say that this behavior is mental illness, "all things being equal"; that is, that it is not an instance of legitimate grief, shock, and so forth. Yet to know if all things are equal presupposes knowing that it is mental illness.

We might try to teach the child with another method. We might escort him through the streets of our cities and the wards of our hospitals to show him what is common to all of the behavior named mental illness. Better yet, we might consult some psychiatric glossary in which all of this looking at cases is summarized for him and merely tell him to look up the definition in the dictionary. We feel that the definition should tell him what is common to the various behaviors labeled mental illness. Note an official definition of psychotic disorders.

These disorders are characterized by a varying degree of personality disintegration and failure to test and evaluate correctly external reality in various spheres. In addition, individuals with such disorders fail in their ability to relate themselves effectively to other people or to their own work.[14]

We then get:

1. personality disintegration;
2. failure to test and correctly evaluate external reality;
3. failure to relate effectively to others;
4. failure to relate effectively to one's own work.

Is this what is common to mental illness? Is this what is common to all the cases subsumed under the name? Could such a definition be learned without knowing any language in the first place? How could we teach anyone what "personality disintegration" means or what "failure to correctly test external reality" means?

In other words, we tend to answer the question, "What is mental illness?" by utilizing our knowledge of what mental illness is; that is, we have to know what "failure to relate effectively to others" is in order to define mental illness; and yet, if we knew such things we should not need a definition of mental illness. The two points which emerge from this are:

1. The diversity of behavior named mental illness resists distillation in a formula or a fixed meaning or calculus.
2. We cannot use the formula exclusively because it has to be interpreted, which requires us to move beyond the list, which presupposes settling the very questions that the list is supposed to resolve.

Is it not possible that the behaviors named mental illness have nothing in common and the search for common properties is misleading? Is it not reasonable that the meaning of mental illness subsists in the ways in which the concept is employed and that such usage can be understood only by inspecting the ways in which users move outside of the definition? Think of a more specific disorder, like paranoid schizophrenia, "characterized by autistic, unrealistic thinking, with mental content composed chiefly of delusions of persecution, and/or of grandeur, ideas of reference, and often hallucinations. It is often characterized by unpredictable behavior with a fairly constant attitude of hostility and aggression." [15]

Does this list give us a picture of paranoid schizophrenia? Are these the exclusive and exhaustive set of properties that all behaviors named paranoid schizophrenia have in common? Consider the following points:

1. We will find actors designated as normal who produce all these behaviors and actors designated as paranoid schizophrenic who produce few. How much of a property does one need to be this or that? Of course, psychiatrists settle such problems, but not because of the definition; the definition settles no diagnostic decisions for them. Rather, they know how to use the terms contained in the definition. Such use is not defined in other definitions ad infinitum; rather, it is known in common by psychiatrists as competent members of the organization of psychiatry as a collectivity. Psychiatrists do not place this known in common knowledge in definitions because they take it for granted; yet the definition could not be used without such knowledge.
2. How, then, do we use the definition? We have to be taught the meaning of autistic, unrealistic thinking, delusions of persecution, and so on. However, knowing what these words mean raises the same problems involved in knowing what paranoid schizophrenia means.

The definition does not define paranoid schizophrenia; it does not give us the meaning of paranoid schizophrenia; it does not help us. However, we are not particularly helped in being told that the meaning of paranoid schizophrenia is in the way it is used unless such use is described as rule-guided, methodical activity. Of course, psychiatrists work concertedly to negotiate a common recognition of paranoid schizophrenia, but this is only because they know how to use the words in the list.[16] Another way of stating this is to say that psychiatrists share a common culture.

What seems to be our problem? We are simply under the spell of a word and of a model of naming. "When your words seem to carry you along so that you seem to have lost the reins and you lose your head to the words, then if you pause, reminding yourself of how words are harnessed together to do the speaker's work, then you regain control." [17]

We lose our heads to the words because we demand absolute precision in the rules (a fixed meaning) and absolute finality in their interpretation. On the other hand, what determines whether there is sufficient precision in the rules is whether the concept is used successfully, with general agreement.

Thus, nothing appears to be common to mental illness in the sense of a set of identical properties of the behavior so called, and while the concept may be used similarly on all occasions and contexts of its use, a search for common uses seems just as misguided as a search for common properties. We do not want a general definition; instead, we desire a description of a particular use on a particular occasion, not a general theory of properties or uses. "And we may not advance any kind of theory. There must not be anything hypothetical in our considerations. We must do away with all explanations and description alone must take its place. . . . The problems are solved, not by giving new information, but by arranging what we already know." [18]

"What is mental illness?" is, then, a misleading question; rather, we must ask how mental illness is used in such and such a context on such and such occasion. To understand such a usage is to comprehend the social organizational form of a context.

> The slogan "Ask for . . . the use!" can mislead us, then if we think that this asking will be settled by a declarative reply, "The use is . . ." The reason that there is no reply is not only that we cannot say what *the* use is since there are many games that could be played with this counter—a point sufficiently emphasized by interpreters of Wittgenstein—but that we could not *say* what a use is since noting that a word has a use is seeing it as a piece in a game. . . . We can . . . try to show what the meaning or use of a word is by assembling a variety of language games that could be played with the word. Failure to understand the meaning of a word is failing to see how it directs us one way and not another— we don't understand what contrasts are being pointed to by the scientist who claims the floor is unsolid because it is made of electrons. In order to appreciate the range of contrasts in a particular game, we may surround it with other games which vary slightly in certain ways. Our interests will not be in games actually played but in imaginary and even bizarre cases, since they point up more sharply the contrasts in the game under investigation.[19]

In order to understand a use we must see it within a context; therefore language games are not equivalent to linguistic games because they are contexts of "meaning," and it is the socially organized ways in which meanings are applied that make particular usages intelligible.

These "games" that are played with concepts are, then, organizations of social actions, and the description of such actions requires reference to the common culture of members. This common culture is what Wittgenstein intends with his notion of forms of life.

> We learn and teach words in certain contexts, and then we are expected, and expect others, to be able to project them into further con-

texts. Nothing insures that this projection will take place (in particular, not the grasping of universals nor the grasping of books of rules), just as nothing insures that we will make, and understand, the same projections. That on the whole we do is a matter of our sharing routes of interest and feeling, modes of response, senses of humor and of significance and fulfillment, of what is outrageous, of what is similar to what else, what a rebuke, what forgiveness, of when an utterance is an assertion, when an appeal, when an explanation—all the whirl of organism Wittgenstein calls "forms of life." Human speech and activity, sanity and community, rest upon nothing more, but nothing less, than this.[20]

Thus, language is ultimately a form of life, a complicated set of human activities, and to know this language is to know the "forms of life" in which it is embedded or which it expresses. Investigating the application and use of ordinary concepts is not a mere linguistic exercise, but eventually reduces to studying the socially organized grounds of knowledge and action.[21]

When jurors, psychiatrists, kinsmen, and all ordinary members decide the sanity of another, their decisions are ultimately based on a socially accredited body of knowledge that they methodically use. This knowledge constitutes their common culture. The problems posed in describing how a member uses "mental illness" are both theoretic and methodological. The theoretic problem is framed by the issue of social order previously alluded to: it requires us to pose as problematic the ways in which members regularly and stably produce the actions which we (observers) encounter in the first instance as mental illness.[22] The methodological issue is one of locating and describing a class of observable actions whose production entails the problematic event which we initially encounter.

Thus, mental illness is possible because members, in very small and ordinary ways, treat certain behavior as "mentally ill" and collaboratively develop systematic ways of recognizing, categorizing, and acting upon such behavior. Mental illness is also possible because those who produce such behavior learn methodically to produce treatments of themselves and others that confirm such categorizations. As sociologists, our task is not to accept such actions as "givens," but rather to describe how they are possible. In the same way that a description of psychiatric usage is not satisfied by reporting the definition used, but requires a description of how it is used, a description of any member's practice necessitates reference to how the practice is accomplished.

II

Assume that defendants are exonerated from criminal charges when they are labeled "insane" or that persons are accepted into psychiatric hospitals when they are labeled "schizophrenic." How is such labeling accomplished?

Note that when we ask how an activity is accomplished, we desire some rule(s) that describes how the activity is organized as a production. Are there rules available for describing how "not-guilty-by-reason-of-insanity" verdicts or "schizophrenic" categorizations are assembled? The labels which we as observers confront are, so to speak, the end points of much socially organized activity that enter into their production. To accept such end points as points of departure for exploring the antecedent conditions or independent variables that influence the labeling process (as in the information that persons of different backgrounds, experiences, or biographies produce different types of labels) is to neglect the socially organized character of the labeling process itself.[23] The question, then, is how to transform the labeling process into an observable phenomenon to extract the rules that organize its assembly.

Imagine that we are required to supply a definition of "not-guilty-by-reason-of-insanity" verdict. Any glossary we consult, whether psychiatric or legal, will provide us with another set of words that is as problematic as the original definition. Note the alternative ways in which the judge defines NGI verdict in his instructions to the jury: the crime was the product of mental illness; or in committing the crime, the defendant did not know right from wrong.

We cannot begin to appreciate such definitions without knowing how such words are used ("product of mental illness," "knowing right from wrong"). Assuming even that a Martian knows what a verdict, or a defendant, or a trial is, would he know the definition of "not-guilty-by-reason-of-insanity verdict" if we told him: it is a verdict which states that the defendant is not judged to be legally guilty of committing the crime because it is decided that his performance of the criminal act was a product of mental illness? A definition of NGI verdict in terms of the legal criterion is not helpful unless we know what it means to apply the constitutive terms of the definition, and this requires further definitions.

If a sociologist then tells us that a specific category of persons (say, Negroes) produce more NGI verdicts than another category (say, whites), he is not particularly informative unless he tells us how such verdicts are assembled; that is, how jurors actually behave under the auspices of the legal definition to make sense out of it, to apply it, and to use it. Any finding such as this that treats the legal definition as equivalent to a juror's definition obstructs sociological inquiry in several ways: (1) it treats the legal definition as for all practical purposes an adequate description of the juror's definition; (2) it accepts as a given a verdict that remains to be described; and (3) it deflects the investigator from such description by encouraging him to search for antecedent independent variables rather than to examine "what is all the time before his eyes," as Wittgenstein phrased it.

To answer what does "not-guilty-by-reason-of-insanity verdict" mean, we do seem to require, not a definition, but a description. We need a description of how jurors use the concept. To say that we require a description of the ways in which jurors use the concept amounts to saying that we must begin to understand the concept as a move in a game. What are the games played by jurors with the concept "not guilty-by-reason-of-insanity verdict"?

If we start with the observed fact that NGI verdicts are recorded in behavior like writing NGI on a slip of paper or in speaking, we pose the problem of how such behavior is possible. A solution will take the form of describing the type of game(s) jurors play with the concept. If verdicts are to be understood as moves in a game and if a description of the game(s) presupposes knowledge of the interpretive procedures employed by jurors in working through their solutions, we must somehow acquire a participant's knowledge of the game while remaining outside of the action as spectators rather than players.

The methods and procedures of jurors in constructing NGI verdicts can be treated as organizations of social actions. The talk of jurors about the mind of a defendant is socially organized and controlled talk: an acceptance of this premise requires us to consult such talk with the intention of locating the principles or rules that govern its production.

Such talk can be analyzed on several levels. In the research in which we are presently engaged, we begin with any statement that a juror produces as a designation of the defendant's legal status ("I say he's guilty because he knew what he was doing") and we attempt to analyze it as the behavioral product or outcome of a particular principle or rule. We start with the statement by asking how it could possibly be produced; that is, what does the production of this particular statement strongly imply about a principle for organizing the production? Put another way, what interpretive rule is presupposed in such a statement to the extent that the production cannot be conceived as plausible without the principle? We assume that a set of rules can be identified whose application [24] will serve to reproduce the behavioral product (NGI verdicts). Certain problems raised by this type of analysis must be considered.

We have not settled the problem of locating analyzable statements in any but a common-sense way. That is, what rules are used to locate statements which "designate the defendant's legal status"? Can such statements be identified purely on the basis of an inspection of their formal properties without reference to the observer's common-sense knowledge of the situation in which they occur? [25] For the present, we accept any statement that conveys an intended solution to the defendant's legal status in conjunction with a reason in support of the statement. However, this is a common-sense solution, since we do not have members' definitions of "statement," "intended solution to the defendant's legal status," and so forth, as available resources.

Second, given the identification of such statements as potentially describable regularities, how does an observer locate the principles capable of generating them? What principles are presupposed in a piece of talk, and how does one "find" them? This appears to be a variant of the problem of determining what we mean when we say "*x*." A peculiar relationship seems to be involved here because it has the character of both necessary and synthetic features. Thus, Cavell suggests that the use of the term "voluntary" in ordinary language (call it A) as in "*x* is voluntary" or "is *x* voluntary?" implies that something is fishy about *x* (call it B) and that the relationship between A and B (between using "voluntary" and something being fishy) is necessary in the sense that to a normal language user to say A necessarily implies B.[26] In the same way, "I know it" (A) necessarily implies that the speaker has confidence in what he is saying (B). The problem is that these are statements (supposedly) about matters of fact, and there is no necessity about matters of fact. Are these relationships between talk and its implications then necessary or synthetic or both or neither?

From the point of view of ordinary language users, statements commit both speaker and hearer to a set of culturally accredited interpretations of the implications of these statements. The relationship between saying "I know it" (A) and having confidence in what you are saying (B) has enough of a necessary character to cause us tremendous surprise if it would fail to occur; yet in depicting a factual matter it raises the possibility of nonoccurrence and thus of contingency rather than necessity. Cavell summarizes the possible options: (1) the implications of our statements are quasi-logical; (2) or, if such implications cannot be construed in terms of deductive or inductive logic, there is some third kind of logic; or (3) some necessity is not logical.

> Something does follow from the fact that a term is used in its usual way; it entitles you (or, using the term, you entitle others) to make certain inferences, draw certain conclusions. (This is part of what you say when you say that you are talking about the logic of ordinary language.) Hearing what these implications are is part of learning the language, no less a part than learning its syntax, or learning what it is to which these terms apply: they are an essential part of what we communicate when we talk. Intimate understanding is understanding what is implicit.[27]

The relationship between such A's (usage) and B's (correct implications of usage) appears to be a synthetic description of matters of fact unless we appreciate that "we do not say 'I know it' unless . . ." sounds more like a rule than a descriptive statement. In other words, given the fact that we want to speak English correctly, the relationship between A and B can be better described as a rule of correct ordinary usage (rather than as a descriptive synthetic statement).

Thus, to study NGI verdicts as socially organized products, we attempt to determine (from the perspective of ordinary usage) the culturally accredited implications of stating that the defendant is not-guilty-by-reason-of-insanity. Each rule that we locate specifies a different set of implications of saying that the defendent is NGI: such implications are not consequences or results, but, rather, each constitutes a different culturally accredited set of grounds for producing such a statement. The quasi-necessary relation between grounds and designation is described in a rule (like a rule of usage) which says: you cannot legitimately call the defendant NGI without implying that you conceive of him in such and such a way. Thus, each rule supplies a condition of correct NGI usage from the perspectives of members of the collectivity of jurors.

These considerations are important for several reasons. First, we want to claim that there are principled grounds for believing that the inspection of mere talk allows one to move legitimately beyond the talk to descriptions of the socially structured environments of actors as seen from within. This leads to the further claim that the study of talk —in the hands of sociologists—can be legitimately converted into a description of the common culture of ordinary members.

In the research previously alluded to, several rules are identified, and without going into detail, their general features can be specified. Perhaps the most popularly understood grounds for deciding NGI verdicts concern the construction of accounts that members warrant as constituting legitimate excuse for a defendant's action. There are several varieties of account (or theories) available to do this job: what they share is the stipulation that the defendant was "unfree" at the time he performed the act.

Another method for deciding NGI verdicts is noted when jurors use the act as an occasion for reviewing the defendant's biography to determine whether the character of the action is discrepant with some conception of the defendant based on a reading of his biography. In these cases, conflict is used as grounds for deciding guilt; that is, an insane defendant should have a biography that supports such conception.

Another procedure available to jurors (as revealed in the research) involves deciding whether the defendant is treatable and using such a decision as grounds for the NGI verdict. Thus, the defendant might lack a legitimate excuse and might have a normal biography (that is, it might not be possible to see him as NGI from the perspectives of other theories), and yet he may be found NGI if it is decided that he is a certain type of person (treatable, "not a criminal type," and so on).

We suggest, then, that the notion of an NGI verdict conceals the different ways in which such verdicts are assembled. Furthermore, jurors appear to produce such verdicts methodically in the sense that each verdict is the product of their application of a particular interpretive principle. To claim that jurors label differently is, then, elliptic, for labeling is a socially organized process of theorizing that is capable of being identified at the most specific levels. The issue for research is, then, not to identify the features of the finished product (that is, the publicly available, completed theory), but rather to describe the activity of theorizing itself. We are able to accomplish this when we can pose the problem of describing the jurors' activities of producing a verdict as methodical activity.

Note also that this type of description serves to reveal that jurors can generate different verdicts from the same evidence. Thus, evidence of a normal biography will be used as grounds for asserting that the defendant could not be insane and deserves a verdict of guilty; while exactly the same evidence is used to decide that he is not a criminal type and hence deserves hospitalization and an NGI verdict. So the decision depends on the theory that the juror invokes to interpret the evidence. In the same way, jurors may use some conception of hospitalization either as grounds for an NGI verdict or to support a more punitive guilty verdict on the assumption that psychiatric hospitals will serve to isolate the defendant more effectively than prisons.

We can see, then, that the notion of an NGI verdict masks the subtle and varying ways in which jurors theorize about the world and that proper understanding of an NGI verdict is attained only when such theorizing is described.

III

One possibility suggested by our analysis of the jury materials is that a member's conception of another as mentally ill presupposes a conception of what constitutes a bona fide, competent collectivity member. Thus, methodical judgments of mental illness can be used to locate conceptions of normal membership. This, then, represents another way of using studies of mental illness, for in analyzing common-sense theories of illness, we are actually collecting material on the conditions under which cultural competence is assigned.

Conceive of what it takes to be assigned cultural competence: sociologically, this is equivalent to describing the parameters of adequate membership. From a sociological perspective, the concept of membership implies that there are rules which persons so classified respect as maxims of conduct and for the nonobservance of which they can be sanctioned. Thus, a sociological description of membership requires some depiction of the rules which persons so classified respect as maxims of conduct and which they feel morally compelled to follow under pain of being redefined as inadequate members.

Any description of social organization presupposes a conception of membership; for example, any description of family is a description of the rules an actor is likely to follow while acting under the auspices of family as a normative order. To define family, we define family membership; and to define family membership, we must describe the typical rules whose observance in action is taken by the typical actor to be a condition of his membership status.

It is not easy to describe the rules that actors respect as maxims of conduct and as conditions of membership status. Of course, we can question people, but since this is the weakest strategy, we might suggest the close and detailed observation of persons in order to discern in their activities their operating conceptions of membership. As an example, let us conceive of our problem as one of tracking down the sociological meaning of age and/or sex. In assigning sociological meaning to age or sex, we are trying to discover what it means from the point of view of an actor to be a member of an age or sex category. Age and sex membership in turn refer to the rules that persons respect as constraints and conditions of their placement in age and sex categories.

How can we locate those occasions on which persons behave in ways that will permit us to make such inferences? How do persons methodically behave to make the doing of age and sex behavior describable?

We say that age and sex are membership categorizations, but hair color, eye color, and weight are not. Can we formulate grounds for such distinctions that are independent of the empirical fact that sociologists are responsive to one set of categories and not to another? Is there anything about the categorization of sex that is inherently more sociological than the categorization of hair color?

It might be said that hair color and associated categories are not socially significant. But certainly persons act as if hair color, weight, and so forth, have meanings and implications for action (obese = jolly, redheads = temper). Thus, these categories are certainly used by other members as grounds of inference concerning the incumbents of the categories.

Can it be said that the persons so categorized do not act on the basis of such categorizations? However, redheads and fat persons are treated in certain ways and presumably often act on the basis of such treatments. For example, a number of bodily properties are taken into account by actors; that is, body image and the self.

When sociologists say that the term "member" does not make sense for inclusion in a hair category but does for age or sex, they are proposing that it is not sensible to speak of one as a member of a hair-color category for various possible reasons. These reasons crystallize around the differences between being a member of a category and being an element in a category.

To say that a characteristic signifies membership in a category is to say more than that it signifies classification and possible implications for behavior, or that the characteristic can be used as grounds of inference and actions. One conventionalist objection might be anticipated at this point: we use sex rather than hair color because it predicts, and so on. However, this is an ad hoc argument that does not provide principled grounds. Also we do not really know if hair color predicts; that if we analyzed survey data by suspending our knowledge of category relevance and treated hair color, weight, and so forth as seriously as we would treat community size, socioeconomic status (SES), and so on, we would probably discover a number of interesting relationships. Is any and all regularity of interest to the sociologist?

Being a member as compared to being an element implies something about one's awareness about the basis of his attachment to the category.

To repeat: membership implies that there are rules that persons so classified respect as maxims of conduct and for the nonobservance of which they can be sanctioned.

Redheads and fat persons do not expect and do not expect others to expect them to be sanctioned for the nonperformance of category-ade-quate behavior. Redheads do not respect the standard of temper, fat people of being jolly, as maxims. They are not sanctioned if they fail to be volatile or jolly. Being placid and redheaded and being morose and fat do not represent moral failures.

The difference between being an element and being a member might, then, be suggested as follows:

1. Both may involve orientations to normative order (blonds are supposed to have more fun, fat persons are supposed to be jolly).
2. However, both can be used by others as grounds of inference and action.
3. Members as compared to elements respect the rules governing category placement as maxims of conduct, as conditions and sanctions, and react to performance failures as moral failures.
4. It is important for members to be good members; that is, in good standing. The adequacy of membership is an issue.

Imagine if elements of categories (ectomorphs, redheads) acted as if they were members, by using body as a normative order, by theorizing about respecting its upper and lower limits as constraints, and so on. That we can imagine it suggests no logical basis for distinguishing between elements and members in the sense that elements may not be conceivable as members at some point; that is, the distinction is not a logical one.

In consequence, the difference between conceiving of something as a member of a category and as an element of a category might be summarized by saying that only members can be good members; elements cannot be good elements. It might be said that a good redhead is the reddest redhead and that blondes can often be seen as moral failures if their blondness is manufactured rather than natural (just as toupees disqualify a person from having good hair). All of this kind of talk appears senseless. It does not seem to make sense to use "good" in these cases. There do not seem to be principles for fulfilling category placement competently in these instances.[28]

Sociologists speak of age and sex as examples of ascribed characteristics of persons. They mean that the individual's membership in age and sex categories is not achieved through these performances, but is conferred on him at birth. What is meant is that the individual has no control over the selection of age and sex properties at birth: these properties are automatically ascribed because others categorize him necessarily into age and sex categories simply by inspecting him as a physical object.

Age and sex are viewed, then, as two sorts of categorizations which are decided on at the individual's appearance. There are an array of other physical properties that actors decide on on the occasion of their first inspection of the individual as an organism; and yet these others are not seen as "membership conferring" properties.

There is no intention here of examining the conditions under which age and sex are singled out as socially significant categorizations while weight and eye color are ignored (though they might be admired and commented on). Instead, we are interested in the ways in which these initial or primordial categorizations are viewed as conferring membership status. Not that we are concerned with the ways in which persons' parents theorize upon the receipt of a boy or girl child, but rather with the question of the meaning of sex and age category memberships for those designated as members.

To examine the meanings of such memberships, we have recourse to several strategies. First, societal members talk frequently and openly through the medium of a language of age and sex distinctions and through such talk inform us about age and sex as normative orders.

Parents socialize children by employing age and sex categorizations; that is, children are reprimanded, encouraged, advised, and conceptualized in terms of age and sex distinctions, and children themselves react to adults in similar ways. Thus, one way to understand the meaning of membership in age and sex categories is to study the ways in which persons speak about, and in terms of, age and sex in doing their routine affairs.

A second alternative focuses on common-sensically understood failures to perform according to the criteria of adequate membership in age and sex categories. That is, on a variety of routine and extraordinary occasions, persons are judged as not fulfilling membership criteria. On these occasions, membership status is temporarily challenged in the sense that one's performance in age and sex categories is discussed as an example of inadequate membership in such ways as to be informative about the criteria of adequate membership.

It is not that one's age and sex properties are literally suspended: rather, one's claims to such properties are denied verbally, and the assertions of the denial serve to express in negative form the principle which the denial negates. Thus, the language of insult and disparagement, to the extent to which it is organized around age and sex distinctions, tacitly conceals the normatively ordered properties of age and sex categories.

When a woman is called a male or a man a female, when an adult is accused of childishness—on these occasions we witness the invocation of age and sex moralities. The study of such occasions requires us to come to terms with the grounds for such abuse; for instance, the depiction of American men as "boys" by certain women begins to inform us about the sex-related meaning of age in America when we get a grip on the specific reasons underlying such descriptions.

We see in this respect how the language of psychiatry functions as a source of such abuse. Thus, not being of the proper age or sex can at this point often be used as grounds for describing age and sex membership. For example, the psychoanalytic description of a castrating woman can be read as a specification of the constitutive properties of a "bona fide member" of the category of woman for certain elements of our society. Moreover, psychoanalytic theory is principally organized around its common-sense description of the conditions of adequate age membership.

We notice also that when persons approach psychiatrists with their "problems," they often use as grounds for detecting such problems some conception of adequate age and sex membership against which they hold their notions of their own performance as imperfect comparisons. Thus, for example, since patients often report to psychiatrists because of their feelings of inadequacy vis-à-vis "supposed" standards of sex-category membership, such complaints, troubles, and regrets tend to conceal notions of adequate sex-category membership.

A third research strategy focuses on the smaller class of occasions on which persons talk about abdicating from their membership in age and sex categories. Though age and sex are ascribed properties, they are not irrevocable or irrefutable; that is, they can be transformed through performance (this is why the ascribed-achieved dichotomy is misleading).[29]

It is not only transexuals who contemplate membership change in these areas but also homosexuals and persons involved in the "aging" process. In all these cases, persons often refuse to accept the terms of their membership categorization, assert their preference for alternatives, and in so doing theorize about age and sex as normative orders. The activities of "keeping young" and, conversely, the attempt to "grow up" both express dissatisfaction with the actor's categorization as a member of an age or sex group. In the activities of "looking older" or younger, we witness actions oriented to an order and governed thereby in its course.

Simply put, our question in the present section is this: In the standard, stable, typical, and repetitive social structures in which we routinely participate, what does it mean for actors to be governed by the standards of adequate membership in age and sex categories? More specifically, how is one behaving when his actions are conducted under the auspices of age and sex adequacy as a maxim of conduct? What does it mean to behave like a male, female, old person, young person? What principles represent adequacy with respect to these categorizations?

These are not philosophic questions; rather, answers to them can be achieved only through research. They suggest that we consult the behavior of persons who are acting under the auspices of such categorizations. We have to locate the occasions when action is governed by such auspices.[30] We have to observe persons behaving when such categorizations are problematic, challenged, being reconsidered, or perhaps on just the routine occasions when such categorizations are being accomplished. All of this presupposes that we can then recognize such occasions.

The relevance of membership to the study of mental illness can be stated as follows: the occasions on which therapists and patients confront one another can be used to elicit material for inspecting the various rules which organize membership assignment in a number of socially relevant categories.

If we accept Garfinkel's basic premise of ethnomethodology, that the activities produced by members are identical to the methods and procedures used by members to make such activities describable (that is, observable and reportable), we can treat the activities done by patients in the presence of their therapists as methods for making such activities describable.[31]

Since patients report for therapy with a set of troubles that they respect as grounds for entering therapy in the sense that such troubles are used legitimately to infer performance failure in some membership category, all occasions of seeking help can be treated analytically as a patient's way of making methods and procedures for performing in a membership category describable.

This is possible because trouble in our society (that is, complaints that warrant psychiatric review) is necessarily linked to an actor's performance in some membership category. Another way of saying this is that all psychiatric troubles are membership troubles: they are problems which a person is experiencing in his attempt to perform under the auspices of some conception of adequate membership. The patient is, then, an occasion for us to locate the operating conception of membership which is instantiated in his activity of "reporting to a therapist."

Conceive of patients reporting the following kinds of troubles: [32]

1. My problem is being a Negro.
2. My problem is having six children.
3. My problem is my hand: it hurts and even though doctors say there is nothing wrong with it, it just hangs like an inert thing and cannot be used.

In the first case, the therapist can legitimately answer, "So what?" for the patient is merely locating his membership status in a category and is not describing the way in which such a categorization gives him trouble. In describing such, he would reveal some behavior that must be done to be an adequate Negro; that is, some behavior which he has trouble doing. Thus, it is only when the patient admits that his trouble is in the way he reacts to whites and the meaning he assigns to most behavior directed by whites against him that we are able to see that his trouble is not in being a member (Negro) but in *being preoccupied with being Negro,* which suggests in turn a big problem for members of many stigmatized categories: to live with your membership in many categories is to behave so as to deny the salience of the category as a routine organizing device. Thus, to be a good cripple or a good blind person is to invoke the rule of sanctioned irrelevance and to behave "as if" the category exerted no constraint.[33]

In the second case, the therapist does not find the woman's reported trouble a membership problem until she indicates that she is unmarried. Since this bit of information shifts her into the category of single woman, we get a view of her conception of adequacy as a member of the category, *single woman,* and the problem she experiences in performing under such auspices. To be an adequate single woman is to control one's affection in such a way that it does not become invariably converted into conception. One feature of being an adequate single woman is to control promiscuity; that is, to manage its effects.

Not only do patients theorize about their membership, but therapists use a primary operating strategy of forcing the patient to formulate his problem as a membership adequacy describable.

Thus, the patient with the inert hand refuses to use the hand as a symptom of membership failure. It is only when the therapist can interpret the injured hand as the patient's bid for attention and support from his environment (especially his mother) that the patient is able to see the hand as a symbol of his failure to perform as an adequate adult. The therapist attempts to convince the patient that his membership failure is a failure to perform adequately under the auspices of the conception "normal adult" because he is doing behavior which is infantile.

In general, the following kinds of problems appear as interesting features of the therapeutic encounter as an occasion of members' theorizing about membership. First, there is the fact that of all the memberships which are available to a patient for assessment and review, there appear to be regularities in the choice of memberships as sources of trouble. Second, as we have noted, talk about failure is talk about the conditions whose removal promises success. The rules governing the production of behavior constitutive of adequate membership are articulated on those occasions when members review and contemplate their failures to do such behavior. Finally, given talk about membership failure, there are a number of resources available for members to depict such failure as a function of this or that. Thus, these occasions are also characterized by the production of members' accounts for specifiying how such failures are possible as the outcome of a set of biographic conditions.

IV

Conceive of the therapeutic interview as an orderly, stable, and typical set of activities. One of the questions we want to ask is: How do therapists do a therapeutic interview in such a way as to make their methods and procedures of doing the activity describable? In what sense is the therapeutic interview a set of methods and procedures for making the therapeutic interview describable? To describe the therapeutic interview as a socially organized process is to describe its common culture; that is, the sets of understandings which must be invoked in order for the therapist and his client to speak together.

It is these common-sense understandings, these taken-for-granted forms of life, that are presupposed in any conception of a therapeutic interview. Indeed, the vast literature on the subject treats this knowledge tacitly as a stable point of reference, as given and as not requiring further description. This is to say that any conception of a question or of an answer in therapy presupposes a set of procedures for doing the questions and the answers, and while such methods and procedures are circulated informally and are part of the common oral culture of psychotherapy, they are not usually described in training manuals. In this section, we want to explore some of the parameters of the common culture of the therapeutic interview.

This can be viewed as another version of Wittgenstein's problem: any characterization of a therapeutic interview as an exchange of questions and answers is not descriptive until we begin to learn how questioning and answering are done in this game. Because questions and answers must be described as methods for doing questioning and answering, such a description constitutes a characterization of the common culture of the interview.

What kind of language game do therapists play with clients? The first thing we will examine is the way in which therapists intend their questions to be answered.[34]

It appears that therapists desire their questions to be heard not as mere requests for information (in some restricted sense of "information") but as requests for "displays." [35] In order for a client to hear a question as a request for a display, he must treat the question from the perspective of a common-sense actor: by employing and applying all sorts of background understandings that he hears the question as evoking.[36] Thus, a common-sense treatment of a question is an answer which treats the question as unproblematic—as a question which conveys a set of background understandings and notions that the therapist and his client understand the question to be eliciting.

To begin to see how we might characterize this common understanding that both therapist and patient assume a question to be invoking, consider:

A father asks his daughter the question, "How was school today?" and she answers, "Fine." This answer has the function of terminating the exchange. To find out more, the father must continue questioning her. In this circumstance, from the point of view of the father, this is an inadequate answer because it builds upon her hearing the question as a request for information (Was school fine today?) and not as a request for a display. The work the question "How was school today?" is designed to do is to invite the daughter to talk, but she refuses to hear the question in that way and instead treats it as a request for literal information. What is her answer designed to do? It can be seen as a method for terminating the exchange, but it also seems an efficient procedure for passing the turn to talk back to the questioner.

The therapist's question is intended to evoke an array of statements, a batch of talk, that he can use as grounds of inference and action.

That the question is not to be heard literally does not mean that the father is not interested in whether school was fine or not, but rather that he is interested in how it was fine.[37]

From the point of view of the therapist, there is a set of possible answers to the question such that some of them constitute grounds for inference and action and others do not. What rule seems to make "fine" an adequate response in this sense?

"Fine" appears to be an answer (whatever that means), and not an occasion for talk. Answers are literal responses to questions: therapists want occasions of talk; that is, displays that use the questions as a point of departure for talk (and not merely as an answer).

Thus, one produces a therapeutically correct response by hearing the question as requiring more than an answer to the question. The questions therapists ask are of this nature: they are intended to summon from the client a display of talk that can be used as grounds of inference for a therapeutic description of the client's "mind," and answers cannot be used in such ways.[38]

One feature, then, known in common by both therapist and client is that a question is heard to be eliciting, not literal answers, but occasions of talk. In the game of psychotherapy, questions are to be treated by clients as occasions for talking.

Parenthetically, our discussion also succeeds in a tentative attempt to isolate psychotherapist and psychiatric patient as courses of action. A therapist is defined by the methods and procedures used to impose such a hearer's rule upon another;[39] this is why a rule of socialization will partially describe "doing therapy" as a course of action. On the other hand, a psychiatric patient is one whose actions are conducted under the auspices of such a hearer's rule and who assembles treatments of the therapist's questions in conformity with such a rule.[40]

Note how much research is conducted along the lines of this kind of question-answer game. Many psychological tests try to explicate this to subjects with the reminder that there are no right or wrong answers. Actually, the so-called projective test consists of a set of stimuli which are designed to provide occasions for seeing rather than literal answers.

So if one would describe what he saw on a Rorschach card as a series of ink blots rather than as a set of butterflies or bats or various animal forms, he would be penalized, not for giving the wrong answer (for it is literally ink blots that are there), but for refusing to accept the rules of the game, viz., that the literal ink blots merely present the subject with the occasion to see other forms and that if he refuses to use

the occasion in this way, he is not behaving as a competent member
(or, he is deliberately suspending his cultural competence, which itself
is a sign of some problem).

If one responded to projective tests literally by reacting to stimuli in
terms of behavioralizing them, one would be judged to be some kind
of creature. In order to take the test, one has to accept and invoke his
common-sense understanding of the test as an occasion for seeing.
The sociological problem here is to describe this knowledge that can
be suspended but must be invoked in order for the game to be played
correctly.

It might appear as if radio interviewing and therapeutic interviews
are similar in that (1) the questions are invitations or occasions for
talking; (2) the interviewer often knows the answer to the question
he is asking; and (3) he is thus less interested in the content of the
answer than in the "display" it evokes. However, in therapy the occasion of talk is not used to fill time or to entertain some population, but
rather it is used as evidence for making assessments of the talker's
mind. Consequently, answers are not viewed as a test, in the sense of
being right or wrong, but as symptoms of some underlying state of affairs.

The therapist's concern in this respect is with the way(s) in which
the talk is done, with what it "really" means, or with what is "really"
being said. Just as "fine" does not tell one "How was school today?"
unless it is understood what it means to say "fine," so all answers to
the therapist's questions remain uninformative until the therapist un-
derstands what it means to produce these answers. In this respect, the
following exhaustive set of questions were asked by a therapist during
an interview:

1. How are you?
2. Could you tell me a little about what's been going on?
3. To what, for instance?
4. Could you tell me a little bit what's been going on since you came
   over?
5. How, for instance?
6. What do you mean?
7. Just wander along and see what turns up.
8. You tend to work at this pretty constantly yourself?
9. When you say you might get upset, what does that mean to you?
10. For instance?
11. You feel in some way the marriage was a way out?
12. Well, but it had that effect.

13. Anything?
14. Well, what thoughts did you have about that?
15. You feel that all these things came first?
16. Well, remember we talked about this in the spring.

Most of the questions attempt to invite the patient to talk. In fact, it might be suggested that the more questions a therapist asks during an interview, the more inadequate for the therapist are the answers; that is, the more they tend to be literal answers rather than occasions of talking.

For the therapist to be able to treat occasions of talking as grounds of inference and action, the client must likewise subscribe to the maxim that his activity of talking is identical to his methods and procedures for making this talk describable. In this game, both players must subscribe to the notion that adequate answers are occasions of talking, because it is only such talk that permits the therapist to describe the patient's mind. The therapist can begin to treat the patient's words as moves in a game only when he has talk available to formulate rough estimates of the parameters of the game. Thus, while mere talking is not in itself a sufficient condition of satisfactory answers, it is a necessary condition.

Examples of the refusal of patients to accept therapeutic questions as invitations to talk abound in the literature of the interview.

Q—How are you?
A—Alive.
Q—How did you happen to come here?
A—The Huntington-Arborway bus.

While the first answer has the form of a pun, the second is so literal as to appear absurd. It reminds us of:

Q—Do you have the time?
A—Yes.

In answering "Alive" the patient refuses the invitation to talk and instead selects from a universe of possible descriptions one that fails to differentiate him from anyone else. In choosing "Fine," in response to "How are you?" the patient is at least selecting from a class which has its complement and is thus choosing some self-description; that is, a meaningful one. In answering "Alive," though, he is deciding on a categorization without a complement. In this way, we might say that "alive" gives less information than "fine" and is less adequate, even though both represent failures to accept the invitation to talk.

> Q—Does it bother you?
> A—It bothers me or I wouldn't be here.

Note the rule we are approaching by inspecting these unsatisfactory answers. In each case, the question is not heard as an occasion for talk, but as a request for literal information. Now we can begin to specify the kind of talk which the therapist is interested in generating: he designs his questions, not to elicit just any talk, but talk the occurrence of which on inspection will reveal possible methods for categorizing the talker's trouble(s). Each of these various inadequate responses fails to provide such a categorization by focusing on the literal question and ignoring its intent and by treating the questioner (therapist) as if his question constitutes a personal trouble for which he wants a solution (which the answer is supposed to provide), rather than as a ritualistic invitation to talk which the patient is expected to seize in order to be informative about his trouble.

In giving literal information, inadequate answers fail to use the resources of the question as a basis for categorizing the talker's trouble. Categorizations generated by the answer generally fail to discriminate the patient from anyone and thus do not appear to supply meaningful information.

In summary, there are certain parameters of the common culture of the interview: (1) that questions are intended and heard as invitations to talk; (2) that answers are treated as occasions for talking; and (3) that the patient's talk is treated as a set of methods and procedures he uses for making his trouble describable.

V

In this chapter we have sought to present and illustrate a program of sociological research in the area of mental illness that succeeds in meeting requirements for adequate and rigorous sociological description.

The theoretic point of departure for this program is framed by the social order problem; that is, events of conduct are described as possibilities that have been realized, as practical accomplishments of members. At every point, the methodological foundation of the program is organized around the naturalistic observation of these routine practical accomplishments.

NOTES

1. Throughout, it is assumed that the reader is familiar with the criticisms of the epidemiological, survey, and anomie approaches to the study of mental illness and that he does not require a repetition of these deficiencies.

2. L. Wittgenstein, *Philosophical Investigations* (New York: Macmillan, 1953).

3. Although Husserl was the first philosopher systematically to enumerate the distinction between the "natural" and the "theoretic" attitudes, the writings of Alfred Schutz and Harold Garfinkel have been responsible for dramatizing the import of the distinction for sociology. See A. Schutz, *Collected Papers: The Problem of Social Reality* (The Hague: Nijhoff, 1962), Vol. I; and H. Garfinkel, *Studies in Ethnomethodology* (Englewood Cliffs: Prentice-Hall, 1967). Anyone who knows the tremendous corpus of published and unpublished writings of Garfinkel will recognize the indebtedness of the present chapter to his conception of the activity of sociologizing, though he is in no sense responsible for the claims and description of the program outlined in these pages.

4. In other words, we do not take this common-sensically known givenness as a scientific description, but rather as a point of departure for inquiry.

5. As Wittgenstein says, "Our investigation . . . is directed not towards phenomena, . . . but towards the 'possibilities' of phenomena." *Op. cit.*, p. 420.

6. This is what a description of mental illness in contrast to an explanation would look like; that is, it would locate the constituents of mental illness as an event without reference to extrinsic facts. In this sense, urbanization, social class, and so forth are not part of the meaning of mental illness (its parameters or criteria). The identity of such parameters is a topic of empirical meaning.

7. For a review of correspondence theories, see E. Nagel and R. Brandt, eds., *Meaning and Knowledge* (New York: Harcourt, Brace, 1965), Section 2. Also Peter McHugh, "On the Failure of Epistomological Truth," paper presented at the 1966 meetings of the American Sociological Association, Miami Beach.

8. Assume for the purposes of the example that we all know how to recognize "ranting," "raving," and the other ordinary terms employed in what follows.

9. Such definitions are not adequate because they presuppose knowledge of the language which is itself intended to be problematic in any adequate description of the learning of language.

10. Of course, this presupposes that we know how to identify "carrying on in exactly the same way."

11. This means that it is not the behavior in deviance (deviant behavior) or in mental illness that is common to all instances of the use of the concept. What is common to all instances of the use of the concept is the fact that the concept is used, and not the behavior to which the concept refers.

12. This is not to say that we are interested in correcting lay descriptions of mental illness, for if this is how we decide, the problem is one of describing how it is that we decide in this way.

13. S. Cavell, "Existentialism and Analytic Philosophy," *Daedalus* (Summer, 1964), p. 463.

14. *Diagnostic Manual: Mental Disorders* (Washington, D.C.: American Psychiatric Association, 1952), p. 24.

15. *Ibid.*, p. 27.

16. Actually, we are giving psychiatry too much credit here; reliability statistics characterize the difficulties they have in achieving such order even through the employment of their common-sense theories.

17. O. K. Bousma, "The Blue Book," in K. T. Fann, ed., *Ludwig Wittgenstein: The Man and His Philosophy* (New York: Dell, 1967), p. 156.

18. Wittgenstein, *op. cit.*, p. 47.

19. J. O'Brien, "The Unity of Wittgenstein's Thought," in Fann, *op. cit.*, pp. 403–404.

20. S. Cavell, "The Availability of Wittgenstein's Later Philosophy," in Pitcher, G., ed., *Wittgenstein: The Philosophical Investigations* (New York: Doubleday, 1965), pp. 160–161.

21. "To understand a concept, a word, put the word in its linguistic context and the whole utterance in its social context and then describe, without preconceptions, what you find; remembering that each word, each utterance, may figure in many contexts. . . . Just as a word gets its significance from the context of its use, so those elements of our experience which we are tempted to isolate (or, failing this, to fabricate) and make the self-sufficient bearers of certain names get their significance too from their setting, from the form of life to which their titles allude." Strawson, in Pitcher, G., *op. cit.*, p. 62.

22. On the problem of social order, this discussion owes much to Garfinkel's unpublished writings on Talcott Parsons.

23. Thus, "labeling" theorists like Scheff and Becker do not describe the labeling process, but affirm that the process exists, using this as grounds for attacking traditional conceptions of mental illness.

24. As Wittgenstein argued, the enumeration of rules is not a sufficient guarantee of their application, because of the problematic character of "following a rule"; that is, this is a contingent rather than a necessary relationship.

25. Thus, Piaget identified "socialized talk" common-sensically, not by inspecting the structural properties of such talk, but by inferring from

other clues that the child in emitting his words "was directing it to others." Such knowledge was possible only because Piaget employed his common-sense understanding of the scene (by observing the child's eye movements and the like).

26. S. Cavell, "Must We Mean What We Say?" *Inquiry* (1958).

27. *Ibid.*, pp. 180–181.

28. There might be rules, but not principles. See G. Ryle, *The Concept of Mind* (New York: Barnes and Noble, 1949), Chapter 4; also Cavell, "Must We Mean What We Say?" on the differences between rules and principles.

29. Garfinkel speaks to this point in *op. cit.*, pp. 116–186.

30. This is possibly the biggest problem in the type of sociological approach being discussed here, for it does not seem possible to locate such occasions which initiate research in any but a common-sensical way.

31. Though Garfinkel does not refer to this as a "basic premise," it obviously is. See *Studies in Ethnomethodology*, pp. 1–4.

32. Based on transcripts of actual troubles reported by patients to a psychiatrist.

33. For this patient, this is how the notion of being an adequate Negro was formulated, though for many others such a formulation would appear to be a "white man's theory." Note also how the rule of sanctioned irrelevance is supposed to be invoked by others who assemble treatments of the member and how members define others as "good people" or not on the basis of whether they invoke the rule (A. Gowman, *The War Blind in the Social Structure* and E. Goffman, *Stigma: Notes on the Management of Spoiled Identity* [Englewood Cliffs: Prentice-Hall, 1963], present material documenting this.) It is still difficult for an observer to decide if one's invocation of this rule is evidence of "universalism" or a selective treatment.

34. We are working with a common-sense conception of "question-and-answer" for the purpose of initiating the following discussion.

35. No assertion of omniscience about therapeutic "intent" is claimed; rather, it is argued that "request for display" in the sense discussed here is part of the ordinary meaning of "asking a question."

36. See Garfinkel, "Studies of the Routine Grounds of Everyday Activities," in his *Studies in Ethnomethodology*, for a discussion of background understandings in conversation.

37. Of course, fathers as opposed to therapists can produce such questions out of a parental sense of obligation to the requirement of producing any question which documents "interest in the child" and then might fervently hope that children hear the question as a request for literal information and for termination. This is one method of doing one's duty as a father; however, fathers will then often get trapped by displays which they did not want to hear in the first place.

38. Of course, answers can be used as grounds of inference in the following ways: that the patient is resistant, defensive, aloof, covering up, and so on; but none of these constitute substantive descriptions.
39. Cf. Harvey Sacks's unpublished "Lectures and Notebooks" for the use of "hearer's rule."
40. This is premature, for it does not exhaust the possibilities for defining "patient" and "therapist" as courses of action.

3

A Common-Sense Conception of Deviance

Peter McHugh

My question here will be: Deviance is an expression of what social process? I will try to show that the sociological import of deviance is its expression of two kinds of common-sense actions: first, a deviant act is an act that members deem "might not have been," or "might have been otherwise"; second, it is an act the agent of which is deemed to "know what he's doing." For the observing member, in other words, a deviant act must occur in a situation where he can conceive that there were alternatives to that act; and it must be committed by an actor who knows what the alternatives were. By invoking these two common-sense rules, a member comes to depict the circumstance or situation in which the act takes place and the agent or person or group committing the act, respectively. This is the process, much elaborated below, by which deviance is conferred upon an act.

This is to say that members, judgers, assessors, and labelers have a notion of the ways in which social structure can generate and limit behavior and beyond that a notion of the actor as an agent of his own behavior. It makes a difference to them whether an act had to occur or not, whether it was structurally possible to do otherwise; and whether an actor knows what he's doing or not, whether the actor can be said to have intended to do what he did. It is on these two common-sense considerations that societal designations of deviance, as well as exemption from such responsibility, depend in any social state of affairs. Some shootings, for example, are thought to be made necessary by their settings, as in self-defense. Here the judging member calls up a version of social structure (in this case the absence of alternative courses of action) in exempting the shooting act. It does not embody the same social transgression as a shooting that didn't have to occur; say, the deliberate murder of a political rival. Other shootings, though occurring in circumstances with structural alternatives, are thought to be committed by actors who didn't know what they're doing, as in wanton mass shootings. In the latter instance, the common-sense focus is not on the aspect of setting, but directly on the mind of the actor, which for the member depicts that actor's intent.

These two criteria of responsibility—"It might have been otherwise" and "He knows what he's doing"—are criteria for the *conventionality* and *theoreticity* of acts.[1] They are the fundamental common-sense rules for deciding what is deviant and what is not and for distinguishing between various kinds of deviance. Whether our interest is in killing, boredom, psychosis, bureaucratic indifference, organized crime, lying, alienation, totalitarianism, stupidity, or delinquency, we first assess the possibility that a particular such act needn't have occurred at all, whether it is conventional; and then if the actor knew what he was doing, whether it is theoretic. And the social units can be of any size or conceptual status, such as persons, groups, bureaucracies, political ideologies, physicians and their patients, spouses and their spouses, and so on.

A deviant act thus is not located by identifying its "effect" (though it may have effects) in the sense that an effect alters something in the world which exists independently of the act under question; for example, the waste and expense that follow upon crime. Criminality may cost a fortune. That may be one of its effects. But criminality as deviance does not *depend* on costing a fortune; it could occur and be so designated whether it cost much or little. Members do not treat deviance pragmatically, according to what are thought to be its consequences. In this regard deviance is typically a moral matter. The social processes of deviance, in which members call one another into question, inhabit the items which are thought to *produce* an act, whatever its effects. Deviance is an upshot of its own production. This is to say, for example, that deviance could occur even if it never had any effects at all. A sole figure on some island, engaged in some perfectly harmless practice, could be called deviant if that practice ever came to public attention. We may share the sentiments of those who decry this punishment of a deed because it "isn't hurting anything," but we are doing so at the sacrifice of the sociological import of punishment, which ensues from the items that are defined as producing the act, rather than from the changes in the world which may follow it. We can call another into question, even punish, without ever attending to the pragmatic consequences of the act upon which we call ourselves into question.

Let me give an example of the difference between effects and upshots.[2] In almost all circumstances serious pool players are quiet when another player takes his shot. They believe a sudden noise will startle the shooter and interfere with his shot. Treat the startle as an effect of the noise in that the noise alters something in the world (the shot). Assume also that any and every serious pool player subscribes to this as an effect of the noise. Then observe two sets of serious pool players, in each of which one player shouts and hence will be said to have startled the shooter. Now it so happens that when one set is composed of professional stage actors, there is no observable difference in their behavior after a shout as compared with their behavior after no shout. Their game proceeds in the same way in each instance. The next shooter chalks his cue as he lines up his shot; the eyes of the players remain on the table; there is desultory talk by those not in the game. Among the other set of serious players, however, there is a distinct difference in their behavior following the shout: they are immediately silent, their eyes moving from the table to the shouter, then to one another; and sometimes they shake their heads and address a comment to the shouter. Among professional stage actors, the shout is accompanied by about the same behavior that can be observed after other shots; among others, behavior is distinctive.

Yet the startle is held by each group to be an effect of the shout. If social deviance depended on the startle as effect—in our terms, on the effect independently of its producing act—the shouting player would be deviant in both sets of players. If deviance were conferred according to the premised effect, both groups would respond as the non-actors do, because both groups hold that the shout produces the startle effect. But there is no special response by professional stage actors. A reaction occurs only when the players are not professional stage actors. If we agree that some differential response must occur in deviance, we can see that in the former case the stipulated effect has nothing to do with deviance. From this we can suggest that it is not the effect in either case, not being the effect in one. Something other than pragmatism is operating here. In both sets of pool players the startle effect is believed to follow the shot, but in only one set is there a startle reaction, a reaction that is therefore only associated with deviance, rather than essential to it. The idea of deviance as effect does not describe the activity, and for good reason: the startle as effect does not describe the conventionality and/or theoreticity of the shout.

This distinction between the social identification and effects of deviance introduces the conceptual and empirical thrust of what is to follow. On the assumption that the reader will be better able to fashion his own usable understanding if he is appraised of this thrust, I will discuss it very briefly here.

I have chosen to locate deviance in its common-sense items of production, not in some formalist classification of its causes and effects (such as biographical factors, group conflict, stratification), in order to meet the sociological principle of describable social treatment. This principle stresses that it is the activity of members as they deal with one another that maintains or changes society by creating, filling, and emptying all the categories, organizations, and units of society, and so to describe society one must describe these dealings. True, the term "stratification" can be a description, once it is descriptively specified. But, (1) it will remain a description of stratification, not deviance; (2) it will not be a sociological description, even of stratification, until it is specified in a very particular way, namely, by depicting the actual, ongoing social treatments of members such that those common-sense treatments can be said to *comprise* the classification we call stratification.

What the principle of social treatment requires, then, is a description of deviance according to its own logic as members do deviance, not according to some other logic of factors external to itself (the cause-effect logic of stratification).[3] We do no more with the idea of deviance than note it, as an undescribed symptom or point of reference for this or that if we talk all around it with terms like stratification or socialization or the social position of the labeler; and even upon abandoning these embellishments, it is necessary to describe it by its own logic, that is, as it is composed of the common-sense methods that enable us to say, "It occurs, it exists, it is a social phenomenon." We must, in other words, do more than merely cite causes and terms, for these are only implicitly descriptive of what members *do*—of the courses of social treatment by which the causes and terms are enacted and take observable shape.[4] It may be that deviant labels emanate from subcultures, or that delinquent histories include certain class affiliations, but to say so is not to depict what is done as deviance or delinquency. We know nothing of deviant behavior—of the acts identified by such a designation—by having described its formal causes. Neither causes nor terms describe the procedures members use in organizing themselves as social actors. They are extrinsic to doing deviant treatment, among all other forms of treatment, and thus cannot serve an analysis of the assessment procedure called deviance. To say that being born into the lower class is biographically selective for the kind of delinquency that comes to the attention of authority is in no way to describe what authority does when it attends. It is only to accept a patina of our own everyday presuppositions about delinquency. How authority treats the matter, and delinquency can be said to *be,* as a socially generated and recognized phenomenon that can be distinguished from the biographical factors said to be its cause, remains unstated. It takes for granted that there is an authority called doing delinquent treatment; that is, it does not describe delinquency-coming-to-attention-of-authority as a course of common-sense action. Being born into the lower class may be related to delinquency, but the two ideas have only been juxtaposed against each other until social treatment has been described.

The same inadequacy is apparent in deviance as effects. To say that an effect of deviance is the existence of prisons, ostracism, or a punch in the mouth is not to depict the doings which warrant turning members into the kinds of offenders who "need" such treatment, or the doings by which such offenders continually reappear in summary tables. It is not even to depict an offender. To note and count the inhabitants of these tables as deviant is to accede to common-sense judgments already made, not to describe those judgments while being made, and of which the inhabitants are mere traces. Surely they must be traces of something, unless a djinn whisks them from one place to another without even a first glance by some membership. But of what? Without its common-sense items of production, with only its causes and effects, we will not have identified, observed, or described deviance and thus will be left holding a conglomerate of causes and effects of nothing.

I will expand on the idea of doing deviant treatment throughout by attempting to show that deviant acts are both conventional and theoretic. That is, they are acts which members deem might have been otherwise and during which the actor can be said to have known what he was doing. In order to point up these essential elements of deviance, I will first treat deviant acts as if they are always punishable. In Part II the assumption will be modified to include other forms of deviance. Part III includes a discussion of the relevance of the ideas presented here for other sociological issues. In Part IV, certain critically important general properties of social rules are distinguished from other kinds of rules.

I

CONVENTIONALITY

To the member, a deviant act is first of all conventional. By conventional I do not mean the ordinary, customary, or commonplace. I do not mean to generalize about the prevalence of deviance. Whether or not deviance is regular and commonplace, *conventional behavior is behavior which a member deems might not have been, or might have been otherwise*. It is essential to the member, in other words, that a deviant act not be inevitable. If he sees deviance, so does he see alternative ways of performing in the circumstance under question. The forms of deviance which are punishable (lying, professional crime, indifference, bribery, spying, bigotry, and so forth) and not the forms which a member calls coerced, accidental, or miraculous (homicide, poverty in underdeveloped countries, brain damage, some versions of psychosis, being hit by a meteor, and so on).[5] In its conventional aspect, deviance is not merely not following a rule but whether the rule can be conceived to have been followable, and followable in the situation in which it was not followed. It is probably their nonconventional similarity that sometimes induces us to draw parallels between, say, saints and psychotics. They share the common-sense notion that they had to do what they did in the situation where they did it. The sociological importance of deviance does not cover nonconventional instances like being maimed in a war or falling accidentally out of a building, although we may be uncomfortable in being around these affairs. A conventionally deviant act occurs in the context of other possibilities, as is attested in the suicidal case by the tenacious and organized devotion to sorting out the self-destructive from the accidental.

Take, for example, a horribly burned face. What do we do with it, about it, as concerning its conventionality? That its owner is stigmatized is surely correct; yet this says little about assigning responsibility for the face. We may expect its owner to manage the interactional scene for us, and in this sense he is held responsible for something, but we needn't hold him responsible for having created the scene, in the sense that the owner of the face will be held to have authored his face.[6] He may have been burned in an accident, or burned by someone else, or lightning may have struck. In any of these cases—accident, coercion, or miracle—we assign responsibility to a situation, that is, to something that "couldn't be helped" and therefore to the nonconventionality of the face, by locating the items of behavior which are said to have produced the face. That the burn "might have been otherwise" is in these circumstances not a possibility for which we hold the owner responsible. His face, in fact, is not causally "his." Instead, he gets treated as a victim, which shifts the locus of inquiry to some other set of conditions and some other author of the face. If it is discovered that his face was burned in a fire at home when he was a child, perhaps his parents' activities will be taken up for their conventionality: Were they out of the house at the time, and did they have to be out of the house? Were they at a movie, a funeral, a hospital? If they were in the house, did they rush out without attempting to save him, or did they make the effort and fail, in which case they too would be absolved because "it couldn't have been otherwise."

It is important to note here that the existence of the conventionality-nonconventionality question makes it impossible to think of deviance merely as the ready assignment of designations or labels, if by that we mean that a term is matched to an act the way the names on a roll are matched to the people in a room. Rather, deviance requires a charge before it can be said to have occurred at all. Something has happened, certainly (or a supposed something—this is not crucial); but the first ensuing question is to find out what happened, and the procedure is to assess its conventionality or not. There being at least two outcomes, the procedure is not univocal. This is to say that at some prior point deviance is a charge, not just a designation. A charge is a call to judgment of responsibility ("what happened?") not the consequence of its exercise ("this happened"). To say someone is a fool, for example, is to implicate some other behavior which in that situation might not have been foolish and presupposes that the foolish act has been weighed against this possibility. To say that a fool rushes in is to suggest that he didn't have to, and to suggest he didn't have to is to indicate some alternative was possible. The reputable poor, though soon parted from their money, are not called foolish, because there are thought to be no alternatives. The poor's loss is deemed inevitable; the fool's not. This sort of procedure is totally dissimilar from saying that a piece of wood is ash, or that a face is horribly burned. (Of course, it is true that members sometimes act as if they are only designating a property, not making a charge. But these designations either presuppose a charge already made, or presuppose that a charge could be made, and might be termed labeling ideology. The analytic process of deviance remains one of conventionality and charge, because it would be incumbent on the member to argue for conventionality if a counterassertion were made. A fool would lose his reputation if it were discovered that he

had been pushed in.) To say that a face is horribly burned is only
to indicate the potentiality of deviance, for such a statement is not
necessarily accompanied by a description of its items of production.
It is an essential analytic feature of deviance that the designation,
name, label ascription, or what have you be some kind of account that
imputes a "choice" among alternatives, not a situationally determined
product. The face is burned, which itself recommends nothing one way
or the other about deviance. The face may have been burned in a war,
that is, accidentally, in which case it is not conventional and not
deviant. Or it may have been burned on the owner's decision that he
was "too beautiful," which a member would probably say was a choice
that might have been otherwise and thus levels a charge. Our next
immediate concern will be to expand on the workings of a charge as a
feature of conventionality.

A charge depends for its existence on being defeasible; that is, it
must be capable of rejection as a characteristic of an observed act. In
other words, it must not be self-evidently correct that the charge is
applicable and deviance occurring, for a charge always bears the possibility that it will be refuted. Being without a nose, if that can be
said to be self-evident, is not comparable in this regard to being without morals, which is always a defeasible charge. The logic of conventionality is that it should be vulnerable to rejection, undoing, refutation. In actual practice it may not be refuted, but in actual practice
this is always a possibility when deviance is at issue. This raises the
question in any particular case that a judgment may be accompanied
by disagreement; for example, a group can be deviant to some and
not others. It is here that moral contests reside.

One import of the defeasibility of a charge is that a member doesn't
"elect" to define an act as deviant, but rather "accepts" such a definition in the sense that any designation of deviance must be conceived
as the outcome of an argument. (The argument needn't be verbal, of
course, nor between two parties. It need only be the consideration of a
contention, insofar as the applicability of a label has to be managed
into existence.) Deviance is a sifted outcome that must be backed.
Take, for example, the classic syllogistic form: "Blux is an actor; all
actors are childish; Blux is childish." The universal premise "All actors
are childish" disguises its own characteristic qua premise; namely, that
it requires some reason, warrant, or justification which does not appear
by inspection in that premise.[7] "Who says?" we might ask, but we
would be more precise to ask "How says?". Is the content of this statement recommended by theological definition, empirical finding, taxonomic inclusion, or what? (This is true also with regard to classic

syllogisms, such as "Socrates is a man / All men are mortal / Socrates is mortal." The more self-evident appearance of these is a consequence of their being hackneyed.[8]) That is, a syllogism requires backing, for there is nothing in the universal that can be said to necessitate agreement by a reading of the statement. It is always possible that even a syllogism will be argued. The existence of this possibility is a feature of syllogistic logic. It obviates a self-evident logic. What a syllogism would require to be self-evident is the following: (1) a beforehand knowledge of the grammar of its terms; (2) a language structure which conforms to that of reality; (3) a perfectly known reality; and (4) immediate knowledge of reality by all users of the language.[9] In other words, for a syllogism to be self-evident would require that everything be known and nothing learned. Furthermore, a beforehand knowledge of terms means that it cannot be self-evident, for such knowledge would comprise a mediating factor between the syllogistic sentence on the page, or utterance in the air, and some reader or hearer. Thus, something else must be "established" before the syllogism.

Suppose that we were discussing actors, and someone uttered the syllogism above. Some such stated or unstated question as "According to what criteria?" will arise or be presupposed, even if it is only directed to oneself. It would bring answers like "I have read about actors," "I have observed actors," "According to psychoanalytic versions of the world," "That's what actors say," "Can't you tell?" and so forth. Or the question might be more directly definitional, as in "All actors? You mean to include the people in community theaters who do it part-time as therapy?" Or it might accept everything but the conclusion: "Well, yes, Blux is an actor, and actors are childish, but Blux is an exception. He is very mature." A charge is used; it is a behavioral and linguistic process; and it must be weighed, justified, made good. That is, it must give evidence, facts, reasons. To make it good is to appeal to something outside the statement on the page or the utterance in the air—some empirical, taxonomic, or statutory rule by which argument is made or presupposed, and the statement given life as a course of action. One can most easily see this, perhaps, in history. Until the sixteenth century, theological propositions were guaranteed and may even have seemed to have been self-evident, but they were, of course, backed up by faith. Suddenly, they needed authority and witness as warrants against a burgeoning skepticism of their immediate self-evidence. Foucault similarly depicts the variety of backing which can be observed to have generated changes in the treatment of madness.

Aside from these formal inadequacies of the syllogism, we can add that the common-sense notions which are the subject matter of sociology are substantial, and so the purely formal feature is inadequate as a description of common sense in any case. Common-sense descriptions are certainly not a calculus, even if the form "All A's are B's" is a calculus, and any notion that they are inadequately formulates deviant processes. Common-sense notions are literally equivocal; they do not even qualify as formal, although they are sometimes treated as if they do.[10] A common-sense canon may be enforced as morally or normatively required, but it does not meet the canons of geometric analyticity, because the following of a rule, alas, does not insure that the performance will be accomplished. And this is a consequence, not of the weakness of men, but of the character of the rules themselves, as we shall discover in a moment. A flagellant theory will not do. Some have called common-sense rules "maps," "blueprints," and "calculi," but these terms should always be enclosed in quotation marks. One cannot get from one social place to another by following common-sense rules in the same way one gets from one number to another by following arithmetic rules. It is an interesting and important characteristic of certain kinds of rules that merely by following them one succeeds, but this characteristic is absent in social rules. By following the rules for multiplying numbers, one has multiplied numbers; by following maps, one follows maps; but by following virtue rules, one may or may not have been virtuous. The simplest kinds of these social rules, say the instructions for eating a salad, are not enough to insure success in the activity guided by the rules. A leafy lettuce salad can be intractable.

This is because, by contrast with maps and arithmetic, common-sense rules can be followed only in the absence of their conditions of failure. Take the bromide "It is better to give than to receive." [11] Now, the rule of which this is a statement incorporates a whole set of conditions which would prevent the activity of giving: the lack of a recipient, nothing to give, no occasion for giving. To succeed to virtuousness here, and thus follow the rule, there must be not just good intentions but a recipient, and a willing one at that; some object to give; and so forth. If these are not present and available, one has not violated the rule, because their unavailability is incorporated by and envisioned in the rule. A common-sense rule depicts a course of action (giving, under conditions of failure that do not obtain) and should never be confused with the statements ("It is better to give than to receive") that are only elliptical references to the rule as a contingent course of action. Imagine how odd it would be, for example, if everyone took the statement as the rule, which would make it impossible to practice giving, everybody refusing to receive.

A statement of a rule may be positive, but it presupposes certain rule-stipulated conditions which will necessarily make a common-sense act fail, and it is only in the absence of these conditions that an act can succeed. Without a recipient, an object, an occasion, following the rule of giving is not possible. A common-sense rule is a peculiar, abstracted transformation of courses of action into structural conditions of failure—conditions which describe and depend on the state of the world as the action occurs. The statement thus is abstracted and cannot fully represent the rule; and the rule, by addressing itself to the limitations of social structure, depicts itself in negatives. It cannot therefore be self-evident or automatically invoked because the activity it guides does not always succeed and because the conditions of failure must be consulted when it does not.[12] These conditions are incorporated by conventionality. We always ask, "What happened?"—"What was the state of the world vis-à-vis rule-stipulated conditions of failure?" before "What shall we do about it?" I suppose this is what makes common sense so awesome to the member and elusive to the sociologist.

A common-sense rule guides the issue of deviance by depicting certain features of the world which, if they obtained, would preclude the activity. For some, American prisons pretty well obviate the possibility of following the heterosexual rule. The rule itself depicts various contingencies (a one-sexed population without conjugal visiting) which require going away from certain acts themselves, say, homosexuality, in any instance of assessment or appraisal of those acts. When such failure contingencies are decided to exist, the rule cannot have been broken, even though behavior is out of accord. The prison, according to those holding the view, is a social structure necessitating the failure of heterosexuality. In fact, the heterosexual rule, conceived as a set of stipulations upon sexual activity, would be said to have been validated, rather than violated, because its conditions of failure existed and the act was not guided by it. Thus, in the prison case, efforts have been made simply to provide the structural alternative to homosexuality in the form of conjugal visiting, not to "rehabilitate" the "sick and deviant" prisoner. It is the condition of the world here which neutralizes the failure and exempts the homosexual act. The deviance, if any, is to be found in some prior item of production.

But these matters are not limited to the dramatic: to eat certain salads gracefully is impossible without using a knife as well as a fork.

An absent knife is a failure condition that can be "seen" in salad eating over and over. Common-sense rules take the form of "only if," the "only" being a reference to sets of failure conditions which are built into the rule.[13] Deviance, thus, can exist only when these conditions of failure do *not* obtain and yet the act fails. Otherwise, the rule has been followed in the sense that it has a grip on the activity.

Here is grist for deviance. Deviance is failure when conditions of failure are absent. A deviant act is a conventional act, whence it is deemed that the conditions of failure (accident, coercion, miracle) are not present, and thus the act under question was not inevitable. If homosexuality persisted after the introduction of visiting rights, it would probably be called deviance. Because the conditions of failure are not present, the act under question is (was) contingent, unnecessary, needless. Not giving can only be deviant if the conditions of failure do not obtain: if no recipient does not obtain, if no available gift does not obtain, and so forth. One stumbles not always out of weakness, but out of the state of things—a state that may or may not coincide with conditions of failure. And until the state of things is deemed to accord with the absence of the conditions of failure as demarcated by the rule, the activity at issue has no moral aspect. This is the equivocal nature of moral rules: they display an emphasis on conditions of failure (an emphasis that necessitates checking on the world), the absence of which becomes the conditions of success. A common-sense success is not a success solely by being a success. It is not like arithmetic. Rather, it is a success because it takes place in a world empty of the conditions of failure, in a world that provides the freedom to do it by not obviating the structural alternatives for doing it. What will be a success is thus represented in the rule largely by the prospects for failure. Failure itself is not deviance. Deviance is to fail in the absence of conditions of failure. The very same act would not be deviant if conditions of failure were present.

In summary to this point: to assess an act as conventionally unnecessary, and to back this assessment with a reason, is to charge deviance. To charge deviance is to move closer to holding alter responsible for the identified act, because it is to say that the rule-given conditions of failure (accident, coercion, miracle) do not obtain—that the actor was "free," his act not fixed by social structure. The potential label, designation, or name is worked out by charging this responsibility and is no more than a tag, a terminological epiphenomenon of the charge. Furthermore, and by way of distinguishing the pragmatic from the deviant feature of an act, although an effect can be assigned to an act (his suicide upset his children), an effect need not be assigned and is therefore inessential to deviance. The actor could be charged even if there were no effects. It is responsibility for the items in its production, not its effects, that must be identified in deviance. Deviance is identified through its common-sense structural "causes"; that is, its conventionality-nonconventionality. To be poisoned by a Borgia is distinctively separable from being poisoned by an oyster, although one could be made equally sick, even dead, by both kinds. The first we take to fall under the conventional rubric "It might have been otherwise," the second under the nonconventional rubric "It couldn't have been otherwise." It is this application of the criteria for conventionality that makes the two incomparable with regard to deviance. The Borgia poisoning, in which we would discursively rule out conditions of failure, would continue on from the charge to an assessment of responsibility. Conventionality and nonconventionality are two common-sense versions of "cause"—they depict for members the indeterminate and determinate consequences of social structure—and as such they delimit reactions to behaviors which are out of accord. They thus generate the possibility of social deviance. There is nothing deviant about an act until it has been called a conventional act.

THEORETICITY

Let us now move on to the second aspect of members' assessment of deviance, which is captured by the phrase "He knows what he's doing." This phrase is suggestive of, and I think helps to resolve, a central and difficult problem in sociology; namely, the problem of the actor as agent of his own behavior. Although it has been called a psychological or at least a social-psychological problem, I shall try to show among other things that this needn't be so if we convert it into a problem about members' treatment of the actor as if here were an agent—a procedure which directly connects with social deviance.

To clarify the following general discussion, I will begin with an example. Note that the same behavior in children and adults can be very differently treated. A physiological description by a child, for instance, may lead to no observable reaction by those around him, whereas the same description by an adult usually does. It is often said by parents that the child is exempted because he is still learning, which may be true, but glosses over our interests. It would bring greater concision to ask the parent what there is about the common-sense state of "learning" that permits of exemption in the child's case. And sooner or later I think we would find that a parent conceives a child not to know what he is doing, in that the child is held to have no theoretic or formulated knowledge as opposed to mere knowledge by familiarity or practical knowledge.

Members generally make a distinction between knowing what they are doing (theoretic action), in the sense that the actor can be said to formulate what he is doing in terms of some rule or criterion, and not knowing what they are doing (practical action),[14] in the sense that the actor is unable to so formulate what he is doing. Russell's distinction between *savoir* and *wissen,* on the one hand, and *connaître* and *kennen,* on the other,[15] corresponds to the difference between theoretic and practical action, respectively. And I think Simmel had it in mind, but primitively and with certain indigestible consequences, when he separated sociability from sociation.[16] The former, insofar as Simmel can be read with our interests in mind, is for the member to envision the form of the activity as it exhibits rules, while the latter is only to participate in the content of the activity. In attending to form, we specifically organize the matter as a procedure as such, while sociation is a sealed preoccupation with the thing itself. Shwayder nicely sums it up by saying that we distinguish between acting in terms of the idea "That's the rule," and not so acting.[17] It is the difference between behavior which is regular and behavior which is rule-guided.[18] According to Bennet, who is discussing generalizations and for which we may substitute action, the move from regular (practical) to rule-guided (theoretic) is comparable to the move from "generalizations which manifest" a rule to "generalizations about" a rule and is "analogous to that of the move from descriptions which are rules to descriptions which refer to rules."[19] Perhaps the distinction is similar to the one between rule-governed, in the way a generalization or law would govern, and rule-oriented, in the way an evaluation or assessment would be oriented. It is to "assess as well as express."[20]

At any rate, it is the contention here that actors themselves make these sorts of distinctions about the activities of one another. Those undergoing psychoanalysis, for example, are directly involved in transforming "acting out" (practical action) into "insights" (theoretic action). In this procedure the analysand is to review his acts in such a way that he displays "That's the rule" behavior about acting out. In so doing he transforms the practical action of regular acting-out behavior, which only manifests or expresses some clinical rule, into rule-oriented behavior, which is an assessment in terms of the clinical rule. Socializing situations, including formal education, are probably the ones where this distinction is a most direct and palpable common-sense concern. So also does it characterize the difference we impute between amateurs and professionals in all fields, as in art: the true poet is not one who only happens upon his work, but who has mastered the rule-guided "discipline" of his craft, even when he chooses to innovate upon it.

This is to say that members assess whether behavior only happens to conform to (or violate) a rule or whether the actor was behaving in terms of the rule. Is the actor conforming to, or violating, the rule as rule, or does he merely happen to conform or not? In other words, can he be thought to have a rule-oriented reason for what he does? In New York City, the parents of preschool children rush them from interview to interview in hopes of getting them into private school, in the belief that public schools won't do the job. The parents are consistently on tenterhooks about their child's behavior at these interviews, even when things went well at the last one. They treat the last one as only coincidentally that, nothing on which to envision the next. This is because, although they may think of the child as a conscientious practical actor in his interview behavior and thus not culpable on these grounds, they do not conceive the child to be a theoretic actor, to be rule-guided, in that he does not attend to an interview as it expresses formulable social properties of which this single interview is an instance. He is thought to have no conception or mastery of the interactional formulations by which the practices of interviews proceed, though he may have a sense of what he's doing while doing it. He is responsive, but not instructible. That is, he is thought not to deal with rules qua rules, of which an interview is one case.

Consequently, parents spend the time before an interview trying to put the child in a good humor, in an attempt to create a scene in which the practical actions of the child will happen to conform to the rule-guided version of correct interview behavior. Argument is avoided, breakfast is gratifying, the child is kept busy on uncranky fun, and so on. And when the interview turns out badly, the parents act as if nothing much can be done about it, the child not having known what he was doing when he did it. The issue of deviance and conformity doesn't really come up. With older children, however, a disappointing session is often followed by remonstration, because the child is thought now to be a theoretic actor and thus to have chosen to do badly. In the first case, deviance and conformity are just not relevant, because it is the parental version of their child that he is only a practical actor. In the second, however, deviance and conformity are at issue, because the child is a theoretic actor. He is now held to be an agent of his own behavior, because he "knows what he's doing." Only here does deviance arise.

I am not suggesting that an actor with knowledge by acquaintance or familiarity—with only practical knowledge—does not know what he's doing in that he is unaware of his milieu and activity: that he is a robot or dope. A practical actor, as with children, can attend to his circumstance in the sense that he could record his experience, write it in a letter, tell it, draw a picture of it, or the like. He can even do these in a way that satisfies him and in a way that could be made intelligible to others, viz., clinical interpretations of schizoid writings. A parrot is surely not unaware when he squeaks, "Polly wants a cracker," nor is Piaget's child when he syncretically interprets mechanical cause and effect. Yet suppose the parrot croaks his line immediately following someone's remark that "a Floridian is looking for a wife." Even those who dislike awful puns might laugh. But they laugh only because it seems like a bad pun; that is, it only happens to be guided by pun rules and thus meets none of the criteria, though it appears to meet all. Any exercise of wit is foreclosed here; it has nothing to do with the quality of wit at all, because the parrot does not formulate the rules by which puns are made. A lout is not forever and always prevented from doing something clever. But he does not link the act to its context; he only acts in a context. We are made to suffer the boring redundancy of a child's joke because, although he can practically engage with the comic, he does not apply the theoretic criterion of repetition.

To be a theoretic actor, thus, is "not merely to satisfy criteria, but to apply them." [21] Similarly, a conformist is not one who happens to satisfy a rule, but one who applies it; and a deviant is not one who happens to violate the rule, but one who defies it. Those who only happen to be one place or another in the conforming-deviant scheme of things are exempted from judgment. They are not even in the scheme. That children are syncretic and egocentric serves not to remove the onus of deviance, but to preclude even the possibility of it, because although children may know the particular objects with which they are dealing (marbles, a mother, some peers), they are thought not to know them as usably rule-guided objects, by which they are organized into general courses of action. Thus, although things and acts can be identified by the nontheoretic actor, rules cannot. He does not act in consideration of a rule.

This is not a strange idea to members, as can be observed in their everyday adoption of it. One common-sense use of this distinction is playing dumb. An actor who explicitly attends to the difference between knowledge by familiarity and theoretic knowledge—that is, an actor who formulates the distinction—can anesthetize his deviance by acting as if his knowledge were only by familiarity: he can act dumb.

He can act as if he doesn't know he committed an offense, and he may get away with it as a result, especially if he is a recruit, neophyte, or newcomer. He gives an impression of practical action by having theoretically organized the distinction. It is a device made available by a theoretic treatment of the materials of deviance themselves, a very sophisticated course of action. Certain features of the guard-inmate "collaboration" in prisons and hospitals can be seen as an exercise of the distinction in order to neutralize it. The offender plays dumb in not recognizing the rule, while the offended plays dumb in not recognizing the offense, or in not recognizing that the offender is playing dumb—by playing dumb about playing dumb, as it were. Of such also is made the plea of temporary insanity,[22] which is a statutory provision for the distinction between theoretic and practical action.

This distinction, if correct, is very revealing of the idea of intentions, motives, and purposes.[23] An actor can be said to have intended to do what he did by being ascribed theoretic status with regard to what he did. If he is held to have behaved in consideration of a rule, and if his behavior can also be said to have been concentional (not accidental, coerced, or miraculous), then so can he be said (according to common sense) to have intended, wanted, or meant to do what he did. That is, he can be treated as an agent of his own behavior, his act as a motivated act. He will be treated as if he is alive to the world around him, and hence the conforming-deviant issue will arise. Here is the paradigmatic deviant. Someone who "knows what he's doing" in this special sense will be held accountable for his acts and responsible for his behavior. He will be considered to have acted from the status of full-fledged membership, which is to take on social responsibility and to give over rights to review. Intentions, as acts which are deemed to be theoretic, are a central feature in deciding on the character of an act—so central, in fact, that an intention to deviance can be deviant, and punishment ensue, in the face of behavior which conforms. This is the theoretic reciprocal of behavior which only happens to conform or deviate. An imputed intent makes the behavior unimportant. Imagine the suburban wife's reaction upon discovering that her husband's fidelity is only a consequence of being unable to find an object for his promiscuous intent. An argument like "But I never *did* anything" would hardly assuage her, though it might amplify her suspicion that he is another kind of incompetent as well. Intent is explicit in criminal cases and can literally make the difference between life and death.

In summary, deviance in this other aspect of common-sense response is committed by one who can be said to be a theoretic actor. A theoretic actor is socially treated as if he acts in consideration of a rule. To be so treated is to have intended to do what was done (if the act is also deemed conventional), which is to assign responsibility for the act. It is this social responsibility which engenders the execrable character of deviance.

Deviance is thus the expression of a process in which behavior is assessed as conventional (or not) and then theoretic (or not). With regard to conventionality, to be deviant the behavior requires that it be deemed unnecessary—not accidental, coerced, or miraculous. When the conventional contingency is realized, the equivalent of a charge has been made. The charge then sticks or not, depending on whether the actor is also treated as a theoretic or practical actor. If the former, he will be said to have known what he was doing by having acted in consideration of a rule; that is, he will be held responsible because he intends to do what he does. If the latter, he will be exempted because he doesn't know what he's doing. Conventionality and theoreticity are the processes by which deviance is recognized, responsibility ascribed, and labels designated. Deviance is an upshot of these processes, because they produce the designations of deviance which follow them.

II

I now want to modify the periphery of what I have been saying so as not to be peremptory about what is deviant and what is not. Although it has been my central purpose to locate the overarching parameters of deviant judgments, not to discuss particular substantive forms of deviance, it is time to redeem certain forms which may have been excluded while pointing up the ideas of conventionality and theoreticity. Deviance has been discussed here as if it were always both conventional and theoretic, and hence punishable. An act that "might not have been," performed by an actor who "knows what he's doing," would usually engender punishment for the offense. These are the kinds of acts, neither inevitable nor unconsidered, for which actors are held directly responsible. Lies, fraud, indifference, professional crime, and disingenuousness are examples from our kind of society that readily come to mind. Yet many other behaviors which we have come to call deviant do not combine in this positive way for both conventionality and theoreticity and are thus more rehabilitative than punishable: mental illness, delinquency, ignorance (as contrasted to stupidity), and so on. There is no overriding reason not to continue to call these deviance, but by applying the two notions of conventionality and theoreticity I think we can see what they share with all deviance, as well as what in particular separates them from the more punishable forms. I think they meet one or the other of the conventional-theoretic criteria, but not both.

Suppose, for example, that someone tells a falsehood, tells something that members believe to be untrue. Imagine our response here, which will be to address the conventionality and theoreticity of the falsehood. Is the falsehood accidental, coerced, or miraculous; that is, is it inevitable and so not conventional? What if "No, no, you're beautiful" had been said to an ugly, crying woman? Being a palliative, we may very well suggest that, socially speaking, the statement could not have been otherwise under the circumstances. We think of some palliatives as being forced by the situation. Even though the speaker knows what he's doing—knows others would take his statement to be false, intends to make a false statement—he is doing something that is made impossible to avoid and thus falls under the common-sense rubric of nonconventional and hence exempted behavior.

Now imagine that the falsehood is treated as a "tall tale." What are we doing here? A tall tale implies that it might have been otherwise, for the teller is conceived not to have had to launch it. He chooses to do so, so to speak. Yet it is also treated as an "exercise of the imagination" in that the teller is thought to get carried away and doesn't have it in mind that he is doing anything in particular. We often excuse him on the grounds that he doesn't know what he's doing, that he's not acting in consideration of rules of truth, that he is without any theoretic intent at all (if we got the impression that it only seems to be a tall tale and the teller has something else in mind like changing the subject, we are, of course, no longer dealing with a tall tale). He is thus not held responsible for telling an untruth because his behavior, while conventional, is treated as not theoretical.

Suppose next that what the speaker is saying sounds like a paranoid delusion, spattered with persecution and aggrandizement. It seems to me that in secular societies there is some empirical division about the conventionality of this. In some places, notably backward ones, such acts are thought to be neither accidental nor coerced nor miraculous, to be not inevitable and thus conventional. In other places, we do believe psychosis to be a result of biographical accident or the coercions of circumstance. Where such an act is defined as conventional, the common-sense observer moves on to theoreticity and whether the actor can be seen to have acted in consideration of a rule. And again there may be a division, although the attribution of theoreticity is not very prevalent in the world today. Some would say no, he is "insane" and that means he cannot be a theoretic actor, which is a more clinical version than yes, he can so be seen, he knows what he is doing. The latter would be assignment of full responsibility, since the act is both conventional and theoretic, but the former would not, since it is only conventional. If the act [24] is thought to be nonconventional in the first place, on the other hand, the actor would be exempted from responsibility right off, and his ensuing treatment would be to rehabilitate without punishing.

Continuing with conventional and theoretic mix, think of the falsehood that smacks of mendacity. It is our notion that a lie is something that might have been otherwise and that the actor knows what he is doing. He knows what he is doing in that he is felt to maximize advantageously a discrepancy in information and that he does this out of a choice that is unencumbered by circumstance. When this occurs, his act is both conventional and theoretic. He can be said to have done it without duress and by intent. The consequence for him will be severe in terms of the treatment he will receive.

One final example. Imagine a man who goes from the tenth floor of a building to the first, without the aid of stairs, elevator, or parachute. The first issue will be to decide what happened, and this will involve asking about "causes" with an eye to their conventionality: Was the act inevitable? Did he trip by an open window? Was he pushed? If it is decided that he tripped, another accidental death. If he was pushed, homicide. In either of these cases it is not the act of going from the tenth to the first floor that is deviant. Rather, the deviance, if any, resides in some prior act of which this is only an extension. It is to be discovered in the items which produced going from the tenth floor to the first.

But suppose these possibilities are abandoned. Suppose the subject is young and athletic, very unlikely to trip, and that no one was in the room when he did it. We have rejected the possibility that the act was not conventional and in doing so accept that the act was conventional. We establish the working premise that it must in some way have been a choice, since it was not inevitable in the circumstantial sense. (Note, by the way, that the procedure is one of abandoning or rejecting certain classifications, and not merely accepting some. This is the heart of the equivocality of moral rules already discussed. We proceed by following rules of rejection until no other interpretation is possible or likely except the one that is left, which transforms the affair into a positive assignment of responsibility.)

So we move on to the theoretic-practical status of the actor: Did he know what he was doing, insofar as he can be said to have acted in terms of the rule about jumping off high places? Could he have observed his act as if he were a third party? If so, the act will be classified as suicidal, for to be a theoretic actor is to intend what happens. If not, if though he could be said to have been "aware," "responsive," "conscious," he could not also be said to have been rule-guided, we will probably adopt our favorite residual category of psychosis, that being the only one left after an exhaustive rejection of all others.

Thus, out of the various configurations of conventionality and theoreticity we come to various forms of deviance. An act can be one or the other, or both, or neither. I suggest that all deviance is generated by some such configuration. The actual configuration in any case remains to be observed.

III

There are several relevant methodological and conceptual issues in sociology that conventionality and theoreticity may clarify. At least I hope they will not be further obscured.

First, this idea of deviance makes it unnecessary to look at the act itself. Since deviance is no more nor less than the way an act is received, empirical observations can be made by observing its reception. It is unnecessary to establish any empirical criteria of deviance except community criteria. We do not have to look at the act itself, or recreate one after it vanishes. This is intuitively important with regard to the physically inaccessible, such as suicide, although the difficulty holds even for acts which are not so terminal. Under this principle, the suicide is its treatment via conventionality and theoreticity, and nothing else. It is the sociologist's special advantage not to have to observe the act or person that members deal with, only the way members do their dealing. It is not necessary to conceive the essential sociological nature of deviance as a transaction between some actual concrete labeled actor and some actual concrete labeling actor. Analytically, the transaction is entirely between labeling actors, even when it so happens empirically that a labeler is labeling his own act. The sociological "actor" is the labeler, whatever the referent act, whoever the concrete person. We need observe no more than conventionality and theoreticity.

Second, we are clarifying the very vague notions of ought, morality, and value. The traditional idea of ought, as something which should be done, barely scrapes the surface of deviant behavior, because it sel-

dom tells us how we actually behave with regard to the acted performances that oughts and values only give us the license to do.
Children ought to do many things, but they are often excused after
not doing them. Adults are, too. Conventionality and theoreticity are
the modes and behavioral uses of morality, of its enforcement and exemption, given the very general and undescriptive character of moral
precepts. They are ways of moral practice, and it may even be appropriate to say that they, as in the suicide case, are the morality. Furthermore, if we proceed, as was suggested, by rejecting certain interpretations before going on to the next, the moral status of any case is
arrived at by rejecting the existence in the world of rule-stipulated
conditions of failure. To be immoral, then, is to reject exemption, and
not just to accept immorality. To add figures may be to add figures,
but to be immoral is to be not moral. This is a consequence of the active logic of conventionality and theoreticity, which is a ruling-out
procedure of conditions of failure and practical action, respectively.

Third, conventionality and theoreticity depict the processes by
which acts fall inside and outside "the norms." To say that profanity is
deviance in one group because it is outside the norms, but not in another because it is inside the norms, is clumsy if not tautological and
can only be applied willy-nilly. How but by fiat would we know we
had a case that something outside the norms was not deviant; that is,
how does the inside-outside conception provide a principled empirical
opportunity to observe an exception? To counter that we look at the
"situation" to see whether a norm is invoked or not is little better, for
it is only to recognize that a norm may not be invoked. It is not a
method for observing how this happens and thus gives no lever for description. To say one will be excused, another not, depending on
whether the situation involves friends, enemies, mothers, spouses, and
so on, is only the barest kind of ad hoc illumination. What is there
about these memberships such that inclusion and exclusion could happen? That is, what formulation of behavior, independent of its particular, boundaried content, makes it possible of characterization in the
first place? We need first to know the analytic properties of deviance,
not the concrete substantive imputations which are their consequence.
To put it even more aggressively: conventionality and theoreticity are
general processes which occur in all groups and all relationships.
They are the linchpins of deviance because they generate the conceptual possibility of particular normative imputations, with the result
that we needn't document one substantive description by another.

To say that falling inside and outside the norms is determined by
the meaning of the act to the member is equally uninstructive. It is so

bland an idea—of course it is the meaning—as to be nondescript. So the meaning of a shout varies between sets of pool players. We have already said this by depicting their behavior. We need to talk of meaning, not as offense against a (substantive) norm, but the rule by which offense comes to be recognized and generated as an offense; that is, we are right back to conventionality and theoreticity. These are the criteria of meaning in a deviant matter because they generate the content of the matter as deviant.

Fourth, it is according to the workings of conventionality and theoreticity that the grades and boundaries of membership are proffered and withdrawn. A full member is a person, group, or collectivity whose acts do not come to be questioned under the rubrics of conventionality and theoreticity. A partial member is one whose act is deemed either conventional or theoretic, but not both. A nonmember is one whose act is both conventional and theoretic. One who never comes under these auspices never engages in behavior that is questioned. One who falls only under one is, presumably, excused in part. Though he may be placed in limbo for a while, he is probably treated as retrievable without having to annul his act, so long as it can be shown that he will not repeat it. One who falls under both, on the other hand, will be excluded until and if his act can be annulled, which is to say that it can be treated as if it never happened. This sort of re-reading is a process which makes it impossible to think of social definitions as frozen in time and place. Rather, a single act can be punished at one point and then fully redefined as exempt at another.[25] It could, for example, be called conventional and theoretic, then nonconventional and practical.

Fifth, conventionality and theoreticity are relevant to preferential rules, not constitutive ones, and hence deviance occurs with regard to preferential rather than constitutive behavior.[26] Deviant behavior does not violate the rules that sociologists describe as necessary for the maintenance of social action. It is instead the kind of trouble that may change or disrupt things without destroying them. Since the judgmental aspect routinely incorporates the possibility that acts may or may not be conventional and theoretic, it cannot be said that the presence or absence of one or another is necessary to the continued survival of the action. Lying, psychosis, and the like are continuous matters for which members are prepared and with which they cope in an organized way. One feature of this organization is the operation of conventionality and theoreticity.

Sixth, it would seem that conventionality is the common-sense version of situation, theoreticity the common-sense version of actor. "Was it inevitable?" is to ask about the causal status of the circumstance in which an act takes place, and "Does he know what he's doing?" is to ask about the causal status of the actor (person or group) who does it. They are common-sense versions of social structure and character, respectively, when the causal status of an event becomes an issue. They conjoin situation and actor so as to produce the social account on which members make inferences, review themselves, assign blame, and so on, when an act needs to be evaluated for deviance.

Seventh, conventionality and theoreticity can be used to study social change, and to compare social units, by applying them to particular items of behavior. At one time, for example, decisions about deviance were mostly the province of lay persons as members of the same collectivity. Now, however, many of these deliberations rest with experts in bureaucratically rationalized organizations, often with rather different results than before. But I would argue that the conventional-nonconventional and theoretic-practical questions continue to guide such decisions and that any differences in result are a consequence of which side of the alternative is accepted as an adequate account. That madness was earlier thought to be a theoretic choice, whereas it is now thought to be only a practical action, probably describes the change in treatment we accord to that state. The questionable behavior, then, may be located in a different cell by the expert, but his deliberations remain in the same matrix. The general analytic status of conventionality and theoreticity makes it possible to go beyond a mere substantive juxtaposition of changes in treatment and toward the links between such changes, because they formulate for us how the treatment of deviance is possible in the first place. They are thus utilized by, and can describe, behavior in and between societies, organizations, persons, towns, economies, or whatever social units and processes one chooses to investigate.

IV

I have tried to depict deviance not as the substantive reception of particular acts, but as the common-sense rules which generate the reception of any act. There are two of these rules, "Might it have been otherwise?" and "Does he know what he's doing?" That they are common-sense rules rests on the claim that members recognize and use them.

These rules are constituted by ruling-out procedures: ruling out (or not) certain circumstances by checking on the world, a procedure which can eliminate those circumstances as causes and so locate an actor of potential responsibility; and ruling out certain features of the actor, a procedure which brings the social realization (or not) of that responsibility. Underlying these matters is the analytic idea that deviance must be conceived in terms of the character of rules and their treatment by members, not concrete acts and their treatment or concrete persons and their treatment. It is the rules to which we look in our creation of moral assessments, enforcements, exemptions, and so on, and in the theoretic case it is from the rules we look to see if alter also looked.

But it would be more than an oversimplification—it would be an error—to depict this procedure of rule-looking as one of matching behavior to rules, as though the process were identical to matching towns and maps or kitchens and blueprints,[27] since matching does not incorporate defeasibility. Now, to say that these latter kinds of rules are not defeasible kinds is not to say that they always lead to actual successes: a rule of multiplication may not be followed as a result of all sorts of mistakes, forgetting, and intervention. This would be to confuse the very thing we are trying to clarify; namely, it is not the act (multiplying) we scrutinize, but the kind of rule by which the act can be a course of action (being guided by rules for multiplying). A man may fail to multiply because he is distracted, because he forgets, because paper and pencil are unavailable, or because he is shot through the heart. But these factors are not built into the rules for multiplying the way they are built into the rules for deviance. They have nothing to do with rules for multiplying, the state of things not being formulated or made relevant by those rules. Yet the state of the world and the state of the actor are part and parcel of moral rules. They are encumbrances which make it impossible to say an act failed or succeeded merely by looking at the act, as arithmetic rules provide. A moral observer cannot grade his subjects by looking at the doing of a behavior the way arithmetic teachers grade theirs by looking at the doing of a multiplication.[28] And again, it is not because observers are weak or uninformed, nor because the moral rules are merely more complex, but because moral rules are incomparably and qualitatively distinctive. We never talk about the "erosion" of arithmetic, for example, but this is easy with morality, because deviance is always a conventional-theoretic charge. Moral rules not only permit but create and require the possibility of argument, denial, and disconfirmation.

NOTES

NOTE: The following have been important sources in formulating this chapter: D. S. Shwayder, *The Stratification of Behaviour* (New York: Humanities Press, 1963); H. L. A. Hart, "The Ascription of Responsibility and Rights," in Antony Flew, ed., *Logic and Language, First and Second Series* (New York: Doubleday, 1965), pp. 151–174; Stephen Toulmin, *The Uses of Argument* (Cambridge: Cambridge University Press, 1964); Jonathan Bennet, *Rationality* (New York: Humanities Press, 1964). I wish also to thank Alan F. Blum, Aaron V. Cicourel, Walter Goldfrank, and Jack Douglas for their helpful suggestions.

1. "Conventionality" and "theoreticity" are technical terms which will be clarified below.
2. See Shwayder, *op. cit.*, pp. 311–320, for a discussion of upshots.
3. These "explanations" do not explain anything. In fact, they do nothing except turn back upon themselves. Lacking description, what is thought to be explained is only an elliptical reference point for allusions to the explanatory factor.
4. This is to say that references to structural causes are no substitute for description. For more complete statements of this argument, see this writer's *Defining the Situation: The Organization of Meaning in Social Interaction* (Indianapolis: Bobbs-Merrill, 1968), pp. 7–20; Aaron V. Cicourel, *The Social Organization of Juvenile Justice* (New York: Wiley, 1968), pp. 1–18.
5. "It makes a great and real difference when the cause of deviant behavior is seen to lie in deliberate choice rather than in accident, inheritance, infection, or witchcraft." Eliot Freidson, "Deviance as Social Disability," in Marvin B. Sussman, ed., *Sociology and Rehabilitation* (Washington, D.C.: American Sociological Association, undated).
6. This is not to discount Goffman. My purpose is to depict processes by which deviance comes to be recognized in the first place; his is to depict what happens afterward. See his *Stigma: Notes on the Management of Spoiled Identity* (Englewood Cliffs: Prentice-Hall, 1963). This distinction also needs to be made for some of the cases described by Freidson, *op. cit.* I might add here that with the exception of professional stage actors, the examples used throughout are not empirically known to concretely represent the points they serve. Perhaps the owner of a burned face would be held responsible. The claim is that if he were, the circumstance of his face would be treated as a conventional one.
7. See Toulmin, *op. cit.*, pp. 94–145.
8. Gilbert Ryle, *The Concept of Mind* (New York: Barnes and Noble, 1949), p. 300. This is to say that, far from being a deduction, the

ascription gains weight only by having been repeated: "An argument is hackneyed, when practice with it or its kin has long since prepared us to use it unhesitatingly and without qualms. [It is] immediately obvious for the same reason that a Latin sentence is immediately obvious when we are quite used to both its vocabulary and to its syntax."

9. Chaim Perelman, *The Idea of Justice and the Problem of Argument* (New York: Humanities Press, 1963), pp. 112–113.

10. Social processes are thus the behavioral siblings of the dialectic logic of rhetoric and argumentation, not of Cartesian deduction-demonstration. It is perhaps this understanding that underlies recent greater interest in linguistics, the dramatic metaphor for social interaction, and even the collaboration of Marxists and Rousseauans in politics as theater.

11. This example adapted from Shwayder, *op. cit.*, pp. 271–273.

12. This is the process which generates moral relativism. A member excuses an act when conditions of failure are present, or by acceding to others' accounts as to what will be considered conditions of failure.

13. It is a mistake to hope that we could list failure conditions $1 \ldots n$ and then match them against an act. This is to beg the issue by denying what has already been suggested: whether we are dealing with an overarching rule or one of its subrules, the process remains the same. It is still a charge and must be worked through, not matched, because it is an argument, not a deduction, and there are failure conditions for failure conditions. Aside from this logic, such a list would be a practical impossibility anyway, there being innumerable sub- and subsubconditions.

14. It may be confusing to use the term "practical action" as a contrast to theoretic action, because practical action has been used to cover all common-sense activity (viz., Harold Garfinkel, *Studies in Ethnomethodology* [Englewood Cliffs: Prentice-Hall, 1967]). But I have chosen to do so in order to indicate that the opposite of theoretic action is not no action at all, or some form of subhuman action, and to suggest that we do have these two kinds of action in connection with the idea of rules, as will be addressed below.

15. Bertrand Russell, *An Inquiry into Meaning and Truth* (New York: Norton, 1940).

16. George Simmel, *The Sociology of George Simmel*, trans., ed., with introduction by Kurt H. Wolff (Glencoe: The Free Press, 1950), pp. 40–57. Simmel errs in limiting pure sociability to certain kinds of activity, such as play and art. If sociability is theoretic action, it can be everywhere. And sociability is probably never pure in the concrete, because it always operates jointly with sociation.

17. Shwayder, *op. cit.*, pp. 238 ff.

18. Bennet, *op. cit.*, pp. 8–21. See also John Rawls, "Two Concepts of Rules," *Philosophical Review* (January, 1955), pp. 3–32.

19. Bennet, *op. cit.*, p. 21.

20. *Ibid.*, p. 23.

21. Ryle, *op. cit.*, p. 28.

22. See "Common Sense Conceptions of Insanity," an unpublished paper by Alan F. Blum.

23. Intentions, motives, and purposes are technically different phenomena, but I will treat them as similar here.

24. The reader should be reminded that I am not talking here or elsewhere about the socially untenanted act per se, but about its treatment. "The act" is always empty until it is given treatment, in our case according to conventionality and theoreticity. I have left implicit the qualifications "treatment of the act," "reception of the act," and so on for ease in reading, but the reader should assume such a qualification in every case.

25. See the author's *Defining the Situation*, for an empirical examination of rereading.

26. Harold Garfinkel's earlier work was primarily concerned with constitutive features. See his "A Conception of, and Experiments with, 'Trust' as a Condition of Stable Concerted Actions," in O. J. Harvey, ed., *Motivation and Social Interaction* (New York: Ronald, 1963). For a general review of constitutive rules, see Shwayder, *op. cit.*, pp. 267–271.

27. It is a different matter entirely to *ask* directions or to *learn* to read maps, because what is being done here is asking or learning, and only incidentally mapping. See Wittgenstein on understanding, *Philosophical Investigations* (New York: Macmillan, 1953).

28. This is not to say that grading a multiplication is so simple or obvious as to be self-evident, which I have tried to show is never the case in any kind of activity. It is only to emphasize the distinctions we have been discussing between these kinds of rules, which involve different kinds of nonself-evident checking procedures.

4

Accounts, Deviance, and Social Order

Marvin B. Scott
Stanford M. Lyman

Historically and analytically, sociology is the study of social order. Viewed historically, sociology emerged in France [1] among a group of thinkers who, seeing disorder all about, attempted to develop the principles whereby society would be orderly, that is, without conflict—a society characterized by co-operation and co-ordination.

Analytically, sociology attempts to answer in more theoretical terms the Hobbesian question of how social order is possible.[2] Despite this recognition, however, the fundamental bases of social order have been neglected in recent sociological thought. The acceptance of the given social order, a somewhat reluctant but nevertheless real commitment to evolutionary theories of social change,[3] and a remarkably heavy research concern with macrosocial structures and local social problems have led to a general begging of the Hobbesian question. Perhaps the time has come to re-evaluate our research priorities.

Briefly put, we are suggesting that a return to the fundamental processes by which human association is possible—language, gestures, and symbols—might help restore to its rightful place the basic question of the sociological discipline.

In studying fundamental processes in terms of their bearing on the problem of order, a strategic research site is the area of deviance. It is our position that studies of deviance are intrinsically theoretical and implicitly solutions to the problem of order. For example, once a sociologist studies, say, the causes of schizophrenia, he has committed himself to a certain theoretical position, namely, that society is not possible if all men are schizophrenic. Further, a study of the causes of schizophrenia is a study of how social order is possible: if, for instance, the researcher shows that a certain pattern of socialization produces schizophrenia, he is implying what kind of socialization is needed to produce normality, and presumably this normal socialization is a condition making society possible.

As mentioned, however, we might do well to focus our concern on the more fundamental processes that underlie such structural phenomena as role relations and socialization. In short, we are suggesting that the study of social order might fruitfully begin by considering the relation of language and gesture to the phenomena of deviance.

But what specifically is meant by deviance? And what fundamental process is most directly relevant if we are to study deviance to understand a solution to the problem of order? First we will answer these questions before elaborating on larger theoretical considerations.

When Is an Act Deviant?

Between the promised and the performed, between the expected and the actual, falls the shadow of deviance. Numerous failures in mutual expectations characterize human association: old friends still violate one another's expectations in enough instances for the matter to generate common interpersonal concern; colleagues and acquaintances often startle one another by their unpredicted behavior; and strangers are approached cautiously in part because of the presumed likelihood that they will do the unexpected. Deviation from the expected, then, is a common feature of society. Yet society, rooted in a notion of predictability, endures these frequent dissociative acts. How is this possible?

Answers to this question might focus on the basic stuff of society—talk. Among the many functions that talk serves is that of restoring estranged relationships, repairing broken engagements, and cementing new gaps in associations. Talk provides mechanisms by which everyday violations of expectations may be excused or justified; it provides a ready-made process by which the label of deviant may be avoided or removed. The form of talk especially devoted to this function is what we will call the giving and receiving of "accounts."

From an interactional perspective the deviant is one whom others label as deviant.[4] When we speak of labeling someone as deviant we do not mean to imply that persons use the term *deviant*. More specific words are employed, such as "queer," "junkie," "troublemaker," and so on. Regardless of the specific terms used, persons ascribed a deviant label share two characteristics. First, the deviant is an individual whose actions, observed or imputed, are perceived as untoward and possibly thought to be a threat to the common good—as that is defined by some group or group agent (like a policeman). Second, deviants are generally held to be in some sense responsible for their deviant action. In other words, deviant acts are linked to an imputed mental element said to reside "inside" the actor, so that presumably he knows (or can be made to know) the reasons for which he acts and the reasons for which he might restrain or inhibit his behavior.[5]

Deviant action and the mental component of this action are inextricably linked in lay beliefs and reflected in ordinary language.[6] Thus language with respect to untoward action is both descriptive and putative.[7] To say, for instance, "Smith hit the girl," is not only to describe the action but also to ascribe responsibility. But note that our ordinary language also permits us to defeat the accusative aspect of the remark: Smith might reply, "I hit the girl accidentally while moving a piano out of the room"; or he might reply, "I hit the girl because she had a knife poised to cut her wrist." In the first case the pejorative aspect of the act is modified by a claim of accidental (that is, unintended) action; in the second case, the action is relieved of its label of wrongfulness because of the higher purpose it served. It follows, then, that the label of deviant can be attached successfully to an actor only if he is unable to relieve himself of the negative interpretation of his intentions. If he is able to offer an acceptable account (an excuse or justification) for his presumed untoward action, his behavior is no longer deviant. When his account is honored, we may say that his deviance has been neutralized.

The sociological study of accounts given to neutralize the attribution of deviance and the conditions and reactions to success or failure in this enterprise have hardly begun. As an initial step toward such investigations, we propose to discuss the nature and construction of accounts and their relation to the structure of law and society.

The General Nature of Accounts

The essence of the argument that follows is that the plausibility and acceptability of accounts depend ultimately on two considerations: the shared common-sense theories of persons and the plausibility of the immediate argument process itself. We may briefly examine these two considerations in terms of the theoretical origins of the subject of accounts. As might be expected, these theoretical roads lead back to Max Weber.

For Weber, what is distinctive about social science (in contrast to natural science) is the concern with the actor's attachment of subjective meaning to the events and things in his environment. The depiction of these meanings constitutes the criterion for an adequate explanation of social phenomena. Specifically, the study of subjective meaning involves an analysis of the actor's *motives*. By motive Weber did not refer to drives, need-dispositions, or attitudes,[8] but rather to "a complex of subjective meaning which seems to the actor himself or to the observer an adequate ground for the conduct in question." [9]

From Weber's all too brief and somewhat ambiguous definition of motives [10] two separate lines of investigation have begun. The first is that which stems from the phenomenologically oriented interpretation of Weber advanced by Alfred Schutz [11] and carried forward in explication and research by Harold Garfinkel.[12] Schutz was particularly impressed by Weber's notion that conduct tends to become routinized, so that the actor's world becomes a taken-for-granted world consisting of recipes for living that "everyone knows." This taken-for-grantedness is part of the "background expectancies" of the actor's everyday world. The task of the sociologist is to uncover the routine grounds of action that the actors themselves are often only partly capable of expressing directly. Garfinkel, in a series of intriguing experiments, has continued exploring the leads opened by Schutz. His research is designed to demonstrate the taken-for-granted expectancies of everyday action, and he has repeatedly shown that the actors are not aware of the routine grounds of their conduct until a breach in expectations occurs. To account for the uniformity of social order, the sociologist in this tradition attempts to locate and describe these taken-for-granted expectancies.

The second line of investigation stemming from Weber's work on motives involves the study of linguistic designations. C. Wright Mills, inspired by Weber's discussion of motives (as well as Mead's social psychology and the work of Kenneth Burke), advances the sociological study of motives in his well-known essay "Situated Actions and the Vocabularies of Motive." [13] According to Mills, motives are lingual devices avowed or imputed to social actors whenever conduct is interrupted directly or inferentially by the actor himself or someone else by the question, "Why?"

Since usage of the term *motive* still connotes a psychobiological re-ductionism, locating it in the actor, and also suggests a dichotomy among explanations dividing those that are real from those that are mere rationalizations,[14] we need a term more appropriate to sociologi-cal formulation. Further, a term is needed that will bring together Schutz's emphasis on the taken-for-granted social recipes that "every-one knows" and Mills's emphasis on linguistic designations. We think the suitable term is *accounts.*

Elsewhere we have extensively discussed the major analytic features of accounts.[15] Here it is only necessary to summarize our previous dis-cussion with some modifications.

Accounts are statements made by social actors to relieve themselves of culpability for untoward or unanticipated acts. There are two types of accounts: *excuses* and *justifications*. An excuse is an admission that the act in question was bad, wrong, or inept, coupled with a denial of full responsibility. A justification is an admission of full responsibility for the act in question, coupled with a denial that it was wrongful.

Four modes of excuses may be perceived as appeals to various re-sponsibility-mitigating agents: the appeal to accidents, the appeal to defeasibility, the appeal to biological drives, and scapegoating. Invok-ing *accident* as a source of one's allegedly deviant conduct mitigates (or relieves) one of responsibility by pointing to the well-recognized hazards in everyday life and the equally well-recognized inability of humans to control absolutely all their own motor responses. The appeal of defeasibility invokes a division in the relation between action and intent, suggesting that the latter was malfunctioning with respect to knowledge, voluntariness, or state of complete consciousness. Invoking biological drives suggests a distinction between the animal and human characteristics of mankind as an explanation for untoward behavior, acknowledging that the former sometimes overrides the latter char-acteristic. Scapegoating, employed for our purposes in a wider context than that familiar to students of racial prejudice, blames others for one's own actions.

Justifications assert the positive qualities of an action in the face of a claim to the contrary. They may utilize a universal counterstatement to the original accusation, claiming that, in contrast to the accuser's position, the act in question is everywhere recognized as acceptable; or, a particularistic defense in which the act in question is recognized as generally impermissible, but situationally appropriate. Four of the well-known "techniques of neutralization," delineated by Sykes and Matza [16] to explain how juveniles commit crimes without feeling like criminals—the "denial of injury," "denial of the victim," "condemnation of the condemners," and "appeal to loyalties"—are generalized justification types that have wider usage than the arena of juvenile delinquency. In addition, the "sad tale" (that is, a selected and distorted arrangement of facts or reconstruction of the biography) is often invoked as a justification. Last, individuals sometimes employ an appeal to self-fulfillment as a justification for behavior that others regard as untoward.

Given these preliminary considerations, the question arises as to the crucial structural form involved in giving accounts and holding others accountable. We shall argue that giving accounts and holding accountable are typically *face games*—and, properly played and resolved, they are the basic mechanism by which social breaches are bridged. Before this argument can be made, we must first consider briefly what is meant by games in general and language games in particular.

Interaction as Game Behavior

To understand both the construction and the acceptability of an account, we may usefully begin by considering Wittgenstein's discussion of language games.[17] According to Wittgenstein, the many kinds of games—card games, football games, baseball games—have no single feature in common. Rather, they resemble one another as the members of a family might, being alike now in this feature, now in that, and again in another. The same may be said for language and, more to the point here, accounts. An account may be fruitfully studied as a move in a social game. The questions facing the actor in any encounter in which an accusation is made are "What social game am I playing?" and "What are the rules of this game, and what is the most efficacious move I can make in order to win, or at least not lose?" Perceived as games, social engagements employ moves, tactics, and strategies, although the interactants themselves may be more or less aware of the game properties and good or poor players. In any case, the accused must estimate his goals and perceptions, the goals and perceptions of his fellow interactants and other relevant persons, and the interpretation that others place on his own action and words.

The minimal arena of game action is that social situation which Erving Goffman[18] has designated variously as a "focused gathering," an "engagement," or an "encounter." The characteristics of an encounter are that two or more persons have come into one another's visual and audial presence and have granted one another mutual rights of cognitive and communicative recognition and response. Any encounter between two or more individuals may be analyzed as a game if the following condition holds true: at least one of the interactants is aware or capable of being made aware that, in realizing his aims in an encounter, he must take into account the others' expectations of him, also the others' expectations of what he expects of them, and vice versa.

Game activity, then, is under way when action is social in the sense that Weber employed this term.[19] Hence we may dispose of that criticism of game theory which holds that it is confined solely to a narrow conception of goal orientations.[20] In social reality and in sociological theory it is recognized that men may rationally proceed to achieve goals other than those associated with eighteenth-century shopkeepers. Men may be primarily interested in saving their own or someone else's face; in securing the unqualified love of another; in gaining compliance from or giving allegiance to another. These noneconomic goals are subject to actor's and alter's cognitive awareness and also to their mutual and respective calculation of means to be employed.

True, an encounter may proceed on the course of interaction without any of the members' becoming especially conscious of any "game" being involved in their own or others' behavior. But should obtrusive information, unexpected events, or untoward behavior intrude on the proceedings, a situation having all the properties of a game might then become a conscious, as well as an active, part of the encounter. In other words, it is in account-giving situations where we are most likely to find a heightened awareness on the part of the interactants, generating a gamelike mode of interaction.

When persons are conscious that the behavior pattern in which they are involved is like a game, they tend to have a sense of sequentiality about their own and their coparticipants' acts. For example, when one person seeks to find out some information about another who desires to withhold that knowledge, their mutual acts are apt to be perceived as a series of covering and uncovering moves.[21] Similarly, when people are primarily interested in protecting their identities against spoilage, their acts are likely to take on the character of face-supporting and protective moves.[22] Each move carries with it strategies and counterstrategies, some of which go undetected by the players.

The game situation is not stable. Its instability exists precisely in the two kinds of contingencies inherent in goal-oriented behavior. First, that of the dynamics of game behavior itself: during the course of any game, the interactants will continually indicate by their behavior that they are in the game, out of the game permanently or temporarily, that they understand or do not understand that they are in a game, or that they are changing the nature of the game. The players communicate these various game states by transmitting an assortment of clues and cues: some obvious, others subtle; some recognized, others missed. That any player will know what is happening depends on his receptivity and perceptivity with respect to ongoing behavior and his past experience and its meanings to him in the game context.[23]

Second, the complexity of interaction in game behavior is indicated by the fact that it operates according to the paired mutuality or complementarity of symbolic interpretation. Thus to make but a single opening move of a game, John must decide in what game he is participating, what game Marsha is playing, what game Marsha thinks John is playing, and what orientation John has toward his imputed interpretation of Marsha's and his own behavior. When third and fourth parties are added, complications multiply. Consider the social function of humor as an element of a game in which one actor is trying to shore up a difficult relationship, as, for example, the relation between a dying patient and a hospital nurse. Both nurse and patient may understand that jokes about death or playful derogations of the hospital, its personnel and services, are techniques that temporarily patch up the fractured state of their different situations; but another patient may regard the entire scene as one of unwarranted impropriety on the part of either the nurse or patient and "enter the game," so to speak, in order to redress what he believes is an imbalance in the relationship.[24] Complexity and causes for error in perception arise because of the very nature of human interaction; that is, the mutual mirror images and interpretations of the players. Complexity and potential misperceptions are enhanced by increasing the number of players and, consequently, of mirror images.

Despite these complexities, however, the interactants may simultaneously participate in different games without confusion. Because the same event has multiple "normal" interpretations, the players are able to interpret that event in different ways without necessarily confusing their association. Thus, two scholars engaged in research on the same topic may meet and carry on a colloquy in which one seeks to maintain "face" of both himself and the other, while the other seeks to establish a more secure relationship. The face-saving moves of the former may so interlock with the intimacy-creating moves of the latter that each will interpret the behavior of the other as complementary and co-ordinative, and both will end the encounter believing that the sought-after goals were achieved.

Moreover, awareness by one player that the other is playing a different and unco-ordinative game does not necessarily result in confusion. Rather, such a situation is more likely to produce conflict. The players will then mobilize stratagems for controlling the situation or avoiding an unwanted outcome. Conflict, including deadly engagements, is usually carried on in what may be viewed analytically as a game context. Only when collective behavior of the type described under such headings as "extraordinary popular delusions" or the "madness of crowds" occurs can we suggest that the game framework is fractured—and even then it may be only a fracture and not a total break.

Confusion and a state of anomie may arise when one interactant cannot fathom any meaning from the other's behavior and thus is left in a state of diffuse anxiety and fear. Such is likely to occur when the interactants employ entirely different and mutually impenetrable universes of discourse and gesture. Examples of such a condition are found in the autobiographical literature of travelers[25] and immigrants[26] and in the accounts of persons placed in captivity in a society entirely different from that with which they are familiar.[27] A lesser state of anxiety, but of the same general type, sometimes occurs when persons of different ethnic, class, or status groups find themselves in situations where they must interact.[28] Even a state of anxiety, however, can lend itself to a game-strategic outlook, as when a player determines that, whatever happens, he will not lose his composure, or when he decides that his own anxiety is an element in a game whose object is to confuse and demoralize him. Thus, for analytical purposes, the state of anomie must be regarded as but a potential element in a game situation.

Face Games

Although game situations are subject to abrupt or gradual shifts, it is possible to delineate the analytic contours of that gamelike encounter most crucially relevant to the giving and receiving of accounts. Following Goffman,[29] we refer to this encounter as a face game.

In face games each participant maneuvers to maximize his own realization of a valued identity, while seeking an equilibrium that will permit others to do likewise. In such games one or both of two objectives are sought. One may be described as "defensive," in which a player seeks to protect his own identity against damage or spoilage;

the other is "protective," in which a player seeks to prevent any damage or spoilage from happening to the identity of the other player(s).[30]

Face games, then, are those which involve the preventing of damage to one's own or another's identity or the salvaging of honor when it has been impugned. In the encounter where the face game is played, one may detect an interchange which (as Goffman suggests) has certain formal properties that indicate its beginning, playing time, and termination. The participants are a minimum of two persons, and the acts or "moves" occur as a serialized taking of "turns" at action. The game event signaling that a face game is about to begin is an occurrence that openly damages the identity of one of the persons. This occurrence can be initiated by the person damaged by the deed or by another person. The event must be one that casts manifest doubt and negative evaluation on the self that has been presented thus far in the encounter. Thus, a person may make a remark that is interpreted by others present to be beyond and beneath the character that he represents himself to be; he may indicate lack of motor skills or body controls that until the event have been associated with his character; he may reveal incapacity to carry out tasks with which he has been previously identified; or he may give way to an emotional state that is regarded as unsuited to his general character.

But whether a face game will be initiated or not is still problematic. Several general considerations [31] will determine if an act is seen as untoward and if a call or anticipated call for an account will be forthcoming—these being two conditions necessary for generating a face game.

To begin, one or more of the participants in an encounter may be seeking excitement, which can easily be generated by "calling down" or "sounding" another. One may even fabricate another's wrongs and challenge him to an accounting—all for the sake of whipping up some action. Thus, the youthful tough turns in anger on another accusing him (falsely) of bumping, of not watching where he is going, demanding an apology. Should the innocent fail to respond apologetically, the situation for action (that is, excitement) is generated. And insofar as one desires the stepped-up excitement of a heated face game, hot action may be provided by challenging easily available authority-endowed role others. For this kind of action, then, students can turn to the administration, inmates to the staff, and juveniles to the police.

If the players perceive an encounter as an opportunity or risk to gain or lose face, we have a second factor determining whether a face game will ensue. Certain conduct of the other might threaten or violate one's self-definition, sense of rightful place, or honor. Thus, an untoward action may be perceived not only as a breach of situational propriety but also as an insult to the character of other participants in the situation. To spit on a person in a New York subway is not only a violation of a city ordinance (against spitting in subways) but also a violation of the victim's sense of honor. Typically, however, the challenge-to-honor act is more subdued. Through the slightest of cues—a look, a smile—one tests the other's willingness to engage in moral combat, or decides whether the insult deserves notice as a character challenge.

A final feature influencing the initiation of a face game involves the restorative actions of those present in the encounter. Again, no more than a look or a word need be necessary to communicate to another that he must avoid or cease an activity lest he be launched in fateful moral combat. The very presence of others—witnesses before whom one wishes to enhance one's own face or destroy that of another—will affect whether an act is perceived as untoward, or worthy of initiating a character contest, or both.

In short, whether a face game will ensue depends on the meaning ascribed to the various actions. This meaning in turn "derives in part from the orientation the player brings to them and the readings he retrospectively makes of them." [32]

In any case, the game itself is begun by a challenge, a "move" made immediately after the untoward event. One or more of the parties present calls attention to the offensive deed, designates the person responsible, and calls for an admission of responsibility or a statement or deed of exculpation. The challenge is one to the "face" (that is, a valued element of the identity) of one of the participants. Responses to the challenge may take the form of an offensive move against the challenger or an offering of apology, explanation, or justification for the deed in question. When the offending party attacks the challenge itself or the challenger, the game is escalated to a counterattack on the face of the challenger. Such a counterattack must be responded to by withdrawal of the original challenge, accompanied either by appropriate face-saving statements or by abject retreat (and, hence, loss of face by the challenger), or by a counterchallenge.

Here, however, we are concerned with face salvage, and hence we shall deal with instances in which the response consists of an offering by which the player in question hopes to restore the characterological *status quo ante*. Emphasis in such an offering may be placed either on the untoward event itself, as when a person challenged about an offensive story insists that it was "merely" a joke or that it had no meaning with respect to persons present or those with whom they intimately identify,[33] or on the actor, as when our storyteller insists that he "must have been drunk," "didn't know what he was doing," or, in making jest, claims to be a true representation of the reprehensible self exhibited by the telling of the story.

An alternative or supplementary strategy is compensation, penance, and self-punishment. By these acts the offender, though unable to establish his innocence, indicates to his co-participants in the interchange that he is rehabilitated and ready to re-enter the group, if not as his old self, at least as one who has paid the penalty for his offensive deeds and is thus cleansed of guilt and no longer required to feel shame. Moreover, he indicates by such acts that he is solicitous for the feelings and sensibilities of others and that when—however unintentionally—he has injured someone or the entire group, he is willing to acknowledge fault and accept or even execute judgment for his untoward act.

When self-punishment is included, the actor signals to the others his calculation of the gravity of his offense and of the punishment appropriate to it if it were to be regarded seriously. Statements such as "I could kick myself," "I hate myself when I do things like that," and "I ought to be shot" express a layman's calculation of punishments suitable to social crimes,[34] for in the arena of face interaction there are no crimes without victims.

Often enough, as the previous examples suggest, the offending party will overstate the punishment for his deed, and by such exaggerated (though only expressive) inflicting of pain on himself he will invite the offended parties to assure him that "it wasn't that bad" and that "he shouldn't be so harsh with himself." By executing judgment and sentence on himself, the offender re-establishes the code of ritual which his deed has threatened and indicates that he is a supporter of the code, as vigilant as his fellows about its violation, and is as willing to punish violators, including himself, as they are.

After the offering is made, the next move is up to the challengers and their allies. If face is to be restored, they must accept the offering and indicate that equilibrium is re-established in the engagement. As suggested in the discussion of the offering above, the offender can so phrase his move of apology, penance, and punishment as strongly to invite acceptance. On the other hand, dramatic failures here can lose the game as well. If an offender so overstates the crime and exaggerates the penalty that the others regard his entire performance as unserious with respect to his offense, they may refuse his offer and even call for an account of that offer. Understatement may also indicate lack of interest in social crimes and sensibilities and thus invite unacceptance. But if conflict is to be avoided, or a permanent rupture in the relationship is undesirable, even a rather unseemly offering may have to be tendered an acceptance.

The terminating move of the game is an acknowledgment of gratitude by the offending party that he has been readmitted to his circle without any permanent loss. This move itself is fraught with delicate aspects that may upset the play and shift it back to the challenge-offering stage. Thus, the offender may not believe that his offer has been fully accepted and instead of ending the game continue to make offerings, adding penances and punishments and calling for further acceptances. This move may, indeed, have positive pay-offs, since it can be taken as a sign of sincerity, a true expression of the state of mind of the contrite sinner against social conduct. A repetition of this offering, however, may also be overdone and signal insincerity, false contriteness, and a desire for social intimacy that overrides propriety. Persons who habitually apologize too much run the risk of exclusion from social circles, since their demand for face is greater than the available supply.

Once the gratitude phase is passed, the game is concluded, and reopening it constitutes a breach of the social etiquette by which it was carried on. Such breaches are themselves sources of loss of face which may not be granted salvage, as when, after the sign of gratitude has been given, one party continues the challenge. It is customary for the latter party to be cut off with a peremptory, "The incident is closed!" (Such a response requires retreat or apology.) The face game is thus an episode that usually interrupts ongoing social intercourse until face has been restored or one party has suffered a loss.

In addition to the elementary forms of face games just presented, certain additional characteristics deserve comment. First, as suggested earlier, face games may be prevented from beginning by the process of *avoidance*. When one's face is likely to be challenged, one can avoid contacts from whom a challenge is likely to arise. Delicate negotiations can be handled by go-betweens who, precisely because of their neutrality, can conduct matters with impunity for all concerned. Further, when an untoward act does occur on the part of the actor or his fellow participants in an encounter, one or all can disassociate with the deed, thus giving it no standing to be interpreted in the engagement.[35] Persons, moreover, who are well known to one another count it as an index of their mutual knowledge that they know what topics to avoid and what information to keep secret; persons who are strangers employ tact and discretion until they have mapped out the social areas of safety open to them.

Second, the elementary forms of the face game do not absolutely define who the initiators and the respondents will be. Thus an offender may challenge himself immediately after the untoward act and monopolize the roles of accuser, judge, defendant, penitent, and guilty party in himself, leaving the others to accept or reject his accusation or offering. Or other parties may assume the protective role for the offender, responding to the challenge by explanations or apologies and also indicating gratitude when their offering is accepted. The offending party, then, can be only an object in a face game in which others have stakes in saving his face. In still another type of situation the offender or others can be subordinate allies to whoever is making the challenge or offering. In short, the face game offers unusual opportunities for an individual to employ multiple roles and role switching as devices to secure his goals.

Finally, face games may be undertaken as part of a larger strategy of exploitation. Thus persons may pose a threat of loss of face to themselves to achieve certain gains that may be obtained thereby. Here the goals sought are praise and favorable identifications for oneself or the social downfall of another. The former is illustrated by the person who employs a strategy of self-derogation as a way of finding greater acceptance; the latter, by the person who commits suicide, leaving behind a note indicating that a certain party has forced him into this ultimate act and thus is irrevocably guilty.[36] In conclusion, face games may be undertaken for their own value or for the pay-offs they have for larger strategies in other games.

We have noted that accounts may be usefully analyzed as moves in a social game. But such an analysis would be incomplete without a consideration of law and pluralistic social structures. We now turn to these matters.

Accounts and the Law

The problematics of deviance, its imputation and disavowal, are well illustrated in the law. To begin, the prohibition of certain acts raises complex questions because of the legal tradition that insists an act must be connected in some manner to the intent of the actor. Activities that are prohibited become legally actionable in the sense of a potentially successful prosecution of the deviant actor only if it can be shown that the actor intended to commit the act and foresaw the consequences. A variety of other interpretations, which appear as accounts, with respect to the same event are possible: that it was an "accident"; that it or its consequences were an unintended result of action undertaken for another purpose; that the seriousness with which the act is viewed varies in the community so that its normative undergirding is problematic; that the act does or does not fall into the category of universally disapproved behavior; or that the act is or is not situationally prohibited.

There are two problems here. The first is that of establishing the unambiguous intent of the accused. Without an establishment of intent, there may not be a crime. Policemen, judges, juries, and other administrators of the law are faced with the necessary task of taking a retrospective reading of the meaning of an untoward act for the actor at the time he committed it. The second problem is that of the objective meaning of the act in the social order. Law is undergirded by norms or a shared consensus of a community. The degree of consensus for the law is inversely related to the degree of value pluralism in a society. To the extent that a society is characterized by a wide divergence in values, a heterogeneity of norms, and a variety of beliefs, a consensus cannot be presumed. The law thus must cope with both the mind-reading problem of intent and the societal survey of consensus.

Jurists and legal scholars typically approach the problem of intent under the rubric of *mens rea*.[37] Two contradictory positions are argued in legal circles. The more orthodox position holds that the accused's act must have been voluntary, that he must have known what he was doing, and that he must have had foresight of the prohibited consequences of his act. Unless the prosecution positively demonstrates that each of these three elements was present at the time of the act, the guilt of the accused is not established. A more recent and less orthodox approach is taken by H. L. A. Hart, who argues, according to the principle of *defeasibility*, that the voluntary character of human action is not understood in a positive but only in a negative way.[38] That is, human action is in fact carried out as mere behavior most of the time, and the voluntary and foresighted character of action can be presumed only if a number of negative conditions are not present. Thus, an accused is guilty only if it is shown he was not insane, not drunk, not under hypnosis, and so on. The problem of subscribing to the orthodox position is amply illustrated in the cases on negligence, recklessness, and errors of omission. In what manner, for example, can failure to do something be a legally actionable instance of negligence? How can the foresight in the positive sense of the orthodox school be established? Most judges, in fact, much as they may officially subscribe to the orthodox position, practice a bit closer to the position argued by Hart; that is, they look for the forms that lack of culpability can take in a particular situation, except in the crime of homicide.

The courts' problem in wholesale subscription to Hart's doctrine is that it opens up a line of personal accountability by which an accused may defeat the central charge against him. The orthodox position has a tendency to relieve judges and juries from the onerous task of ascertaining and evaluating the mental state of the accused at the time of the untoward deed by substituting for him a homunculus, the reasonable man. It is argued that if a reasonable man would have contemplated that a prohibited harm was likely to result from his act, and this harm did occur, the accused stands convicted. The unorthodox position puts the real actor into the legal retrospective reading at all times and insists that his unimpaired foresight be the substantial question before the judge or jury.

The law is posed with a real dilemma when it either seeks to substitute the reasonable man for the real actor or opens itself to considering the accounts for his own behavior offered by the actually accused person or his witnesses and representatives. The reasonable-man doctrine substitutes such an extraordinary actor-homunculus for the real actor that at least in many instances ordinary men and jurists find it difficult to punish the accused for his failure to act in accordance with the behavior imputed to this legal chimera. In addition to this problem, ordinary men and jurists may also recognize that to act for a reason is not necessarily to act after deliberation about the situation.[39] The rational-man model of behavior seems to presume just such a deliberating person—a person unlikely to be encountered in everyday life and even less likely to be found deliberating in those situations where the majority of crimes occur.

Despite the easy-to-demonstrate discrepancy between the reasonable-man doctrine and actual behavior, this typification of responsibility often proves adequate for the practical purposes at hand. Given the necessity of mass-organized "justice," jurors and others find it useful to invoke the rule-of-thumb maxim of the "reasonable man," while the same jurors (in nonlegal situations) will employ other maxims for constructing the intentions for an action.[40]

In contrast to the traditional legal model for constructing intention, Hart's position of defeasible culpability might open the court to consider whatever negating circumstances an accused might offer. But the possibility that any account of impaired consciousness and foresight might relieve the accused of guilt—and, in addition, the jurists' suspicion of the accused's or his lawyer's knowledge of the pay-offs that would arise from invoking just the right account to defeat the charge of culpability—tends to lessen their willingness to adopt an unambiguous juridical acceptance of the defeasibility doctrine. In a celebrated English case involving the death of a police constable who jumped onto the running board of the accused's car and was killed in the crash that ensued after the driver panicked, the Lord Chancellor insisted on the legal rectitude of invoking the reasonable-man doctrine in place of giving official recognizance to the accused's own account of his behavior because, if the intention of the accused were to become an issue, it would be impossible for the prosecution to circumvent the accused's simple denial that he intended to kill the policeman.[41] That the invoking of the proper account for an untoward act is likely to be part of the process by which a defense attorney negotiates the relationship between himself and his client and also reconstructs the relevant aspects of the biography of the latter is nicely illustrated in Traver's novel *Anatomy of a Murder*. The lawyer presents in a seemingly objective manner all the possible defenses against the charge of intentional homicide and subtly assists the client to choose just the one that might defeat the accusation most efficaciously in the given situation.[42]

In the place of the reasonable man some juridical scholars, following Hart, would have the judge and jury adopt a doctrine of empathy by which they would apprehend the defendant's state of mind by vicariously taking his role. Guilt or innocence is then assigned on the bases of the jurors' "indwelling understanding" of the situation in which the accused found himself and their evaluation of what they might have done or been restrained from doing therein. While this assignment to juries seems to come closer to recognizing the nature of human behavior, it poses dilemmas of gravity and standards. Jurists may be faced by persons accused of crimes so heinous as to tax their sympathetic abilities beyond capacity, such as Albert Fish, who murdered children and ate them, or John Reginald Halliday Christie, who was a necrophiliac, or Adolf Eichmann. Moreover, excuses or justifications of prohibited acts may or may not enjoy respect among the community of jurors or a presiding judge. Thus an account that invoked an identity understood by psychiatrists might fail to impress peers.

One other aspect of the intent problem faced by courts considering accounts arises when the actor is a body of persons rather than a single individual. The typical situation is that of mobs, crowds, or excited groups who engage in forbidden acts. Their collective behavior seems not to lend itself to individual decomposition, as scholars such as LeBon and Freud have so pointedly argued.[43] Yet they may be tried in a jurisdiction that requires an assessment of individual innocence or guilt. Even when collective excitation is not an issue, however, the decisions of deliberative bodies sometimes come under judicial inquiry. The usual situation is that of conflicting statements over the intent of a legislative enactment that imposes a harm, annoyance, special duty, or obligation on a class of persons. The latter, haled into court for noncompliance, may insist that the legislation is not only unfair and discriminatory but also venal because it singles out the classified group for special treatment. The representative of the state may insist that the legislation has a reasonable public purpose and that no malevolent intent exists. Whose account is to be believed?

Consider the famous case of a Chinese laundryman, denied through a local ordinance a license to operate his business, who having refused to retire from the occupation was arrested, tried, found guilty, fined, imprisoned, and then appealed the lower courts' decision to the U.S. Supreme Court.[44] The Court invalidated the administration of San Francisco's laundry licensing ordinance when it discovered that though the law was "fair on its face," it operated to affect adversely an entire group, the Chinese. This consequence of the law, the Court argued, demonstrated an intent prohibited in lawmaking. The makers of the ordinance insisted in vain that their intent was to prevent fire through the regulation of hazardous businesses and that the social imbalance created by the licensing procedure was an unintended consequence.

There are two problems here. First, the courts must distinguish between purposes and consequences. Clearly not every consequence of an action undertaken by a person or a group is intended by them to come about. There may be unforeseen events or unanticipated consequences of purposive action.[45] Although some legal scholars [46] have hinted that the intent of a legislature may be read by noticing the outcome of the legislation they pass, both legislators and ordinary men might deny that so easy a discovery can be made. Some legislators may be astonished at the results of the laws they pass; others may be ignorant of them; and still others may claim that nothing like what happened was intended.[47] But, granting the distinction between purpose and consequence, actors, individual or collective, may be held responsible for more than that which they intended.

The second issue is ascertaining, irrespective of purpose, the span of consequences for which actors should be held responsible. Legal terms like "gross negligence" suggest that there are situations where legal and common-sense standards of foresight coalesce and where they may not be overlooked. When in such an instance an excuse of unintentionality or lack of cognition is presented, it will not be honored. However, it is by no means clear that jurists have unambiguously established the perimeter bounding the area of consequences for which an actor may be held responsible.

Moreover, what is "one of the thornier aspects of judicial review" [48] for higher-echelon judges is also a problem for the ordinary man. He, too, in his everyday life must distinguish between another man's intentional acts and the consequences and also decide just for what span of consequentiality others shall be held responsible. This is made all the more complex if the society is marked by a plurality of values, norms, and beliefs.

Accounts, Pluralism, and Power

The ability of an account to re-establish sociation is at the outset dependent on its comprehensibility and acceptance by others. To the extent that everyone in the audience to whom an account is given shares a common universe of discourse and a common basis of beliefs, an account is likely to be routinely acceptable. But in pluralistic societies in which consensus on a wide range of matters cannot be presumed, accounts are likely to be problematic and their acceptance not readily predictable. Pluralism may entail differences in language and employment of argot, differences in identification of persons and objects, differences in beliefs about just what is acceptable and unacceptable behavior, and differences in hierarchies of value-importance. The pluralistic society suggests the existence of a multiplicity of identities and meanings and a context of situated moralities wherein universal rules of ethics are less if at all relevant.

Three issues in pluralistic societies are relevant to the presentation and acceptability of accounts. The first is the relation of pluralistic meanings and moralities to the power structure. The plural elements of a society do not possess equal power or authority. In fact, in most societies, plural or not, we can speak of a power elite that possesses certain rights over others and that expresses a given value pattern and morality. The value pattern and moral beliefs of the power structure tend to take precedence over all other value structures and moralities, at least in all situations in which individuals and groups come into contact with and must acknowledge at least formal compliance to the authority of the power-holding group. In such situations there is not only a potentiality for confusion in communication and contradiction in morality but also the hazard of suffering pain or deprivation from failing to indicate agreement with the moral structure of the power holders.

Typically certain functionaries act as agents of and representatives for persons or groups outside the pale of legitimated morality. In modern societies this task usually falls to the attorney—although clergymen, professors, and psychiatrists sometimes act in this capacity.[49] The task of these functionaries is to legitimate the accounts of persons untutored in, or out of sorts with, prevailing beliefs when these persons come under the interrogatory scrutiny of the minions of law or authority of the larger society. Lawyers and other functionaries often find it necessary to recast the behavior, reconstitute the beliefs, and reconstruct the morality of their clients in order to bring off a successful defense. The actual behavior and beliefs of the actors in the untoward event in question are thus sometimes wrenched out of original context and pressed on to what for some, at least, is a Procrustean bed of publicly acceptable action and morality. Abstruse legal rhetoric is itself used to mystify so that the inevitable gaps between different value and belief positions in the conflictful pluralistic society will appear to be bridged. The language of law—like a magical incantation—creates the illusion of consistency and coherence.

The second issue with respect to pluralism is that which focuses on the degree of social compartmentalization existing in any plural society. At the outset we may note that it is possible at least to imagine a plural society composed of groups that have no contact whatsoever with one another, but do acknowledge common membership in the same society. Such a society has been envisioned in the past and in South Africa as the solution to problems of race contact and the protection of minorities,[50] but rarely if at all has it been achieved. In such a society, however, account problems would be reduced to a minimum, since persons with reciprocally different expectations and beliefs would not come in contact with one another and thus would not come under interrogatory scrutiny of one another. But such perfect social apartheid is nearly impossible to bring about in contemporary societies because of the coexistence in them of independent cultural and social groups and interdependent tasks. Getting a living, preparing for an occupation, enjoying the fruits of one's labor, and seeking after or dispensing services provide just those opportunities wherein peoples meet.[51]

It is in these contacts, crossing cultural and social groups, where individuals will be likely to violate others' expectations and be called to account. At one time a Roman Catholic clerk, for example, might have refused to eat the meat set before him at his boss's Friday dinner and might have been subjected to inquiry by his host. A student who is a marijuana user may light up a "joint" at the coffee shop where he is talking over problems with a professor and earn a look of shocked dismay and a statement of searching disapproval which evokes the need for him to justify his behavior. A Negro man in college may fall in love with a white coed and be asked by Negroes and whites alike how he dares to love one of another race. An adolescent may refuse his friends' urgings to join with them for a night of revelry and fun, claiming a prior interest in his studies, only to have his refusal rejected on the grounds that on week ends fun should take precedence over studies.

In each of these instances we have examples not merely of normative conflicts but also of more subtle conflicts over the intensity of commitment to and ecology of action for potentially untoward behavior. Catholics at one time were expected to observe a double standard with respect to the prohibition on eating meat on Fridays, living up to the church's edict when at home, but permitting themselves lapses when at the homes of others. Similarly, marijuana users and Negroes might be expected to give ample expression to their beliefs in the positive aspects of the drug experience and racial emancipation without acting in such a manner as to give a widely visible display to these beliefs.[52] A call for accounts here is not merely a question, "Why are you doing this?" but rather, "Why are you doing this now?" or "Why are you using this situation as a vehicle for your moral expression?" A successful account not only will have to excuse or justify the particular act but also do the same for the degree of normative commitment which the act indicates and the situation chosen for action. Given the different milieus from which the interactants are drawn, the construction of an efficacious account is by no means easy.

The third issue emerges from the elementary observation that pluralistic societies are not typically static. Two dimensions of their dynamics may be noted. The first, on which we have already touched, is their interdependency, which is likely to throw together persons of several distinct social or cultural backgrounds. The second is their tendency for change and reconstitution with respect to the statuses of the several groups vis-à-vis one another. Pluralistic societies in the contemporary era are not like the Estates of France during the *ancien régime* [53] in that the several groups might hold now a less respectable, but soon a more respectable, position in the society.

The point with respect to accounts is their right to be requested, their establishment of social identity, and their efficacy to change in accordance with the changing status of the group involved. Situations of account confusion are especially acute when a group is in transition from one status position to another and is undergoing a collective identity crisis. Racial groups provide numerous examples. During the 1920's the Japanese in America insisted on their identity as "free white persons" in order to circumvent naturalization and franchise barriers, but found that few others would accept this definition of their racial status.[54] The Chinese have often surprised naïve but well-meaning whites by being offended when they are referred to as "Chinamen," refusing to recognize the latter term as anything but pejorative.[55] And contemporary Negroes sometimes take umbrage when they are referred to as Negroes, preferring such recently resuscitated identity pegs as Afro-American, African, or black. Identity switching is not only a tactic in the negotiation of account acceptability but also a source of confusion to both speaker and hearer when several identities are equally available. If a mutually agreed upon identity cannot be established, the giving and receiving of accounts may break up into conflict or show signs of anomie.

In addition, status transition may involve a revocation of previously established conditions of accountability. As Negroes assert their equality with whites in America, they refuse to behave according to, or apologize for violation of, the etiquette of race relations familiar to white southerners. In another instance, users of LSD were once a law-abiding group, but since the passage of recent legislation, they must excuse or justify their drug use with respect to the law. And in a society in which automation is replacing workmen with machines, groups that disdain work altogether may feel it unnecessary to excuse their defalcation from the Protestant Ethic.

Finally, status transition may make some accounts inefficacious where once they would have done nicely. An excellent example is the career of the term "colored person" as a polite euphemism for Negro. While at one time persons might excuse their offensive remarks about Negroes by recasting them as "colored" persons, today use of that term may invite a call to account. In a related sense some Negroes who might have once apologized for their language style by meek reference to their ghetto background today take it as a badge of honor for which no apology need be offered and no account requested.

Pluralism, then, affects accounts through the operation of unequal power available to the several group or value interests, the contacts between normatively distinguishable groups, and the mobility of status groups within a society. At any given point in history a society may be more or less pluralistic in any of three senses just discussed. When status groups are mobile, contacts between discrepant groups frequent, and the legitimacy of the power elite questionable, accounts are highly problematic, and even the opening negotiation of identities and the right to call for accounts will be ambiguous. Such a society is likely to experience a sense of fractured consensus, a bewilderment of identities, and a frustration in the enforcement of account liability.

Conclusion

Since accounts are employed to restore fractured sociation, we may say that in general accounts are offered as part of a face or relation-building game. The relation in question may range from a highly formalized and nonintimate one (such as in cases at law where the accused seeks to retain his membership in the company of respectable citizenry) to a very localized and intimate one (such as that in which the accused seeks to retain his identity as "beloved one").

Note, however, that social actors are sometimes unaware that their actions are such that an account is expected. This is especially the case if an encounter proceeds between persons of different cultures, subcultures, or status groups. Even in social engagements between persons of the same social class and cultural milieu there may arise situations in which one or both parties are unaware of their liability to accounts. Consider the case of a middle-class coed on her first date with a "sophisticated" senior. She may be unaware that a refusal on her part to engage in sexual relations requires an account. But once she discovers that an account must be offered, there are several strategies open to her. She may reverse the accountability and insist that her refusal is not an account-requiring act, while the young man's insistence on having sexual intercourse on the first date does require some justification. Or she may invoke one of several kinds of universally recognized criteria for refusal, such as stating that she is in her period. Still another tactic is to exculpate oneself from any blame by pointing to specific attributes of the situation: that "nice girls" don't do "that" on a first date; that she doesn't feel well; or that she is having family problems and is not in the mood.

The last-named tactic points up a peculiar quality of accounts. Some statements about self or situation are so well understood in the mind-life of the community and refer to conditions so ubiquitous that they may be invoked to cover a multiplicity of untoward acts. Among these is the common statement, "I'm having family problems," which is an account efficacious enough to cover deviancies and failures as different as crimes and sexual inadequacy. Cognizance of the widespread workability of certain rhetorics constitutes a basic background expectancy of society so that individuals can fashion an account quickly and effectively in a variety of situations.

In general, however, the fashioning and acceptability of accounts are functions of the social composition of any society. The presentation of self and self-rescues constitute interaction rituals rooted in the group identity of an individual. Depending on the social make-up of any society, there will be a homogeneity or heterogeneity of group identities and a commonality or variation in the very nature and legitimacy of accounts. To the extent that there is a culturally homogeneous power elite presiding over a society, one set of account forms will have greater precedence and rectitude over others. For those who come from culturally or socially discrepant groups, public accounts— in order to be efficacious—will have to be restructured for presentation before the holders of power or their representatives. In a highly pluralized society certain functionaries are likely to serve as account-makers and modifiers for all persons and groups who do not readily adhere to established account procedures. Misunderstandings and punishments are most likely to arise when the excuses or justifications for the untoward acts of a socially or culturally discrepant group cannot be negotiated at all by the respective advocates for the holders of power and the social transgressors.[56]

Furthermore, the dynamic aspects of society modify the efficacy of any established account procedure. Homogeneous societies may be "invaded" by culturally distinct peoples or suffer withdrawals of support from indigenous inhabitants who redefine themselves and their social aims, and either or both will drastically affect the nature and acceptability of accounts. Plural societies may restrict contact between their culturally distinct inhabitants and thus reduce confusion in accounts, but even apartheid is likely to break down under the insistent pressures of secondary contacts and task interdependence. Finally, the rank order of social groups in any society is rarely static. Hence, the legitimacy of various forms of behavior and the accounts offered for them are changing aspects of society.

The comparative structure of societies, and especially the comparative study of social ethics and intrasocietal values and beliefs, constitutes crucial areas of sociological research in the study of accounts. Especially valuable for demonstrating and comprehending the dynamic and fragile aspect of accounts are societies undergoing internal social estrangements and rearrangements—such as in the United States. In these societies sociologists will find the elements of social change by which one moral order replaces or shares the moral order of another.

These societies are social laboratories for research on alienation, conflict, reidentification, redefinition, and reintegration.

Our discussion also suggests a fruitful line of research for the sociology of law. Law distinguishes the prohibited from the permissible among the activities of humans not only by designating certain acts as illegal but also by dignifying certain motives as lawful. Thus law provides an inventory of intentions which are, in fact, the efficacious excuses or justifications for alleged crimes. But the law, by insisting on the mental element for criminal behavior, opens its practitioners, clients, and subjects to a problematic situation: ascertaining and evaluating the motives of the accused person. The establishment and judgment of the actor's intent call for the knowing and judging of "other minds" [57] under extremely onerous conditions—absence of direct observation, conflicting statements, and a situation in which the accused has a vested interest in establishing an excusable or justifying intent; while his accusers and judges, cognizant of his interest, are in a state of hyperconsciousness and suspicious awareness of his preferred intent. Sociologists interested in law might well turn their attention to the resolution of the conflicting philosophical systems of legal thought on the subject of *mens rea* with the actual practices in legal situations. Sociological theory has much to offer this research already. The sociological tradition inspired by the phenomenological work of Alfred Schutz,[58] and elaborated in the recent writings of Harold Garfinkel [59] and Peter Berger,[60] suggests the role of biographical reconstruction in determining and judging other people's actions and intentions. The courtroom is an arena of empirical research for establishing the praxeological [61] basis of these already developed concepts and for noting the process by which one institution of modern societies maintains and re-establishes the moral order.

Let us conclude by noting that the study of accounts—by which individuals and groups bridge the gap between the promised and the performed, the expected and the actual, and the surprising and the routine—focuses attention on a basic mechanism of social order. The threads of human association are constantly being rent by unexpected deeds and untoward acts. If there were no way by which individuals might salvage their identities and repair their broken relationships, social relations would indeed be treacherous, perhaps even coming to approximate Hobbes's state of nature.

Moreover, we must recognize that in modern societies accounts function not only to salvage the ego but also to restore the person; that is, that set of societal identities that we present in everyday life.

Thus accounts are given in every kind of social relationship, from the most trivial and fleeting (like bumping into a stranger) to the most important and life-sustaining (such as excusing or justifying the taking of another's life in a court of law). Accounts cut across class and status lines and modify power relationships. Their presentation may bind up the wounds of conflict or open the interactants to continued hostile engagements. And, finally, accounts rest on a fundamental acceptance of a bargaining process by which humans agree that their irregular and asymmetrically reciprocal wrongs to one another may be made up for by some form of restitution. Thus the fundamental "social contract" by which individuals and groups agree to the rules of bargaining and negotiation of accounts constitutes a basis for the moral order and a solution to the Hobbesian problem.

NOTES

1. In a paper for the San Francisco International Exposition of 1915, Durkheim himself was very emphatic on this point, writing, "To set forth the role which belongs to France in the establishment and development of sociology is almost tantamount to writing the history of this science; for it was born among us, and, although there is no country today where it is not being cultivated, it nevertheless remains an essentially French science." See Émile Durkheim, "Sociology," in Kurt H. Wolff, ed., *Émile Durkheim, 1858–1917* (Columbus: Ohio State University Press, 1960), p. 376.

2. This argument is most cogently presented by Talcott Parsons in *The Structure of Social Action* (Glencoe: The Free Press, 1949), pp. 89–94.

3. See Kenneth E. Bock, "Evolution, Function and Change," *American Sociological Review*, XXVIII (April, 1963), 229–237; and Marvin B. Scott, "Functional Foibles and the Analysis of Social Change," *Inquiry*, IX (1966), 205–214.

4. Howard S. Becker, *Outsiders* (New York: The Free Press, 1963), especially pp. 1–18.

5. This is also true for the mentally ill. Mental illness is a "reason" for behavior, and acknowledging one's own mental illness is an excuse for untoward behavior as well as a signal of "cure." See Thomas Scheff, *Being Mentally Ill* (Chicago: Aldine, 1966), pp. 80–101.

6. Behind this deceptively simple remark stands the whole of "analytic philosophy," that modern school of philosophical inquiry spawned by Ludwig Wittgenstein in his epoch-making *Philosophical Investigations* (Oxford: Basil Blackwell, 1958). For a general statement on the fundamental principles of this school, see Antony Flew, "Philosophy and

Language," in Antony Flew, ed., *Essays in Conceptual Analysis* (London: Macmillan, 1956), pp. 1–20.

7. See H. L. A. Hart, "The Ascription of Responsibility and 'Rights,'" in Antony Flew, ed., *Logic and Language, First Series* (Oxford: Basil Blackwell, 1960), pp. 145–166.

8. Weber was not uninterested in attitudes, however. He published a detailed program for essaying the attitudes of industrial workers and tortuously explored the realm of attitudes while seeking to avoid psychological reductionism. See Paul F. Lazarsfeld and Antony R. Oberschall, "Max Weber and Empirical Social Research," *American Sociological Review,* XXX (April, 1965), 185–199, especially pp. 190–192.

9. Max Weber, *The Theory of Social and Economic Organization,* trans. by Talcott Parsons and A. M. Henderson (Glencoe: The Free Press, 1947), pp. 98–99.

10. See Parsons, *op. cit.,* pp. 44–51, 579–639.

11. See Alfred Schutz, "Commonsense and Scientific Interpretations of Human Action" and "Concept and Theory Formation in the Social Sciences," in his *Collected Papers,* ed. by Maurice Natanson (The Hague: Nijhoff, 1962), I, 3–98.

12. Harold Garfinkel, *Studies in Ethnomethodology* (Englewood Cliffs: Prentice-Hall, 1967).

13. First appearing in *American Sociological Review,* VI (December, 1940), 904–913, the essay is reprinted in C. Wright Mills, *Power, Politics and People,* ed. by Irving L. Horowitz (New York: Ballantine, 1964), pp. 434–452.

14. Harry Stack Sullivan, for example, recognizes words as lingual symbols of action, but still divides accounts into creditable motives and "personal realism." He writes: "Actually in a very long psychiatric career I would say that I have come to have more and more affection for the rationalization which ends with 'just because'; the more words that follow, the harder it is to figure out how much is personal verbalism—rationalization, as it is called—and how much is an important clue to something that one ought to see." See his *Interpersonal Theory of Psychiatry* (New York: Norton, 1953), p. 191. In contrast, Mills notes: "The 'real' attitude or motive is not something different in kind from the verbalization of the 'opinion.' They turn out to be only relatively and temporally different." *Op. cit.,* p. 446.

15. Marvin B. Scott and Stanford M. Lyman, "Accounts," *American Sociological Review,* XXXIII (February, 1968), 46–62.

16. Gresham M. Sykes and David Matza, "Techniques of Neutralization," *American Sociological Review,* XXII (December, 1957), 667–669.

17. Wittgenstein, *op. cit.,* pp. 31e, 32e.

18. Erving Goffman, *Encounters* (Indianapolis: Bobbs-Merrill, 1961), pp. 7–19.

19. Weber, *op. cit.*, p. 88.

20. See Jessie Bernard, "The Theory of Games of Strategy as a Modern Sociology of Conflict," *American Journal of Sociology*, LIX (March, 1954), 411–424, especially pp. 413–415.

21. For an empirical and theoretical statement on such information games, see Marvin B. Scott, *The Racing Game* (Chicago: Aldine, 1968).

22. Erving Goffman, *Stigma* (Englewood Cliffs: Prentice-Hall, 1963).

23. Thus certain categories of persons—for example, homosexuals and paranoids—are more likely to be game-aware at all times than others. See Marvin B. Scott and Stanford M. Lyman, "Paranoia, Homosexuality, and Game Theory," *Journal of Health and Social Behavior*, IX (September, 1968).

24. For an extended discussion of this example, see Joan P. Emerson, "Negotiating the Serious Import of Humor," *Sociometry*, XXXII (June, 1969), 169–181.

25. See, for example, Etsu Inagaki Sugimoto, *A Daughter of the Samurai* (Rutland, Vt.: Charles E. Tuttle, 1966).

26. Many instances are reported in William Carlson Smith, *Americans in the Making* (New York: Appleton-Century, 1939).

27. An excellent example is Paul Edwards, ed., *Equiano's Travels* (New York: Praeger, 1966, originally published in 1789), especially pp. 30–31.

28. A nice example involving race is related by the Negro poet M. Carl Holman, "The Afternoon of a Young Poet," in Herbert Hill, ed., *Anger and Beyond* (New York: Harper and Row, 1966), pp. 138–153. For numerous insights about socal class in this respect, see W. Lloyd Warner and Paul S. Lunt, *The Status System of a Modern Community* (New Haven: Yale University Press, 1942). For a full-scale description of a game orientation between teacher and student involving the former's imagination of the embarrassment and anxiety he was causing the latter, see Willard Waller, *The Sociology of Teaching* (New York: Wiley Science Edition, 1965), pp. 326–332. For a literary illustration, see Herman Melville's "Benito Cereno," in *Great Short Works of Herman Melville* (New York: Harper and Row, 1966), pp. 182–259.

29. This section leans heavily on Erving Goffman's "On Face Work," *Psychiatry*, XVIII (August, 1955), 213–231.

30. Fred Davis, in his work on "deviance disavowel," deals with the manner in which interaction with the stigmatized is "normalized." But when the normalization process itself goes awry, account-giving situations with the attendant face-game framework are generated. Thus we are suggesting that Davis' theoretical statement is but a special case to be subsumed under the more general framework of face games. See F. Davis, "Deviance Disavowel: The Management of Strained Interaction by the Visibly Handicapped," *Social Problems*, IX (1961), 120–132.

31. In exploring these considerations, we are closely following the leads of

Erving Goffman. See his essay "Where the Action Is," in his *Interaction Ritual* (Garden City, N.Y.: Anchor, 1967), especially pp. 239–258.

32. *Ibid.*, p. 244.

33. An example is the joke that slurs a racial group. In polite circles, it seems to be necessary to preface such a joke by an explanation or apology not only to the parties listening but also, vicariously, to the offended racial group, whether any of its members are present or not.

34. In very serious breaches, the individual may take the ultimate recourse of suicide in an effort to project a new and more favorable imagery of self. For a discussion along these lines, see Jack D. Douglas, *The Social Meanings of Suicide* (Princeton: Princeton University Press, 1967), pp. 284 ff.

35. The problem of managing studied nonobservance of one's own violations of social rules deserves more attention. One obvious element is that studied nonobservance is itself noticeable by others and thus requires them studiously to nonobserve not only the untoward deed but also the offender's studied nonobservance of it, if interaction is to proceed smoothly. See the discussion of this and related phenomena in Erving Goffman, *The Presentation of Self in Everyday Life* (Garden City, N.Y.: Doubleday, Anchor, 1959), pp. 233–237.

36. See Douglas, *op. cit.*, pp. 310–319.

37. For an illuminating discussion, see Graham Hughes, "Criminal Responsibility," *Stanford Law Review*, XVI (March, 1965), 470–485.

38. Hart, *op. cit.*

39. See D. S. Shwayder, *The Stratification of Behaviour* (New York: Humanities Press, 1963), pp. 95–102.

40. The whole question of the social construction of meaning is clearly examined in Douglas, *op cit.*, Part IV.

41. Director of Public Prosecutions vs. Smith, 1961, A.C. 290. This case is discussed in Hughes, *op. cit.*, pp. 473–477.

42. We are indebted to the discussion in Thomas J. Scheff, "The Negotiation of Reality: The Process of Assessing Responsibility," Working Paper No. 6, Social Science Research Institute (Honolulu: University of Hawaii, 1967), pp. 13–16.

43. Gustave LeBon, *The Crowd* (London: Ernest Benn, 1952, originally published in 1896); Sigmund Freud, *Group Psychology and the Analysis of the Ego* (New York: Bantam, 1960).

44. Yick Wo vs. Hopkins, Sheriff, 118 U.S. 356 (1886).

45. See Philip Selznick, *TVA and the Grass Roots* (Berkeley: University of California Press, 1953), pp. 253–259.

46. See, for example, the discussion in Joseph Tussman and Jacobus Ten Broek, "The Equal Protection of the Laws," *California Law Review*, XXXVII (September, 1949), 341–381.

47. Tussman and Ten Broek (*ibid.*, pp. 343–356) suggest that judges may organize the classifications made by legislative bodies into categories

of reasonableness, suspicion, and prohibition. The first would include all classifications which are reasonably related to a public purpose and not prohibited or suspect; the second would include classifications which, while not necessarily prohibited, are suspicious because they suggest the latent motive prohibited to lawmakers of exercising prejudices against tribal, racial, or other groups popularly subjected to prejudice; the last would include classifications whose very invocation is so unreasonable to any public legislative purpose as to prompt a presumption of prohibited intent.

48. *Ibid.*, p. 367.

49. See Talcott Parsons, "The Law and Social Control," in William M. Evan, ed., *Law and Sociology* (New York: The Free Press, 1962), pp. 56–72.

50. See J. A. Laponce, *The Protection of Minorities* (Berkeley: University of California Press, 1960), pp. 67–96. For South Africa, see Ernest Cole with Thomas Flaherty, *House of Bondage* (New York: Random House, 1967).

51. See Alain Locke and Bernhard J. Stern, eds., *When Peoples Meet* (New York: Hynds, Hayden, and Eldredge, 1946); and Everett C. Hughes and Helen M. Hughes, *Where Peoples Meet* (Glencoe: The Free Press, 1952).

52. The increase in human contacts between normatively distinct groups appears to have put a premium on reserve and imperturbability in contemporary America. For an extended discussion, see Stanford M. Lyman and Marvin B. Scott, "Coolness in Everyday Life," in Marcello Truzzi, ed., *The Sociology of Everyday Life* (Englewood Cliffs: Prentice-Hall, 1968).

53. See Ferdinand Tonnies, "Estates and Classes," in R. Bendix and S. M. Lipset, eds., *Class, Status and Power* (Glencoe: The Free Press, 1953), pp. 49–63.

54. See Raymond L. Buell, "Some Legal Aspects of the Japanese Question," *American Journal of International Law*, XVII (January, 1923), 29–49.

55. Walter Kong, "Name Calling," *Survey Graphic*, XXXIII (June, 1944), 296–304.

56. One fruitful area of study for this phenomenon is that of colonized peoples. In this respect see J. S. Furnivall, *Colonial Policy and Practice* (New York: New York University Press, 1956). An excellent illustration of the personal breakdown of an individual living inside a plurality of cultures overseen by a culturally homogeneous power elite will be found in Wulf Sachs, *Black Anger* (New York: Grove, 1947).

57. See J. L. Austin, "Other Minds," in *Philosophical Papers*, ed. by J. O. Urmson and G. J. Warndek (Oxford: Clarendon Press, 1961), pp. 44–84.

58. Schutz, *Collected Papers;* also *The Phenomenology of the Social World,*

trans. by George Walsh and Frederick Lehnert (Evanston: North-western University Press, 1967).

59. Garfinkel, "Commonsense Knowledge of Social Structures," in *op. cit.*

60. Peter L. Berger, *Invitation to Sociology* (Garden City, N.Y.: Double-day Anchor, 1963), pp. 54–65.

61. The key figure in the science of praxeology—that is, the study of *methods* employed by social actors in going about their daily routines —is T. Kotarbinski. A brief statement of his position is found in Henry Hiz, "Discussion: Kotarbinski's Praxeology," *Philosophy and Phenome-nological Research,* XV (December, 1954), 238–243; see also H. Gar-finkel, "Some Sociological Concepts and Methods for Psychiatrists," *Psychiatric Research Reports,* VI (October, 1956), 191.

5

Rules of Conduct and the Study of Deviant Behavior: Some Notes on the Social Relationship

Norman K. Denzin

In his insightful analysis of deviant behavior, Howard S. Becker points to the important fact that social acts are not deviant in and of themselves.[1] Rather, it is the imputation of deviance to ongoing social acts by some audience that leads any form of behavior to be termed or labeled "deviant." The proper study of deviant behavior then becomes, Becker argues, the study of audience reaction and the study of the rules that audience members evoke when they evaluate any set of interactions. Thus dual emphasis on rules and audience reactions has become the central focus of that school of deviant behavior now known as the labeling or societal reactions approach.[2]

While this approach has gained wide popularity among social scientists, it has been subjected to little critical analysis or empirical investigation.[3] The intent of the present discussion is to examine seriously the relevance of rules of conduct for the study of deviant behavior. It will be indicated that rules themselves are of a wide variety and that their differential application leads to quite different forms of and reactions to deviant behavior. In brief, it will be suggested that the sociologist must distinguish three different types of behavioral rules in his study of deviant behavior. Central to the thesis will be the notion that sociologists have too quickly focused attention on public forms of deviance and have thereby failed to give adequate attention to the more ephemeral forms of misconduct that daily surround us. In short, I shall argue for a shift in attention to what Goffman and Becker have termed secret or normal deviance.[4] The rationale for this position derives from the fact that only a small percentage of any population ever comes to the attention of formal social control agencies. Yet we daily reaffirm our moralities and value structures by placing ourselves apart from others whom we regard as deviant. In this respect, our attention shifts to the social relationships and situations in which routine, taken-for-granted daily interactions occur.[5] It will be proposed that much of what the labeling theorists claim as support for their position (for example, differential reactions by social control agencies to observed deviance) in fact finds its locus in our daily interactions. We must return to the mundane and routine forms of behavior to establish a solidly grounded theory of deviance. In short, a complete theory of deviance must account for misconduct that does not come to the attention of broader agencies of social control.[6]

At the heart of any social order, I will suggest, lies a multitude of recurring and symbolically sustained moral orders, or little social worlds. At the center of these worlds are social selves and social relationships. Sustained by consensual systems of communication and symbols, the daily vocabularies of motives and meanings that bind us together and give order to our conduct arise. It is in the moral or social world of daily experience, and the social relationships that arise out of and give substance to such orders, that our conceptions of right and wrong, correct conduct and deviance, appear.

To summarize, I will propose a refocus in labeling theory such that daily forms of interaction are given central attention. I will delineate the variety of rules that play upon our daily conduct, treat the nature of social worlds and social relationships, and indicate under what circumstances we feel a public and private deviant will be created.

A word of qualification is in order. I am not challenging the efficacy and theoretical base of the labeling theorists. Rather, I hope to extend the boundaries of their interactionist perspective to areas as yet not systematically treated.

Rules of Conduct: Prior Formulations

At the heart of any social order lies a bundle of recurrently validated rules of conduct.[7] Ultimately derivable from some set of values, or preferred lines of action, these rules specify for the participants involved appropriate and inappropriate ways of behaving toward that group's valued social objects. A rule of conduct is, then, a guide for action that is recommended, not because it is "pleasant, cheap, or effective, but because it is suitable and just."[8] The existence of such rules impinges on our daily conduct in two fundamental ways. First, the rules specify moral obligations of conduct for us. They define the moral character of our selves and when employed establish us as upholders of the social order. Thus, when a husband co-operates in celebrating the anniversary of his marriage by purchasing a gift, he at once celebrates the basis of his relationship while reaffirming his commitment to that relationship.

Second, rules specify the types of expectations we may hold alter to when he acts toward us. What we mean by patterns of deference, or avoidance and presentational rituals, references the obligatory feature of rules. Nurses, for example, may expect to receive orders from physicians, but cannot in turn give such orders.[9] The rules of conduct governing their relationship are thus asymmetrical, and if a nurse violates this asymmetry she challenges the sacred value of the relationship and the attendant selves involved.

Thus, when rules of conduct are violated, both parties involved run the risk of embarrassment and self-discreditability. Both actor and recipient are threatened; their selves have not been upheld. Hence, we point to a central feature of rules of conduct: they are daily reaffirmed through the rituals of interaction and communication. They adhere not so much to participants as to the situations and occasions of interaction. Their meaning arises only when persons translate them into ongoing lines of action. To be precise, rules of conduct are situationally and relationally specific.

These rules may take many forms. In the past, two generic types have been treated. The first are those that are formalized into laws and enforced by specialized bodies, such as the police and the courts. We shall call these rules of substance, or more properly, rules of the civil-legal order. These formalizations, which may be expressed by law, official morality, or codes of ethics, commonly govern conduct in public settings and exist to protect the objects designated by them.

It is these rules of the public-civic order that have most centrally concerned Becker in his analysis of the outsider.[10] In turn, his examination of these rules has given rise to the contemporary concern of the sociologist with social control agencies and the public deviant. He states:

> All social groups make rules and attempt, at some times and under some circumstances, to enforce them. Social rules define situations and the kinds of behavior appropriate to them, specifying some actions as "right" and forbidding others as "wrong." When a rule is enforced, the person who is supposed to have broken it may be seen as a special kind of person, one who cannot be trusted to live by the rules agreed on by the group. He is regarded as an outsider. . . . Rules may be of a great many kinds. . . . I shall mainly be concerned with what we can call the actual operating rules of groups, those kept alive through attempts at enforcement.[11]

Stating his interest in the analysis of rules that are routinely enforced, Becker proceeds to focus on the natural history of such rules; for example, the ways in which they become translated into legal codes and standards. While he also treats lesser formalized standards of conduct, his emphasis is clear: the public rules and their public definers and enforcers.

The thrust of Becker's conceptions discussed above has been to validate sociologists' contemporary interest in social control agencies and the public deviant. Thus, we now read of the abortion clinic and its clientele, the prostitute, the blind and their social agencies, the drug addict, the homosexual and the courts, and so on. In short, his perspective has properly led sociologists away from an unfruitful interest in peculiarities of the deviant and has forced them to deal with the conditions under which deviants are created by public reactions.

In one sense, then, his perspective sets the stage for our own. Only I suggest a renewed interest in the deviant who does not come in contact with the public agencies of social control.[12]

Goffman, on the other hand, has focused on what we might call ceremonial rules, or rules of civil propriety.[13] These are specifications that guide conduct in matters felt to have secondary importance in their own right. Their official function is to maintain the moral and social order of those expressing them. These are what we commonly call rules of etiquette. They govern polite, face-to-face interaction among persons when they are in both public and private behavior settings and may range from statements on proper dress to how one introduces himself to a stranger. It is in these rules and their violation that Goffman derives his theory of mental illness. He suggests that what we mean by mental illness is behavior that routinely and regularly violates the rules of polite, situational, face-to-face interactions. Hence he speaks of the structure and function of situational proprieties and delineates such rules as those governing the acquaintanceship process, body idiom, visual interaction, face work, and so on.

We express these rules daily, he insists, through our verbal utterances, our gestures, the spatial location of our bodies when in another's presence—when we refrain from touching another, or refuse to intrude into his personal space. We also express them by the ways in which we perform our daily tasks. Deference to another's wisdom or special skill evokes a sense of respect for that other, and by such actions we reaffirm the moral worth of his self. Last, we may express these ceremonial rules by our rituals of communication. The form of greeting or leave-taking statements, and even the order in which one speaks (for example, deferring to another's prominence or position), suggests an adherence to these rules.

In short, through a ritualistic adherence to ceremonial rules, we show deference and demeanor to alter. That is, we show our appreciation of him as a person by how we either avoid him or present ourselves to him. Conversely, we establish our own worth to him by our demeanor strategies: by our deportment, dress adornment, and bearing. By challenging these ceremonial rules, Goffman suggests, we place ourselves in the position of an outcast; we have failed to support our society's moral order and the moral worth of the selves in that society. Those who challenge these rules, Goffman states, end up in our mental hospitals.

> The ultimate penalty for breaking the rules is harsh. Just as we fill our jails with those who transgress the legal order, so we partly fill our asylums with those who act unsuitably—the first kind of institution being used to protect our lives and property; the second, to protect our gatherings and occasions.[14]

The concern of Goffman and Becker with rules of conduct has thus taken two directions. Becker, more than Goffman, examines civil-legal rules and the natural history of such rules as they are translated by audiences into deviant definitions. His concern, thus, immediately directs us to one type of rule violation and one type of deviant. Goffman's formulations, on the other hand, lead us into the vague realm of daily interactions wherein persons play by rules of etiquette. His deviant is the mental patient; Becker's the marijuana user and jazz musician. Somewhere in between stand the majority of society: those persons who from someone's perspective are deviant, but not deviant enough to be brought fully into public light. It is to these persons that we direct our attention. The rules of daily-relational interactions must be discussed.[15]

Rules of Relationships

It is suggested that there is a third category of rules that Goffman and Becker have not attended to, and these may be called *rules of relationships,* or *relational proprieties.* Reference is made here to the fact that in enduring, long-term social relationship the categories of rules Goffman has categorized under civil proprieties become radically altered, redefined, and at times made irrelevant. For example, Goffman discusses the way in which males and females in our society attempt to control the information they give regarding themselves when in another's presence. He states:

> Before entering a social situation, they often run through a quick visual inspection of the relevant parts of their personal front, and once in the situation they may take the extra precaution of employing a protective cover, by either crossing the legs or covering the crotch with a newspaper or book, especially if self-control is to be relaxed through confortable sitting. A parallel to this concern is found in the care that women take to see that their legs are not apart, exposing their upper thighs and underclothing.[16]

Rules of this order are classified by Goffman under requirements of body idiom and involvement shielding. The implication from his treatment of this type of rule is that it represents a rule of behavior that governs all persons, whenever they are in another's presence. He uses data from his observations in mental hospitals to demonstrate their violation:

> The universality in our society of this kind of limb discipline can be deeply appreciated on a chronic female ward, where, for whatever reason, women indulge in zestful scratching of their private parts, and in sitting with legs quite spread, causing the student to become conscious of the vast amount of limb discipline that is ordinarily taken for granted.[17]

It is suggested that rather than assuming that violation of these rules occurs only among persons labeled mentally ill, they are violated daily in enduring social relationships. For example, it is not at all uncommon for married males in our middle-class society to routinely expose the upper portions of their body on a sunny week-end afternoon when working on their lawn. Nor is it unusual for married males and females drastically to relax the rule of body scratching when enjoying an evening of television. In fact, it is not at all rare to see either the female or male in various stages of undress when preparing for an evening at the concert, or in the last preparatory stages of a dinner party at one's home. In short, not only do enduring social relationships sanction the violation of situational rules of civil propriety but, in fact, these relationships are built on a deliberate violation of such rules. This, of course, is not meant to suggest that marriage represents flagrant violations of all rules of conduct, for this is not so. In fact, as representative of one class of relationships, marriages are built on a unique order of moral and civil rules, actually sanctioning that which is not allowable in polite society.

It is suggested, then, that there exists in our civil society a category of behavioral rules that have as yet not been systematically examined. These are rules of relationships and are representative of rules that in some indirect, yet systematic, fashion represent analogies to the previous two categories of rules. Further, it is suggested that it is the violation of relational rules that quite frequently leads a given set of audience members to impute deviance to an ongoing set of interactions. Rules of conduct have relevance and meaning only when they are fixed in specific interactional and relational contexts. The categorical statement that groups have rules of conduct, without an interactional-relational specification on the part of the investigator, makes the notion of deviance by labeling at the very least a vacuous statement.

I turn now to the nature of social relationships. Briefly, it will be indicated that relationships are of great variety, that the rules attached to them are widely varying, and that the rules which grow up around them in fact represent specific translations of civil-legal and polite interactional standards into the morality of the relationship. In addition, I will suggest the conditions under which each relational-partner comes to view the other as deviant and enacts rules defining him as such.

The Nature of Social Relationships

That a good deal of daily human interaction takes place in either the symbolic or physical copresence of another cannot be denied. Despite the recurrent regularity of this phenomenon, we as sociologists still lack the appropriate imagery and symbols to conceptualize the wide degrees of variation that occur when humans carry on interactions in this recurrent sense. It was Simmel who defined the dyadic relationship as one in which strains toward totality, intimacy, and sentimentality were present.[18] Weber paralleled this position when he defined a relationship as existing when there was a high probability that two or more persons would come together into copresent interaction.[19] Cooley's distinction between the primary and secondary relationship represented one of the few attempts to introduce a qualitative distinction into this concept.[20] The vast theoretical and research literature on the "other"—reference group and otherwise—has contributed to our understanding of those relationships that are abstractly symbolized, but not actualized in daily, face-to-face interactions.

Even Goffman, the one contemporary sociologist who has persisted in analyzing forms of copresent interaction, has been too limiting for our purposes. His world of study fundamentally constitutes interaction among the unacquainted, the stranger, and only infrequently the friend. His humans are actors, ever on a stage searching for action and dramaturgical support. Seldom does he show us a picture of social men caught up in "safe patterns of interaction," in which his front could drop and he might for the moment feel at ease. Given this bias, it is not surprising that his attention would fall on rules of etiquette and their functions for polite interaction. In a world where no one can trust the other, protective devices must be created to save the moral worth of these tenuous objects called selves.

Becker, on the other hand, has extensively examined the rules of conduct that adhere to ongoing relationships, but his focus has been on the deviant. Hence, we have in neither of these theorists a thoroughgoing concern with daily forms of recurrent interaction among persons who are not outsiders, or in some other sense a public deviant.

My thesis is: the range and types of social relationships that characterize human interaction have remained largely unconceptualized by the sociologist. We have as yet not adequately described the effects of such relationships, nor have we sufficiently come to grips with the ways in which these ranges of experience are created, stabilized, and dismissed by persons themselves.

We take as our problem, then, the study of the social relationship and its effect on the creation of private and public forms of deviance. We shall adopt as our perspective that of the "acting other" and assess the effects of these experiences as the persons involved perceive them.

SOME DISTINCTIONS AND DEFINITIONS

A relationship shall be said to exist between two or more persons when those persons engage in recurrent forms of either symbolic or copresent interaction. The emphasis on symbolic deserves special attention. For a relationship to exist, the parties involved must share the same or a similar set of reciprocal definitions about the other. Further, these definitions must extend through time such that the influence of the other does not disappear when out of his physical, face-to-face presence.

There may be, then, those relationships that exist on merely a symbolized level, with face-to-face interaction never occurring, or having occurred once but never again. The widow's continuing love for her deceased husband is but one example. The minister who daily speaks with a higher being and the student who carries on internal conversations and dialogues with his absent professor are others. We shall call these relationships with the absent other.

There are, further, those relationships which combine face-to-face recurrent interactions (for example, copresence of other) with symbolized images of the other. The love relationship described by Simmel is an example. The marriage dyad, the employer-employee relationship, and the friendship between close acquaintances are other instances of this type of relationship.

We have distinguished two basic types of relationships: those that exist on the purely symbolic level and those that combine the symbolic with recurrent face-to-face interactions. Additional definitions and distinctions are needed. Earlier we defined a relationship as a condition represented by reciprocality of interaction and/or symbolizations of the other. It is apparent, however, that this statement must be modified. There are those relationships that are not reciprocated on either a symbolic or face-to-face basis. The wife who carried on a dialogue with a deceased husband in no way is engaging in a reciprocated relationship. Her dialogue is only in the form of an internal forum or discussion with that other. He never speaks out directly. Teenagers who belong to fan clubs represent another instance of this case. Letters to their idol are returned by a secretary and not the idol himself. And even though that person (the idol) may have extreme influences on such personal matters as dress and vocabulary, his reciprocal influence on the fan is indirect, to say the least. The employee who idealizes his relationship with an employer is another type of unevenly reciprocated relationship.

Clearly any relationship between two parties will never represent *unilinear* reciprocation. The idealized, romantic love theme in American culture, which describes two lovers forever intertwined in an enduring relationship, represents an ideal that few relationships ever attain. We can speak, then, of relationships that are reciprocated and those that are nonreciprocated. Further, we can talk of those that are reciprocated, but unevenly so. Thurber's description of the Walter Mittey complex represents this type.

When a person is in a relationship that is reciprocated, no matter how unevenly, he shall be said to be *in-relationship*. The marriage dyad illustrates this case. Husbands and wives are not expected to be looking for other relationships of the sort represented by marriage. They are locked in that relationship, notwithstanding what may be differential commitment and involvement of each in it. It is frequently the case that persons in-relationships will find themselves for a period of time *out-of-that-relationship*. The wife who leaves for a vacation while the husband remains at home places her husband in the uncomfortable position of both being in and out of the relationship at the same time. The symbolic demands of the relationship remain constant, but the important element of physical copresence has been removed. This is well represented in the movie *The Seven Year Itch*, and middle-class morality abounds in tales of the indiscreet husband who acted out-of-relationship when his wife was gone. To summarize, thus far, we have suggested that persons are either in or out of relationships that are either reciprocated or nonreciprocated.

In some instances we will find persons who are in-between-relationships. This is well illustrated by the searching divorcee, the broken engagement, and the man out of work. In such instances, peculiar symbolic demands will be present. Having acquired the perspective and vocabulary of the previously "involved other," the person feels a sense of internal collective behavior, not knowing whether to drop that perspective completely or to search again for a similar other. Friends and acquaintances of such persons also feel peculiar demands. Fearing the potential embarrassment that may arise by bringing up the absent other, they know not how to handle this peculiar person.

In many senses a strange type of constrained freedom falls upon persons in this category. They are permitted to search, to be indiscreet (up to a point), and even on occasion to bring that other up in conversation. These are the moments of revealing truth when the harsh reality of relationships comes to the surface. To have embedded one's self in another's personality and then be forced to withdraw that self is painful. All of us, at one time or another, fear such occurrences and are acutely sensitive to the demands of those who suffer through such occurrences.

We can speak of further types of relationships. There are those that are idealized, as in some marriages and love affairs; those that are nonreciprocated and rejected; those that are over and past; and those that are purely symbolic, yet recurrent in a symbolic sense. In addition, there are those that are reciprocated, yet truncated in either a situational or role-specific sense. The employer-employee relationship, for example, is situated both by time and place. Consequently, in these instances, we find both parties locked into only a few identities or images of self. The relationship has a restricted effect on the selves of both parties. Further, there are those relationships that are long-standing and reciprocated on both the symbolic and copresent levels, as well as those that are long-standing and nonreciprocated or unevenly reciprocated. The bartender-customer relationship may be long-standing, but only unevenly reciprocated.

TIME, PLACE, AND INVOLVEMENT

To recapitulate, I have suggested that relationships may be analyzed by their duration, location, and degree of mutual involvement. Those relationships that are time-specific, place-specific, and involvement-specific represent what we commonly observe in encounters with strangers, employers, civil-legal authorities, clients, customers, colleagues, and passing acquaintances. On the other extreme, when we observe a relationship existing beyond specific situations, of long duration, and resting on many levels of involvement, we have the case of friends, lovers, and relatives. Yet, such a distinction as this, while conceptually attractive, is much too gross. It is beyond the scope of the present discussion to treat each of these types of relationships in the detail they deserve. The purpose, so far, has been to suggest the tremendous variety of relationships that may be generated and briefly to distinguish analytical dimensions for their treatment. It is now necessary to return to our theme of deviance and the relationship. But first we must turn to the morality of relationships.

A word of qualification must be inserted. Unless otherwise indicated, the types of relationships we will be discussing are those in which multiple identities are evoked and which are of long duration, typically enacted in a variety of different situations. Paradramatically we are treating what Cooley called primary relationships and what we call *relationships of substance*. Marriages, long friendships between colleagues, mutual acquaintances, and the like represent what we are treating. We ignore any detailed treatment of the stranger relationship, the fleeting encounter between the unacquainted, as well as the highly formalized relationship in the bureaucracy.[21] Ours are the relationships one enters into with confidence, feelings of safety, sincerity, and, at times, intimacy.

Analytically the discussion will be heuristic and more suggestive than definitive. In the areas of interaction and deviance under analysis, little in the way of systematic evidence may be brought forth. I hope to develop a framework which will permit others to treat more comprehensively an area that heretofore has received little attention.

Relational Morality and Propriety

Each social relationship may be viewed as a peculiar moral order or social *world*, to use Shibutani's term.[22] Contained within such relationships are special views of self, unique vocabularies of meaning and motive, and most importantly symbol systems that have consensual meaning only to the participants involved. Analytically we may note that in relationships of long duration rules surrounding the following dimensions will be developed. First, rules will arise specifying acts of deference and demeanor that direct the participants' behavior when alone and in public. Second, mechanisms for regulating knowledge, secrecy, and personal problems endemic to the relationship will be developed. Third, task structures will evolve to specify who does what, when, where, and with whom. Last, specifications concerning the proper conduct of ego and alter when not in the other's presence will be developed.

These are interactional dimensions on which rules of conduct will be built.[23] Their existence thus serves to give order, rationality, and a sense of predictability to the relationship. I will suggest that violations of these specific rules leads relational members to feel a sense of embarrassment, irritation, annoyance, and, at the severest extreme, self-threat and publicly designated deviance.

Before turning to these dimensions of the relationship, let us examine a number of other characteristics. First, each relationship represents a universe of social experience and discourse that is unique with those involved. The meaning of a nonverbal gesture, of the trite phrase "I love you," of time, past occurrences, and broken selves are all contained within these little worlds.

Second, relationships may validate, redefine, or make irrelevant the rules from any other moral order—be that civil-legal, polite propriety, or another relationship of the same class. Herein lies their signal importance for the student of deviance, for they represent the ways in which members of any society make that society's rules of conduct meaningful in their daily interactions. Hence, each social relationship potentially contains a set of deviant values and ideologies which, if ever let out, would brand the member-participants as outsiders and deviants.

Third, the rules of conduct on which these relationships rest fundamentally refer to the ways in which the social self is to be defined and treated. To sanction the violation of a rule of etiquette is to say that for the selves involved such rules are irrelevant.

Fourth, these relational rules of conduct and their attendant moral orders are neither situationally nor personally abstract. They have reference only within the context of the relationship and are shaped and altered every time a new participant, a new situation, or a new problem arises. Thus, marriage partners may not sanction public quarreling among themselves, viewing this as indiscreet and character-damaging for their relationship. Yet, they will surely do so in private and quite likely sanction it when done by other people, although they may well apply their own relational rules to that couple, branding them as relationally deviant for the transgression. They are unlikely, however, to make public this interpretation to the perceived transgressors.

This brings us to our fifth point. By applying their relational rules to others, members of a relationship establish their own uniqueness and reaffirm the rationale for the rules' existence. Thus, we can point with fond pleasure to the embarrassment felt by a quarreling couple, when in our presence, and pride ourselves for our sense of character propriety.

Sixth, by applying our relational rules to others we uniquely uphold our society's general values. That is, while we may reject a specific rule of etiquette or civil-legal rule, we have replaced that rule with another that permits us to act orderly and quite frequently within the boundaries of permissible public and private behavior. In a very general sense, no societal value or rule of conduct is expected to be perfectly enacted and followed. Our society, in fact, allocates rewards to persons who have reinterpreted its values in unique ways. Thus, for example, while the motorcycle gang known as Hell's Angels systematically violate nearly every imaginable rule of propriety, our society at large has rewarded them quite extensively for their specialness and their sense of character, charm, and style.[24] They, of course, are simultaneously branded as deviants and heroes. But in this peculiar definition we see brought forth the unique translatability of rules of conduct. You can be highly rewarded for publicly disavowing them if you do so with character and style.

The severe societal reactions that fall on the rapist and philanderer represent the other extreme. While they may do what many males secretly desire, their action lacks the style and character to bring both distaste and honor. Similar problems seem to arise for the mentally ill, the indigent, the Negro (notwithstanding soul), the mentally retarded, and the occupationally and educationally incompetent.[25] We can find little in the way of glamour in their actions; and if we did, few of our moralities would sanction them.

Seventh, since relationships develop their own moralities and special world views, it can be seen that they quite soon begin to take on a life of their own. In short, an element of supraindividuality emerges and settles around the member-participants.[26] Marriages, for example, immediately have forced on them not only the values of their members but special values from the broader society. It is assumed that marital partners do certain things and assiduously avoid others. This element of supraindividuality leads to a number of important consequences. First, for all persons involved, a special sense of self is evoked and created. Second, an implicit demand is placed on each person to maintain that moral order, oftentimes at great personal loss. Goffman phrases these demands as follows:

> It seems to be a characteristic obligation of many social relationships that each of the members guarantees to support a given face for the other members in given situations. To prevent disruption of these relationships, it is therefore necessary for each member to avoid destroying the other's face. At the same time, it is often the person's social relationship with others that leads him to participate in certain encounters with them, where incidentally he will be dependent upon them for supporting his face. Furthermore, in many relationships, the members come to share a face, so that in the presence of third parties an improper act on the part of one member becomes a source of acute embarrassment to the other members. A social relationship, then, can be seen as a way in which the person is more than ordinarily forced to trust his self-image and face to the tact and good conduct of others.[27]

An element of trust and reciprocity develops in the relationship. I will show shortly that refusals to validate this moral order lead to feelings of rejection, embarrassment, lack of trust, and perhaps only general irritation on the part of one or both of the relational partners.

A third consequence of this supraindividuality in the relationship is the fact that rules will develop to permit *relational-release,* or escape from its demands. These rules of release may be of any duration, and, as in divorce, be forever binding. At cocktail parties marital partners may momentarily release the other from certain restrictions and permit conversations and actions not otherwise sanctioned. These are episodes in which nonself-conduct is sanctioned. However, a very restrictive sense permeates these episodes, for no matter how free the release is, the person will ultimately be held accountable for his actions during this sequence. Such is the case because his actions must always be related back to his major relationship. Hence, his actions, while reflecting momentarily on a nonself, ultimately reflect on his relationship and the character of the other self that permitted his conduct. We all stand to lose a great deal when our relational partners act to excess in nonself episodes.

Fourth, just as all relationships build in conditions for release, so too do they develop procedures for handling and preventing embarrassment.[28] So when a husband engages in an extreme nonself episode, the wife typically has at her disposal a variety of motives and explanations to account for that conduct. Occasionally, however, nonself episodes will be severe enough to prohibit attaching any reasonable explanation to them. In these situations the relationship may virtually collapse and abruptly disappear. Even if such severe consequences do not occur, many relational partners hold this threat over their partners.

Thus, we see that a sense of security and fear permeates all relationships. If we step too far out of bounds, it may disappear. If we are judicious and careful, the sense of security that alheres to these social orders will be maintained—often past our lifetime.

Given these characteristics of the relationship, we now turn to the rules surrounding deference, demeanor, knowledge, tasks, and public behavior.

DEFERENCE AND DEMEANOR IN THE RELATIONSHIP

Each social relationship, whether it be at work, at play, or among friends, will contain specifications (often implicit) of deference and demeanor for the involved participants. Deferentially, we will observe rules restricting avoidance and presentational conduct, and in acts of demeanor standards of modesty, sincerity, and discretion will appear as ways of permitting the appropriate selves to be presented.

These rules may be *symmetrical* or *asymmetrical*, as when a wife defers to her husband's role.[29] Their enactment will reveal the underlying morality and vocabulary of the relationship, as can be seen in the case of a wife deferring to her husband. Both deference and demeanor may be expressed, not out of respect, but because of custom, tradition, or for dramaturgical reasons. Thus, an employee may call his employer by a nickname when out of his presence, but when they are face to face he uses a formal term.

The two categories of deference that deserve special attention are the *avoidance* and *presentational rituals*. By avoidance rituals we refer to norms governing "how far one can intrude into another's personal space." Each of us is located in a sacred space with ourself at the center, and elaborate rules are operative in our culture to admit some persons into that space and to keep others out. Thus a marital partner, a new lover, and an old friend may differentially caress, pat, and otherwise touch the other's body. Each relationship will have its own avoidance rituals, which may go no further than specifying that secretaries and employers sit at nonintimate distances from one another.

Presentational rituals of deference involve the use of special salutations, "touch systems," and different ways of noticing the other's presence, thereby according him the status deemed necessary and appropriate. The use of nicknames among friends implies a degree of sincerity, intimacy, and prior acquaintance. To use a nickname or a first name when a formal name would be appropriate denies the recipient of deference to his proper respect.[30]

Through acts of deference, then, we may alter our sense of respect for him. In short, we communicate to him what kind of self we have defined him as being. Through acts of demeanor we establish the definitions of self we want alter to validate and give deference to. Thus by dress, style of speech, nonverbal gestures, and, on occasions, through direct declarations we stake out our interactional identity.

Taken out of a relational context, deference and demeanor have little relevance for our analysis. But by viewing each relationship as a unique moral order we can see that within each, special rules of deference and demeanor will exist. Special "touch systems," manners of dress and undress, the use of nicknames, salutory rituals, and other presentational strategies will grow up within them. When in-relationship and alone, the members will be expected to adhere strictly to these rules. In public, these rules will undergo translation and as such will dictate the collective presentation of selves of the members. Consequently, rules of deference and demeanor that are ascribed to relationships by outsiders will constitute for those outsiders their basis of classifying that relationship.[31] Conversely, it will specify for the outsider how he is to act toward the members, individually and collectively. In short, relationships take on a supraindividual quality, and membership in them provides a source of labels and directives for action by both insider and outsider.

PROBLEMS OF KNOWLEDGE

Not only will each relationship evolve rules of deference and demeanor that direct their own and others' behavior, but specific strategies for controlling knowledge about the relationship will be established.[32] By controlling the amount and type of knowledge it gives off publicly, a special sense of respectability will be sought and maintained.[33] To achieve this respectability, or dramatic idealization, the relationship will find that it must classify the range of situations and persons it comes in contact with as either safe or unsafe, trustworthy or untrustworthy.[34] While these rules will often be implicit and never formally voiced, we will observe across situations and audiences specific attempts to monitor the kinds of information given off such that a specific definition of the relationship is maintained. Not only will audiences and situations be classified, but so also will knowledge about the relationship be classified. Some topics will simply be taboo to outsiders and hence subject to the strongest rituals of secrecy. These may include dark secrets out of the past, strategic secrets integral to the relationship's ongoing existence and performances, and inside secrets that are made known to a select few.

When discrepant information leaks out, potential problems are imminent, and under these situations we can predict attributions of deviance to arise—from both the inside and the outside.

TASK DECISIONS

A sense of dramaturgical collusiveness is likely to develop around the relationship to dictate also how its work is to be handled, both privately and publicly. Husbands and wives may have private and public divisions of labor so nearly opposite that role reversals can be observed at certain times. Because each relationship creates its own divisions of labor, we can expect outsiders viewing that relationship to perceive varying senses of familiarity and unfamiliarity, comfortableness and uncomfortableness, depending on the particular arrangement.

NONRELATIONAL CONDUCT

Rules, again implicit, will develop to govern a participant's behavior when not in the presence of alter. Typically aided by an elaborate symbolic order, relational partners will find that they can convey their relational status nonverbally. Thus, marriage rings, maternity clothing, and a well-kept demeanor can convey for the female varying degrees of the marital status (for example, expecting, looking, and so forth). For the male, being clean-shaven and well dressed represent two strategies of communicating marital status and occupational security.

Communicating one's relational status poses several problems. First, if correctly located, one finds that he must act as if his relational partners were present. In these situations, conversational strategies and interactional maneuvers become severely restricted or widened, depending on the perspective. If the incorrect relational status is imputed, similar problems may arise. The person may be deliberately masquerading as another type of person, wishing to be labeled as out-of-relationship. This seems to be the case for married males searching for homosexual contacts, married males "looking around," males looking for another job, married females looking for another partner.

When we examine nonrelational conduct, we must simultaneously keep in mind the perspective of the relationship being presented (or not presented) and those viewing the presentation. There seem to be ritual occasions when one can look for another relationship without recriminations (such as conduct at conventions, in certain bars, on vacation); but basically once involved in a relationship, a person finds that he is held accountable for that relationship wherever he goes. Relational partners will thus develop strategies for communicating their status when out of the other's presence and will hold alter accountable to the same rules.

Problems for the relationship will arise when the partners fail to agree on these rules, and under these circumstances varying degrees of relational impropriety will be perceived—again by both the insider and the outsider looking in.

Perceptions of Relational Impropriety

Now the basic question guiding our discussion will be, "Under what conditions will relational partners define themselves and others as deviant?" We are necessarily led to this question by virtue of our earlier propositions which held that relationships redefine society's legal and moral orders and that many forms of public and private deviance find their locus in the relationship.

THE RELATIONAL CONCEPTION OF DEVIANCE

To answer our pivotal question, a number of related issues must be looked at. First, we should make clear our conception of deviance. We agree with the labeling theorists and define deviance as any behavior that is so defined by the self or a set of others. We restrict this definition, for the moment, however, to relational deviance. That is misconduct that is not formally treated or recognized by broader society or its social control agencies. Conceiving deviance in this relational fashion leads us to picture a continuum of potential deviant reactions to any relationally perceived act.[35] At the most extreme end of our continuum are publicly acclaimed, validated, and legislated labels of deviance. The criminal, sexual deviant, and political anarchist represent this form of the societal reaction. Next, we may conceive of the deviant acts that are regarded as self-threatening, or character-damaging, but the reactions to them are handled interactionally, seldom made public. Criticisms of dress, drinking behavior, or nearly any self-attribute fall in this category.

Third, we have the egregious errors which cause *embarrassment* to those present and involved in the action at hand. Loss of poise, the presentation of an inappropriate identity, or misinterpretation of alter in an interactional sequence gives rise to feelings of embarrassment, and again these are problems that are handled interactionally,[36] often through rituals of avoidance.

Fourth, we may consider actions that are *irritating*, but not embarrassing. For females this often takes the form of criticizing another's sense of style and fashion. For males, it may include irritation at another's drinking patterns, his style of speech, and so on. Clearly we cannot restrict these to sexual dimensions. The point to be made, however, is that various locations in the age-sex-status structure of one's society lead one to view actions by certain others as inappropriate, incorrect, and irritating. We typically handle irritation by ignoring it, or staging situations in which the likelihood of such occurrences is significantly reduced.

Fifth, we have actions that everyone engages in, feels bad about afterward, and hence is led to excuse in the conduct of others. Drinking to excess, repeating a favorite story, falling into a mood, and the like

represent these occurrences. These are the daily, taken-for-granted actions that we all engage in and dutifully accept on the part of
others.[37]

Sixth are actions that are perceived as legitimate, ordinary, and routine in one interactional sphere, but if viewed from the outside may
evoke public labels of deviance. What criminologists term "white-collar crime," and what members in an organization perceive as ordinary,
represent this category of relational deviance. Dalton has elaborately
described actions such as this. He reports the following instances of
what would be viewed as misconduct by certain outsiders:

> A foreman built a machine shop in his home, equipping it with expen-
> sive machinery taken from the shop in which he worked. The loot in-
> cluded a drill press, shaper, lathe and cutters, drills, bench equipment,
> and a grinding machine.
>
> The foreman of the carpenter shop in a large factory, a European-
> born craftsman, spent most of his workday building household objects—
> baby beds, storm windows, tables, and similar custom-made items—for
> higher executives. In return, he received gifts of wine and dressed fowl.
>
> An office worker did all her letter writing on the job, using company
> materials and stamps.
>
> An X-ray technician in a hospital stole hams and canned food from the
> hospital and felt he was entitled to do so because of his low salary.
>
> A retired industrial executive had an eleven-unit aviary built in fac-
> tory shops and installed in his home by factory personnel. Plant carpen-
> ters repaired and reconditioned the birdhouses each spring.[38]

Commenting on these actions, Becker illustrates our point concerning
relational deviance:

> Dalton says that to call these actions theft is to miss the point. In fact,
> he insists, management, even while officially condemning intramural
> theft, conspires in it; it is not a system of theft at all, but a system of re-
> wards. People who appropriate services and materials belonging to the
> organization are really being rewarded unofficially for extraordinary con-
> tributions they make to the operation of the organization for which no le-
> gitimate system of rewards exists. . . . The X-ray technician was allowed
> to steal food from the hospital because the hospital administration knew
> it was not paying him a salary sufficient to command his loyalty and hard
> work. The rules are not enforced because two competing power groups
> —management and workers—find mutual advantage in ignoring in-
> fractions.[39]

Bringing actions such as these to the public eye involves the kinds of complex negotiations that moral entrepreneurs and provocateurs are so skilled at.[40] We shall only incidentally be concerned with those full-blown reactions, however. Our interest thus lies in the more ephemeral interactional reactions of embarrassment, self-threat, and irritation that routinely occur when social relationships are brought forth in emergent encounters and occasions.

SYMBOLS, ENCOUNTERS, AND OCCASIONS: WHENCE THE ACTION?

The statements above on the nature and evocation of relational misconduct suggest that the reality of a relationship exists only on the occasions when members present themselves for public interaction. In some senses this is correct; that is, the copresence of two or more relationships in a behavioral situation necessarily gives rise to an interactional encounter. In these encounters between relationships we observe the confrontation of varying moralities and proprieties, and herein lies a part of what Goffman calls "the action." [41] That is, in these encounters, which typically evolve into occasions or gatherings of significance, the approbations of deviance and misconduct arise.

Relationships have other realities, as well. Of equal significance are the symbols we carry with us that represent our characterizations of the selves, moralities, and relationships in which we and others are involved. Man, we suggest, maintains a sense of security and predictability in his interactions by fondly isolating certain images of self and other in his mind and recurrently calling forth these images. To use Cooley's phrase, "The other exists for us in our imaginations of him." In these internal and silent conversations, we stake out views of self, challenge the other's morality, test lines of action against his perspective, and carefully prepare ourselves for the next set of interactions with him.

Placed in the context of relationships, we see that each participant will carry images of that relationship in his mind and routinely govern his conduct by these symbolizations. Conversely, he will transpose those images on all other persons he encounters who are defined as being in his same "kinds" of relationship. In short, the perspectives we carry with us derive fundamentally from our focal relationships.[42]

Given these conditions, it can now be seen that in any given encounter, whether in the same relationship or when relational partners confront others, the symbolic images of what is "right and proper" will govern any conceptions of misconduct that emerge out of that encounter.

MISCONDUCT WITHIN THE RELATIONSHIP

We turn now to the problem of under what conditions a relational partner will view the other as acting inappropriately. Earlier we saw that rules of conduct develop around the dimensions of deference, demeanor, knowledge, tasks and conduct in public. It was suggested that because relationships take on a life of their own, each member will feel obliged to sustain that moral order in some degree, on all occasions, public or private. We noted that perceptions of relational deviance may range from feelings of "this is routine" to irritation, embarrassment, extreme self-relational threats, and public accusations of deviance. Taking the role of any relational member, we can now hypothesize the following conditions as giving rise to perceptions of misconduct.

Our first, the most general, hypothesis states that misconduct will be perceived whenever any relational member fails to uphold the moral order of his relationship. More specifically, however, we can suggest the conditions under which any, or all, of the reactions above will occur.

Generally speaking, the routine, taken-for-granted, and hence forgivable reactions can occur when a relational partner acts on a rule that is unclear, forgotten, or infrequently evoked. This seems to be the case when errors of public etiquette are violated; when a husband calls his wife by a long-forgotten nickname; and when a relatively unimportant date is forgotten (like a distant relative's birthday). Under these conditions, initial feelings of minor or faked irritation may appear, but soon disappear when the transgressor explains his mistake. These are the kinds of interactional errors that daily surround us and keep us mindful that everybody forgets, or is impolite occasionally.

Feelings of *irritation* arise when the relational partner fails to aid the other member in carrying off a routine act, or when a member acts to excess in an area that has little consequence for subsequent interactions. Thus, the husband who expects his wife to initiate laughter after his favorite joke and finds that his spouse has become engrossed in another conversation will feel mildly irritated, but not likely embarrassed.

Embarrassment, which is the most interesting case, seems to arise when a relational member enacts an inappropriate identity, loses poise during a public encounter, and/or makes the wrong interpretation of the situation and those present.[43] Presentation of an *inappropriate relational identity* may arise when a husband violates a deference or demeanor rule. Thus he may become excessively attentive toward his wife when having drinks with friends, causing embarrassment to both relationships. To his relationship, embarrassment arises because he has publicly violated their "personal touching code" and in a very direct sense has involved his wife in a silent sexual act which is now public. To those looking on, several degrees of uneasiness are likely to be felt. Should they counterreact by similar "touching" actions? Would it be appropriate to suggest a termination of the encounter? Can they discretely avoid "noticing" the action going on before their eyes? Can they shift the encounter to a mutually engrossing topic and hence "lift" the transgressors out of their impropriety? These represent at once interactional strategies and repressed reactions the "viewers" are likely to feel.

Such encounters generate a peculiar interactional tenseness, for no one is likely verbally to give notice to the misconduct. An encounter is thus likely to ensue that is entirely nonverbal. Given the peculiar meanings often attached to the same nonverbal gestures, it is quite probable that no one will know for sure what the other is thinking.

In one sense, the evocation of an inappropriate relational identity increases the probability that one or all of the persons involved will suffer a loss of poise. Speaking of poise and the individual actor, Gross and Stone state: "Personal poise refers to the performer's control over self and situation, and whatever disturbs that control, depriving the transaction, as we have said before, of any relevant future, is incapacitating and consequently embarrassing." [44] Loss of poise, we suggest, deprives the enacted relationship of the deference and appreciation it demands from those viewing its performance. This is the case because if any one of the relational selves is challenged, the collective self of the relationship is also challenged. Hence relational partners stand to lose a great deal when one of their attendant members begins to act inappropriately in public.[45] Private transgressions are, of course, a different matter. In these situations embarrassment is likely to be felt if an absent other is symbolized and brought forth in the encounter. To bring that other into the transaction is to make it public in some degree, even if he is not physically present. Hence, it is not uncommon to hear the phrase, "Don't you ever do that in public!"

Several conditions can give rise to a loss of poise and hence to embarrassment. The situation can be misread, leading to situationally inappropriate conduct. Thus students in the home of their professors may act overly personal and drop their usual formal-name basis with the faculty. On these occasions, reciprocal embarrassment will be felt (if the act is viewed as incorrect), and both parties will be observed to draw back into themselves and deliberately reduce the "openness" of the contact. On other occasions relational partners may find that they are without the usual props they employ when staging performances for visiting teams. Hence, on a particularly important occasion they may find themselves without liquor, appropriate "snacking" materials, or the kind of music that would make the encounter flow as desired. At other times the wrong props may be present and thereby foster a definition of the relationship that is out of character. In these instances, both relational partners will feel uncomfortable and perhaps even embarrassed. The presence of liquor and drinking equipment before friends who do not drink raises an inappropriate identity structure for both parties. Commenting on the role of props for such occasions, Gross and Stone note:

> The porcelain dinnerware may always be kept visibly in reserve for special guests, and this very fact may be embarrassing to some dinner guests who are reminded that they are not so special after all, while, for other guests, anything but the everyday props would be embarrassing. Relict props also present a potential embarrassment, persisting as they do when one's new life-situation has been made obsolete. The table at which a woman used to sit while dining with a former husband is obviously still quite serviceable, but it is probably best to buy another.[46]

Loss of poise may also arise when the relational partners have inappropriate *equipment* present during their encounters. Following Gross and Stone, we distinguish props from equipment by the degree of mobility accorded them during an occasion.

> If props are ordinarily stationary during encounters, equipment is typically moved about, handled, or touched. Equipment can range from words to physical objects, and a loss of control over such equipment is a frequent source of embarrassment. Here are included slips of the tongue, sudden dumbness when speech is called for, stalling cars in traffic, dropping bowling balls, spilling food and tool failures.[47]

On certain occasions we can observe faulty, noisy, inappropriate, and otherwise intruding forms of equipment challenging the character and selves being presented. On the evening of a prenuptial dinner I observed an unusual intrusion of equipment from the outside that challenged the ritual nature of the occasion. A former boy friend of the bride-to-be's sister had been circling the house for several hours, peering into the back yard where the event was being staged. The yard had been strung with Japanese lanterns to give the effect of a garden party, and suddenly, just as toasts were being offered to the couple-to-be, the boy friend crashed into the light pole and brought all the lanterns down with sparks and explosions. Collective behavior spread and curses filled the air, rapidly followed by profuse apologies from the mother of the bride to all the guests. Although lights and order were soon restored, the ritual nature of the occasion had been challenged and so severely damaged that it soon collapsed. The mother felt she had been offended by a "punk teenager," but of most importance her presentation had been damaged and the sacred character of her family and soon-to-be married daughter had been severely flawed.

A fourth factor which may lead to relational embarrassment is the presence of incorrect dress on the part of one or both of the members. "*Clothing* must be maintained, controlled, and coherently arranged. Its very appearance must communicate this. Torn clothing, frayed cuffs, stained neckties, and unpolished shoes are felt as embarrassing in situations where they are expected to be untorn, neat, clean, and polished.[48] On any given occasion each relational partner is expected to be so dressed that a consensual definition of the relationship can be conveyed and maintained. Being out of dress thus challenges the definition and gives rise to potential embarrassment to all persons involved. In some situations we will find that the failure to pay due respects to another's dress can create mild feelings of embarrassment and irritation. A new dress that goes unnoticed by a close friend may lead the presenter to feel irritated and regard the viewer as inconsiderate. The failure to notice new, novel, and uniquely arranged equipment and props can also create this reaction. A sensitive feel for the importance of these objects and a knowledge that one accords deference by ritually noticing their presence lead some relational partners to develop a division of labor in this regard. Thus, wives are expected to notice new furniture, drapery, tableware, and the like, and husbands may be given the territory of books, records, and mechanical devices. We can observe peculiar forms of cajoling and "notice-taking rituals" in this respect, for one partner may notice an object in the other's domain and subtly communicate his discovery. In some settings the owner of the object will call attention to its presence, and here we see the rituals of deference being tightly drawn. Having an object called to one's attention requires that one can respond properly. Thus, conversational strategies of a quite traditional variety are brought forth, and such phrases as "Oh, how nice!" or "I wish we had that!" can be heard.

A last condition which potentially gives rise to relational embarrassment is the failure to keep one's body under proper control. This, of course, relates to our earlier discussion of the relational touch system and rules of deference.

The body must always be in a state of readiness to act, and its appearance must make this clear. Hence any evidence of unreadiness or clumsiness is embarrassing. Examples include loss of whole body control (stumbling, trembling, or fainting), loss of visceral control (flatulence, involuntary urination, or drooling), and the communication of other "signs of the animal." [49]

In any relational social structure, normative standards arise to specify correct and incorrect body control. The intentional or unintentional violation of these rules challenges the ritual order of the presented relationship. Few effective strategies are available to cover these indiscretions. While such motives as fatigue, drunkenness, and boredom can be evoked, they seldom work. Typically what is observed is the designation of such conduct as "nonself" behavior. Placing it in this category also implies that it is "nonrelationally" relevant, and all persons can be absolved of responsibility when exposed to the episode. On some occasions we observe an entire phase of the encounter being written out of existence. All members agree to forget what went on. It was a nonencounter. Expressions of grief, extreme drunkenness, and overaffection seem to fall in this category. It must be remembered, however, that these are strategies that may or may not work. That they are called into existence suggests that the character of the presented relationship has been strongly challenged.

Feelings of *self-threat* are more severe than reactions of irritation and embarrassment. In situations where the ritual and moral value of the self is challenged, the entire relationship underpinning the self is badly damaged. It seems axiomatic that all the conditions that create embarrassment also can create self-relational threats. Thus, unnoticed props and equipment, misidentified selves, improper body control and dress, lead back to the relationship itself.

But more importantly, we observe in these actions a disconcern for the relationship itself. This brings us to the question of conduct when out of the physical presence of alter and when one is in-between relationships.

Husbands who behave indiscreetly, wives who flirt with other males, employees who derogate their employers, and children who tell "tales" behind their parents' back convey by their actions a basic disrespect for the relationship they are representing. These are situations where relational-release cannot be sanctioned and hence the actor must be held accountable for his misconduct. On these occasions the character of one's own relationship is threatened, for if husbands respond in a like manner to an indiscreet wife, they open the way for similar actions by their own spouse. In short, they are forced to condone these actions if they do not respond in a recriminatory manner.

When a person commits an act which is defined as inappropriate to the moral order of his major relationship, he is most likely to be defined as a relational deviant. Indiscreet husbands, fiancés who cheat, employees who steal, and children who "rat" on their parents soon find themselves defined as untrustworthy. Extreme avoidance rituals are enacted, exclusion from friendship circles begins, and they soon learn that they have transgressed a very important ritual order. Having once traveled beyond that outer boundary of respectability, they may never return. Search as they may for the old friends and the trusting wife, they will soon find that for them that relationship is over and done. In short, they have dangerously broached the territory of the public deviant. On occasion they may be permitted to return, but, as Jackson has shown with the alcoholic, having once left, things are never the same again.[50]

Perhaps more than any other kind of transgression, the relational threat makes all persons aware of the fragile order of their moral worlds. We have only to read the daily lists of divorces and letters to Dear Abby to be reminded of this fact.

Several conditions can potentially give rise to a perceived relational threat.[51] First, the behavior of one of the relational members may change over time and lead to a breakdown in the accommodation patterns between that person and the other members of the relationship. A father who enjoys poker parties with his cronies may increase his involvement in such activity so that he spends only a few evenings a week at home. Soon his children and spouse begin to feel excluded from his interactional circle and counter by leaving him out of their affairs. Almost without notice, it may occur to both parties that all sense of accommodation has collapsed and a relationship of substance no longer exists. Each responds by charging the other with inappropriate conduct, and unless counterforces are established, the relationship may disintegrate. Similar problems seem to occur with the wife who displays signs of mental illness, the drinking father, and the married male who insists on working eighty hours a week at his office.

Second, the potential deviant may bring his actions to the eyes of influential outsiders, and their perceptions are then fed back into the relationship. Social workers, physicians, close friends, distant relatives, and even legal authorities may take on such a role.[52] The veracity of their definitions may lead the other relational members to view the potential deviant's actions in a different light. They may attempt to foster changes on his part, and if he is unsuccessful in validating his actions, ascriptions of deviance may appear *within* the relationship. Under these circumstances, the moral order of the relationship is challenged, and unless changes occur, a public deviant may be created. At the very least, exclusion rituals will be set in motion and a moratorium may be established. A "trial period" of conduct will be set up, and the potential deviant is then given a period of time to prove himself worthy of relational membership.

A third condition for the relational threat arises when the rules of conduct begin to undergo change within the relationship. One of the members may adopt a new perspective and begin acting on what appears as unreasonable and unacceptable grounds in the opinion of the other members. One occasion reported to me involved the introduction of certain illicit drugs into a marriage that had long sanctioned the excessive use of alcohol for purposes of relational-release. The wife refused to accept this new definition, and the husband refused to change his line of action. Collective behavior in the relationship occurred and lasted until a compromise was established.

In this situation, the wife felt that the morality of her relationship was being threatened because the conduct of her husband when under the influence of drugs was quite unlike anything he theretofore had engaged in. Hence, we see that the introduction of new perspectives and new lines of action can potentially threaten the stability of any relationship. Keep in mind that the transgressions we are dealing with carry greater implications for the relationship than the momentary acts of embarrassment discussed earlier.

Relational Morality and the Broader Social Order

Having discussed the circumstances under which varying degrees of relational impropriety will be sensed, let us now turn to the relationship between relational moralities and perceptions of deviance by the broader social order. In short, we move away from the forms of deviance and misconduct that never come to the public's eye. It will be indicated how involvement in a relational social structure can lead to varying reactions by members of society's social control agencies. We are dealing with the situations when public deviance is either ascribed to a relational member or rechanneled back into the relationship.

ASCRIPTIONS OF PUBLIC DEVIANCE

Speaking abstractly, we may hypothesize that the greater the involvement in a relational social structure, the lower the probability of deviance ascription by members of social control agencies. That is, when we observe what by public standards would be an act of deviance, we predict that labeling will not occur if the potential deviant is highly involved in a relational network. Several contingency factors must be noted, however. First, we must consider the degree of societal legitimacy and power attributed to the offender and his relationship.[53] Under conditions of high power and high legitimacy we would predict the lowest rates of public deviance. This hypothesis is supported by research in the areas of both delinquency and mental illness. Kitsuse and Cicourel have shown that in an upper-class Chicago suburb acts of delinquency were written off as routine conduct among the youth of that area.[54] The typical approbation given by the chief of police was that "good kids don't get in trouble." In lower-class areas the reverse would have occurred. When rates of publicly diagnosed and treated mental illness are considered, the classic findings of Hollingshead and Redlich indicate similar conclusions. The higher the social class of the potential deviant, the lower rates of publicly ascribed mental illness.[55]

We observe similar processes operating under conditions of high political influence but relatively low social status. Thus members of powerful street gangs are less likely to be booked and charged for delinquent offenses than are members of less prestigious and powerful gangs.[56]

These data suggest that we may most profitably view any social structure as a complex arrangement of varying moral orders and relational statuses. Persons bound into powerful relational structures can expect relative immunity in the face of public deviance, while those lower in the moral hierarchy may be penalized for the very actions that found their source in persons from above.

Under other conditions we may observe ascriptions of public deviance, but to a lesser degree, because the deviant is involved in a relationship. Thus Bittner shows that police in skid-row areas are less likely to pick up and charge a law violator if he can show relational membership in an occupational or family structure.[57] Similarly, once booked and treated by a social control agency, the deviant will remain in that status for a time directly proportional to the strength and prestige of his ongoing relational structures. Thus mental patients are more likely to be released soon after admission if they can show relational need and if pressure from their relationships can be made public. Under conditions of little or no involvement in a relational structure, we can predict a much longer degree of hospitalization, incarceration, or treatment.[58]

As a person moves through the life cycle we can expect to observe varying moments of high and low public deviancy potential. In fact, the structure of our society's social control and treatment agencies directly corresponds to variations in the life cycle. These arrangements reflect an implicit belief that one's relational involvements will vary by his age. Thus, with a great deal of ease and relative immunity we can place our aged in retirement homes, our retarded in special institutions, and our juveniles in detention homes.

THE COMMUNICATION OF RELATIONAL IMPROPRIETY TO AGENCIES OF SOCIAL CONTROL

The statements above suggest a number of conditions under which one's relational status at the moment will affect his perceptions by agencies of social control. I wish now to examine those conditions when members of relational structures will bring into the public's eye a case of deviance.

Earlier, a number of conditions were suggested that would give rise to a sense of self or relational threat. It would seem that we could pursue these same dimensions one step further and hypothesize that as the relational deviance exceeds the tolerance limits of the involved members, the probability of exposing it to the outside increases. Hence, when embarrassing acts persist and increase in regularity, it may become apparent to relational members that they can control the deviant no longer. When a relational act remains confined to the relationship, public denouncement is less likely than if it recurrently comes to the eye of other friends and acquaintances. We can all handle deviance at home, but when it occurs publicly it causes embarrassment to the entire relationship. And relationships, we have suggested, can tolerate only a certain degree of public embarrassment.

Intrusions by third parties can bring in new perspectives and also disrupt the accommodation that has evolved between the potential public deviant and his relational partners. Sampson, Messinger, and Towne suggest that the intrusions of mothers-in-law into husband-wife dyads often brought a wife's deviant acts out into the open and ultimately led to hospitalization.[59] However, this would seem to be but a special case of bringing a new perspective or line of action into the relationship.[60]

On occasion we will observe relational partners deliberately staging situations such that one of the members can be formally and legitimately excluded. This would seem to be best represented in acts of betrayal, which Goffman has shown to operate in certain phases of the mental patient's moral career.[61] Betraying another relational partner seems to represent the extreme point of termination for the relationship. The betrayer has shifted his alliances to another moral order and is now searching for a convenient and socially acceptable exit from his present relationship. Thus, actions which formally were accommodated and accepted begin to be viewed in another light, and the betrayer begins to evoke a morality that would not sanction such actions. The betrayed soon finds himself in the uncomfortable position of no longer having the self-and-relational support he formerly expected from his partner. For an act of betrayal to be successfully carried off, the betrayed must not know why he is being excluded and who the actual betrayer is.[62] Thus, as Goffman suggests, third parties in the form of relatives, members from social control agencies, and friends will be brought in to bear the brunt of the responsibility. The strategy for this action is clear: no moral responsibility can be placed on the betrayer, and the betrayed can now be shown to be morally incompetent, and hence no longer deserving or fit to be a member of his focal relationship. He becomes the perfect mark, to be culled out by our agencies of social control.[63] Of course, once he has been shown to be morally unfit, all responsibility for maintaining the former relationship is removed from the betrayer. He or she is now free to enter into any other relationship. Thus, having dispensed with a burdensome and troublesome partner, he can begin a new life in another moral order. To summarize, I am suggesting that in the case of betrayal, the betrayer employs the label of public deviant as a convenient means of terminating the relationship. In some situations we find that a member of a relationship will deliberately seek out a label of public deviance. This is most frequently the case in voluntary admissions to mental hospitals. The prepatient comes to view his own actions as deviant and no longer morally acceptable to himself or his relational mates. Under these circumstances amicable resolutions are made, with both partners agreeing that this is the proper and correct line of action. The relationship is thus not terminated, but only held in abeyance for the duration of treatment or incarceration. When this occurs, the relationship role in its relational social structure is likely to go unthreatened. Friends will feel that the partners took the proper action, and no lasting aspersions will be cast on the relationship's over-all legitimacy and morality.

These are all instances when the matter of relational deviance rises out of the relationship and comes to the public's eye. On these occasions, I suggest, the fragile morality of the relationship is most severely tested. Depending on the degree of commitment and involvement held by the relational members, these social orders may either dissolve and disappear or take on renewed strength and vigor as a result of the publicity they have received. It would seem that the relational responses to such instances would also vary by the nature of the public label and public reaction. Hence, in cases of relational impropriety we would predict lower rates of dissolution than when one of the relational partners committed an action that challenged the legal and moral order of his broader society. In short, if the public reaction is primarily limited to a relational social structure (like a character flaw indicative of mental illness), milder forms of exclusion and lower rates of relational collapse will occur than if the action comes to the attention of an entire community, organization, or work group.

Rules of Conduct and the Study of Deviant Behavior: Some Implications and Suggestions

In this chapter I have suggested an area of analysis that labeling theory, as set forth by Becker, Goffman, and Scheff, has as yet to deal with systematically. It was suggested that the proper application of labeling theory to the area of deviant behavior must consider the complex interrelationship between rules of the civil-legal order, rules of polite, face-to-face interaction, and rules of social relationships. The application of the labeling theory has no meaning until we can specify the actual interactional-situational relational context of the rules and audiences under analysis. I have also suggested that contemporary studies of deviant behavior, employing the labeling perspective, have focused in an excessive fashion on rule violations of the civil-legal order. Studies of drug use, parole violations, juvenile delinquency, police behavior, and so on either have examined the social organization of social control agencies that legislate civil-legal codes and rules or have examined forms of deviance that by definition involve few of the complex negotiations most typical of the wide forms of deviance common in our society. Few persons ever come in contact with the courts and legal institutions, but many persons are defined by some set of others as deviant; and it is my position that it is persons of this order that any theory of deviant behavior must be held accountable for. In short, a shift in the focus of attention has been proposed.

To this end I introduced the concepts of relational deviance and relational morality. I suggested that perceptions of relational deviance may range from the taken-for-granted response that "everyone does this at one time or another anyway" to feelings of irritation, embarrassment, and finally self-relational threat. The great majority of relational acts that are perceived as deviant evoke reactions of irritation and embarrassment. They are infrequent and are typically kept private.

Any social order, I suggest, is routinely maintained by the kinds of interactional rituals treated in this chapter. Publicly to acclaim a person as deviant and move him into a formal treatment agency is an extreme act, indeed. The fact that such actions occur infrequently suggests that social order and social control are not so much maintained by the law and the agencies of social control as some have suggested. In short, from our perspective, social control becomes self-control and relational control. Each person in the social structure is finely attuned to the moralities and demands of his focal relationships and acts to uphold those microcosmic social orders. He does so because to do otherwise would be to deny himself the degree of self-respect, intimacy, and security that is rightfully his.[64]

The perspective offered here has several disadvantages. If, as I suggest, attention should be shifted from the civil-legal institutions to the more ephemerally sustained social organizations and moralities I have called social relationships, a fundamental analysis confronting us is to uncover the range and variety of relational moralities that are operative in any social order. Such a shift is difficult, if only for the fact that every existing relationship represents a unique moral order—a unique transformation, if you will, of rules of conduct from the legal and polite interactional sides of the continuum. The language and imagery of the social relationship must then be examined.[65] In our studies, of course we will find regularities across relationships—if not by social class position, perhaps by occupation, by cultural setting, by ethnic position, by age-sex grading, and so on. Having identified regularities across relationships and situations, we must then inquire into the differential consequences of rule violation and rule evocation for deviant careers. We need not be overly concerned with the more glamorous and exciting forms of deviance, such as drug use or homosexuality, to become aware of the fact that nearly every person has at some point in his life trajectory engaged, perhaps even regularly, in some form of behavior that by someone's standard is deviant. It is not unreasonable to assume that weekly bowling groups, or poker clubs among middle-class or lower-class males, or bridge societies and weekly teas among middle-class females represent, from someone's point of view, behavior that violates a relational or polite code of behavior. These are offered as instances of serious behavior forms, the engagement in which allows the participants to do "something" their ordinary interactional circle disapproves of. Goffman has suggested that all persons are at some points in their interactive careers normal deviants.[66] That is, they have escaped the stigmatizing label of public deviant. The present discussion builds on this point by suggesting that all persons are seen as deviant in the sense that they systematically violate one set of rules while building another set that legitimates those very rules initially violated. Beyond this, it is suggested that the more common forms of deviance we observe and study in any society or community come initially from defined violations of relational proprieties. If, as I suggest, all persons systematically break or violate rules of one of the three orders described, the comprehensive analysis of deviant behavior becomes a study of rule violation at all three levels. Rather than focusing primarily on the public deviant, as much of the research to date has done, we must examine persons labeled as deviant either by virtue of the fact that they have violated rules of polite society in a regular fashion, or because they have violated the rules of those symbolically recurring and reciprocated face-to-face interactions termed social relationships.

The present discussion has implications also for the study of deviant careers, for the role of the self in interaction, and for the socialization process. The study of childhood socialization, for example, becomes one lever by which the sociologist can identify the translation of society's rules into the process of self-construction in the child. Socialization at this level would indicate the ways in which families, as unique interactional units, construct their own moral worlds that sustain and tolerate a wide variety of rule-violating conduct, while at the same time punishing other forms of deviance. We might also attempt to identify the range of social relationships a "normal" member of any social order "routinely" enters into. At what point in the age cycle, for example, is a person expected to be maximally "locked" into a relational social structure or structures? Carefully conducted case studies of a variety of relationships would begin to reveal the nature and form of these moralities repeatedly stressed in our discussion. We might also want to inquire into the strategies of relational negotiation that all persons are forced to engage in. When is it appropriate to enact a given "relational morality," and when is it inappropriate?

The study of deviant careers, given the present perspective, would focus on the ways in which persons, once defined as deviant, attempt to carve out enduring and self-sustaining social relationships that sanction the behavior they have either voluntarily or involuntarily been cast into as a result of the labeling process.

But perhaps more importantly, the investigation of deviant behavior becomes, as the labeling theorist indicates, a study of social interaction and of the ways in which rules of conduct emerge and are differentially defined and applied by the groups under investigation. In short, the study of deviance becomes social interaction and the situationality of interaction. Such an interpretation, it is suggested, lends further validity to the interactionist-labeling theory perspective by forcing the investigator and theorist to extend the boundaries of his observations to the actual behavioral nexus of social conduct and the rules on which that conduct is based.[67]

NOTES

1. Howard S. Becker, *Outsiders: Studies in the Sociology of Deviance* (New York: The Free Press, 1963).
2. See Stephen P. Spitzer and Norman K. Denzin, eds., *The Mental Patient: Studies in the Sociology of Deviance* (New York: McGraw-Hill, 1968), where the labeling perspective of symbolic interactionism is more fully elaborated and applied specifically to the mental patient.
3. See *ibid.*, "Issues and Problems in the Sociology of Mental Illness," pp. 461–473, where problems not treated in this chapter are discussed. See also Alexander L. Clark and Jack P. Gibbs, "Social Control: A Reformulation," *Social Problems*, XII (Summer, 1965), 398–415; Jack P. Gibbs, "Conceptions of Deviant Behavior: The Old and the New," *Pacific Sociological Review*, IX (1966), 9–14; David J. Bordua, "Deviant Behavior and Social Control: Recent Trends," *Annals of the American Academy of Political and Social Science*, CCCLXIX (January, 1967), 149–163; Judith Lorber, "Deviance as Performance: The Case of Illness," *Social Problems*, XIV (Winter, 1967), 302–310; Eliot Freidson, "Disability as Social Deviance," in Marvin B. Sussman, ed., *Sociological Theory Research and Rehabilitation* (Washington, D.C.: American Sociological Association, 1966), pp. 82–93; Daniel Glaser, "National Goals and Indicators for the Reduction of Crime and Delinquency," *The Annals*, CCCLXXI (May, 1967), 104–126; Roland L. Akers, "Problems in the Sociology of Deviance," *Social Forces*, XLVI (June, 1968), 455–465; Richard J. Lundman, "Labeling Theory: Its Past, Its Present and Its Future," unpublished M.A. thesis, Department of Sociology, University of Illinois, 1968. The most recent compilation of research and theory representing the "labeling-interactionist perspec-

tive" is Earl Rubington and Martin S. Weinberg, eds., *Deviance: The Interactionist Perspective* (New York: Macmillan, 1968).

4. Becker, *op cit.*, pp. 18–39; Erving Goffman, *Stigma: Notes on the Management of Spoiled Identity* (Englewood Cliffs: Prentice-Hall, 1963), pp. 130–135.

5. See my *Symbols, Relationships and Social Groups* (Chicago: Aldine, in press), where this notion is more fully explored.

6. A number of the problems to be discussed later in this chapter were treated in an earlier version. See my "Rules of Conduct and the Study of Deviant Behavior; Some Notes on College Youth and Mental Patients," paper presented to the 63rd Annual Meeting of the Midwest Sociological Society, April 19–21, 1968, Omaha, Nebraska.

7. I draw heavily upon Erving Goffman's "The Nature of Deference and Demeanor," reprinted in his *Interaction Ritual: Essays in Face-to-Face Behavior* (Chicago: Aldine, 1967), pp. 47–95, in the following section.

8. *Ibid.*, p. 48.

9. *Ibid.*, p. 49. This is Goffman's example.

10. Becker, *op. cit.*

11. *Ibid.*, pp. 1–2.

12. See, for example, Jack D. Douglas, "The General Theoretical Implications of the Sociology of Deviance," to appear in John C. McKinney and Edward A. Tiryakian, eds., *Theoretical Sociology: Perspectives and Developments* (New York: Appleton-Century-Crofts, 1970). This paper has provided one of the perspectives employed in the present chapter. See also Donald W. Ball, "The Problematics of Respectability," Chapter 11 in the present volume. The thrust of Douglas' and Ball's perspective is to move beyond the public deviant and into the dynamics of daily, routine interactions wherein the forms of deviance we treat in this chapter appear.

13. Virtually all the essays in Goffman, *Interaction Ritual*, point in this direction. See also his *Behavior in Public Places* (New York: The Free Press, 1963).

14. *Ibid.*, p. 248.

15. A theorist who stands between Goffman and Becker is Thomas Scheff. See his *Being Mentally Ill* (Chicago: Aldine, 1966) for a modified social systems theory that merges Becker's view of the outsider with Goffman's perspective on rules of etiquette. In general we feel that Scheff has moved too rapidly to the social systems level and hence has also ignored the more routine forms of deviance that do not receive treatment by agencies of social control. See also Edwin Lemert, *Human Deviance, Social Problems, and Social Control* (Englewood Cliffs: Prentice-Hall, 1967).

16. Goffman, *Interaction Ritual*, pp. 26–27.

17. *Ibid.*, p. 27.

18. George Simmel, *The Sociology of George Simmel,* trans. by Kurt Wolff (New York: The Free Press, 1950), pp. 118–135.

19. Max Weber, *The Theory of Social and Economic Organization,* trans. by A. M. Henderson and Talcott Parsons (New York: The Free Press, 1947), pp. 118–120.

20. Charles H. Cooley, *Social Organization* (Glencoe: The Free Press, 1956), pp. 23–31.

21. For a treatment of the stranger relationship which draws on Simmel's formulations, see Margaret M. Wood, *The Stranger: A Study in Social Relationships* (New York: Columbia University Press, 1934).

22. Tamotsu Shibutani, "Reference Groups and Social Control," in Arnold M. Rose, ed., *Human Behavior and Social Processes* (Boston: Houghton Mifflin, 1962), pp. 129–147.

23. This in no way represents a comprehensive list of dimensions around which rules will evolve. This is a highly tentative formulation, pointing to what are felt to be salient problems for the relationship.

24. See Hunter S. Thompson, *Hell's Angels* (New York: Ballantine, 1966).

25. That societies create "surplus populations" for purposes of upholding occupational, moral, and ideological structures is suggested in Bernard Farber, *Mental Retardation: Its Social Context and Social Consequences* (Boston: Houghton Mifflin, 1968), pp. 3–42, 260–271.

26. Simmel, *op. cit.* See also George J. McCall and J. L. Simmons, *Identities and Interactions* (New York: The Free Press, 1966), pp. 167–201.

27. Goffman, "On Face Work," in his *Interactional Ritual,* p. 42.

28. Goffman, "The Nature of Deference and Demeanor."

29. *Ibid.*

30. See Edward Gross and Gregory P. Stone, "Embarrassment and the Analysis of Role Requirements," *American Journal of Sociology,* LXX (July, 1964), 1–15.

31. In this sense we are suggesting that membership in a focal relationship represents for any person a "master status" which overrides virtually all his other involvements. See Becker, *op. cit.,* pp. 32–33, for a discussion of master statuses and the public attribution of deviance.

32. On knowledge and the relationship, see Simmel, *op. cit.,* pp. 307–376; Ball, *op. cit.;* and Erving Goffman, *The Presentation of Self in Everyday Life* (Garden City, N.Y.: Doubleday, 1959), pp. 77–237.

33. Ball, *op. cit.*

34. The following treatment of secrets is taken from Goffman, *The Presentation of Self in Everyday Life,* pp. 141–144.

35. Ruth S. Cavan has suggested a continuum similar to our own in "The Concepts of Tolerance and Contraculture as Applied to Delinquency," *Sociological Quarterly,* II (1961), 243–258. However, her bias is in the direction of formal-societal reactions.

36. Gross and Stone, *op. cit.,* suggest the above-mentioned treatment of embarrassment.

37. In one sense this form of deviance is represented in Harold Garfinkel's investigations of routine deviance in daily interactions. See his *Studies in Ethnomethodology* (Englewood Cliffs: Prentice-Hall, 1967), especially pp. 35–75.

38. Excerpted from Becker, *op. cit.*, p. 125. See Melville Dalton, *Men Who Manage* (New York: Wiley, 1959), pp. 199–205.

39. Becker, *op. cit.*, p. 126.

40. See Douglas, *op. cit.*, on moral provocateurs.

41. Goffman, "Where the Action Is," in his *Interaction Ritual*, pp. 149–270. Contrary to Goffman's view which sees "action" occurring in the race car, on the stage, and on the top of a mountain, we suggest it lies instead in the vibrant moral orders and interactional encounters between relationships.

42. See Shibutani, *op. cit.*, on this point. We have avoided employing his conception of social world because it implies interactions with any "other" who may share some interest in a person's activities. Thus, he applies the concept of world to interest groups, cults, political parties, occupational groups, and so on. Therefore, while we adopt many of Shibutani's notions of the social world as a referent for interaction, we have restricted its abstractness and termed it a moral order.

43. The following section draws nearly exclusively on Gross and Stone, *op. cit.* For another view of embarrassment, see Goffman, "Embarrassment and Social Organization," in his *Interaction Ritual*, pp. 97–112.

44. Gross and Stone, *op. cit.*, p. 6.

45. In this sense we view relationships as performing teams. See Goffman, *The Presentation of Self*.

46. Gross and Stone, *op. cit.*, p. 9.

47. *Ibid.*

48. *Ibid.*, p. 10.

49. *Ibid.*

50. Joan K. Jackson, "Alcoholism and the Family," in David J. Pittman and Charles R. Snyder, eds., *Society, Culture and Drinking Patterns* (New York: Wiley, 1962), pp. 472–492.

51. Some of the following notions were originally expressed in Spitzer and Denzin, *op. cit.*, p. 463. See also Ernest Becker, "Socialization, Command of Performance and Mental Illness," in *ibid.*, pp. 31–40; and David Mechanic, "Some Factors in Identifying and Defining Mental Illness," *ibid.*, pp. 195–203.

52. This process is well illustrated in Harold Sampson, Sheldon L. Messinger, and Robert D. Towne, "Family Processes and Becoming a Mental Patient," in Spitzer and Denzin, *op. cit.*, pp. 203–213.

53. See Scheff, *op. cit.*, for a similar statement on power and public ascriptions of deviance; also Becker, *op. cit.*

54. John I. Kitsuse and Aaron V. Cicourel, "A Note on the Uses of Official Statistics," *Social Problems*, XI (Fall, 1963), 131–139; Aaron V. Cic-

ourel, *The Social Organization of Juvenile Justice* (New York: Wiley, 1968).

55. August B. Hollingshead and Frederick C. Redlich, *Social Class and Mental Illness* (New York: Wiley, 1958).

56. See Frederick M. Thrasher, *The Gang*, abridged ed. (Chicago: University of Chicago Press, 1963). For similar observations in the area of organized crime, see John Landesco, "Organized Crime in Chicago," in Ernest W. Burgess and Donald J. Bogue, eds., *Contributions to Urban Sociology* (Chicago: University of Chicago Press, 1964), pp. 559–576. The best statement of the conflict theory of deviance which the present discussion implicitly draws upon is George Vold, *Theoretical Criminology* (New York: Oxford University Press, 1958).

57. Egon Bittner, "The Police on Skid-Row: A Study of Peace Keeping," *American Sociological Review*, XXXII (October, 1967), 699–715; also by Bittner, "Police Discretion in Apprehending the Mentally Ill," *Social Problems*, XIV (Winter, 1967), 278–292.

58. This must be seen as a tentative hypothesis only. For suggestive data in this regard, see Ozzie G. Simmons, James A. Davis, and Katherine Spencer, "Interpersonal Strains in Release from a Mental Hospital," in Spitzer and Denzin, *op. cit.*, pp. 376–384.

59. Sampson, Messinger, and Towne, *op. cit.*

60. On misperceptions of these new perspectives, see Gustav Ichheiser, *Misunderstandings in Human Relations: A Study in False Social Perceptions* (Chicago: University of Chicago Press, 1949).

61. Erving Goffman, *Asylums* (Garden City, N.Y.: Doubleday, 1961), "The Moral Career of the Mental Patient," pp. 125–169. See especially pp. 131–146.

62. For an excellent treatment of such strategies, see Goffman, "On Cooling the Mark Out: Some Aspects of Adaptation to Failure," in Rose, *op. cit.*, pp. 482–505.

63. *Ibid.*

64. In one sense we are suggesting a shift in the metaphorical perspective of the sociologist of deviance. Rather than employing the "systems," "dramaturgical," or "threat" metaphors of a Goffman and a Scheff, we are suggesting an image of social man that routinely finds him in nonthreatening interactional quarters which he has created for himself. In such circumstances, a systems metaphor with its implicit demands of equilibration and stability has little relevance. Nor does a "threat-action-drama" metaphor. On metaphors and the sociological game, see the following unpublished papers by Peter K. Manning: "Sociology as a Game of Games" (October, 1967) and "Metaphors as Mirrors" (April, 1968).

65. For one of the few studies focusing on the language and imagery of relationships, see Donald Horton, "The Dialogue of Courtship in Popular Songs," *American Journal of Sociology*, LXII (May, 1957), 569–

578. See also Scheff, *op. cit.* These studies suggest that a profitable line of inquiry for the sociologist would be the analysis of public art forms that systematically define proper conduct in a variety of relationships. Thus, the popular song recurrently treats problems of love, hate, divorce, betrayal, and embarrassment.

66. Goffman, *Stigma*, pp. 130–146. See also Howard S. Becker, *op. cit.*, pp. 20–21, where secret deviance is discussed.

67. In this last respect, we feel that our perspective begins partially to solve the deficiency that Polsky has suggested permeates most, if not all, current studies of deviance. He notes that we know very little about the back-stage actions of the criminal and the convict because we study him only after he has been caught (while in jail or on probation, for example). Polsky's corrective is to go to the natural settings where such deviance occurs and study it before it becomes public. Our perspective would go one step further and examine forms of deviance that virtually never become public. See Ned Polsky, *Hustlers, Beats and Others* (Chicago: Aldine, 1967), pp. 117–149. See also Donald W. Ball, "Conventional Data and Unconventional Conduct: Toward a Methodological Reorientation," paper presented to the Pacific Sociological Association, Long Beach, California, March, 1967. For strategies of methodological conduct in these settings, see my *The Substance of Sociological Theory and Method: An Interactionist Interpretation* (Chicago: Aldine, tentative title, in process), especially Chapers 9–13.

6

The Social Construction of Legal Doctrine: The Case of Adolf Eichmann

Ted R. Vaughan
Gideon Sjoberg

On May 23, 1960, Prime Minister David Ben-Gurion announced in Israel's Knesset that Adolf Eichmann had been captured and turned over to governmental authorities and would stand trial in that country. This announcement set in motion a chain of events, the controversy about which has not yet abated.[1] For Eichmann had been pursued for fifteen years, eventually captured by Israeli nationals in Argentina, and delivered to authorities in the State of Israel because of the nature of his alleged participation in an unprecedented crime: the German Nazis' destruction of the European Jews during World War II. The Nazi crime has informed the conscience of twentieth-century man. And the Jerusalem trial represented a major attempt to confront this unprecedented phenomenon, for Eichmann stood as a symbol of the Nazi era.

Statement of the Problem

The Eichmann trial was no ordinary criminal case, for Eichmann's participation in genocide was no ordinary crime, Eichmann, as we will see, was an "extreme" rather than a "deviant" case.[2] At issue in the trial was neither the fact that genocide had been committed nor the fact that Eichmann had been involved in this action. There was no basic disagreement on these matters. At stake was the interpretation of the meaning of participation in such action. Inasmuch as the action was genuinely unprecedented, judicial meanings could not simply be assigned to the act or the actor; they were perforce constructed.

Our main problem is to analyze the process by which a particular legal doctrine was constructed. We use the term "legal doctrine" rather than law because Eichmann was tried on the basis of an already extant Israeli statute. The very nature of this case makes it possible to focus our attention on issues which are ordinarily not examined by sociologists.

We shall analyze the Eichmann trial and the emergence of this legal doctrine within a "moral contest" frame of reference and shall detail this case from the perspective of the contestants in a more or less natural history account.[3] The protagonists are Eichmann and his defense attorney and the Israeli prosecutors. In the anomalous middle ground stand the Israeli judges. But the situation is more complex than this. Inasmuch as Eichmann was a citizen of Germany abducted from Argentina, these countries (and various subgroups within them) were involved, as was the United Nations.

We shall discuss (1) the nature of genocide and then (2) in some detail the major issues among the key contestants in the trial. After this presentation of basic data we can analyze the construction of legal doctrine by answering three questions:

1. What was done? Here we are primarily concerned with the process by which the extreme crimes that Eichmann committed were reduced to the "traditional categories" of Israel's legal system. The logic of how this process was carried out—for instance, the use of analogy —is of considerable theoretical importance in understanding the construction of social meanings.

2. How was the moral contest resolved? That Eichmann, "a man without a country," was engaged in a contest with a nation-state had a bearing on the decision-making process, as, indeed, it appears to be in the resolution of many other kinds of moral contests.

3. How was Israel's decision legitimized? The Israelis were faced with a dilemma which is frequently encountered in the history of legal thought: whether to adopt "universalistic" criteria or "particularistic" criteria in order to justify one's actions. Although the Israeli prosecutor and judges were ambivalent in their reasoning (they acknowledged, for example, some transnational considerations), their pri-

mary justification seems to have been in terms of the moral basis of the nation-state.

We believe our analysis places the Eichmann trial in a somewhat different light and hopefully opens some new avenues for sociological exploration. The writers who have analyzed the case of Eichmann seem to have overlooked the major dilemma in this trial. By appealing to national (and ethnic) considerations, the Israelis translated the problem back into some of the traditional nation-state categories, and thus they unwittingly undermined at least to a degree one of the very principles they were striving to establish: that of building a legal doctrine which would serve as a standard for judging cases such as Eichmann's and would hopefully even build constraints which would prevent such cases in the future.

The Nature of the Crime

Although much controversy surrounded the Eichmann trial and its aftermath, there has been no serious challenge to the central facts of the case. From the time the Nazis came to power, the persecution of the Jews was the official policy of the German state.[4] Predicating their actions on widespread anti-Semitism in Germany, the Nazis within two months of their ascension to power organized and legalized economic boycotts against the Jews and within two years relegated them to inferior status in the whole of social life via the infamous Nuremberg Laws. Official persecution and harassment of the German Jews continued until the *Anschluss,* when the strategy was changed to systematic forced emigration.

The first large-scale efforts to expel the Jews from the Reich occurred in Austria. While the earlier persecution and expulsion had been official state policy, these efforts were largely unco-ordinated. But in Vienna a central co-ordinating office for Jewish emigration was established on the recommendation of Adolf Eichmann, who became its first head. The various steps requisite to expulsion and simultaneous confiscation of property were organized on an assembly-line basis:

A Jew would enter the office of the *Zentralstelle;* he was still somebody, having a job or a shop, an apartment to live in, some property or cash in the bank, his child still registered at school. As he proceeded from window to window he was stripped of all these things one by one. When he finally left the building he was jobless, his property had been requisitioned, his child crossed off the school roll and his apartment taken away. All he had now was a passport with the letter "J," valid for two weeks. It was his task to find a foreign visa. He was expressly told that if he were to be found in Austria after the passport expired, it would still be valid but only for a single, one-way journey: to a concentration camp! [5]

This procedure, so well received by Eichmann's superiors, served as a model for other centers, including the Central Office in Berlin which Eichmann came to head. However, the forced emigration of large numbers of Jews under German control proved to be impossible, and alternative measures for forced relocation (the Madagascar and "Nisko" Plans, for example) were discussed, but not acted on.

With the outbreak of the war and the closing of the borders for emigration and the simultaneous increase in the number of Jews in territories occupied by German troops, a new phase in Jewish persecution was initiated. This involved the concentration of Jews in a relatively few large ghettoes. The Germans' task of surveillance and control was thereby simplified. Although the plan for the total extermination of the Jews (the "Final Solution") was not formalized until late 1941, concentration of the Jews in a few locations greatly facilitated their deportation to the death camps.

The Final Solution of the Jewish problem began with the wholesale shooting of Jews located in the Soviet territories occupied by the German army. While this practice was never completely abandoned, the principal means of destruction was by gassing in the killing centers in the East. Millions of Jews were sent to such camps as Majdanek, Treblinka, Chelmo, Belzec, and Auschwitz between the early part of 1942 and the end of the war. In all, it is estimated that at least six million European Jews, approximately one-third of the Jewish population of the world, were killed by the Nazis.[6]

While murder is as old as the human race, genocide involved, as Gideon Hausner observed in his opening address in Jerusalem, "a new kind of murder."[7] Indeed, genocide does not fall into the typical normal-deviance continuum. It is an extreme case which is identified by two key characteristics: (1) genocide was official policy of the German nation-state wherein there was a calculated decision to systematically destroy a people within that social order, and (2) not merely because they were enemies of the state but because they were defined as subhuman. As Hannah Arendt has written: "It was when the Nazi regime declared that the German people not only were unwilling to have any Jews in Germany but wished to make the entire Jewish people disappear from the face of the earth that the new crime, the crime against humanity—in the sense of a crime 'against

the human status,' or against the very nature of mankind—appeared." [8]
But we must emphasize that those who participated in this act of
human destruction were carrying out the official policy of the German
state; they were acting in accordance with the rules of the dominant
societal standards.

To be sure, this German policy regarding the Jews evolved over
time, and we shall briefly comment on the patterning of events, particularly as these relate to Eichmann.[9] The implementation of the various stages was carried out chiefly by the *Schutzstaffeln* (SS), of
which Adolf Eichmann was a member. The Nazis endeavored to destroy all evidence of the organizational apparatus that was responsible
for implementing their Jewish policy; nevertheless, considerable information on the organization of the SS has been amassed. It evolved
from a small cadre charged with Hitler's protection to the party's
equivalent of the Stadt administrative system. The SS came to be composed of twelve offices, all of which were in one way or another involved in the extermination process. One of the twelve was the Head
Office for Reich Security (RSHA). This office in turn was divided into
seven bureaus, one of which (Bureau IV) was the Bureau of the Gestapo, the secret state police. The Bureau of the Gestapo was further
divided into two parts, Division B being concerned with sectarian
groups. In turn, this division had four sections, one of which (Section
4) was concerned exclusively with "Jewish Affairs." Section IV-B-4
was headed throughout its existence by Adolf Eichmann.

The afore-mentioned facts with respect to the organizational structure responsible for the holocaust were so agreed upon that they were
not, in the main, challenged by the defense in Jerusalem. The real
problem in the trial was not to establish Eichmann's guilt to punish
him. Eichmann's participation in genocide, an act in which he was admittedly implicated, is fundamentally incommensurable with conventional reasons for punishment. The foremost problem encountered
here was that of understanding the incomprehensible. Clearly, the various contestants interpreted the meaning of Eichmann's participation
—especially the relationship of the individual to the group—in markedly different ways.

Major Issues in the Trial

Eichmann was charged under the provisions of Israel's Nazis and
Nazi Collaborators (Punishment) Law of 1950 with fifteen counts of
crimes against the Jewish people, crimes against humanity, and war

crimes. To these charges Eichmann pleaded "not guilty in the sense of the indictment." [10]

But even before Eichmann entered his plea to the charges, the defense raised a number of objections to the trial. These objections served to challenge the very basis and legitimacy of the trial. The court's decisions with respect to these issues were of vital significance, for they decidedly influenced the outcome of the moral contest between the protagonists. The major issues fell generally in one of the following broad, but interrelated, categories: (1) jurisdictional problems, (2) the legal status of the Israeli law under which Eichmann was charged, and (3) the problem of the defendant's guilt.

JURISDICTIONAL PROBLEMS

1. The lack of impartiality of the Israeli judges. The first objection raised by the defense challenged the jurisdiction of a court composed of Israeli judges to sit in judgment of Eichmann. Because the judges were identified with the Jewish people, this might undermine their impartiality. "This may be possible and arises out of the fact that the Jewish Nation was concerned in this catastrophe of extermination." [11] The defense argued further that public opinion, which in this case was the "world at large," had to be convinced of the impartiality of the court.[12] Since "people of a certain importance in world public opinion had voiced their fears" of prejudice and had suggested a neutral tribunal, the defense attorney argued that this was sufficient for the judges to declare that they had no jurisdiction in the case.[13] Finally, the defense argued that the nature of the case directly involved the judges:

> Here we do not speak about an ordinary crime, an ordinary offense. Here we have to deal with acts which were carried out not from a purely criminal disposition of any kind. Here we are dealing with a problem which actually means participation in political activities. These are political activities which are of political interest to the Jewish people and the State of Israel.[14]

The prosecution countered these arguments by quoting at length from a defense of the Nuremberg trials against similar objections. At Nuremberg it was argued that a judge could be impartial to the accused, although he could not be expected to be impartial to the crime. If this were not the case, the prosecutor argued, no judge could try a spy, for inasmuch as the spy represents the enemy country the judge would not be neutral to the issue.[15] The issue of neutrality constituted the thrust of the prosecutor's argument to the court:

> No one can demand that you be neutral toward the crime of genocide and if the defense believes that there is a person in the world who can be neutral towards this crime this judge is not fit to sit in judgment.[16]

To the defense attorney's objection to the possibility of bias on the part of the judges, "the court finds and each judge finds himself fit to sit in judgment." [17] The court detailed its reasons as follows:

> The subject of the indictment is the responsibility of the accused for the acts described in the indictment. And when these acts are being clarified, it will not be difficult to safeguard the interests of the accused according to the procedure of our Criminal Court Ordinance, that everyone appearing before the court is innocent and his judgment will be declared only in accordance with the evidence brought before this court. Those who sit in judgment are professional judges, used and accustomed to weighing evidence brought before them and do their work in the public eye and the criticism of the public. Learned lawyers and counsels defend the accused. And as far as the fears of the accused regarding the background which is the background of the case, we must only respect what has been said and holds good in all courts: that when a court of judgment sits to judge, the judge is still a human being, flesh and blood with feelings and senses, but he is ordered by the law to restrain these feelings and senses, because otherwise there will never be a judge to sit in a criminal case where the abhorrence of the judge is aroused, like treason, murder, or any other serious crime. It is true that the memory of the catastrophe and the holocaust stirs every Jew, but when this case has been brought before us, it is our duty to restrain these feelings when we sit in judgment in this case. And this duty we shall keep.[18]

2. The abduction of Eichmann. A second objection raised to the Jerusalem court's jurisdiction concerned the kidnaping of Eichmann by Israeli nationals in Argentina.[19] In 1950, after hiding out after World War II in Germany, Eichmann made his way to Italy, where he obtained an Argentina visa in the name of Richard Klement. At the time of his capture, he had resided in Argentina for ten years under this alias. In May, 1960, after months of surveillance by Israeli nationals, Eichmann was captured and then was held for a period of several days, during which he signed a statement in which he agreed to stand trial in Israel. He left Argentina in a plane ostensibly chartered for the purpose of transporting a gravely ill person out of the country. Argentine authorities were unaware of Eichmann's abduction.

In his oral pleadings the defense counsel argued that Eichmann had been kidnaped on instructions of the Israeli government. Consequently, the means by which he was brought to trial were illegal. Dr. Servatius argued that "since a court cannot base its jurisdiction on an illegal act of state, the courts of Israel do not have jurisdiction to try the defendant." [20]

Anticipating the prosecution's arguments of precedent for the action and the jurisdiction, the defense contended, "One must not bring these precedents before this court, and they do not apply to this case because the kidnapping in this case was altogether different." [21]

In his lengthy written brief to the court, Servatius contended that Israel's failure to use extradition channels constituted a violation of international law.[22] And one court observer noted:

> There is an accepted and firmly established principle in the law of extradition of the majority of countries, known as the "principle of speciality," that the right to punish, of the state requesting extradition, is limited in each specific case to the offence or offences for which the extradition is asked. Hence the person extradited enjoys a personal immunity from any prosecution for any other offence committed before his extradition.[23]

The prosecution rejoined by citing numerous precedents supporting the argument that a court does not inquire into the circumstances under which a person has been brought before it:

> A legal doctrine has developed in England and the United States, that the method of bringing the accused into court is irrelevant to the matter of the competence of the court itself. Infringement of the sovereignty of a state by the capture of a man within its borders and his subsequent transfer abroad—this can be subject for discussion between states. And in fact they were the subject for discussion between the State of Israel and the Argentine in this case. But in all the authorities which I quote shortly, it has been laid down that it is not for the accused to argue against the competence of the court. That is a matter of the state which has been affected.[24]

In other words, the prosecution reasoned that "the circumstances of the arrest and the bringing of the accused to the court are not relevant when the question of competence is discussed." [25]

In its decision on the matter of abduction issued in the sixth session, the court overruled the objection raised by the defense:

> And regarding the arguments about the circumstances whereby the accused was brought to this Court: We found that this Court is competent

to sit in judgment, and therefore according to the law, there is no importance to the way the accused was brought within the jurisdiction of this Court.[26]

In the court's *Judgment* at the conclusion of the trial, the reasons for the ruling were indicated:

It is an established rule of law that a person standing trial for an offense against the laws of the land may not oppose his being tried by reasons of the illegality of his arrest or of the means whereby he was brought to the area of jurisdiction of the country. The courts in England, the United States and Israel have ruled continuously that the circumstances of the arrest and the mode of bringing the accused into the area of the State have no relevance to his trial, and they consistently refused in all cases to enter into an examination of these circumstances.[27] [There follow twelve legal pages citing precedents for this decision.[28]] To sum up, the contention of the accused against the jurisdiction of the Court by reason of abduction from Argentina is in essence nothing but a plea for immunity by a fugitive offender on the strength of the refuge given him by a sovereign state.[29]

THE LEGALITY OF THE ISRAELI LAW

The law under which Eichmann was tried, the Nazis and Nazi Collaborators (Punishment) Law of 1950, was itself a major issue in the trial. The law provided for the punishment of acts committed by the Nazis in Germany and German-occupied Europe between 1939 and 1945. The defense objected to the law on the grounds that it was contrary to international law. The defense contended that the Israeli law violated international law in that it specified punishment for actions which took place outside the boundaries of Israel, prior to the establishment of the state, against persons who were not Israeli citizens, and in the course of duty on behalf of a foreign country.[30] Thus, formally, the law contains extraterritorial and retroactive features as well as provisions for the intervention of one state in the internal affairs of a sovereign country.

1. The problem of extraterritoriality. According to generally accepted principles of international law, a state's power to punish crimes committed outside its borders is limited to cases in which a clear linking point can be established between the state and the crime. The issue between the defense and prosecution revolved about this point.

The defense contended that the law did not meet the exceptions cited above: "The law of the nations (international law) does not extend the sovereignty of the case or category of cases such as this one. It is inadmissible to try foreign citizens. This is not recognized by the territorial jurisdiction principle nor the law of the nations principle, nor of the principle of personal protection." [31]

The defense contended further that the International Convention on Genocide (1948) established "the jurisdiction of the Courts of the state in whose territory the act was committed." [32] Thus, Servatius was contending that only German courts had jurisdiction in the case, for only Germany satisfied the territorial requirement.

The prosecution countered with the assertion that the territorial principle enjoyed no special status in international law: "It is not true to state that there is only one principle here which gives authority to the court, and that that is the territorial principle. There are many principles." [33] Moreover, the prosecution cited several judicial precedents which sought to establish the claim of countries to jurisdiction for crimes against their nationals, wherever committed.

In addition, Hausner contended that a crime such as genocide requires universal jurisdiction:

> Some crimes have always been considered to strike at the welfare of humanity at large, for they are not limited to specific geographical units. Piracy is an example of an offense that may be committed in various places, on land, in ports and on the high seas. It transcends the boundaries between states, and affects so many communities that its due punishment is a matter of universal interest. It has always, therefore, been the law that a pirate can be tried by any country into whose hands he falls, for he is "an enemy of mankind at large."
>
> The perpetrator of a crime against humanity is considered to be on a similar level. His offense is not aimed at a particular part of society; it is a crime against the human race. It is, therefore, within the power of any civilized state to try him; indeed, it is actually a duty of every sovereign power to act as a guardian of international peace and, in discharge of this duty, to put such offenders on trial before its courts. [34]

The argument of the defense that the Israeli law conflicted with international law was rejected by the judges on several grounds:

> Our jurisdiction to try this case is based on the Nazis and Nazi Collaborators (Punishment) Law, a statutory law the provisions of which are unequivocal. The Court has to give effect to the law of the Knesset, and we cannot entertain the contention that the law conflicts with the principles of international law. For this reason alone Counsel's first contention must be rejected. [35]

The court added, however, that it failed to find the Israeli law in conflict with the principles of international law:

> The power of the State of Israel to enact the law in question or Israel's "right to punish" is based, with respect to the offenses in question, from the point of view of international law, on a dual foundation: The universal character of the crimes in question and their specific character as being designed to exterminate the Jewish people. . . .
>
> The abhorrent crimes defined in this law are crimes not under Israel law alone. These crimes which afflicted the whole of mankind and shocked the conscience of nations are grave offenses against the law of nations itself ("delicta juris gentium"). Therefore, so far from international law negating or limiting the jurisdiction of countries with respect to such crimes, in the absence of an International Court the international law is in need of the judicial and legislative authorities of every country, to give effect to its penal injunctions and to bring criminals to trial. The authority and jurisdiction to try crimes under international law are *universal*.[36]
>
> . . . No less important from the point of view of international law is the special connection the State of Israel has with such crimes, seeing that the people of Israel—the Jewish people—constituted the target and the victim of the crimes in question. The State of Israel's "right to punish" the accused derives, in our view, from two cumulative sources: a universal source (pertaining to the whole of mankind) which vests the right to prosecute and punish crimes of this order in every State within the family of nations; and a specific or national source which gives the victim nation the right to try any who assault their existence.[37]
>
> The "linking point" between Israel and the accused is striking and glaring in a "crime manifest against the Jewish people," a crime that postulates the intention to exterminate the Jewish people in whole or in part. Indeed, even without such specific definition . . . there was a subsisting "linking point," seeing that most of the Nazi crimes of this kind were perpetrated against the Jewish people; but viewed in the light of the definition of "crime against the Jewish people," as defined in the Law, constitutes, in effect, an attempt to exterminate the Jewish people. If there is an effective linking point (and not necessarily an identity) between the State of Israel and the Jewish people, then a crime intended to exterminate the Jewish people has a very striking connection with the State of Israel.[38]

But the defense had attacked the principle of protection, claiming that Israel was not in existence at the time the acts were committed. To this argument, the prosecution asserted that "the informal nonexistence of the State does not change the situation" and went on to argue, in effect, that the claim of nonexistence was somewhat spurious.[39] For example, the State of Israel had grown from the Jewish community in Palestine which had received international recognition since 1917. And Hausner went on to state:

> Your Honors, if British and Americans could sit in judgment for crimes not committed on their own territory and their subjects were not the victims, they had no interest whatsoever in the whole case, and only because the victims were allies. More so is it the privilege of a court in Israel to sit in judgment on a man accused with the intention to exterminate the Jewish people. The Jewish people to us are not an ally today and may not be an ally tomorrow, political or economic; today an ally, and tomorrow maybe an enemy. If they could sit in judgment and be competent to judge because the victims were allies, our right is moral and legal to try a man who tried to exterminate the Jewish people, our flesh and blood. And no one will question this right and authority.[40]

The argument over the nonexistence of the State of Israel led directly to another objection: the retroactive nature of the law under which Eichmann was being tried.

2. The problem of retroactivity. The objection by the defense that the State of Israel could not legitimately invoke the principles of protection or passive personality inasmuch as it did not exist at the time of the catastrophe raised the problem of the retroactive nature of the law under which Eichmann was tried. The defense simply argued that the acts for which Eichmann was being tried were made punishable well after these were committed. "This law," Servatius said, "is a *post factum* law. It has been promulgated after the fact, and therefore it cannot be applied." [41] In essence the defense's argument echoed that taken by the defendants at the Nuremberg trials.[42]

The prosecution's rejoinder pointed out that Nazi Germany "violated the principles of justice in general, and by a series of crimes without precedent created a vacuum." [43] This legal vacuum could only be filled by a law that would have to be formally retroactive. But such laws were only formally retroactive, for the laws that have developed since the end of the war are legal moral principles that are basic to the maintenance of a moral order.

> Mankind has no alternative but to declare formulations of principles for international law, and say that these principles were valid at the time the crimes were committed, and apply to these crimes—because otherwise there would have been no law in regard to which these crimes could have been amenable to justice.[44]

The judges also rejected the defense's contention that the court's jurisdiction was restricted by the retroactive nature of the law:

> We have said that the crimes dealt with in this case are not crimes under Israel law alone, but *are* in essence offenses against the law of nations.[45]
>
> . . . The penal jurisdiction of a state with respect to crimes committed by "foreign offenders" insofar as it does not conflict on other grounds with the principle of international law, is not limited by the prohibition of retroactive effect.
>
> It is indeed difficult to find a more convincing instance of a just retroactive legislation than the legislation providing for the punishment of war criminals and criminals against humanity and against the Jewish people, and all the reasons justifying the Nuremberg judgments justify *eo ipso* the retroactive legislator.
>
> The courts in Germany, too, have rejected the contention that the crimes of the Nazis were not prohibited at the time, and that their perpetrators did not have the requisite criminal intent.
>
> The retroactive application of the law to a period precedent to the establishment of the State of Israel does not in itself constitute in respect to the accused a problem on which we have already dwelt above.
>
> What is here said of a Court which did not exist at the time of the commission of the crime is also valid with respect to a State which was not sovereign at the time of the commission of the crime. The whole political landscape of the Continent of Europe has changed after the War; there, too, boundaries have changed as has also the very identity of States that had existed before, but all this does not concern the accused.[46]

3. *"Acts of State."* The crime with which Eichmann was charged differs from other criminal acts in that this crime involves the state as its perpetrator. Thus, the state is not punishing an individual who violates its statutes. The state through its directive organs is the initiator of the criminal act. And this issue confronted the court in Jerusalem just as it did the court at Nuremberg.[47]

Eichmann's defense attorney argued that Israel's court lacked jurisdiction on the doctrine that an act performed by a person in his official state position must be considered an act of state for which he is responsible. The acts for which Eichmann was accused were committed in the context of accomplishing the Final Solution, a plan that originated in Hitler's decision to exterminate European Jewry. And Hitler's plans, it was argued, had the force of law. Therefore, according to Dr. Servatius, such acts were "acts of state" for which the defendant could not be responsible:

> If there is place for expiation, it should be incumbent upon the state which has acted through the instrumentality of the accused. The state was involved in actions, and it is the state which is responsible for the aftermath of its activities. Here we devolve responsibility without guilt, as the accused is to be responsible for the actions in which he was involved through the state, and by the state—who was dragged into them by the state.[48]

In his written plea the defense attorney made additional arguments with respect to the involvement of one country in the internal affairs of another. A foreign state does not dominate and does not sit in judgment of another sovereign state. A state may not try a person for a criminal act that constitutes an "act of state" of another state without the consent of such other state to that person's trial.[49]

The prosecutor pleaded that the court should decide that an act of state is not a defense:

> If we agree to the theory of acts of state as a justification, as a defense, then all those who fulfilled Hitler's orders had a justification for the terrible crimes, for atrocities, and the conscience of the world will not put up with it.[50]

He went on to reason that "crimes against international law are committed by men, not by abstract entities; and only by punishing individuals who commit such crimes can the provision of international law be enforced." [51]

The judges concurred with the prosecution with respect to the "act of state" argument and cited the decision of the International Military Tribunal at Nuremberg as a precedent.[52] They added:

> The contention of Learned Counsel that it is not the accused but the state in whose behalf he has acted that is responsible for his criminal acts is only true in its second part. It is true that under international law Germany bears not only moral, but also legal, responsibility for all crimes that were committed as its own "Acts of State," including the crimes attributed to the accused. But that responsibility does not detract one iota from the personal responsibility of the accused for his acts.[53]
>
> In his written brief learned Counsel has based himself on the exclusive interpretation of the term "a crime against humanity" given by the Nuremberg International according to Art. y (1) of the Charter, which excludes from its jurisdiction many crimes of this kind which had been committed by Germany before the outbreak of the war.[54]

THE GUILT OF THE ACCUSED

The issues discussed above concerned the jurisdiction of the court and the legal status of the law under which Eichmann was tried. Only after the court had overruled the objections of the defense with respect to these issues did Eichmann enter his plea of "not guilty in the sense of the indictment." The sense in which he was guilty formed the basis for the major contest in the trial. Although the prosecution sought to establish the nature and amount of suffering by the Jews under the Nazis, the key issue at stake was Eichmann's responsibility in this suffering.

Eichmann's defense was essentially that he acted as any other citizen would have acted in the same or similar situations. That is, he did what the authorities of the state instructed him to do. Under examination Eichmann observed: "I always regarded myself, as well, as a good peace-loving citizen; because had I not been a good, peace-loving citizen, I would have behaved like a hooligan or a rowdy and there would have been reports about such behavior." [55]

The central point of the defense was that Eichmann was only the executant of policies and orders made by legitimate governmental authorities. His actions were those of a functionary without initiative. Thus, for example, the people designated for deportation were not selected by Eichmann. This matter was determined in accordance with Germany's citizenship law. Eichmann did not determine citizenship and did not formulate the deportation policy. Deportations were ordered by a higher echelon in accordance with the policy determined by the Reich.

Furthermore, the defense contended, Eichmann did not determine the policy for the labor camps or ghettoization. Policies affecting these matters were made by persons at the highest level. In turn, these persons of higher rank than Eichmann received their orders directly from political authorities. Eichmann was responsible only for police measures and technical matters associated with these orders.

Discussing what the defense attorney considered to be the "main count in the indictment," which contained the charge of the extermination in the death camps, the defense sought to dissociate the accused and his office from actions regarding these death camps. The accused's area of competence was police matters, the defense contended. The death camps were not even under the jurisdiction of the Head Office for Reich Security. The camps were under the administration of the Head Office for Economy and Administration. Eichmann admittedly visited the death camps, but only to report to his superiors on the nature of the operations.

The defense concluded that Eichmann's participation in the extermination of the Jews was only as an instrument of the state. Participation was carried out under the constraint of orders from his superiors to whom he owed unconditional obedience. If Eichmann had failed to obey, he would have been subject to rigorous sanctions—possibly death.[56]

In reply to the presiding judge's question, "Do you have anything . . . which points to the fact that in the extermination of the Jews . . . that he [Eichmann] revolted, internally, rose up, internally, against the extermination?"[57] Servatius replied: "As far as I understand the attitude of the accused, in light of our conversations, he repudiated continually the order, if we consider his internal attitude toward it, but he simply carried out the order under duress."[58]

The prosecution painted a very different picture of the defendant. Hausner sought to demonstrate that Eichmann was not simply a bureaucrat who carried out the orders of his superiors, but, rather, one of the major figures in the extermination process who, while acting under general orders, "initiated, planned or organized and implemented the extermination of the Jews in Europe."[59] "We shall prove that the accused overstepped his instructions, that he was eager to fulfill those orders—more than they were intended."[60]

One thrust of the prosecution's argument was to demonstrate the centrality of Eichmann's position and power. The prosecution stated that Eichmann was the "driving force of the gigantic enterprise of the final solution,"[61] that "Eichmann had full authority over the fate of those Jews who were temporarily spared for labor,"[62] and that "in the capital of each satellite country or occupied territory a representative sat who was formally subordinate to someone else, but who actually received direct instructions from Eichmann."[63]

More specifically the prosecution argued as follows:

He controlled the ghettos and extermination centers; his position in the RSHA was unique. He could pass over the heads of his superiors and deal directly with Himmler. His nominally humble status as the chief of a subordinate department did not reflect his powerful position. Through his concern with Jewish matters, he was granted comprehensive and potent authority which brought him into contact with Ministers of the Reich and heads of the conquered governments, with the elite of the German army and the top men of the Foreign Office. In all that pertained to Jewish affairs he operated with all the power and authority of

Himmler and Heydrich behind him. We shall present documents showing that in Jewish matters, the RSHA, the Central Security Office of
the German Reich, was in fact Adolf Eichmann.[64]

Not only was Eichmann's office empowered with initiative in decision making but Eichmann was portrayed by the prosecution as a
zealous, pathological anti-Semite. It was said, "The signal to start the
operation came from above, but once it was given, he proceeded
relentlessly" [65] and "His lust to send the last Jews to their death, his
inviolable resolution to implement the enterprise, his haughtiness and
arrogance in carrying out his designs—this is the true Eichmann." [66]
Also, "He took the initiative in extermination operations for which he
had been given no orders whatsoever, and carried them out because
of his dedication to the task in which he saw his life's mission." [67]

Before the trial and anticipating that Eichmann might plead insanity, Hausner ordered that he be examined by psychiatrists. One of the
tests applied had been devised by the well-known Hungarian psychologist Professor L. Szondi, who was asked to interpret the results:

> The person who took the test, he said, revealed in all phases a man
> possessed with an urge for power and an insatiable tendency to kill.
> "You have on your hands a most dangerous person," Dr. Szondi wrote.
> In every single group the subject had unerringly picked out the most
> negative types as those most appealing to him. Dr. Szondi said that this
> had never happened before in his twenty-four years of practice, in the
> course of which he had tested more than six thousand criminals. He re-
> quested a full case report.
>
>   Other psychological tests produced similar results. They all confirmed
> that Eichmann, though legally sane and fully responsible for his actions,
> was possessed of a dangerous, perverted personality, with an unusual
> and unlimited capacity for using his fellow men as objects for the attain-
> ment of his goals.[68]

In reaching their verdict, the judges dismissed the defense's version
in favor of the prosecution's interpretation of Eichmann's position and
personality. They concluded:

> We reject absolutely the accused's version that he was nothing more
> than a small cog in the extermination machine. We find that in the
> RSHA, which was the central authority dealing with the final solution
> of the Jewish question, the accused was at the head of those engaged in
> carrying out the final solution. In fulfilling this task the accused acted in
> accordance with general directives from his superiors, but there still re-
> mained to him wide powers of discretion which extended also to the

planning of operations on his own initiative. He was not a puppet in the hands of others: his place was amongst those who pulled the strings.[69]

With this we reach the heart of our discussion of the inner motives which prompted the accused in his activities. That he was merciless in all his deeds is almost undisputed. . . . [70]

To summarize this chapter we shall state that the accused closed his ears to the voice of his conscience, as was demanded of him by the regime to which he was wholeheartedly devoted and to which he had sold himself body and soul. . . . He acted within the general framework of the orders which were given to him. But within this framework, he went to every extreme to bring about the speedy and complete extermination of all Jews in the territories under German rule and influence.[71]

The court found Eichmann guilty on all counts listed in the indictment and sentenced him to death. He was hanged on May 31, 1962.

Analysis of the Data

The trial, judgment, and execution of Adolf Eichmann have been widely discussed, and the case continues to be a matter of considerable debate. The lack of agreement on the nature and results of the trial derives in large part from the divergent expectations which the participants and other interested observers have had with respect to what the trial should have accomplished.

Israel's objectives were not totally consistent and were not necessarily shared by other interested parties. According to Prime Minister Ben-Gurion's pretrial statements, the principal purpose of the trial was to teach certain lessons to the world. The non-Jewish world should be instructed on what it did or permitted others to do to the Jews. "We want to establish before the nations of the world," Ben-Gurion proclaimed, "how millions of people, because they happened to be Jews, and one million babies, because they happened to be Jewish babies, were murdered by the Nazis. We ask the world not to forget it." [72] In addition, the Jews in Israel and throughout the world should be instructed on what the non-Jewish world had done to them. "It is necessary that our youth remember what happened to the Jewish people. We want them to know the most tragic facts in our history." [73] Implicit in this instructional purpose was the objective of understanding the phenomenon, for without understanding, the lessons could hardly be properly taught. The principal value in understanding the Eichmann case would be the prevention of the recurrence of such a catastrophe in the future. Indeed, Attorney-General Hausner in his concluding statements contended that the execution of Eichmann would act as a deterrent to genocide in the future and, by implication, that the legal grounds for such action would contribute to the development of international law.[74]

Inasmuch as international law has historically evolved primarily through the actions of the courts of individual states that involve international problems, some commentators have advanced the argument that international law was extended in the Eichmann trial. The official observer of the International Commission of Jurists was of this opinion. He concluded:

> The Eichmann trial is a manifestation of international criminal justice. This form of justice which is said still to be in the first phases of its evolution, in a primitive stage, is usually handled by the states. They perform their task by applying international law, either directly, or by virtue of their municipal legislations which adopt international rules by incorporating them into their own systems.[75]

Other critics, however, have reasoned that the Eichmann trial, far from having a positive effect on the development of international law, had an adverse effect on such law. That Israel showed an unwillingness to subordinate her own "national interest" in a case that involved the world community was, the critics asserted, a restriction on the development of international law. One commentator stated: "That goal [the development of international law] is especially set back whenever a state insists that a question that international institutions already appear to be capable of answering is essentially its own business, that it can act, and that there is nothing the international community can do about it."[76]

Despite such opposed evaluations of the trial, a legal doctrine was produced in Jerusalem—a legal doctrine that served to justify the execution of Eichmann and one that may serve as a precedent in future court actions. A principal aspect of this doctrine affirms that the particular group offended can properly sit in judgment of the person(s) deemed responsible for genocide, although the act is defined as a crime against humanity or the international community. In a sense, of course, this doctrine reaffirms the ancient norm that the relatives or survivors of the victims of an offense not only can, but should, judge and punish the offender.

Yet, that a doctrine was produced is itself an important fact. As Papadatos has noted, "the problem which arises in this case is not how to avoid certain of the consequences—even the least terrible ones—of this criminality, *but how to envisage it at all.*" [77] The crime was regarded in all quarters as unprecedented, as an event that transcended the conventional categories of understanding. Furthermore, the problem of envisioning the meaning of genocide was complicated by the tension of contradictory demands placed on Israel. Despite this state of affairs, the doctrine was produced. The problem of the Jerusalem court and of this chapter concerns the process by which a genuinely unprecedented phenomenon—and in this particular case, moreover, such an unprecedented phenomenon that all our sensibilities demand action to prevent its recurrence—is made comprehensible. We look now at the process by which this transformation was accomplished, how and why the contest was resolved as it was, and how the trial and judgment were legitimated.

What Was Done?

There are probably several approaches applicable to the problem posed, but the most common procedure seems to be to work with what is already available and with that with which one is already familiar. That is, a situation that seemingly calls for a new level of understanding is responded to in conventional ways. This is what the Israelis did when they decided to try Eichmann in an ordinary criminal court in a single nation-state. That the court functioned in the legal confines of a given state, that of Israel, channeled the course of events. The procedures for understanding the phenomenon and structuring the response to it were largely established by this decision. Some specific consequences for understanding emanate from this imposition of legal categories, but, in the main, legal reasoning would seem to be quite similar to other reasoning processes when an unprecedented situation is encountered.

One significant aspect of the legalization of the effort to comprehend genocide was that comprehension became somewhat secondary —not secondary in the sense that it was not of prime importance (the extremity of genocide would not permit that), but secondary in the sense that the attempt to understand the phenomenon was approached through technical legal disputes. The legal issue of jurisdiction exemplifies this. The prosecution argued, for example, that Israel had jurisdiction over Eichmann because the case was in some respects similar to (and therefore understandable in terms of) other cases in which legitimate jurisdiction had been established. The defense argued the converse: The case was not comparable to (and therefore not understandable in terms of) any prior situation. This theme recurred, as the court arguments presented above clearly show, in each of the major legal issues.

Examination of the trial record reveals, furthermore, that the judges, the "duly" constituted arbiters of the legal controversies, opted on each occasion for the prosecution's interpretation of the nature of the act. And through the adoption of this interpretation, the court gave general juridical sanction to a process of subsuming the unprecedented into established categories of legal understanding.

But the process of assimilating the unprecedented into conventional categories for the purpose of understanding and action is fundamentally problematic. An effective rhetoric is demanded in any case. In this instance, however, the process was further complicated by certain particularistic dimensions. Israel claimed a unique right to prosecute Eichmann. But if the act of genocide could plausibly be placed in a conventional legal category (such as murder), existing international law would have been applicable in the case. There would have been no need for the admittedly extraordinary legal position (like abduction) assumed by Israel. Thus, Israeli officials were confronted not just with the problem of making genocide understandable in order to accomplish other objectives; they had also to preserve the extraordinariness of the crime in order to legitimize and justify their unique claim and their extraordinary actions. Officials of the State of Israel had to attend simultaneously to these two contradictory demands.

One step in the dual process involved the placement of Eichmann in a legal category which would give a nation-state legitimate authority to try him. As suggested earlier, the decision to try Eichmann in a conventional court of law implied that genocide would be treated as if it were similar to a conventional crime. The very logic employed in the trial served to make Eichmann comparable to a murderer and genocide comparable to murder. The prosecution, for example, sought to assimilate the Eichmann case into traditional legal categories through the logic of analogy which, as Berman has argued, is the most pervasive form of legal reasoning.[78]

Reasoning by analogy of precedents, the prosecution went to considerable lengths to justify its position on each of the major issues. With respect to the matter of abduction, for example, numerous precedents were cited in defense of Israel's position. The precedents uniformly supported the contention that the manner in which a suspect is brought before the court has no bearing on the court's jurisdiction over him once the suspect is in the custody of the court. Through citation of a variety of precedents, the prosecution clearly implied that genocide and Eichmann's role in it were essentially similar to conventional, understandable crime. Furthermore, in each instance the court not only subscribed to the prosecution's argument but made reference to additional precedents in order to demonstrate the strict legality of the trial. It was not enough, however, to treat Eichmann as if he were a conventional murderer, for such treatment would not have established Israel's singular right to try him.

Perhaps the most direct means by which the prosecution sought to justify and legitimize Israel's trial of Eichmann was by comparing him to a pirate and genocide to piracy.[79] This explicit analogy was employed to place the offense in a category with universal jurisdiction. The jurisdiction of Israel was argued on the contention that Eichmann fell within the purview of the laws of piracy, an offense that any nation can legally punish. Inasmuch as no other nation had sought to try Eichmann, Israel, using the analogy of piracy, justified her claim in terms of the punishment of a universal crime; that is, she acted as the representative of humanity at large. Reasoning by analogy stresses consistency and continuity,[80] and Israeli officials employed it as a primary means for incorporating the Eichmann case into the traditional legal categories of the nation-state. Although the differences between Eichmann's crime and that of piracy may seem apparent, the prosecution further utilized the logic of analogy as a means of reducing the unfamiliar to the familiar.

Even the claim of universal jurisdiction did not sufficiently legitimize, to the Israelis themselves, the extraordinariness of the actions taken or the uniqueness of their right of prosecution. For, while arguing on the one hand for the universal nature of the crime, Israel simultaneously claimed pre-emptory jurisdiction on the grounds that she alone could properly represent the Jewish victims. Inasmuch as the "people of Israel—the Jewish people—constituted the target and the victim of the crimes in question," [81] the judges reasoned, this "linking point" established the right of Israel to try Eichmann. And the judges concluded: "If there is an effective linking point (and not necessarily an identity) between the State of Israel and the Jewish people, then a crime intended to exterminate the Jewish people has a very striking connection with the State of Israel." [82] Thus, Israel claimed a dual legitimacy: universal jurisdiction in terms of a crime against humanity and particularistic jurisdiction on the grounds of a crime against the Jewish people.

In the process of justifying their right to try Eichmann, the Israelis

placed him principally through the logic of analogy in the legally responsible category of murderer; not that of a conventional murderer,
however, but the murderer of an entire people—the Jewish people.

The logic of analogy is associated with, although not coterminous
with, the process or "logic" of simplification.[83] Even after Eichmann
had been placed (through the logic of analogy) in a category of the
court system of the nation-state, and more specifically in the Israeli judicial system, Israel still was faced with the problem of making Eichmann—still yet an extreme case—comprehensible.

Through the process of simplification, the prosecution sought to
make Eichmann understandable by demonstrating that Eichmann was
similar to the "normal" murderer at least in that he was in a position
to have committed the offense and he had the requisite motivation to
have done so.[84] One facet of the prosecution's argument was to show
that Eichmann was not just a small cog in a giant machine. The prosecutor argued that while operating under the umbrella of general orders, Eichmann was competent to act in terms of his own initiative.
Throughout the trial, the prosecution's argument emphasized Eichmann's singular responsibility in the catastrophe. The prosecution always spoke as if the situation would have been very different had
Eichmann not been present. He was depicted as culpable in the same
sense as the murderer who shoots his adversary. Only Eichmann was
much worse because his victims were so numerous.

The other side of the argument was to demonstrate that Eichmann's
attitudes and values led him to pursue monstrous actions. These were
seen as deriving from his violent anti-Semitism. Conventionally, we
understand murder in terms of the motivations and intentions of the
murderer. In order to comprehend how a crime of this magnitude
could have been committed by a person, we (at least in the Western
world) tend to think in terms of gross abnormalities. And the understanding of Eichmann's actions was argued in terms of his abnormality: "His lust to send the last Jews to their death, his inviolable resolution to implement the enterprise, his haughtiness and arrogance in
carrying out his designs—this is the true Eichmann." [85] Or "The accused closed his ears to the voice of his conscience." [86] Consistently,
this was the manner in which Eichmann was described: a man with a
dangerous and perverted personality.[87] Thus, the Israelis attempted to
make Eichmann comprehensible by portraying him as a pathological
monster—and a monster is believable as a participant in genocide.

Eichmann, presented as a pathological personality, was transformed from an extreme case into a deviant, but understandable, case
—someone whom the prosecution and the court in Jerusalem, as well

as the publics in various nations, could comprehend. It would have been somewhat more difficult for Israel's officials to have acted had they accepted as a fact that Eichmann was a normal person functioning within the context of an "abnormal system."

There were other forms of simplification which were instrumental in reducing Eichmann's actions to manageable and understandable proportions. The legal setting with its contestlike structure serves also to simplify issues. After all, one of the principal objectives of the prosecution and the defense is to win. In order to win, the participants selectively abstract from the complexity and ambiguity of social reality the facts that support their particular point of view. Although the judges are supposed to weigh the evidence which is presented, and ideally the prosecution and the defense should expose the deficiencies in arguments and evidence of the other, the combative arrangement nonetheless emphasizes winning at the expense of understanding the viewpoint of the opponent. The prosecution portrayed Eichmann's position and acts as totally devoid of any moral dilemma, while the defense consistently presented Eichmann as no more than a rather minor executant of orders which he carried out uncritically. Neither approach seems to have provided a basis for extending our understanding of genocide.

The testimony of witnesses further simplified the nature of the crime of genocide by focusing on Eichmann's concrete actions. In one sense, the witnesses were providing empirical indicators of genocide as they pointed to Eichmann as the person responsible for numerous specific acts of horror. Eichmann was described as almost single-handedly responsible for the extermination of the Hungarian Jews even after the order had come to terminate the deportations to the death camps. Eichmann gave orders for the murder of the children of Lidice. Eichmann gave the order to the *Einsatzgruppen* to "kill by shooting" in the occupied areas of Russia. Eichmann would not make exceptions even for persons who were only fractionally Jewish. Eichmann was personally responsible for the murder of a Jewish boy who had stolen fruit from his garden. The simplification process here was breaking up the genocide process into its constituent acts—the empirical indicators of this broad, nonunderstandable, unmanageable phenomenon—which were so difficult to understand as one process. Vivid descriptions of the concrete events afforded some leverage in at least giving the impression of understanding the phenomenon of genocide.

Over all, then, Eichmann was translated, by the logic of analogy, from a man participating in an incomprehensible phenomenon into a category of the nation-state judicial system. And through a process of simplification—a process which has several dimensions—the Israeli court came to characterize Eichmann in terms of understandable, albeit abnormal, categories and acts. It was the tension between the simultaneously incompatible demands of justification and comprehension that produced a new category of legal meaning: the legally sane, and responsible, pathological monster. In Western jurisprudence, at least, a person who is adjudged to be pathological is not fitted into the categories of the nation-state's legal structure. The dynamics of this case were such, however, that the category was not only constructed but acted upon. In the process of arriving at a solution to the dilemma, the court and the various participants lost sight of some of the most essential features of genocide.

How Was the Moral Contest Resolved?

We must now address the question of how Israel was able to determine the conditions of the trial and consistently resolve the moral contest in her favor. If we carefully examine Eichmann's defense, we find that his moral argument was not clearly distinct from that which the prosecution employed. Eichmann defended himself in terms of what he did for Germany. Duty or obedience to the nation-state and its supreme leaders was for Eichmann the highest moral virtue. He stated:

> My guilt lies in my obedience, my respect for discipline and military obligations in time of war, my allegiance to the colors and to the service.
> It is not I who persecuted the Jews with avidity and fervor; this was done by the government. The whole prosecution could only have been carried out by the government, never by me. I accuse those in power of abuse of my obedience. Obedience was exacted then, just as it will be exacted in the future, from those under orders.
> Obedience is praised as a virtue. I would therefore request that my having obeyed be the sole fact that is taken into account, while sight is lost of those whom I obeyed.[88]

As long as the nation-state is accepted as the ultimate basis for legal norms, Eichmann's defense is not as highly improbable as was pictured by the prosecution. Thus, from the nation-state perspective—the perspective generally assumed by Israel—justice was not the automatic outcome of the judicial process, but a highly problematic result. After all, Nazi Germany had been accepted as a legal entity with power to constrain its citizenry to act in its behalf. Although there is no question, from the standpoint of humanistic values, about Eichmann's guilt, many of the justifications Israel employed in the trial, based as they were on the appeal to the ultimate authority of the nation-state, opened up the question of mitigating circumstances. Israel, however, did not accept the argument of mitigating circumstances. In the immediate sense, Israel was in part able to attain her objectives in the trial because the trial involved more than a "moral contest." It involved a "power contest" as well. In this power contest, Israel and Eichmann were in an unequal power relationship. Eichmann was, in one sense, a "member" of a nation-state that had been destroyed. It seems unlikely that Israel would have acted as she did if Eichmann's status had been markedly different, if Eichmann had been strongly supported by a powerful nation-state.

Apart from an internal controversy in Argentina, which resulted in that state's taking the case to the United Nations (which, after lengthy discussions, passed a resolution calling for an Israeli apology, but not the return of Eichmann, to Argentina [89]), no nation lodged an official protest against the Eichmann trial. On the contrary, public opinion, in the West particularly, supported the unequal power contest in Jerusalem. Western nations were also bound by certain moral considerations to support Israel's position. They could not readily chastise Israel for seeking to support some of the principles that had emerged at the Nuremberg trials.

The Israelis were able to construct the new category of meaning and respond to it in part because their greater moral and political power made for an unequal contest. But, more importantly perhaps, the new category of legal meaning, converging as it did with traditional categories, was from the perspective of the Israelis, as well apparently as other publics, altogether plausible. The Israelis were committed—as are others—to their particular categories because of their implicit acceptance of the belief system of nationalism and the social structure of the nation-state.

How Was Israel's Decision Legitimized?

As suggested above, the moral and power factors were closely intertwined in the Eichmann case. Although Israel could not have enforced her judgment on Eichmann without her superior political power, it is also clear that the representatives of Israel's government were highly conscious of justifying and legitimizing their actions to publics throughout the world.

The process by which Israeli officials sought to legitimize their actions is a complex one and is rent by several dilemmas. The central one was whether the Israelis should justify their actions in terms of particularistic, or situational, in contrast to universalistic criteria.

The Israeli officials acknowledged the presence of nonsituational factors in several ways. They argued, for instance, that the statute which served as the basis for trying (and punishing) Eichmann reflected the principle that there were crimes against humanity. Moreover, the Israeli judges reasoned, as noted above, that because of their "professional" commitment they could transcend the demands of nation-state categories in arriving at a fair judgment in the Eichmann trial—that their professional orientation made it possible for them to be "objective." [90]

Although we recognize these appeals to universalistic criteria, it is also clear that Israel emphasized the situational criteria. In practice and in theory these took precedence over the universalistic ones. First, the very procedures of the court, imbedded as they were in the legal structure of the Israeli state, were oriented to situational rather than universalistic criteria. Second, Israel could not systematically appeal to universalism inasmuch as she justified her jurisdiction over Eichmann in particularistic (ethnic) terms, an ethnic identification which was directly linked to Israel as a nation-state. Actually, Israel's justifications and actions gave rise to some significant dilemmas, even within the context of nation-state categories. For the prosecution argued that while Eichmann could be tried by Israeli judges, he could not be defended by an Israeli lawyer.[91]

The emphasis on situational factors gives rise to still other dilemmas. For example, the Israeli officials, by portraying Eichmann as pathological and overzealous, sought to make him understandable in part at least in order to justify or legitimize their own actions. But given the fact that genocide was defined in Jerusalem as a crime against humanity, Eichmann need not have been pathological in order to have been punished. Would not there have been even greater justification to punish Eichmann for his actions had he been viewed as a normal person? It would appear that a normal, in contrast to a pathological, man would more likely grasp or comprehend the constraints of nonsituational norms (that is, crimes against humanity). We must remember that the Israeli officials accepted the presence of transnational norms as a key working premise in their prosecution of Eichmann.

Implications

We believe that the Israeli officials were grappling with a problem of central interest and concern to mankind everywhere. For here we explicitly have an instance where a man was punished because he committed crimes against humanity, not because he violated the norms of a particular society. More specifically, the phenomenon encountered in Jerusalem is powerful testimony that occasions arise when the welfare of mankind overrides one's duty to a particular social order (that is, nation-state).

Although we agree with the Israeli officials that the idea of "crimes against humanity" is a viable social imperative, our analysis also suggests some of the moral issues which man encounters as he seeks to act in accordance with this kind of constraint. The Eichmann case points to the kinds of problems any particular nation-state will face as it seeks to punish individuals for crimes against humanity within the traditional legal framework of the nation-state system. Thus, the many writers who have analyzed the Eichmann trial seem to have overlooked the central dilemma: that Israel relied heavily on certain key nation-state categories at a time when Eichmann was defending his actions in terms of his duty to the nation-state.

Also, the Eichmann case brings into question the tendency of sociologists to rely solely on nation-state categories in their efforts to theorize about or to investigate empirically social deviation. Although philosophers through the centuries have wrestled with the idea of "transocietal" norms, sociologists have for the most part ignored the issue. And although the problem of transocietal norms must be recast in more sociological terms, it is one that cannot forever be neglected. We hope that this chapter has at least brought to light the fact that this problem can be studied in rather empirical terms.

NOTES

1. The capture, trial, and execution of Adolf Eichmann have created a continuing debate. Perhaps the major negative assessment of the trial is Hannah Arendt's *Eichmann in Jerusalem*, rev. ed. (New York: Viking, 1964). The principal spokesman for the Israeli position is Gideon Hausner's *Justice in Jerusalem* (New York: Harper and Row, 1966).

At the time of the trial, Hausner was Attorney-General of Israel and prosecuted the case. These works have produced hundreds of reviews, including book-length critiques. See, for example, Jacob Robinson, *And the Crooked Shall Be Made Straight* (New York: Macmillan, 1965).

For an authorative account of Eichmann's capture, see Moshe Pearlman, *The Capture of Adolf Eichmann* (London: Weidenfeld and Nicolson, 1961).

2. For a discussion of the difference between deviant and extreme cases, see Gideon Sjoberg and Roger Nett, *A Methodology for Social Research* (New York: Harper and Row, 1968).

3. In interpreting the moral contest, we employ a Meadian framework which emphasizes the actor's construction of action from the elements in the situation. Mead can be reinterpreted to deal with the phenomenon of social power, although most sociologists using this perspective have ignored this aspect of the Meadian framework. See George H. Mead, *Mind, Self and Society*, edited, with an introduction, by Charles W. Morris (Chicago: University of Chicago Press, 1934).

4. For our discussion of Nazi policy vis-à-vis the Jews, we have relied heavily on Raul Hilberg, *The Destruction of the European Jews* (Chicago: Quadrangle, 1961), and Gerald Reitlinger, *The Final Solution* (New York: Beechhurst Press, 1953).

5. Hausner, *op. cit.*, p. 38.

6. Hilberg, *op. cit.*, p. 767.

7. "Eichmann, Adolf, *defendant*—Transcript of the Trial in the Case of the Attorney-General of the Government of Israel v. Adolf, the son of Adolf Karl Eichmann, in the District Court of Jerusalem. Criminal Case Number 40–61" (Washington, D.C.: Microcard Editions, Inc.), Session 8, Ch. I. The transcript includes the following statement: "This is an unedited and unrevised transcript of the simultaneous translations and, as such, should not be regarded as stylistically perfect or devoid of linguistic errors." We have relied heavily on this record for our data. That it is an unofficial translation presents certain problems. Yet, we have attempted to be cautious in our use of the materials. The quotations we have employed are not isolated instances. In almost every instance, we could have used additional quotations to document the same points. Thus, we feel certain that the evidence we present is not the result of linguistic errors. Additionally, we have compared the translation with Hausner's account which, while not written when he was the Attorney-General, does follow the official court record. On occasion, when the former Attorney-General's account was more precisely stated, we have cited this work in lieu of or in conjunction with the transcript of the trial.

8. Arendt, *op. cit.*, p. 268.

9. For a discussion of Eichmann's role in the Nazi system, see Hilberg, *op. cit.*, especially pp. 184–185.

10. Transcript, Session 8, Ch. 1.
11. *Ibid.*, Session 1, E1.
12. *Ibid.*, Session 1, F1.
13. *Loc. cit.*
14. *Loc. cit.*
15. *Ibid.*, Session 1, I2.
16. *Loc. cit.*
17. *Ibid.*, Session 6, A1.
18. *Loc. cit.*
19. *Ibid.*, Session 1, F1.
20. *Ibid.*, Session 1, H1; Session 5, G2.
21. *Ibid.*, Session 1, H1.
22. *Loc. cit.*
23. Peter Papadatos, *The Eichmann Trial* (New York: Praeger, 1964), p. 57.
24. Transcript, Session 1, J1.
25. *Ibid.*, Session 1, L2.
26. *Ibid.*, Session 6, A1.
27. *Ibid.*, Judgment, Section 41.
28. *Ibid.*, Sections 41–50.
29. *Ibid.*, Section 52.
30. *Ibid.*, Section 7.
31. *Ibid.*, Session 1, F1.
32. Papadatos, *op. cit.*, p. 48.
33. Transcript, Session 3, K1.
34. Hausner, *op. cit.*, pp. 313–314. See also, Transcript, Session 4, O1–P1.
35. Transcript, Judgment, Section 10.
36. *Ibid.*, Sections 11, 12.
37. *Ibid.*, Section 30.
38. *Ibid.*, Section 32.
39. *Ibid.*, Session 3, VI; Hausner, *op. cit.*, p. 315.
40. Transcript, Session 4, T1.
41. *Ibid.*, Session 1, GL.
42. Hausner, *op. cit.*, p. 315.
43. Transcript, Session 2, R1.
44. *Loc. cit.*
45. *Ibid.*, Judgment, Section 16.
46. *Ibid.*, Section 27.
47. Hausner, *op. cit.*, pp. 317–318.
48. Transcript, Session 1, G1.
49. *Ibid.*, Judgment, Section 28.
50. *Ibid.*, Session 5, C1.
51. *Ibid.*, Session 3, E3.
52. *Ibid.*, Judgment, Section 28.
53. *Loc. cit.*

54. *Ibid.,* Section 29.

55. *Ibid.,* Session 102, V1.

56. *Ibid.,* Session 114. The defense's argument with respect to the nature of Eichmann's guilt is summarized in Hausner, *op. cit.,* pp. 398–404.

57. Transcript, Session 114, W1.

58. *Loc. cit.*

59. *Ibid.,* Session 3, G1.

60. *Ibid.,* Session 5, B2.

61. Hausner, *op. cit.,* p. 391.

62. *Ibid.,* p. 394.

63. *Loc. cit.*

64. Transcript, Session 8, Chapter III–3.

65. Hausner, *op. cit.,* p. 392.

66. *Ibid.,* p. 395.

67. Transcript, Session 8, Chapter III–4.

68. Hausner, *op. cit.,* p. 7.

69. Transcript, Judgment, Section 180.

70. *Ibid.,* Section 226.

71. *Ibid.,* Section 241.

72. *New York Times Magazine,* December 18, 1960, p. 7.

73. Quoted in Arendt, *op. cit.,* p. 10.

74. Transcript, Session 120, E1.

75. Papadatos, *op. cit.,* p. ix.

76. Yosal Rogat, *The Eichmann Trial and the Rule of Law* (Santa Barbara, Calif.: Center for the Study of Democratic Institutions, 1961), p. 42.

77. Papadatos, *op. cit.,* p. 103 (emphasis added).

78. Harold J. Berman, "Legal Reasoning," in *International Encyclopedia of the Social Sciences* (New York: Macmillan and The Free Press, 1968), IX, 197–204.

79. Hausner, *op. cit.,* p. 314.

80. Berman, *op. cit.,* p. 200.

81. Transcript, Judgment, Section 30.

82. *Ibid.,* Section 32.

83. Schutz recognized that typification plays a central role in ordering (and simplifying) the social world. However, Schutz did not proceed far enough in his analysis. He does not seem to be aware of the relationship between the logic of analogy and the construction of types, and he does not recognize the presence of various aspects of (or dimensions to) the simplification process. We have discussed certain facets of the construction of meaning which seem to have been overlooked by such writers as Schutz, Weber, and Mead. We hope on another occasion to pursue these problems in greater detail. On this topic, see Alfred Schutz, *The Collected Papers,* Vols. I and II (The Hague: Nijhoff, 1962–1966).

84. We might contrast our over-all discussion with that of Sudnow, for in-

stance. David Sudnow, "Normal Crimes: Sociological Features of the Penal Code in a Public Defender Office," *Social Problems,* XII (Winter, 1965), 255–276. Sudnow's emphasis is on the application of existing types by various officials, whereas we are principally concerned with the construction of types. Sudnow suggests that when officials encounter special or highly unusual cases, the application of this typification pattern breaks down (pp. 274–275). Although we would assume that new types are created under certain circumstances, Sudnow nonetheless implies that there is continuity in the original typification scheme. This pattern in turn leads us to believe that there are "logical" procedures for placing extreme or highly complex cases in pre-existing categories. We would hypothesize that the officials whom Sudnow discusses make use of the logic of analogy and that of simplification (with its various dimensions) as a means of "normalizing" special cases.

85. Hausner, *op. cit.,* p. 395.
86. Transcript, Judgment, Section 241.
87. Hausner, *op. cit.,* p. 7.
88. Transcript, Session 120, I1.
89. Hausner, *op. cit.,* pp. 460–463.
90. Transcript, Session 6, A1.
91. Hausner, *op. cit.,* p. 301.

7

Guilt and Guilt Neutralization: Response and Adjustment to Suicide

James M. Henslin

The data on which this chapter is based were gathered in the course of a broader study dealing with the general problem of how primary-group relatives respond and adjust to suicide. Among other topics, changes in religious practices, in work routines, and in daily interactions, as well as the awareness of suicidal intent, the patterns of death announcements, and patterns of grief response, were investigated. The aim of this chapter is to examine a narrower portion of this broader study, "suicide-connected guilt"; that is, guilt that arises among survivors after someone has suicided. If by this topic and in our analysis we have veered out of the ordinary confines of sociology, let us hope that we can swim in these atypical waters without "going psychoanalytic," on the one hand, or being afraid to venture into a new area, on the other.

Guilt, as employed in this chapter, is used in the sense of an actor's blaming himself in some way regarding some aspect of a death by suicide, this blame being conceptualized such that it is broad enough to include both blaming the self as a causal agent in the death and also blaming the self for ways in which one did or did not treat the deceased while he was living. Neither the intensity of the guilt nor the success of the methods by which guilt is attempted to be neutralized or handled will be the subject under discussion, although we may from time to time touch upon them, but the guilt itself and the techniques for handling this guilt, the strategies for neutralizing guilt as a means of adjusting to suicide, are the topics of this analysis.

Sample

The sample on which this study is based is a continuous sample, consisting of all cases of death adjudged to be suicides in St. Louis County between January 1, 1967, and August 20, 1967, a total of 44 suicides.[1] Interviews were conducted in 25 of these cases. The 19 cases in which interviews were not held break down in order of frequency into the following categories:

1. Could not locate: 7
2. Refused the interview request: 6
3. No interview requested: 3
4. Appointments made, but not kept by the interviewer: 2
5. Agreed to be interviewed, but no date was set: 1

Of the seven that could not be located, category (1), there were probably only three cases in which members of the primary group had either moved geographically or were in other ways unlocatable. Four of the cases involved persons with unlisted phone numbers, who probably could have been interviewed either by first contacting them by letter or by visiting them unannounced, thus substantially reducing the number in this category.

Category (2), consisting of "refusals," appears, on the surface at least, to contain cases that have particular elements that set them apart from cases in the other categories. This category includes the suicide of a prominent physician's only son, a wife who committed suicide after an argument with her husband, the only case of a combination murder-suicide, a son who committed suicide within weeks of his brother's suicide, a widow who first said she "wasn't ready" to be interviewed and later said she objected to this type of research, and one case in which outstanding characteristics are not readily evident. This category appears to be significant for our study in that it may contain survivors whom one might expect to have experienced greater sorrow, hurt, or guilt.

The three cases in category (3), in which no contact was attempted, do not appear to have any outstanding characteristics about them, but were not contacted because of lack of time.

Category (4) includes the two cases for which I made specific appointments but which were later determined to be beyond the time imposed for the termination of interviewing.

In the single case in category (5), no interview date had been set, but a future interview had been promised, which also would have extended beyond the termination date.[2]

The *interview rate,* then, since interviews were conducted in 25 of the 44 cases, is 57 per cent. Wherever time and information on primary-group members permitted, requests for interviews were made with more than one person who knew the suicide. A total of 74 such requests were made, with 61 accepting the request and 13 refusing it. The 61 include, in addition to the 58 respondents interviewed, the two appointments I did not keep and the one that was accepted for a later date. The *acceptance rate* (61/74) thus is 82 per cent, which, in my view, is a very satisfactory rate for this type of sensitive research.

Methodology

Because I am convinced that methodological procedures that could be of great value to other researchers if they were shared are too often lightly glossed over with the result that the experience is "lost" to others when it had at least the potential of being cumulative, I will go into some detail at this point. Coroner's records were examined in each case of death adjudged to be a suicide in St. Louis County during this time period.[3] Information about the type, place, and time of death, and personal characteristics of the suicide such as his age, marital status, and occupation, were gathered. Additionally, wherever possible, the names, addresses, and phone numbers of surviving relatives were abstracted. Interviews were then requested with close primary relatives, the order of preference usually being: first the spouse, then an adult child, then parents or siblings. Where these were unavailable, friends of the deceased, various sorts of in-laws and employees and witnesses were contacted. All interviewing was done between February 10, 1968, and April 11, 1968, with the mean lapsed time between the occurrence of death and the date of the interview being eleven months ten days and the range being six months twenty days to fourteen months seventeen days.

In each instance where a telephone number was available, the prospective respondent was telephoned for an appointment. I introduced myself over the telephone, using as identifying tags both the titles "doctor" and "sociologist," and gave my affiliation. I then told the prospective respondent that research was being conducted on family adjustment to suicide, and I asked him if I "could speak to him at some time." An appointment was then made, usually for the next day. Most appointments were set up just this simply and easily, with it becoming obvious that the title "sociologist" was meaning next to nothing to the typical respondent, but that the title "doctor" was opening a lot of doors.

After the first two interviews, which were conducted separately, but awkwardly, with the wife waiting for a couple of hours in an adjoining room while I interviewed her husband, and her husband leaving the house while I interviewed her, it became apparent that I needed an assistant to help with the interviewing. It is interesting to note that even the sex of the assistant was dictated by the requirements of the research, as was evidenced by my third appointment, one with a twenty-five-year-old widow. (This was one of the fourteen "open" cases, the only one of this type that I interviewed, and the results are not included in this chapter.) The appointment was for the evening, and when I arrived, I was greeted by a uniformed upholder of the Pagedale, Missouri, law in a (to make a severe understatement) "not too gracious manner." The policeman was an acquaintance of the widow in question and was the officer who had been called the night she found her husband dead of carbon monoxide. It turned out that after she had accepted the appointment, she checked with him, and he was convinced that "anybody visiting widows at night has to be up to no good." She later apologized for his behavior, and I conducted the interview. However, this incident made it evident that the "presentation of an acceptable front" demanded more than just a male researcher, preferably a research team composed of both sexes.

Accordingly, I hired an assistant,[4] and the following became our standard procedure: When an appointment was made, to keep the appointment-making process as simple as possible, no mention was made of an assistant. My assistant and I would then arrive at the appointed time and introduce ourselves at the door. After being seated in the living room, I would read a standard introduction to the research, as follows:

> There has been increasing interest and concern on the part of doctors, researchers, and public officials in the problem of suicide in our country. As a result, researchers are investigating various aspects of this problem.

Family adjustment is a relatively unknown area and is the purpose of this study. You have been included in our sample, and we consider it a privilege to interview you because this will lead us to greater understanding. We would appreciate your honesty and frankness in answering the questions, although you do not have to answer any questions you do not wish to. You will be completely anonymous. All information is considered a privileged communication and will be kept by us in the strictest confidence. Your identification with this questionnaire will be only a code number.

After reading this, I would then ask if the second respondent (ordinarily the person least related to the suicide) would mind speaking with my assistant. At this my assistant would stand, and the second respondent would rise in response to her standing. Either the respondent or my assistant would then suggest that they go into the kitchen "to talk." Thus, in each case where there were two respondents present, two simultaneous interviews were obtained. By using this technique, no interviews were conducted in the presence of a second respondent, thus maximizing anonymity, expressivity, and, hopefully, the validity of the responses.

In five cases it was known in advance that only one respondent would be home. In three of these cases, I visited and conducted the interviews by myself; in two cases my assistant did so. In those cases where we both arrived but only one respondent was home, I would conduct the interview, and my assistant would remain, usually also taking notes.

The mean time it took to administer the twenty-page interview schedule, consisting of approximately one-half closed and one-half open-ended items, was two hours eleven minutes, with the range being forty-five minutes to four hours twenty minutes. In two cases, with the explicit permission of the respondent, the interviews were taped. Taping the interviews was discontinued, however, due to a lack of resources for transcribing the tapes.

The Search for Meaning after a Suicide

People seem to need a feeling of "fit" in their interpersonal relationships and in the events that occur in their lives, that is, a feeling of consonance of one event with another, or a sense of consonance between their own self-definitions and their role or place in an event; for example, a fitting of a particular event into a more general category or into an accepted pattern of viewing causation. Usually each culture offers such consonance to its members by providing its own commonly accepted and acceptable explanations, orientations, interpretations, and meanings for events. For certain events or types of events, however, an individual's culture may not offer such readily available views, although it may provide indications or "cues" as to the direction where these explanations may be found.

In cases where society does not prescribe its acceptable orientation toward a significant event, it is probable that there is a general searching for the why of the event, a search for "meaning," an attempt to understand the event in its consequences for one's life, this being especially so regarding a significant negative or loss-experiencing event.[5] If this is so, and one theory of the function, significance, and universality of religion rests on similar reasoning,[6] we can expect there to be an intense search for meaning in the case of suicide occurring in a culture where suicide is not an expected event and, accordingly, does not have any concomitant built-in explanation for the act; that is, where suicide is not the prescribed or accepted course of action following certain circumstances as it would be in some cultures, as, for example, in traditional Japan following certain types of "losing face," or in the Trobriand Islands for a person who is publicly known to have had sexual relations with a proscribed person.[7]

In any event, following a suicide in our culture, persons who have been in a primary relationship with the suicide are left wondering why the death took place, wondering why the individual committed suicide. Respondents search their lives, and especially their recent interaction with the deceased, attempting to analyze their role in the events that led up to the death, being especially concerned with whether their actions or interaction were causal in some way. They are left with a feeling of "wondering why he did it and what made him think of it in the first place" (S031–20).[8] Basically they feel that the suicide "is evidently caused by something or other—some kind of a problem" (S031–20), and they search their lives to determine their own place in the make-up of that problem.

This search for meaning and for cause leads them continually to review their interaction with the deceased, mentally to restructure or reconstruct the past in order to determine to their satisfaction how these and other events might have led to the suicide. The following two respondents well illustrate this process of tortured searching and researching the past and one's role in it in order to understand the suicidal act. The first, the widower of a fifty-year-old woman, looks for the elusive answer in immediate past events. His wife had wanted to go to Texas for a visit, where she thought she would be happier than at home with her husband. He consented, went to the depot, and re-served a seat for her on the railroad car for the trip; but when he re-turned home, his wife abruptly said, "I don't think I'll go." She did not go, and a few days later, when he was at work, she committed suicide by carbon monoxide. He reported:

> But I often think, "Well, well, if I had forced her to go or made some excuse: 'Well, go ahead, have a visit;' " you know—would it have made any difference, see? I've had that on my mind a lot of times. But that's somethin' we don't know, see. But would it have made any difference, or would it have helped her? . . . But I don't know. I guess one never knows, you know. Would it have been the right thing or the wrong thing? Would she have been happy down there like she was before? Or would she have tried to commit suicide down there? See, that's some-thin' I don't know. Nobody knows, I guess, really." (S009–6.)

The second respondent, after his twenty-five-year-old son's suicide by handgun, is left with the same basic, plaguing questions, and in searching for a satisfactory answer, he reconstructs events going back much further:

> I've wondered where it began if it was suicide. Was it in grade school? Or college? Or was it all this girl? Could I have done something differ-ent? Or wouldn't it have helped? Wondering which is right and which is wrong. . . . I think this thing or that thing could have been done to change the course of events. But you just don't know. I even thought: "If we hadn't moved from (X Town) to (Y Town) years ago." (S016–18.)

This attempt to understand, to fit the death into an acceptable pat-tern of meaning by reinterpreting or reconstructing the past, leads to particular problems in the case of suicide. Although there are cultur-ally acceptable ways of interpreting most deaths, which serve as "ad-justment mechanisms" for those who have experienced the death, these are ordinarily unavailable when the death is by suicide. For ex-ample, accidents can be defined as "something that couldn't be helped" (S030–20), or they can even be defined as "normal," as in the following:

> If he'd been driving and killed in a car wreck—that's an everyday thing. But this was special, and there had to be something wrong—whether with me or the family—if a car wreck—*a normal way people die*—and his personality—figured he'd never do something like that, and couldn't really believe he could have done it. It's an *unusual way,* and *is evi-*

dently caused by something or other—some kind of a problem. (S031–20.)

But, as this respondent is saying, suicide belongs to an entirely different category, being viewed as something that "could be helped" and, therefore, ordinarily could have been prevented. Furthermore, it is viewed as an unusual or "not normal" type of death, which, in combination with the view that it was preventable, further removes or insulates the survivor from the usual or normal ways of defining death— ways that would ordinarily function for the individual's adjustment.

One such culturally allowable definition of death that survivors of suicide are ordinarily cut off from is to define death as "God's will." Such a definition removes causation beyond the control or responsibility of either the deceased or the respondent, allowing easier acceptance of the event. Thus: "If it had been an accident, it would have been easier on the family. They would have accepted it as God's will and let it be done with" (S033–20). Since, however, in suicide the deceased is viewed as the one who performed the act—that is, the suicidal act is defined as having been under the control of the deceased —such a conceptualization of the death is ordinarily unavailable to respondents.

Additionally, this particular definition of death that society offers for its members' adjustment, that of viewing death as "God calling the individual," which, when sincerely subscribed to, can lead to a good fit between the event of death and one's view of that event, not only is typically unavailable for significant others of a suicide but can even further complicate the response to death for those holding such a theological view: [9]

> Well, I would have felt in my own mind that God had called him from the earth and that He had a reason for calling him, and that we could have accepted it as Christians that it was the will of God, and that we could feel in our hearts that God, in His tenderness, had taken him up with Him. I can't feel this was the will of God. I can't feel completely, either—from Lutheran teaching—we don't know if God has forgiven his sins and whether his soul has departed to heaven or to hell. (S024–20.)

By searching for meaning for the event of suicide, by questioning and reconstructing the past while holding the definition that suicide is a caused act that could have been prevented, in being forced into looking for relevant causes for that act and examining their own role in that causal process, and also in being cut off from the usual ways of viewing a death that society offers for adjustment to the death, persons in such a situation are extremely prone to feelings of guilt. It is to such feelings that we now turn.

Guilt Following Suicide

Guilt by significant others following a death has been investigated almost exclusively by those who are psychiatrically oriented. Their studies point to guilt as a normal or common response following any death.[10] Of the 58 respondents in this study, 25 explicitly acknowledged guilt feelings following the death of the suicide; that is, when asked during the psychiatric symptom inventory part of the interview if they had felt guilt, they replied in the affirmative. Additionally, 23 of these 25 at various points in the interview made unsolicited statements expressing guilt feelings, while only 2 did not. Five other respondents refused to acknowledge guilt feelings when pointedly asked if they had experienced them, but during the course of the interview they had already made statements expressing guilt. Thus 30 of the 58 respondents demonstrated feelings of guilt by either explicitly acknowledging guilt and/or making statements concerning guilt. The range of expression of this guilt is amazingly broad, varying from those who only verbally acknowledged having experienced guilt at some point after the death, and who volunteered no explanatory or illustrative material, to those whose guilt has led them to suicidal thoughts, plans, or even attempts.[11]

The major areas of guilt evidenced by these respondents concerned (1) not being aware of the suicidal intent, (2) feeling they should have been able to prevent the suicide, (3) feeling that perhaps they had done something to cause the suicide, and (4) noncausal actions that were regretted.

The first major area of felt guilt, that of not being aware of the impending event, is one that is experienced particularly by close relatives of the suicide. For example:

You feel you should have seen signs of something. (S028–18: wife.)

I think I should have been more alert to see what was going on. (S007–14: husband.)

I had a sense of guilt in not sensing this was coming. (S023–7: son.)
. . . I felt guilty because I didn't see that she was feeling so bad about Dad's death. (S023–18.)

They feel that because they were closely related to the suicide, they should have been closely perceptive of his feelings also and that therefore they failed him by not being aware of his intentions. This feeling of failure is very adequately expressed by the following respondent:

> Since I was with him so much, I could have been more aware of what was going on. I felt I could have asked him what was wrong. (S054–18: sister.)

The response above is closely related to the second area of guilt in that it is always spoken of in terms of possible consequences of such awareness: that if they had been aware, perhaps they could have done something to have prevented the suicide. Some respondents have vague, nonspecific feelings that they could somehow have taken preventive steps, as: "I felt like I should have been able to stop his suicide" (S010–18). Others are convinced there are specific steps that they could have taken which would have prevented the suicide and feel guilty because they didn't take them. For example, the following respondent was in Texas when she received a telephone call from her mother in St. Louis:

> The day she died, Mom called me on the phone. She said, "Dad didn't care" and "she didn't know how she was going to go on" and "nobody was going to hurt her anymore," "she'd been hurt for the last time." She told me to be a good wife first and then a mother, that she had made the mistake of being the other way around. She talked to the baby on the phone, and she never did this. To this day I wonder why I didn't call someone and tell them. (S003–14.)

This particular situation has created guilt problems for her husband also:

> I've kept wondering if we could have done something to prevent it. If I had let my wife intervene between her parents, then she may have been able to stop the death. I feel guilty about this. (S004–17.)

The respondents above, in speaking about suicide intervention, have referred to nonphysical intervention. One respondent, however, had the opportunity to intervene directly and physically to prevent a suicide but was stymied by a rather interesting form of fear of embarrassment:

> (Name) came out with a towel wrapped around his wrist and started running. I stood up. I knew in my mind what he was going to do, but I

was kind of embarrassed to holler out. I thought he would stop when he got to the cliff—like in cowboy movies. And he did slow up at one point, and then he ran full speed and did a swan dive over the cliff just like a person would at a swimming pool. (S047–6.) I felt some personal guilt: If I had tried to tackle him, I probably could of gotten him. (S047–8.) He had a white tee shirt, and I can still see him sailing into the air. (S047–12.)

The third major area of guilt involves actions which respondents think might in some way have been causal in leading to the suicide. Respondents, as explicated above, search the past in order to gain an understanding of the event of suicide, and, in so doing, they mentally re-examine and reconstruct their own interaction with the deceased. When such re-examination leads to guilt of this type, it is usually expressed in general terms, such as the following:

> It runs through your mind: "Could I have done something to cause him to do such a thing?" (S030–18.)

> You have a feeling like: "What could I have done? . . . Where did you fail? If it's your fault."—feelings like that. (S028–18.)

There are probably any number of interaction events that routinely take place between people such that if one suicides, the other can interpret his part of the interaction as causal concerning the death, resulting in guilt feelings that he must contend with. Interactions that respondents seem to have a propensity to interpret in this way are those that took place immediately or shortly prior to the death.[12] A good example of this is a wife who had put up with her husband's alcoholism for approximately twenty years. She had become extremely upset with her life situation, and two weeks prior to her husband's death had experienced facial spasms. She went to a psychiatrist who told her: "Tell people to go to hell," and, "Don't take things so seriously." When she returned to her home, as the doctor had suggested, instead of arguing with her husband, she told him to go to hell. She added, "It seems that that's when he lost the will to live" (S019–12). He suicided within a couple of weeks.

Others, in searching for explanations of the death that might have causally involved their actions in some way, uncover any number of aspects of their interaction, such as moving the mother-in-law to their own home (S020–7), spending too much time at work and not enough with the deceased (S021–20), criticizing the deceased's behavior (S054–18), and failing to have forcibly placed the deceased in a mental hospital (S019–13; S018–8).

Another type of searching regarding causality involves a particular *Weltanschauung*. As above, regarding the theological view concerning suicide and eternal judgment that can lead to increased guilt feelings (S024–20), so this *Weltanschauung* involving causation can lead to guilt feelings:

> I used to think if you do something wrong you would have to suffer. Ever since (Name) died, I have wondered what I could have ever done wrong to have her taken from me. (S017–16.)

What this respondent seems to be saying is that she is suffering, and in her view when someone suffers, it is because one has done wrong. Since she is suffering concerning the suicide of her mother, she wonders what she has done wrong to have caused her mother "to have been taken from her." This particular *Weltanschauung* dictates searching for wrongdoing whenever there is suffering, and since there already exists a propensity to look for complicity in suicidal deaths, it greatly complicates the situation for the respondent.[13]

The fourth major area, that of interaction interpreted in a noncausal sense, is one that can also lead to intense guilt feelings for a respondent. The best example concerns a wife who was jealous of the amount of time her husband was spending with his best friend. In a heated argument over this, she said, "I'll live to spit on his grave" (S044–16). A few weeks later her husband's best friend committed suicide, and she added, "I don't think I will ever get over that" (S044–18). It might be parenthetically added that her statement not only caused guilt feelings for her but also created such severe adjustment difficulties between her and her husband that they did not speak to each other for months, and she herself subsequently attempted suicide.

Persons feeling suicide-connected guilt are not limited to experiencing a single type, of course, but can experience all four types, as the following respondent comes close to demonstrating:

> Wondered if there was something I could've done to have prevented it, or if I let him down in some way. (S031–7.)

> Feeling guilt that there was something I could've done or wasn't close enough to him. (S031–20.)

There is also a fifth type of guilt, which could be subsumed under the last type above, consisting of only a single case. It differs from the other types, however, in that the guilt does not concern interaction that took place prior to the death, but concerns a feeling, or, rather, the lack of "proper" feeling, after the death. This case involves a sister-in-law who intensely disliked her husband's brother. She said that she felt guilty because she didn't care that her brother-in-law had committed suicide, that she "felt guilty because she didn't feel guilty" (S033–8).[14]

Having briefly examined the guilt that these respondents expressed, and having gained some idea of the types, intensity, and range of such guilt feelings, we will now turn to ways in which the respondents handle or attempt to handle their guilt feelings: their techniques of guilt reduction or neutralization.

Guilt Neutralization

The guilt neutralization techniques used by these respondents are: (1) defining others as being responsible for the suicide; (2) viewing impersonal factors as suicidogenic; (3) denying the suicide; (4) emphasizing the inevitability of the act; (5) emphasizing the uncertainty of purposive human acts; (6) emphasizing the irrevocability of the past; (7) minimizing the suicide; (8) conceptualizing the act as good; (9) defining altruism as the suicide's motive; (10) atoning for wrongdoing; (11) using thought transference; (12) conceptualizing the deceased negatively; and (13) using "guilt neutralizers."

We will first discuss the major or primary technique of guilt neutralization, that of defining others as being responsible for the suicide, with the self being defined as guiltless or relatively guiltless. A common form that this technique takes is for the respondent to analyze past events concerning the deceased in such a way that he can point to someone other than himself who was involved in these events as being the direct or primary cause of the suicide. Almost anyone can be selected to be so viewed. For example, a sister-in-law of the deceased locates the blame for the death with the deceased's sisters when she says:

> If his sisters had not picked on him because he drank—if his sisters had left him alone—things wouldn't have built up so much. (S042–16.)

This respondent is saying that the responsibility for causing "things to build up," which in her view led to the suicide, lies with someone other than herself. It is easy to see that if she can maintain this definition of events, she can hold her own guilt to a minimum.

In another case, the respondent, a friend of the suicide, places the blame with the suicide's wife, saying:

> She drove him to it. She would never go anyplace with him. Ninety percent of the time he was without her. She didn't participate in the fun when she did go—like in the pool she wouldn't play tag. (S044–15.)

Insight into the inner dynamics of familial interaction concerning the use of this neutralization technique is gained by the following:

> Things have changed here at home. Since there was no note, everyone is trying to blame everyone else. Oh, not on the surface, but you can tell. They are all saying, "I did this *for* him" or "You did that *to* him." (My parents) don't say so in so many words, but they are accusing each other. Mother protected him too much, and Daddy was too harsh. (S054–16.)

It is interesting to note that this respondent, a seventeen-year-old sister of the victim, while insightfully analyzing how her parents are handling guilt, is utilizing the same technique herself when she says, "Mother protected him too much, and Daddy was too harsh."

In using this technique, not only can one define others as being directly causal in the death but one can also define others as having certain attributes which the self does not have, such as knowledge or power, which, if they had been properly utilized, could have prevented the death.[15] A brother-in-law of the deceased, for example, emphasizes his own lack of knowledge as opposed to the amount of knowledge possessed by the physician who had been caring for the deceased. He said:

> His doctor never told us the things that were wrong with him, and now I think he should have so we could watch him. (S035–14.) . . . Doctors should inform the party taking care of a person in this condition as much about the person as possible so they would know what to expect. (S035–20.)

Another respondent is of the same opinion and said:

> I think they (psychiatrists) could give the family a couple of hints. (S012–13.)

These respondents mean that in their view psychiatrists and doctors in charge of a suicidal patient have knowledge both of the patient's potential for suicide and preventive measures that can be taken and, as such, have the resultant responsibility or duty to so inform the family. They feel, however, that the doctors did not do so in their cases. This definition of the doctor's failure makes the respondent's burden of guilt easier to bear since he can define himself as being without such knowledge and thus without the responsibility which accrues from such knowledge.

In a closely related way, if the respondent can define himself as being powerless, relative to others, he can hold himself guiltless of complicity in the act. Although the following respondent still manifests some guilt feelings, she has quite effectively neutralized them by such a defining process:

> I wasn't really surprised. I felt maybe it was partly my fault—that I wasn't understanding or patient enough the day before. . . . On the other hand, the police could've done something, too. They have more control. They could've put her in jail or anything. When I picked up my gun, the policeman said, "Well, I see she finally did it." (S032–6.)

This respondent is holding her guilt to a minimum by favorable self-comparisons with the agents of social control, the police. She is asking what sort of power she has over people and is answering that she has little such power, but that the police have comparatively great power. The police are even able to incarcerate if they wish to. Therefore, if one is going to place blame, one should place it with those who hold the power to have effected a different course of action. And she also seems to be saying by her final statement that if the police, those who should feel guilt, have such a flippant attitude about the situation, why should she feel guilty?

Another form that it takes is to locate a "guilt hierarchy," an ordering of responsibility in which the respondent views himself as having played only one of many roles in the event. While this necessitates acknowledging some responsibility, the advantage is that when the responsibility for the act is distributed among many, the respondent need feel only partly guilty; he doesn't need to bear all or even a major part of the responsibility. One respondent, the suicide's brother, spread the guilt around in the following manner. He said, in answer to the question if he blamed anyone:

> First myself: (Name) and I were so close. We were roommates in college. I felt I could have been closer—could have talked to him—helped straighten him out—find out what his problems were.
>
> Dad: We couldn't talk to him about problems. I still can't. Can't talk with Mom either.

(Deceased's girl friend): She could've stopped going with him—quit leading him on. She knew his feelings for her and held it over him. I blame part of it on his drinking heavily for the last six months. He drank four or five hours, day in and day out. When he drank, problems built up in him. (S031–19.)

In his particular hierarchy of guilt, the respondent does place responsibility with himself, but it was apparent in the interview that his not having to feel sole responsibility for his brother's death was a definite help to him. (It is interesting to note that his mother is added rather parenthetically in this hierarchy and that the suicide is not blamed at all: "his drinking" is blamed, but not the drinker.)

The following respondent has been more successful in neutralizing her guilt, and her ordering of the guilt hierarchy is fascinating. She said:

Who's to blame? Me, for not letting her in when she just about knocked my door down? The hospital for letting her go in her state of mind? Or the police for giving her back her pills and guns so she could do it again? Or (her lover) for not understanding her, or telling her to get off his back? But her, first off, for trying to take something only God has given us. (S032–13.)

In listing her hierarchy of guilt, this respondent points out that in her view responsibility for acts leading to the suicide are not isolated with any single person, but are distributed among several actors who had been in contact with the deceased. Moreover, in making the analysis above, the respondent, although listing herself first ordinally, conveniently lists herself last causally. Such a conceptualization should prove effective in neutralizing guilt, as indeed it has in her case.

The response above brings us to another form that this technique of guilt neutralization takes, that of defining the suicide himself as the responsible actor. The respondent above, in continuing her answer, made clear that she was placing the guilt for the act on the person committing the suicide when she said: "(Name) did it herself: nobody did it to her. She did it to herself" (S032–13).

Another respondent, taking the same tack, said: "In (Name's) case, he did it himself. That you can't blame on others too much" (S043–17). These respondents are saying that when they can define the suicide as bearing the primary responsibility for the act, they do not have to look for guilt in themselves.

When a respondent is convinced that such definitions of responsibility, with concomitant de-emphasis of causal self-involvement, are valid, this major technique of guilt neutralization, defining others as being responsible for the act, is extremely functional in overcoming guilt and in leading to adjustment to the suicide.

A second major technique of guilt neutralization is to locate responsibility or cause for the suicidal act in nonhuman or impersonal factors, situations, or circumstances. Such a conceptualization of cause is functional for adjustment in that it eliminates the need to locate responsibility or blame with any person, including the self. The respondent above also illustrates this technique when he says: "To me the time and place just happened to be right. Two minutes either way could've changed the whole thing" (S043–14). He is saying, in other words, that the suicide was caused by a combination of circumstances; in this case, circumstances of time and place. The importance of such a conception is that the cause then lies in circumstances that belong to the external situation, not to individuals, with the result that there is no need to place the blame with anyone. This respondent was corroborated in his view when he checked with doctors about the causes of suicide and was told that anybody, given the right situation, could commit suicide (S043–9). He then took what appears to be a rational approach by methodically seeking possible reasons for the suicide in the circumstances that he knew applied to his friend: he wrote down the "things he thought might have contributed to it," and in a short while he "had a page full" (S043–15).

Another respondent, using this technique, finds the causal locus in a completely impersonal, nonguilt-determining factor, the season of the year. He said:

> The winter was part of my wife's problem—probably wouldn't have happened if it had been summer. You're more depressed when you can't get out. (S007–16.)

With such a causal view, it is obvious that no blame need accrue to anyone since the season of the year is viewed as an impersonal, nonhuman situation over which one has no control and therefore no associated responsibility.

A slightly variant form of this same technique is used by a respondent who views internal forces as causing the individual to commit suicide:

> I had no guilt. And, as I said before—and I honestly believe it at this time—there was some mental incompetency to make the man do what he done. (S024–8.)

It is almost as if, in this respondent's analysis, "mental incompetency" is a "thing" that causes the act of suicide. Such a reification, of course, again eliminates the need for locating responsibility with people, including the self.

Finally, in locating the cause in nonhuman situations, though this appears difficult to do for reasons stated earlier, some respondents are able to conceptualize God as being behind the act. Thus:

> I felt maybe this was God's way of doing things. And I felt . . . he wasn't responsible and wasn't himself because he had been sick for so long. (S053–8.)

Although the suicide is viewed in this case as physically pulling the trigger, no blame or guilt need be charged to his account since "he isn't responsible because he wasn't himself"; that is, it was not "his self" that pulled the trigger. Rather, the act is conceptualized as being in God's hands, thus removing responsibility entirely beyond man and, it should be noted, quite effectively erecting a protective shield around the self.

A third technique of guilt neutralization is that of suicide denial.[16] If a death categorized as a suicide by the coroner could be conceptualized as "not suicide" by an individual, that individual would not have to deal with the problems that the category "suicide" entails, and guilt reduction could take place. In addition to suicide, there are two other forms of violent death in peacetime, homicide and accident, and we find deaths judged to be suicide reconceptualized into both categories.[17]

The first, that of reconceptualizing the adjudged suicide as a homicide, is the form of the suicide denial technique used by the father of a twenty-five-year-old son who shot himself (S016). By examining the lengths to which this man went, we can see the importance of such a technique for an individual so involved. He first blamed the police department for purposely hiding information and for filing a false police report. He attributed as motive for such action that "half the police department laid the girl his son was going with, and the department had to protect itself." He accused his son's girl friend of knowing more than she admitted, intimating a plot between her and her husband for insurance money. He attempted to have an inquest held to determine the cause of his son's death, but was refused the inquest when the coroner stated that he was satisfied with the police report. He then accused the coroner of having ulterior motives in his decision. Finally he attempted to have the FBI brought in to investigate the case, but he failed in this also when the FBI informed him that they would have to have a basis for investigating the entire police department if they were to enter any such case. Though he went to such lengths, this respondent unfortunately was not only unsuccessful in persuading others to accept his definition of his son's being a homicide victim but also oscillated in the interview between viewing the death as a homicide and viewing it as a suicide. Additionally, he was markedly unsuccessful in neutralizing his acutely felt guilt. It is not difficult, however, to see that such a conceptualization of the death, if successfully held, would be extremely functional in neutralizing guilt since the slayer would bear the blame, and not the self.

If suicide could be reconceptualized as an accident, the event could also be viewed as being outside the control of either the respondent or the deceased. Moreover, this might enable some respondents to "plug into" the theological view of "God's will." At least this is the view of one respondent who said:

> The family wouldn't have asked why he did it. If it had been an accident, it would have been easier on the family. They would've accepted it as God's will and let it be done with. (S033–20.)

And we do find such reconceptualizing of the death with some respondents. The following respondent, for example, continually spoke of her brother's death as being due to suicide, openly acknowledging that he had purposely shot himself; but at one point in the interview she inadvertently presented an entirely different view of the act—a view that she was perhaps even unaware that she held—when she said, "Actually, we went right from the scene of the accident to the funeral home" (S053–7).

In another case such reconceptualizing is done consciously and overtly:

> To me it was an accident. (Researcher: How's that?) It's something I didn't know about ahead of time, something you weren't prepared for. That made it an accident. (S014–20.)

This respondent has picked out as the essential characteristic of the category "accident," "something one does not know about ahead of time"—something one is, accordingly, unprepared for. She finds this characteristic present also in the case of her husband's suicide, emphasizes it, and, because of this analogous aspect, identifies the one with the other: *ergo* to her this suicide is an accident. Notice that this respondent does not deny that her husband's death was by suicide—that is, she does not deny the correctness of the objective category in which the coroner has placed the death—but, rather, she says, "To me it was an accident." The reason such a reconceptualization makes it easier for an individual to handle the death is probably that pinpointed by the following respondent:

> I think a suicide is harder to justify in your mind. An accidental death is like an act of God, and a suicide is by your own hand. (S015–20.)

A fourth technique of guilt neutralization is to emphasize inevitability, to conceptualize the suicide as having been an inevitable event. If a respondent can be convinced that a suicidal individual would "find a way" regardless of what steps were taken to prevent the act or that if it hadn't happened when it did it would have happened later, guilt may be considerably reduced. Thus:

> I just reasoned it out that if he wanted to do that, he'd find a way, and I couldn't do anything about it. (S010–18.)

> If it hadn't happened then, it would have happened some other time. (S055–8.)

Insight into one way by which such a conceptualization can come about is given by the following respondent who, concerning his mother-in-law's suicide, says:

> When we saw the note, I had a little better understanding as to how lonely she was. She gave a reason in it for why she did it. We felt better —felt there was nothing we could have done to have prevented it. (S020–7.)

Thus, by emphasizing the inevitability of suicide, by conceptualizing a suicide event such that one feels there was nothing one could have done to prevent it, one need feel no guilt. The extreme form of this technique would be to emphasize inevitability to such a degree that one feels that it would be only by accident that the suicide wouldn't have taken place, as:

> I accept the fact that it was what (my son) had wanted to do. If he set out to do it, he would just do it. Like (my other son) said at the inquest: "It would have been an accident if he hadn't done it." (S056–20.)

A fifth technique of guilt neutralization is to emphasize the uncertainty of the consequences of purposive social action. Although a man may perform a given activity in order to accomplish some end, in order to bring about some desired result, he frequently cannot be certain of the outcome of his action. Although his desired consequence may be the result of what he does, so might any number of other consequences. By emphasizing this uncertainty in man's life, an individual who feels that he perhaps could have acted differently toward the deceased, even where he realizes that perhaps his different act(s) might have prevented the suicide, still does not know for certain that it would have done so. Thus, if he emphasizes uncertainty, he need deal only with the possibility of guilt, and he does not have to face the absolute certainty of guilt itself.

This is the neutralization technique used by the man quoted earlier (see page 198) who said he didn't know for certain that even if he had forced his wife to go to Texas, she wouldn't have committed suicide anyway. He means that although one could say that a different course of action would have prevented the suicide, it is just as valid to interpret the possible consequences of the same act by saying that it would not have prevented the suicide.

Since there is this uncertainty connected with the outcome of what man does, not only can one not say for certain what the outcome of a given act would have been but it is also logically possible to view the consequences of a different course of action as making matters worse than they actually did turn out. The father of a suicide (quoted on p. 198) is utilizing this variant of this technique when he says: "But it could have been much worse if we had done it the other way" (S016–18).

A sixth technique is to emphasize another characteristic of man's life in this world, the irrevocability of the past. As explicated earlier, after a suicide one tends to search the past in order to clarify the causal chain leading to the suicidal act. This searching of the past, as in the quotation above, can lead to a brooding about "what might have been," about how one might have acted differently, and can in this way intensify guilt feelings One way of mitigating these feelings is to emphasize that there is no going back into the past in order to alter any acts whatsoever, that although one can in retrospect see how one could possibly have done things differently, there is just nothing that can now be done to alter them. Events are irrevocable: the past is past. Thus:

> I think this thing or that thing could have been done to change the course of events . . . but you can't turn back the clock. (S016–18.)

. . . Facts are facts. They remain the same . . . but there's no erasing events that took place. (S016–19.)

This technique also seems to function as a reminder to the self that not only is it futile to think about the unfortunate course events took but also one should live in the present, where one is able to change events.

Another neutralization technique is to *minimize* the suicidal act or some aspect of it. In using this technique, respondents look for ways in which the suicide could have been worse. By emphasizing these "possible worse aspects," they look at the actual event as being comparatively not too bad. This favorable comparison lessens their need to find guilt in themselves for their possible complicity in the death. One respondent, in utilizing this technique, de-emphasizes the means of death by saying that there are "worse ways to die than she chose" (S003–20). Another minimizes the suicide event by emphasizing three aspects of his stepfather's suicide:

Really, the way I felt was [1] he was a very sick person and that [2] he only had a very short time to live anyway, and, actually, [3] because of his condition, it was fortunate that just the one person was killed. (S029–8.)

This respondent is referring to the intense, continual pain his stepfather experienced from a malignant brain tumor, which pain and pressure "could have made his mind snap" (S029–8), leading him to kill others during the process of taking his own life. If one can so conceptualize a suicide, it follows that one's personal responsibility is diminished, with much lessened pressure toward, and in this case complete isolation from, guilt feelings.

An eighth neutralization technique is to define the suicidal act as *good* in some way. This defining goes beyond the technique last cited in that the respondent does not by favorable comparison minimize some aspect of the death, but, rather, he conceptualizes the death itself as a blessing of some sort, as a higher good. Where suicide is so conceptualized, there is no need for guilt since one need not feel guilty about someone's receiving a blessing.

There are any number of such "blessings" that a survivor can discover if he so conceptualizes the death. For example, the suicide can be viewed as now being with a loved one who had preceded him in death, as:

She wanted to die so much that you can't feel bad that she did it. I
don't ever think of her as a suicide, just that she finally got the things
she wanted most in life—to be with her husband. (S022–16.)

Where such conceptualization exists, an effective guard between the
self and guilt feelings can be erected. Some respondents exert considerable effort to use this technique, as is illustrated by the sixty-five-
year-old widow who emphasizes the peace her deceased husband has
attained by being "the first to go":

You have to take the long view and feel that he is at peace. So I'm the
one who is not at peace. I tell myself that it's lucky that he's the one
who went first because he wouldn't have been able to adjust to my
death as easy as I have to his. (S055–20.)

The suicide can also be viewed as having finally attained the peace
and happiness that he was unable to find in this life: "I am more relaxed about (my son) because he never found peace here: he was always so unhappy" (S056–16). The neutralizing capability of this
technique is demonstrated by noting that this last respondent, the
mother of a seventeen-year-old suicide, not only does not express guilt
regarding her son's death but even displays a feeling of greater content-
ment concerning him since he is dead. She had worried greatly about
him during his teen years because he never seemed to fit in with others and was always searching for something that continually eluded
him; but since she defines him as now having attained the happiness
and peace he was looking for, she feels more relaxed about him.

Since our culture frequently views a suicide as choosing to die, a
primary survivor can emphasize this feature of the act to the point of
viewing the choice in positive terms, as:

You feel it's the way the person wanted it. It's her choice, as gruesome
as it may seem. (S003–16.)

My wife and I told ourselves: "That's the way she wanted it. And if she
wanted it that way, that's the way she should have it." (S020–13.)

This last quotation hints at a process of arriving at such a reconceptualization of the death. The following example illustrates more
clearly how such a reconceptualization can take place:

She was a very unhappy person, and maybe in a way God letting her finally succeed was a blessing. . . . It seems that the few pertinent hours
she needed to conclude her act, the information of where she was, was
unavailable. That's why maybe it was God's blessing. (S032–7.)

This respondent, after kicking out her roommate, had refused to let her back into her house, even though she had shouted, cried, and beaten on the front door. After her roommate had left by cab, the respondent belatedly realized that since her roommate had attempted suicide a couple of weeks previously, she might do so again. She became alarmed and attempted to locate the cab company that had taken her away. Failing to do so, she alerted the deceased's boy friend, who also failed to identify the company. Prior to this, the deceased had called her boy friend, but he hadn't asked from where she was calling. By the time they finally located the motel to which she had gone, she was dead. This respondent views the facts that since the deceased had been unhappy and since people were frantically searching for her but nobody was able to locate her, which provided her with the time she needed to conclude her act, as meaning that it must have been divinely ordered that she not be located before she had completed her death; that is, it is a blessing from God.

Emphasizing the "blessing aspects" of a suicidal death can even be carried to such an extreme that interfering with the death can be construed as selfishness on the part of the interferer. Thus:

> I feel, when I think about it rationally, that she wanted to be with Pa, and if she wanted it that badly, I wouldn't deny her that. It would be selfishness on my part to keep her alive for my sake when she wanted to be with Pa. (S021–13.)

A ninth technique of guilt neutralization is to conceptualize the suicide as having been motivated by altruism. If the attributed motive for the suicide (and this seems to be the one most frequently attributed to the suicide by the survivors) is that of flight—a flight from problems and a flight from persons creating these problems, whether they be close relatives, lovers, friends, employers, or whoever else might have complicated the individual's life—the motive is actually being defined as one of hostility or hatred. That is, the individual is viewed as having committed suicide to get away from persons around him—persons whose acts he disliked so much that he chose death rather than to remain with them. The survivor who attributes such motivation to the suicide is then faced with the greatly disturbing problem of asking himself in what way he might have complicated the life of the suicide, if he in some way contributed to his "flight into death"; and this type of questioning, as we have seen above, can lead to severe guilt feelings.

One way to overcome the problems inherent in this type of thinking is to restructure the past by attributing the opposite motivation to the suicide: to conceptualize the motive as being altruistic—to define the suicide as having acted out of love for the survivor; that is, the individual suicided because he loved the respondent and wanted to spare him some given pain or hurt. A man whose wife of thirty-three years committed suicide demonstrates the relief he finds in this view, as well as his need to hold constant to this definition of reality, when he says:

> Her love was so strong for her husband and her family that she chose that (death by suicide) as a way out to save them that grief and agony. I'm sure this was part of her plan. I'm sure of that. (S008–6.)

A female respondent, regarding her husband's suicide, is also relieved through this definition: "He just didn't want to be a burden" (S030–15). Again, where such a definition of motivation can be successfully applied, a survivor need not feel guilt: the individual suicided out of love for him, not to flee in hatred from him.

There are persons who do not gain comfort in such conceptualizations of the event, but feel guilty about some particular thing they have done and find relief only in atonement for that act—the tenth technique we shall discuss.[18] The best example of this is the following:

> (At the funeral parlor) my brothers and sisters wanted me to see a doctor, but I wouldn't go. (Researcher: Why?) I wouldn't leave him because I felt that I had neglected him at the time when he needed me most. (S034–9.)

This respondent felt severe guilt feelings because she had been visiting at her next-door neighbors when her brother shot himself. She felt that if she had been home taking care of her sick brother, he would still be alive. She chose to atone for her felt failure by performing the very same action, that of "staying with him" or "not leaving him," on the very next chance she had, which happened to be when his body was lying in state. Even though she was showing signs of strain, and her siblings felt she should see a doctor, she refused to leave and instead remained by his side for hours on three consecutive days. I assume that if she had left him again on this last occasion when she could physically be with him, this would have intensified her guilt; but staying with him under these circumstances helped to mitigate it.

The eleventh technique is thought transference, a term adopted from the following respondent:

I'm a great believer in "thought transference." (Researcher: Thought transference?) When I find myself thinking about (my husband) and that I didn't recognize what was obviously there (his suicidal intent), and I feel guilty, I might redecorate the house—deliberately—or do a mathematical problem. You don't think about things or concentrate on your feeling then. (S055–11.) . . . I get my mind off me by "thought transference." I project my thoughts into more constructive ways. (S055–18.)

This respondent felt intense guilt for not recognizing suicidal symptoms in her husband and for not, accordingly, getting him the help he needed. She openly verbalized both her guilt feelings and the avoidance technique she has developed to deal with them. Whether such an overt avoidance technique actually overcomes guilt, or whether it merely postpones the confrontation for a time, is not the judgment here—just that it is a technique used by a respondent to handle guilt, and one that she feels is successful.

The twelfth element of guilt neutralization is not really a guilt neutralization technique but, rather, a guilt preventive factor. It differs from those discussed previously in that it is not something that develops following a suicide, but consists of feelings that existed prior to the suicidal act that insulate a person from experiencing guilt: a strongly negative affect toward or conceptualization of the deceased. Just how negative affect toward the deceased shields someone from guilt, I cannot say, but it seems to be the case, at least in this sample, that those who expressed dislike of the deceased did not feel guilt concerning his suicide. It could be that when one dislikes an individual, and that person suicides, one does not feel the compulsion to examine one's own life in relation to the deceased, but only examines the deceased's life to see what was wrong with him. (One can, however, easily conceive of a person who disliked another, and when that other suicided, felt guilt because of his dislike. No such cases turned up in the sample, however.)

In any event, the respondent who best illustrates this protection from guilt is a brother of a suicide. He neither acknowledged guilt in the psychiatric inventory nor in any way whatsoever expressed guilt during the interview. Some of his statements will illustrate the way he felt about his brother, and perhaps they will demonstrate how such negative affect provides protection from guilt. He said:

I'd visit my brother at his house. Any time you made a corrective criticism, for example, "You're ruining your health with drink," he wouldn't

listen. (S036–7.) . . . My brother knew I resented some of his ways.
. . . I was outspoken in my own way. I might say to him: "You can't
solve anything by drinking. You should grow up." 'Course these kind of
people you can't tell anything—I don't know how I could have changed
anything that took place. (S036–11.) . . . He stunk from whiskey as he
lay dead in the car—just reeked from it. . . . I respect life and don't believe in wasting things willfully, even time. And this kind of irritated me
with my feelings toward my brother—wasting himself with drinking—
didn't overcome it and get back on his feet. (S036–13.)

Another respondent who also neither acknowledged guilt feelings
nor expressed them in any way had a similar attitude toward the deceased. In this case, the respondent was a brother-in-law to the same
suicide as in our last example:

He was only a brother-in-law of mine by marriage. He really wasn't nothing to me. I didn't have no use for anybody who drinks and makes his
wife suffer so she almost had to go to one of those places for the insane
for a while. (S049–8.)

Although such negative feelings concerning the deceased are able
to protect a person from guilt, they do not necessarily do so. In one
case the respondent, the sister-in-law of the deceased, felt extremely
negative about her brother-in-law. She disliked almost everything
about him. Just as in the two cases above, she also did not have guilt
feelings about the death, but, as mentioned in the "Guilt Following
Suicide" section above, she "felt guilty because I didn't care"
(S033–8). It is interesting that not feeling guilt can create guilt: at
the death of a relative it is the cultural expectation that one should
feel bad that the person is dead, perhaps even guilty about the death,
and since she felt neither, this in itself led to guilt.[19]

There is a final type of guilt neutralization technique yet to be discussed, that of seeking aid from guilt neutralizers. By guilt neutralizers I mean persons, professional and nonprofessional, who in some
way help alleviate or reduce guilt felt by an individual. Included in
this category are both professional guilt neutralizers, such as psychiatrists, clergymen, doctors, and suicide specialists, and also a related
nonprofessional cadre, consisting primarily of friends and relatives,
but including others.

Some persons, after a suicide, feel an extreme, compulsive need to
seek out such guilt neutralizers. The following respondent is excellent
for illustrative purposes because he explicitly recognized his guilt feelings, specified his need for guilt neutralization, and revealed how such
neutralization took place through interaction with guilt neutralizers.

This respondent is a fifty-eight-year-old male whose wife had committed suicide in January. He was guilt-ridden because his mother had been living with him at the time, and he was "thinking that others might think that it was because of my mother that she did it." His wife's family lived in Baltimore, and six times between January and July, approximately once a month, he flew the round trip from St. Louis to Baltimore. Such an expenditure, on an annual income of $6,-000 and following recent funeral expenses, was not easy for him to afford, and it illustrates his great need for acceptance by his wife's relatives, his need for assurance that they did not blame him for his wife's death (S007–12). He stated that "things felt more normal" after he spent his July vacation with his wife's family and added:

> I talked to her family. I didn't know how they actually felt about it, but they seemed to be taking it all right. (S007–20.)

Being reassured by his wife's family was not sufficient. He also had to know that his friends were not blaming him for his wife's death:

> My friends helped the most—that you're sure that your friends think the same of you. (Researcher: Think the same of you?) Yeah. I had a little doubt—thought they might not understand the thing—but everybody's been pretty nice to me. (S007–20.)

While interacting with his friends and relatives, he picked up cues that he could interpret as indicating what his friends and relatives thought about his complicity or innocence in his wife's death. He found this reassurance with his relatives when "they seemed to be taking it all right" and with his friends when they were "pretty nice" to him. Receiving such reassurance in interaction became for him an effective means of relieving his guilt.

Many other respondents, whether they purposely seek them out or not, come in contact with guilt neutralizers. In general, the techniques used by guilt neutralizers parallel to a remarkable degree the techniques of guilt neutralization used by the respondents themselves. Some respondents have been assured that they had no control over the death (S024–11, 12); there was nothing more that they could have done for the deceased (S053–19); the suicide in some way had something to do with God's will or God's plan (S024–12; S037–20). Others have been advised not to speak about the death because such speaking would "create problems" (S024–11) and to get involved in nonrelated activities so they won't have time to think about it (S034–11).

To alleviate guilt, guilt neutralizers frequently emphasize the inevitability of the suicide. One respondent was told that her leaving her brother alone had not affected the event one way or the other:

My brother realized I was blaming myself, and he said, "No. He would have found another time when you were away from the house." And my sister and doctor said the same. (S034–12.)

Inevitability can be so emphasized that it is virtually indistinguishable from fatalism, as with the respondent who was told that his failure to tackle the person running toward the cliff hadn't affected the event at all:

(My greatest help was) the priest and people saying, "If it was to happen, it would happen." (S047–20.)

Another respondent was told that her husband's suicide was inevitable, but that her marrying and living with him in his late years had prevented it for a period of time:

My friends flatter me by saying this would have happened to him years ago if it hadn't been for me. (S055–15.)

Another technique used by guilt neutralizers is to emphasize the unpredictability or the uncertainty of the consequences of purposive social action. The respondent who was bothered by his failure to intervene in the jump from the cliff was given the following counsel shortly after the suicide:

If you'd have ran after him, and he'd run off the cliff anyway, then you'd really feel worse. (S047–8.)

What he was actually told is: "If you had tried to tackle the individual running toward the cliff, you might have missed him, and he might then have gone over the cliff. If this had happened, then you'd never be certain that if you hadn't gone after him he might have stopped before jumping, but since you did go after him, he felt chased and jumped. Then you'd really have something to feel guilty about."

The use of guilt neutralizers,[20] whether professional or nonprofessional, as with the use of the previous guilt neutralization techniques explicated above, does not say anything about its success. Just as with the other techniques, mitigation of guilt by using guilt neutralizers depends on the successful implementations or acceptance of particular protective definitions or conceptualizations: the definitions proffered by guilt neutralizers must be accepted by the respondent for his guilt to be alleviated. In some cases respondents are unable to accept the definitions guilt neutralizers offer because they feel that friends don't really mean what they say, but are "just trying to console you," and this "doesn't satisfy your mind or soul" (S020–6).

People are not limited to any one technique, of course, but can utilize these varying techniques in combination. In fact, it seems to be typical that they are not used singly, but in combination. For an example of this, we can look at the case of the sister of a suicide who has handled her guilt feelings quite excellently. Within a week of her brother's funeral she visited a psychiatrist friend who explained that her brother had been sick with schizophrenia. By utilizing the psychiatrist friend as a guilt neutralizer, she was pointed toward another neutralization technique: locating causes in impersonal factors. In addition, she was quite convinced that she had done everything that she possibly could have done for her brother, going into quite some detail in the interview concerning the help that she had tried to give him. She finally defined herself as helpless because of his illness, concluding that she was unable to influence him at all (S053–12, 13). By utilizing these various techniques, this respondent felt certain that she had no complicity in her brother's death, and, accordingly, she felt no guilt in the matter.

Theoretical Conclusions

One of the more useful sociological principles is one that was first put forth many years ago by W. I. Thomas: "If men define situations as real, they are real in their consequences." The meaning of what Thomas so succinctly stated is that, as far as social consequences are concerned, objective situations do not exist apart from a perceiver of the situation, and it is, therefore, not the so-called "objective" situation that determines man's actions, but rather his perception of that situation. Accordingly, the social scientist must be interested in how people perceive or define situations if he is going to understand man's behavior.

In this chapter we have leaned heavily on Thomas' "definition of the situation" in investigating guilt following suicide. We have seen that the origin of guilt does not lie in some objective basis, such as particular acts, but rather in the way in which a person defines his acts and the causal consequences of those acts for the suicide. Thus, it is entirely possible for an individual to appear to an observer to have

been very active in the direct causal chain of events leading to the suicide (for example, locking the door and refusing to allow one's pleading, crying roommate to enter, then watching out the window as she
leaves in a cab, knowing that she had shortly before attempted suicide,
and having her commit suicide a few hours later), and yet be troubled
by very little guilt, feeling only that one "perhaps wasn't understanding or patient enough" (S032). On the other hand, it is just as possible for a person to appear to an observer not to have been involved in
any causal chain leading to a suicidal death, and yet for that person
to define his acts so that he feels he has been responsible for the death
and consequently experiences much guilt.[21]

We have investigated how people construct reality for themselves
concerning their causal relationship to a suicide, examining their techniques of guilt neutralization. We have seen that guilt can be reduced
or even eliminated by particular definitions of one's own and others'
acts, events, and their consequences. Having examined these techniques of guilt neutralization, we can conclude that if the following
definitions of the situation can be successfully applied by an individual, he will experience no guilt, regardless of how his acts in actuality
or in the opinion of others may have contributed to the suicide: [22]

1. *He defines other persons and/or impersonal factors as the causal
agents that led to the suicide.* In his view there is neither anything
that he did nor anything that he neglected to do that led to the suicide. In addition, he defines his own acts toward the person who committed suicide as good.

2. *He defines the suicide as inevitable.* He views the suicide as having been impossible to stop, looking on himself as having been powerless in the face of this crushing inevitability. He had neither the
knowledge nor the power to stop the suicide.

3. *He defines the suicide in positive terms.* He minimizes the suicide event itself and/or emphasizes certain consequences of the suicide as good. He can, for example, view the deceased as now being in
a better state than previously, defining suicide as the means by which
God took the individual to Himself. He also defines altruism as the
motive for the suicide: the suicide was not seeking to escape from
him, but rather he suicided out of love and concern, attempting to
spare him some hurt or pain.

According to this analysis, a person who defines the suicidal situation in this way has no need for a negative judgment on himself, and
guilt will not develop. In cases, however, where the individual has not

successfully applied such definitions to himself and to the suicide event and therefore feels guilt, he can use elements of the methods outlined above to help mitigate his guilt. Additionally, he can use other guilt neutralization techniques, such as atoning for any felt wrong, thought transference, seeking out guilt neutralizers, or emphasizing the irrevocability of the past and the unpredictability of the consequences of purposive human acts.

This analysis applies to suicidal deaths where the deceased was of some consequence for or significance to the survivor, where he was a "significant other." In cases where the deceased was not of personal significance, there would ordinarily be no guilt (such as persons whose suicide one only reads about). One is probably protected from guilt in such cases by holding definition of the situation No. 1 above, wherein, not having a personal relationship with the individual, one feels no causal connection between one's own actions and the events that occurred in the life of the suicide and automatically projects the cause to sources external to oneself.

To maintain definitions, one needs validation of some sort. In line with dissonance theory, if one is defining oneself as guiltless, we would expect that person to seek out others who agree with the definition that he wants to maintain. We would expect him to seek guilt neutralizers, persons who agree that he is not responsible for the death and convincingly offer some sort of evidence or reasoning that this is so. It is also probable that one is either enabled successfully to apply, or prevented from applying, guilt neutralizing definitions of the situation because of the causal views current in one's culture or subculture and the prevailing definitions of the consequences of one's actions by significant others. These factors, however, remain uninvestigated.[23]

Also uninvestigated, and of vital interest, is the question of how guilt and definitions of the situation change over time, the groping or emergent construction of meaning or reality. To investigate this question, future research should be so designed that at least two or three measurements can be taken: one shortly after the suicide (there being greater rapport and co-operation after the funeral than before), and the other a follow-up interview at some specified time, say, three months later. Ideally a third measurement should be included, say, at the end of a year. There are indications that some people wrestle with these questions for a remarkably long period, that some who have experienced a suicide are still reconceptualizing the event five and ten years later.[24] The research design would ideally also take this into account.

NOTES

1. This does not include 14 "open" cases which occurred during this period, most of which were judged to be "open as to suicide or accident." It is probable that most of these cases were actually suicides, but the coroner's decision as to which are and which are not suicides is being accepted here as the operational definition of suicide. This begs entirely the question of how decisions to categorize a death as "suicide" or as "not suicide" are made—an intriguing question but one that is not in the domain of this present chapter.

   For related research on the problems involved in classifying deaths, see W. B. Donovan and G. Nash, "Suicide Rate: A Problem of Validity and Comparability," *Marquette Medical Review*, XXVII (1962), 15–159; Jack D. Douglas, *The Social Meanings of Suicide* (Princeton: Princeton University Press, 1967), especially pp. 161–231; Raymond I. Harris, *Outline of Death Investigation* (Springfield, Ill.: Charles C Thomas, 1962); R. E. Litman *et al.*, "Investigations of Equivocal Suicides," *Journal of the American Medical Association*, CLXXXIV (1963), 924–929; O. Richardson and H. S. Breyfogle, "Medicolegal Problems in Distinguishing Accident from Suicide," *Annals of Internal Medicine*, XXV (1946), 22–65; O. Richardson and H. S. Breyfogle, "Problems of Proof in Distinguishing Suicide from Accident," *Yale Law Journal*, LVI (1947), 482–508; K. Rudfeld, "Sprang han, eller feldt han? Bidrag til belysning af graenseomradet mellem selvmord og ulykker" ("Did He Jump or Did He Fall? A Contribution toward the Explanation of the Margin between Suicide and Accident"), *Sociologiske Meddelelser*, VII (1962), 3–22; A. W. Stearns, "Accident or Suicide?" *Journal of the Maine Medical Association*, XLVI (1955), 313–320 and 336–337 *passim;* A. W. Stearns, "Cases of Probable Suicide in Young Persons without Obvious Motivation," *Journal of the Maine Medical Association*, XLIV (1953), 16–23; N. Tabachnick *et al.*, "Comparative Psychiatric Study of Accidental and Suicidal Death," *Archives of General Psychiatry*, XIV (1966), 60–68.

2. As is readily apparent, the total cases contained in categories (1), (3), (4), and (5) could have been substantially reduced by further effort. Categories (3), (4), and (5), for example, could have been eliminated entirely. Although I wanted to work at reducing these cases, I was unfortunately prevented from doing so because of certain administrative difficulties.

3. I wish to express my sincere appreciation for the fine co-operation of the coroner of St. Louis County, Mr. Raymond I. Harris, for making available case materials on each suicide. I also wish to thank Mr. Daniel Grobelny for his generous help in developing the interview schedule and Dr. Paula Clayton for her stimulating ideas during the initial phase

of the research. Special thanks are due Drs. Robert Hamblin and R. A. Laud Humphreys for their assistance in solving certain administrative and professional problems that developed during the course of this research.

4. I am very grateful to Miss Christine Sanborn, who served as my assistant. She demonstrated remarkable expertise in interviewing, even salvaging a couple of interviews that were nearly "unsalvageable."

5. Lindesmith and Strauss posit that it is "characteristic of human beings to seek explanations of the past, and to 'rethink' incidents and discover new meanings in them" and that searching for meaning "abound(s) in times of personal crisis when the individual is questioning himself about where he is going and must consequently consider where he has been." Alfred R. Lindesmith and Anselm L. Strauss, *Social Psychology*, 3rd ed. (New York: Holt, Rinehart, and Winston, 1968), p. 128.

For related sources on the social bases of reality construction, see Peter L. Berger and Thomas Luckmann, *The Social Construction of Reality: A Treatise in the Sociology of Knowledge* (Garden City, N.Y.: Doubleday, 1966); Burkart Holzner, *Reality Construction in Society* (Cambridge: Schenkman, 1968); and Thomas J. Scheff, "Negotiating Reality: Notes on Power in the Assessment of Responsibility," *Social Problems*, XVI (Summer, 1968), 3–17. Scheff analyzes "the process of reconstructing past events for the purpose of fixing responsibility," a "negotiation of reality" (pp. 3 and 6).

6. Talcott Parsons analyzes religion as an adjustive mechanism in providing emotionally satisfying meaning to frustrating human experiences, such as "making sense" out of the occurrence of death, in "Sociology and Social Psychology," in Hoxie N. Fairchild, ed., *Religious Perspectives in College Teaching* (New York: Ronald, 1952), pp. 286–337.

7. Bronislaw Malinowski, *Crime and Custom in Savage Society* (Paterson, N.J.: Littlefield, Adams, 1964), pp. 77–80.

8. Quotations from respondents' interviews will be designated by the ordinal sequence of the interview and the page on which the quotation was recorded; for instance, "S031–20" refers to the thirty-first suicide interview, the particular quotation being located on page 20 of that interview.

9. The question of whether religious perspectives intensify or ameliorate the grief process is suggested for empirical investigation by Bernard Steinzor in his "Death and the Construction of Reality," in J. G. Peatman and E. L. Hartley, eds., *Festschrift for Gardner Murphy* (New York: Harper, 1960), pp. 358–375.

10. Lindemann concludes that a normal part of bereavement is a preoccupation with feelings of guilt: Erich Lindemann, "Symptomatology and Management of Acute Grief," *American Journal of Psychiatry*, CI (September, 1944), 141–148. For an analysis of how children's searching for cause in the death of a parent leads to guilt, see Bettie Arthur and

Mary L. Kemme, "Bereavement in Childhood," *Journal of Child Psychology and Psychiatry*, V (June, 1964), 37–49. See also Albert C. Cain, Irene Fast, and Mary E. Erickson, "Children's Disturbed Reactions to the Death of a Sibling," *American Journal of Orthopsychiatry*, XXXIV (July, 1964), 741–752; and S. Rosenzweig, "Sibling Death as a Psychological Experience with Special Reference to Schizophrenia," *Psychoanalytic Review*, XXX (1943), 177–186. For a study of guilt over anticipated death, see Stanford B. Friedman *et al.*, "Behavioral Observations on Parents Anticipating the Death of a Child," *Pediatrics*, XXXII (October, 1963), 610–625.

The only studies that I know that deal with guilt by significant others following a suicide are by Albert C. Cain and Irene Fast, "Children's Disturbed Reactions to Parent Suicide," *American Journal of Orthopsychiatry*, XXXVI (October, 1966), 873–880, and "The Legacy of Suicide: Observations on the Pathogenic Impact of Suicide upon Marital Partners," *Psychiatry*, XXIX (November, 1966), 406–411.

The "commonness" of the phenomenon of guilt by survivors following death is illustrated by a recent death. A ninety-seven-year-old male died of "natural" causes. His family had been extremely close to him and had done what appeared to be everything humanly possible for him: he had lived with them, they had had a warm, cordial relationship, and they had provided him with the best of medical care. Yet they felt guilt when he died, even expressing their guilt to others. From a personal communication with Mrs. Adeline Sneider, May 27, 1968.

11. There is one further degree, of course, in the severity of guilt following suicide, but it is one that would prevent the person from becoming a respondent in our sample: that of successful or completed suicide. For example, the brother of an individual in our sample killed himself by jumping off a cliff because of feelings of guilt. He felt guilty because it was his gun that his brother had used to shoot himself.

Suicidal preoccupations, threats, attempts, and successes because of guilt following a death are also mentioned by Arthur and Kemme, *op. cit.*, and Cain, Fast, and Erickson, *op. cit.*

12. For an analysis of children's search for specific incidents that immediately preceded the suicide of one of their parents and the resulting guilt, see Cain and Fast, *op. cit.*, especially pp. 875–877.

13. This type of causal view is common among certain segments of our society. Friedman *et al.*, *op. cit.*, p. 614, encountered this causal orientation with parents of children suffering from leukemia who blamed themselves, saying, "It's God's way of punishing me for my sins."

The correlative positive form of this causal view is that if one is experiencing good things, then one must have done good things, that there is a reciprocal relationship between doing good and receiving good. A popular example of this is contained in the song "Something Good" from *The Sound of Music* where the vocalist says that since she now has someone loving her she must have done something good in the past.

14. This type of guilt was also encountered by Cain, Fast, and Erickson, *op. cit.*, p. 745, and by Friedman *et al.*, *op. cit.*, p. 617.

15. Sykes and Matza analyze neutralization techniques used by juvenile delinquents both to justify their behavior and to overcome guilt for such behavior. Their first technique, "denial of responsibility," is very close to the first two analyzed above. There are also further parallels between the neutralization techniques used by delinquents and those used by significant others of a suicide. Gresham M. Sykes and David Matza, "Techniques of Neutralization: A Theory of Delinquency," *American Sociological Review*, XXII (December, 1957), 664–670.

   Neutralization techniques as symbolic adjustment devices for drug addicts, alcoholics, juvenile delinquents, the police, and other law enforcement officials are discussed by Lindesmith and Strauss, *op. cit.*, pp. 397–399. See also their section on "normal coping devices," pp. 330–333.

16. A related possible technique, but one that was not present in my sample, is "death denial," to deny that the person has died. Arthur and Kemme, *op. cit.*, p. 45, discuss this reaction to death in cases where admitting the death would lead to "catastrophic insecurity." Another technique, also one that did not show up in this sample, is that of confession. Probably the most common form is private confession, as to a priest, but another variant is public confession, as illustrated by a letter to the *Sunday Visitor*, May 12, 1968, p. 12 (my thanks to Miss Susan Smith for drawing my attention to this reference), and possibly this is part of the motivation of Bishop James A. Pike, concerning his son's suicide, in his article "The Other Side," in *Look*, October 29, 1968: Part I, pp. 43–58, and November 12, 1968: Part II, pp. 51–62.

17. For a classification of modes of death differing from that commonly found in our culture—natural, accident, homicide, and suicide—see the one based on a psychological point of view: unmeditated, premeditated, and submeditated, as explicated in Edwin S. Shneidman, Norman L. Farberow, and Robert E. Litman, "A Taxonomy of Death—A Psychological Point of View," in Norman L. Farberow and Edwin S. Shneidman, eds., *The Cry for Help* (New York: McGraw-Hill, 1961), pp. 129–135. See also, Edwin S. Shneidman, "Orientations toward Death: A Vital Aspect in the Study of Lives," in Robert W. White, ed., *The Study of Lives* (New York: Atherton, 1963), pp. 201–227, where they are renamed as unintentioned, intentioned, and subintentioned.

18. Arthur and Kemme, *op. cit.*, p. 42, cite an interesting case of atonement by an eleven-year-old boy who felt guilty for disobeying his now deceased mother and who began to comply "with requests she had once made of him to do household chores—requests which he had formerly resisted."

19. Friedman *et al.*, *op. cit.*, p. 617, found that some parents felt guilt because they did not "feel worse" over the anticipated death of their child.

20. It should be mentioned that my assistant and I frequently "played the role of guilt neutralizers." Reassurance was often sought from us that the respondent had no guilt in the death. This reassurance was, of course, given in each case, regardless of the researcher's personal opinions to the contrary.

21. Such a "definitional approach" carries with it the possibility of understanding behavior from the point of view of the actor involved and can avoid imposing one's own views onto the actor. This phenomenological approach allows one to get at "the reality people create by their interpretation of their experience and in terms of which they act. If we fail to present this reality, we will not have achieved full sociological understanding of the phenomenon we seek to explain." Howard S. Becker, *Outsiders: Studies in the Sociology of Deviance* (New York: The Free Press, 1963), p. 174.

    The "definitional theory" utilized in this chapter appears to be equivalent to "personal construct theory" as developed by Kelly and applied by him to understanding motivations for suicide. See George A. Kelly, "Suicide: The Personal Construct Point of View," in Farberow and Shneidman, *op. cit.*, pp. 255–280.

22. Additionally, as earlier analyzed, denial that the death was by suicide can prevent guilt, as can a strong negative conception of the deceased.

23. Also uninvestigated are larger cultural components, whose presence or absence would dictate resultant feelings following given events. "Guilt cultures" versus "shame cultures" would be apropos in this connection. See Ruth Benedict, *The Chrysanthemum and the Sword: Patterns of Japanese Culture* (Cambridge: Riverside, 1946), pp. 222–223.

24. I am grateful to Miss Christine Sanborn, who noticed this happening with a personal acquaintance and brought it to my attention.

8

The Use of Religion in Constructing the Moral Justification of Suicide

Jerry Jacobs

Since Durkeim's success in establishing the etiological approach as the model methodology of sociology (and simultaneously legitimizing the existence of sociology as an independent discipline), little attention has been paid by sociologists to the motives, morals, or individual condition of any particular suicide. The search for the "essential characteristics" of suicide through the collection of many complete case histories of suicides was abandoned in favor of seeking an explanation of the "causes" of social suicide rates.

> Statistical efforts should take quite a different direction. Instead of trying to solve these insoluble problems of moral casuistry, they should notice more carefully the social concomitants of suicide. For our own part, at least, we make it a rule not to employ in our studies such uncertain and uninstructive data; no law or any interest has in fact ever been drawn from them by students of suicide. . . . Disregarding the individual as such, his motives and his ideas, we shall seek directly the states of the various social environments . . . in terms of which the variations of suicide occur.[1]

The study of suicide has since proceeded in this fashion, not only among sociologists but among other disciplines as well.[2] For sociologists, the acceptance of the etiological approach has been perhaps more universal, and this methodology has been traditionally applied not only to the study of suicide but to the study of all social phenomena. So tenaciously has sociology held to this model that it is not infrequently assumed of those proceeding by methods other than those suggested by Durkheim in *Suicide* that they are, by definition, not doing sociology. Sociologists concerned with the individual, his motives and ideas, are suspect. The acceptance of Durkheim's *Suicide* as a model methodology has only recently come under serious attack from within the discipline itself.[3] The author also feels that a re-evaluation of the etiological approach is long overdue. However, it is not the purpose of this chapter to understake a general critique of Durkheim's methodology. Those interested in such a critique are referred to the authors footnoted above. I will be primarily concerned with Durkheim's statements regarding the "insoluble problems of moral casuistry"; "disregarding the individual as such, his motives and his ideas"; and whether or not concerning oneself with those problems is to concern oneself with "uncertain and uninstructive data" from which "no law or any interest has . . . ever been drawn . . . by students of suicide." It was the acceptance of these propositions that led sociologists into the general practice of interpreting social suicide rates. The author believes that a more instructive line of inquiry is to study the moral prohibitions against the taking of life (one's own or that of another) and how the individual must overcome these prohibitions if he is to succeed in bridging the gap between thought and action. Many contemplate suicide. Few, however, succeed in it. The process whereby one is able to succeed has been discussed by the author in a prior work based on the analysis of the suicide's motives and ideas as expressed in suicide notes and diaries.[4] That analysis dealt primarily with how the suicide was able to overcome the moral constraints implicit and explicit in social norms. Overcoming the constraints of social norms is only one important moral issue that the individual contemplating suicide must contend with.

Another moral issue faced by the suicide is more directly associated with religion per se. The topic of religion and suicide has generally been dealt with from one of three broad perspectives: how religion works to prevent suicide by specifically prohibiting it, how religion affects social suicide rates as a result of the relative extent of social integration between members of any particular religious sect, and how religion may work to encourage suicide by sanctioning it in certain circumstances.

Examples of the condemnation of suicide by various religious sects are numerous. The Koran is explicit in its prohibition of suicide. "The question is asked: 'What ought one to think of suicide?'" And the answer is: "It is a much greater crime than homicide." At yet another point, the faithful are enjoined: "Neither slay yourselves, for God is merciful toward you, and whoever doth this maliciously and wickedly, He will surely cast him to be broiled in the hellfire." [5]

Although there is no specific prohibition of suicide in the Old or New Testaments, Catholics, Protestants, and Jews are clear in their prohibition of it. The idea (discounted by Durkheim) that the perspective of religious teachings toward life, death, and the hereafter has little or nothing to do with suicide rates of Catholics, Protestants, and Jews is not adhered to by all. For example, in a discussion of suicide in Jewish history, Dublin notes:

> This interesting phenomenon [the low rates of suicide among Jews] can be explained by the attitude of the religious Jew toward life and in the philosophic outlook of Judaism. Suicide is unthinkable—and it is unthinkable because throughout the Old Testament runs the theme of the sacredness of life. . . . Their usual attitude is expressed by Job who, when his wife wished him to give up the struggle against adverse fortune and bade him "curse God and die," answered in the true spirit of submission: "Thou speakest as one of the foolish women speaketh. What! Shall we receive good at the hand of God and shall we not receive evil?" And naturally the temperament whose faith is strong enough, when beset with trials and tribulations, to maintain that "the Lord gave, and the Lord hath taken away: blessed be the name of the Lord," is not one inclined toward suicide. [6]

Catholicism is even more explicit in its prohibition of suicide. In this case, the act is considered a mortal sin and, as with Mohammedanism, a graver crime than homicide.

> The church . . . eventually adopted the extreme view, holding Judas Iscariot's betrayal of Christ as a lesser sin than his suicide. From permission to kill in defense of one's life, the inference was drawn that suicide is indeed more reprehensible than homicide. [7]

So explicit is the prohibition of Catholicism and Protestantism against suicide that Durkheim believed that the restraints against it were equally binding for the adherents of both and, therefore, could not per se explain the differences found in the suicide rates.

> Both prohibit suicide with equal emphasis; not only do they penalize it morally with great severity, but both teach that a new life begins beyond the tomb where men are punished for their evil actions, and Prot-

estantism just as well as Catholicism numbers suicide among them. Finally, in both cults these prohibitions are of divine origin; they are represented not as logical conclusions of correct reason, but God Himself is their authority. Therefore, if Protestantism is less unfavorable to the development of suicide, it is not because of a different attitude from that of Catholicism. Thus, if both religions have the same precepts with respect to this particular matter, their dissimilar influence on suicide must proceed from one of the more general characteristics differentiating them [8]

If the assumption above is a convenient one to make in the furtherance—indeed, maintenance—of the argument that the relative degree of social integration in these religions is the general characteristic differentiating them, it is nevertheless a questionable one. There is good reason to suppose that the religious constraints on Catholics and Protestants with respect to suicide are in fact differently binding and might effect the higher rate of suicide among the latter. Douglas has dealt with this aspect from one perspective.[9] The author will deal with it from yet another later in this chapter.

This leads us to the third and last broad perspective on religion and suicide noted earlier: the way in which religion may work to encourage suicide by sanctioning it in specific instances. Perhaps the most frequent reference to this last perspective is suttee, the Hindu widow's act of self-immolation on the funeral pyre of her husband. Through this act she becomes "the goddess Sati herself, reincarnate; the sakti, or projected life-energy of her spouse." For the widow to go on living, according to this doctrine, insures that she survives in the realization that she is "unreal, non-existent, false, untrue, improper; . . . bad, wicked, evil, vile." [10]

Apart from this and other obvious forms of religiously sanctioned suicide, such as the Japanese hara-kiri, are the less obvious historical exceptions to Christianity's abhorrence of suicide. "Exaltation of 'suicide' in early Christian philosophy may be found in the calculated improvidence of martyrs and the enthusiasm for death on the part of ascetics, as well as in the glorification of suicide committed in the defense of virtue." [11]

An earlier example is found in the ambiguities of Roman law. While certain suicides were punishable, as in the case of a master's or the state's claim on the life of a slave or soldier, other suicides were exempt. Some examples of exemptions were suicides caused by "impatience of pain or sickness, some grief or by another cause." [12] In short, the range of acceptable suicides for persons other than those considered property was great. Some indication of this acceptability is given by Cicero: "God Himself has given a valid reason as He did . . . to Socrates and . . . Cato, and often to many others, then of a surety your true wise man will joyfully pass forthwith from the darkness here into the light beyond." [13]

Even the Jews seem to have allowed for certain exceptions to the sacredness of life. Four instances of suicide are found in the Old Testament: Samson, Abimelech, Ahithophel, and Saul.[14] Whereas Saul ordered himself slain by his armor-bearer, the first three were cases of persons taking their own lives.

It should be noted in concluding this discussion that notwithstanding the exceptions (some of which are noted above), Catholicism, Protestantism, and Judaism have all taken (to one extent or another) a common stand in attempting to discourage suicide. In spite of the universality of the prohibition invoked by the major religions against suicide, not everyone shared in this moral indignation. Perhaps the most eloquent argument in the defense of suicide came from Hume, who, having noted the absence of prohibitions against it in either the Old or New Testament, held that in order to be a crime, the act of suicide must be a transgression against God, society, or the self. Having argued well that it was none of these, he concludes:

> If suicide be supposed a crime, 'tis only cowardice can impel us to it. If it be no crime, both prudence and courage should engage us to rid ourselves at once of existence, when it becomes a burden. 'Tis the only way that we can then be useful to society, by setting an example which, if imitated, would preserve to every one his chance for happiness in life and would effectually free him from all danger or misery.[15]

To the extent that the Pope and not Hume held sway over the minds of Christendom, the former view was by far the favored one, except, unfortunately, in the minds of the suicides themselves. For although few are capable of marshaling so eloquent a defense of suicide as Hume, many others have of necessity tried. The suicide's need to resolve, to his own satisfaction, the moral prohibitions against suicide is the central concern of this chapter.

The critical question is whether or not the individual who has in desperation reached the point of entertaining suicide as a possible resolution to his problems is able to resolve to his own satisfaction the binding effects of the social and religious moral prohibitions against it. An interesting sociological problem is how he succeeds in doing so.

The following process, based on the author's previous works, describes the ordering of events by which the individual is led to become "suicidal":

1. A long-standing history of problems.
2. A more recent escalation of problems; that is, the inability to resolve old problems at the same time that many new ones have
   been added.
3. The progressive failure of available adaptive techniques for
   coping with old and increasing problems, which leads the individual to feel a progressive isolation from meaningful social
   relationships.
4. The final stage—the days and weeks immediately preceding the
   suicide—at which time the individual feels he has experienced an
   abrupt and unanticipated dissolution of any remaining meaningful relationships and the prospects of ever establishing them in
   the future. He experiences, in short, "the end of hope." [16]

In brief, the potential suicide feels the necessity of taking his own
life because, from his perspective, he has attempted (to no avail)
every other possible alternative available to him for dealing with his
problems. Death is seen as the only answer, the only possible resolution to the unbearable and insoluble problems of life.

Having been subject to this sequence of events and come to the
conclusion above, one is now able to entertain the ten-point process
described in the author's previous work (see footnote 4) by which the
potential suicide resolves the social prohibitions against suicide. Having succeeded in this, it remains only for him to resolve the moral restraints implicit or explicit in religious prohibitions. This leads to a
fourth important and badly neglected perspective from which to view
suicide and religion: the way in which religious dogma, intended specifically to discourage suicide, is interpreted by the suicidal person in
such a way as to encourage it. The processes noted above deal with
the way in which the suicide convinces himself that he is blameless
and without sin (the contradictory edicts of religious dogma notwithstanding) by convincing himself that he has no choice. The act in the
final analysis is seen as a case of necessity. Since sin (mortal or otherwise) presupposes that the individual has a choice and elects, for
whatever reason, to do wrong, he is blameless, inasmuch as he has not
chosen to kill himself, but feels rather that he must. Since freedom is
"the recognition of necessity," the potential suicide feels just prior to
the act that he is finally free. An account of the final entry in the
diary of Ellen West notes:

On the third day of being home she is transformed. At breakfast she eats
butter and sugar, at noon she eats so much that—for the first time in

thirteen years!—she is satisfied by her food and gets really full. She takes a walk with her husband . . . is in a positively festive mood, and all heaviness seems to have fallen away from her. . . . In the evening she takes a lethal dose of poison and on the following morning she is dead. "She looked as she had never looked in life—calm, happy and peaceful." [17]

An excerpt from a long suicide note written by a physician, relating his thoughts and setting his affairs in order, reads:

Although I am upset now, it is surprising how calm I feel about ending it.

Toward the end of the same four-page typewritten note it says:

I am quite determined and less afraid. 2500 MGM of seconal and some _____ [illegible] ahead of this should do the trick.[18]

Part of another suicide note reads:

Oh Bob I love you, you too Betty, Mary, Ralph and Jim. Just remember that mother wanted the best for all of you, to play with you, go places with you. I miss all the good times. *I can't stay locked in this room forever. I want to be free.*[19]

The anticipation of a final relief is a general condition to the suicide's taking place. An excerpt from a rather lengthy suicide note reads:

There must be a reward for this miserable experience called life. Life would be utterly pointless without it. . . . *Be consoled (my wife) by the happy thought that leaving this world is a release from sorrow.*[20]

Another note, a case of murder-suicide, reads:

To the police station: I have now been unemployed for four years and we are starting to lack even the necessities. *We have decided to go with our children into the hereafter where no unemployment exists and where one is not surrounded by creatures and human beasts.* We ask that you don't get mad at us for doing this, because we have no other solution.[21]

Part of another note reads:

Somewhere in this pile is your answers. I couldn't find it. Mom, you should have known what was about to happen after I told you my troubles. *Now I will get my rest.*[22]

An excerpt from the diary of a suicide reads:

What's the use? *Death only holds forth relief.* I cannot look back on a really happy day. Lighthearted and merry have I been on occasion, but seldom a day without morbid thoughts sometime or another.[23]

However, prior to actually attempting to take his own life, the individual may beg God to spare him the necessity of resorting to suicide. After all, only God has the right: "The Lord giveth and the Lord taketh away."

I want to move to Canada. God, I know I can't live here anymore. No, not in this horrible city. It is wicked, it is cruel. I can't escape it. No, not even in my dreams. What is a dream? Which is the nightmare? Sleep promises escape from this misery—only sleep too is deceitful. Who will end it all for me? I try, but I cannot. I don't even have strength to end this pain. This ceaseless, unrelenting pain. Why was I ever born? What a cruel trick my mother played on me. Is there no limit? I will seek my relief in the grave. God, why? Why do you do this to me? Are you God or are you the Devil? God must be a Devil! Yes it is the Devil I have been speaking to. *If there is a God, please let him hear me and end my agony.* Who is my father? Is he the Devil? No, I am the Devil and there is no death, there is no end. *God, please release me in death.*[24]

Another example from the diary of a suicide reads:

I have just crawled out of bed. Can't sleep. . . . *The last rest is all I pray for now. Oh, God, how many times have I asked you to take me, take me, take me?*[25]

Sometimes the request to have their lives taken is addressed to a husband or other loved one, instead of to God. These are, after all, next in line for the "right" or "duty" to do so. This would be especially true in the case of the nonbeliever. It is no accident that most murders and nearly all cases of murder-suicide are "family affairs."[26]

In the diary of a suicide before she took her own life, we find this entry:

Life has become a prison camp for me and I long as ardently for death as the poor soldier in Siberia longs for his homeland. The comparison with imprisonment is no play on words. I am in prison, caught in a net from which I cannot free myself. . . . I am in Siberia; my heart is icebound, all around me is solitude and cold. My best days are a comic attempt to deceive myself as to my true condition. It is undignified to live on like this. *Karl, if you love me, grant me death.*[27]

In both cases above, the expectation is that one's problems will be resolved in death. This discussion of the way in which death is viewed as the only respite to life's problems leads us to the specific way in which religious dogma may work to encourage suicide. There would be little point in resolving one's problems in this life, only to incur a new set as bad or worse in the hereafter. The suicide's ability to convince himself that death will reduce or eliminate his problems is the final ingredient for the previously described peace and calm found among suicides immediately preceding their act. It is in his search for a means of achieving this outlook that religion holds a promise. The suicide is able to acquire this optimistic outlook toward the hereafter by adopting one of several situated interpretations toward existing religious dogma. I will list these forms of interpretation and give illustrations of each from the suicide's or suicide attempter's own accounts as taken either from suicide notes and diaries or detailed case histories.

First, the suicidal person who had previously been a diligent churchgoer and considered himself religious may abruptly cease attending church and, at the same time, start considering himself a nonbeliever. In doing so, he disposes of the prospect of Heaven and Hell and simultaneously secures for himself all the benefits of the atheist with respect to any future problems. It is one way to resolve the ambiguities implicit in the Heaven and Hell schema and insure that suicide is in fact the ultimate solution to life's problems. From this perspective, one is able to view suicide as a way to "end it all." By excluding the possibility of a future existence, one excludes the possibility of future problems as well. The case histories of fifty adolescent suicide attempters, studied by the author, offer several examples of this form of resolution. Excerpts from the case history of a seventeen-year-old girl who attempted suicide by ingesting about forty Sominex tablets provides an interesting case in point. The case record reads:

> Mother feels that Mr. M. didn't take Joan's suicide attempt very seriously—"he's very cool about most things." Mother states that she was very upset, but not really shocked since Joan had discussed suicide many times in the past. Mrs. M. believes the prospect of going to Hell had frightened her out of it before.

Joan says:

> She does not consider herself to be a religious person, although some of her friends are religious. She used to be very religious, but no more. "It

wasn't doing me any good. . . . People always talk about hearing God speak to them, but I never heard God talk to me."

Joan seemed to have begun losing interest in religion within several months of the attempt.[28]

Another example is that of a fourteen-year-old Caucasian male would-be suicide whose case history notes:

Tom participates sometimes in activities sponsored by the Congregational Church where he used to attend regularly. Tom claims to be an atheist "right now." He thinks that when a person dies, he's just dead.[29]

Another solution to the problem of the hereafter is illustrated by the suicidal person who suddenly "gets religion." These cases were more numerous among the fifty adolescent suicide attempters noted above than were those who abruptly abandoned religion. Among these were those who may have previously attended church to one extent or another, but did not count themselves among the faithful. Many felt in retrospect that they were hypocrites. They generally felt a distressing ambiguity about whether or not they would go to Heaven. It is not uncommon for such persons suddenly to make such inquiries as: "Does God forgive anything?" or "Will God forgive suicide?" It is generally the case that those to whom the question is put, believing that He does, or anxious for the convert, or for whatever other reason, will answer, "Yes, if you really believe." At this point, the person does all that is within his grasp to "get religion" and "really believe."

The following are some examples taken from the case records.

A suicide note left by a sixteen-year-old Caucasian girl who attempted suicide by ingesting twenty-five to thirty Dilantin capsules reads:

Please forgive me, God, I am so mixed up or else I don't know what I really want of life. I love Mom, Joan, Lucy and everyone else in the world so much. I thought and almost fully convinced myself that I was not fully wanted or accepted in the world. . . . In my heart I know there is a Christ everywhere in the world that is being with everyone, every second of every day, and He represents God in every way. I know that in my brain (mind) I think evil things about different situations and sometimes I think that Christ never existed. But my heart is always strong and that when I think that Christ never lived I know that in my heart He did. I love God and Jesus Christ and the world so much that it really breaks my heart to see that I am trying to kill myself. . . . No matter what I said to Mom and Joan and everyone else, I love Mom more than myself. I think I didn't mean the things I said in anger or other-wise to people. I am sorry for all the things I ever said that were sar-castic or mean. Mother thinks that there is no Hell or Heaven and I know there is a Hell and Heaven. I don't want to go to the devil, God, so please forgive me to what I have just done. Frank Jones says that if I believe in and accept Jesus that I would go to Heaven. Some people say that if you ask forgiveness to God for things you do to yourself or others, that He would forgive you (if you believe in Jesus and love him). . . . If I were to live I might never have been at peace with "myself." . . . Heaven is so peaceful and the earth is very troublesome and terrifying.[30]

In this case, as in the one below, both the adolescent and her mother reported that the girl's serious preoccupation with religion began abruptly within the last year.

The following statement is taken from the verbatim accounts of a transcribed therapy session with a sixteen-year-old Caucasian girl who attempted suicide by ingesting thirty-one Miltown tablets.

Doctor: Have you had any religious experiences?
Teenager: Billy Graham Crusade in 1963. [This was a year before the attempt.]
Doctor: Umhm.
Teenager: That's when I really accepted Jesus.
Doctor: Did you have an experience?
Teenager: I started to cry. I started to realize that I'd been a hypo-crite for all those years, saying I was a Christian, but I'd been beat-ing up on kids and stuff like that. That isn't a Christian.
Doctor: Umhm.
Teenager: And lying—that isn't Christian. And stealing.[31]

The account goes on to describe the ways in which she has since tried to become a "good Christian."

A third position is that of the atheists whose past outlook, being consistent with their present needs, requires no revisions. However, even the atheists may have a second thought and take some added precaution "just in case." An example of this is a seventeen-year-old Mexican-American male who attempted suicide by ingesting twenty-five "reds" (Benzedrine capsules). The case history notes:

Jimmy does not consider himself to be religious, nor are any of his friends. He doesn't know if suicide is a sin or not, but in either case, he believes that sin is forgiven and that there is no life after death. Jimmy doesn't attend the Catholic Church or any other, but said he was plan-ning to go to confession next Saturday.[32]

Another adolescent, an eighteen-year-old Negro male who attempted suicide by drinking battery acid, related the following to the interviewer:

> Between the ages of fifteen and sixteen, James attended the Four Square Church very regularly with his father to please him. After he left his father, his church attendance ended. James does not consider himself religious. He does not believe in an afterlife; "If you're dead you're dead." However, during the interview, whenever he hesitated about answering certain personal questions, he told the interviewer that he would "tell that to a priest." In fact, he thought someone should let a priest know that he was in trouble so that he could come to the hospital and James could confess his sins to him.[33]

A fourth position that may be taken is that of the religious person who, although he is aware that suicide is a mortal sin and that he is going to Hell for it, tries to kill himself anyway. This seems to be contradictory to the position previously outlined by the author, in that it is generally held that one's personal situation is unlikely to improve in Hell. However, a closer analysis reveals that the suicide's position in such cases is equivocal. He is not certain that he is going to Hell, or, if he is, he is not certain that things are worse there. The very ambiguity of death allows at least for the possibility that things will be better. Such a view is not a difficult one to risk, if one is already convinced that things couldn't be worse than they are at present. The following example of this line of reasoning is taken from the diary of a suicide:

> I am sad and lonely. Oh, God, how lonely. I am starving. Oh, God, I am ready for the last, last chance. I have taken two already, they were not right. Life was the first chance, marriage the second, and *now I am ready for death, the last chance. It cannot be worse than it is here.*[34]

Another note, this one from a case of murder-suicide, reads:

> Dearest darling Jane (his separated wife): Don't hate me for taking the life of our son. I have tried in so many ways to send him off with someone, but he would just cry when I speak of it. He said I want you. He wants me. *I'm going to Hell and he wants me.* What do you do with a loving son like that? Let him suffer or take him with you? . . . Why did God give me this brain? Why doesn't He stop me? He puts us on this earth and we do what is best, good and bad. I just wanted one more chance. . . . If I only had one more chance. *Will God give me one more chance?*[35]

Having noted that his wife would not give him another chance and that the friend with whom his wife ran off would not give him another chance (he called the friend to tell him he was about to kill himself, to which the friend replied, "I'm sorry you have to do it this way"), he asks, "Will God give me another chance?" At the opening of the note his going to Hell seems a certainty. However, by its closing there is at least a possibility that God will give him another chance.

Still another note reads:

> *They say you go to Hell for taking your life* . . . there was only one thing I wanted and I drove her so far away that there is no sense kidding myself anymore. . . . *Maybe where I'm going it won't be so lonely.*[36]

A further example from the case histories of adolescent suicide attempters is the account of a sixteen-year-old Caucasian male, who attempted suicide by ingesting forty aspirins:

> I knew I'd go to Hell, but I didn't care what people thought. I probably did hurt my parents, but I didn't do it to make them feel bad.

The record continues:

> He is a "half and half" religious person. He is Catholic and used to attend Catholic Church every week. He had had a spotty attendance ever since the family moved to L.A. about a year ago. He believes that suicide is a sin, but "sometimes you don't care." He believes in Heaven and Hell, but "sometimes I'm doubtful." [37]

Another short suicide note, one of the few the author has encountered with an element of humor, reads:

> Good-bye kid, you couldn't help it. Tell that brother of yours, when he gets where I'm going I hope I'm a foreman down there. I might be able to do something for him.[38]

The humorous element aside, it is clear that if he does become foreman he might be able to do something for himself as well. In any event, he hopes so.

A subset of the perspective noted above—the possibility (if not certainty) of a better life in the next world—is to be found in notes requesting that the survivors pray for them or that God forgive them. Here, as in the form cited above, the very ambiguity of death allows for a renewed hope for a better life in the hereafter. The following are some examples of this:

> I know I am mentally ill . . . and know this is the only way out. *I ask forgiveness of God* and my beloved family. I love them all, but life is not worth living the way I am. I just can't go on the way I am. . . . I have killed myself. *God help me.*[39]

> Dear Mary: I'm just too tired and sick of trying to continue. Sorry it had to be this way. I'm sure everything will work out for the best. Keep everything as quiet as possible. Say I had a heart attack. As ever, Bill. *God forgive me.* And God bless you and John.[40]

> Dear Brothers and Sisters: I am so sorry to do this thing, but I am very sick and unhappy and cannot continue on. *Please do not feel sorry for me because I am sure I will be better off.* . . . *Pray for my soul and God bless you all.* Bob.[41]

> Nobody needs to put flowers on my grave. They did nothing for me while I was alive. *My dear Hedeli forgive your father. He had no choice. May God forgive me.*[42]

> Everything was tried to save me. Forgive me, and don't feel badly. Grant me rest. *Pray God be merciful to me.* The lake shall be my grave. Your tired M.[43]

Still another kind of salvation in the hereafter that the potential suicide may entertain centers around the idea of a happy reunion. This may take one of three forms: their returning in an old or new form to rejoin those on earth; their remaining in Heaven and the others joining them; or their joining those already deceased. The following is an example of reincarnation, the first form of reunion.

> Dear Sister, don't be afraid for my sake. *I will soon come back or you will soon hear from me.* Love, Idy.[44]

The notion of the dead communicating with the living is not so novel as one might suppose. For example, Bishop Pike claimed that his son (a suicide at the age of twenty-two) gave him the following message after his death:

> I am sorry I did this. I had problems. I wanted out. I wish I had carried on and worked on the problems in more familiar surroundings.[45]

The Bishop, addressing an overflow audience at a Berkeley church, went on to say: "If Christ talked to his disciples after his death, then why can't we all do the same?" [46]

The adolescent suicide attempters also provide examples of this reincarnation interpretation of religious dogma. Mary H. is a sixteen-year-old Negro girl. Her case history states:

Mary does not consider herself to be a religious person, but she does attend the Methodist Church. . . . One of the most important aspects of her religion is that she believes in reincarnation.[47]

It need hardly be pointed out that reincarnation is not an important aspect of Methodist teaching. However, such religious contradictions were not uncommon among the adolescent suicide attempters. For example, parents had in several instances pointed out to the adolescent after the attempt that suicide was a mortal sin. At this point the adolescent began to feel very guilty and to act as though he had never heard of this before (even though suicide was specifically prohibited).

Another example from the case histories of the use of reincarnation is that of a fifteen-year-old Jewish boy, who until moving to Los Angeles about a year ago attended an Orthodox synagogue regularly. His mother also claims that until that time she had kept a kosher home. The case history notes:

Milton claims that he is not religious at all and that most of his friends aren't either. He does, it seems, believe in reincarnation. Having mentioned this, he refused to discuss it any further.[48]

The following are two examples of the second form of reunion:

Dear Edna and Fritz: I thank you both for your kindness, patience and care. I can no longer stand my nervousness. I am sorry to make you who have been so good to me suffer. All the people with whom I've been in contact were not very nice to me. Please forgive me everything I've done to you. . . . *May God forgive me,* I can't stand it any longer. *We will meet in the afterlife.*[49]

My dearest darling Rose: *By the time you read this I will have crossed the divide to wait for you. Don't hurry.* Wait until sickness overtakes you, but don't wait until you become senile. *I and your other loved ones will have prepared a happy welcome for you.*[50]

An example of the third form of reunion reads:

Cause I'm very very lonesome for my wife, brothers and sisters and fear blindness.[51]

Granting that it is not religious prohibitions that prevent suicide and that it is caused by the nature and ordering of the individual's problems, religious teachings may exert a kind of temporary holding effect on the individual. If things do not improve with time, however, any religious prohibition may be resolved by one or another of the alternatives being discussed here.

> Oh I know I must be wrong, but if so, why does God let me live? Life is unbearable to me now, and if things don't get better, something happens.[52]

In concluding this discussion of the way in which religion is used to construct the moral justification of suicide, the author hopes that he has demonstrated why the study of the role of morality in suicide is not "an insoluble problem," nor is it destined to produce "uninstructive data." In fact, it has already shown every evidence of offering a "law" of considerable interest.

It is strange that Durkheim should have believed otherwise. After all, the basis on which we were advised to seek the "causes" of suicide rates (as opposed to the "essential characteristics" of suicide) is that the stability of suicide rates is indicative of some greater underlying truth which will explain the "why" of social suicide rates, if not the "how" of suicide.

> The suicide rate is therefore a factual order, unified and definite, as is shown by both its permanence and its variability. For this permanence would be inexplicable if it were not the result of a group of distinct characteristics, solidary one with another, and simultaneously effective in spite of different attendant circumstances; and this variability proves the concrete and individual quality of these same characteristics, since they vary with the individual character of society itself.[53]

Yet the stability of rates is taken to be a sign of weakness, when it is found in the categories of motives attributed by officials to suicides.[54] Durkheim goes on to argue:

> What are called statistics of motives of suicides are actually statistics of opinions concerning such motives of officials, often of lower officials, in charge of this information service. Unfortunately, official establishments of fact are known to be often defective even when applied to obvious material facts comprehensible to any conscientious observer and leaving no room for evaluation. How suspect must they be considered when applied not simply to recording an accomplished fact, but to its interpretation and explanation! . . . The value of improvised judgments, attempting to assign a definite origin for each special case from a few hastily collected bits of information is, therefore, obviously slight.[55]

Having made much of this point in an attempt to belittle the official designation of motives and their potential to explain the "causes" of suicide rates, Durkheim says nothing of how the "improvised judgments" of officials were any more valid when it came to assigning the cause of death in any particular case to "suicide." Certainly, these officials were unaware of Durkheim's definition of suicide. Even if they had been aware of it, one cannot help but wonder on what basis they would have decided who fitted the definition. The definition reads: "The term suicide is applied to all cases of death resulting directly or indirectly from a positive or negative act of the victim himself, which he knows will produce this result." [56] In order to make a reasonable choice in assigning the cause of death, it would be required that one be able to establish whether or not "at the moment of the acting the victim knows the certain results of his conduct, no matter what reason may have led him to act thus." [57] We are told that the above-mentioned may be established by "an easily recognizable feature, for it is not impossible to discover whether the individual did or did not know in advance the natural results of his action." [58] How one went about establishing this easily recognizable feature is an element in the discussion that is conspicuously absent. Indeed, one wonders why "it is not impossible" to discover whether, at the time of his act, the individual is aware in advance of the outcome of that act (or aware of anything else), if we do as Durkheim repeatedly suggests we do and not concern ourselves with the individual, his motives, or his ideas.

There is a considerable literature on the problem of establishing the individual's intent with respect to the act of suicide.[59] Rather than acknowledge and deal with this problem (especially after he specifically stipulates in the opening of the book that his case rests on the scientific establishment of and adherence to a definition of suicide based on intent), Durkheim ignores his own definition for the remainder of the book and somehow overlooks the fact that the officials responsible for compiling the statistics on which his work is based have also ignored it.

I have already indicated why I believe a study of the individual's motives and morals is not only useful but essential in the search for a better understanding of suicide. The data presented in this chapter, and their analysis, offer one encouraging way of pursuing such a study. However, it need not be limited to this. It can also provide a means of explaining social suicide rates. The following discussion is intended to caution the reader not to use the author's analysis in this way even if it seems expedient to do so.

It may be argued that Durkheim and others concerned with the interpretation of official rates have, in the course of establishing the "legitimacy" of the etiological approach, excluded themselves from another means of "succeeding" in this undertaking, by placing the study of the individual and his morals, motives, and intentions outside the realm of legitimate inquiry. I referred in the previous sentence to the possibility of "succeeding" in the interpretation of rates. By this I meant that it is possible to make a convincing case for the correspondence found between the rates and certain social phenomena. Such a correspondence and its accompanying explanation constituted for Durkheim the establishment of "causes." The author feels that the widespread acceptance of these assumptions and procedures is unfortunate, not only because there are good grounds on which to question the validity of rates (are there actual suicides to constitute the statistics representing the rates of suicide given in the categories of age, race, sex, religion, and so on) but because it is possible to explain the correspondence found between the rates and any number of social phenomena in an equally convincing manner. Not only is it possible to explain the rates in a variety of ways but it is impossible, using this approach, to know which, if any, of these alternatives is correct, since there are no grounds outside the interpretation itself by which to resolve such a question.

For example, it is possible, using the author's sources of data and form of analysis and Durkheim's own arguments, to explain the descending rates of suicide found among Protestants, Catholics, and Jews, but for reasons completely different than Durkheim supposed. To do so requires only that we try to view religious teachings, not as Durkheim saw them, but as they are seen by the potential suicide. Such a perspective has already been outlined in this chapter. By adopting this approach, we can provide a reasonable and consistent alternative to Durkheim's hypothesis and explain why suicide rates range from high to low among Protestants, Catholics, and Jews. Such an explanation would also eliminate the very loose reasoning Durkheim was obliged to resort to in order to resolve the Jewish question. For example, among the three major religions, Jews alone have no specific moral prohibitions against suicide.[60] One needs to infer these prohibitions from the "sacredness of life" argument. Neither do Jews place much emphasis on the hereafter and Heaven or Hell;[61] yet they are somehow restrained. Then, too, we are told that, although the Jews are more educated (a condition predisposing to suicide), the nature of their education is different.[62] However, the nature of higher education among Catholics and Protestants is the same.[63] These and

many other logical inconsistencies too numerous to list here are not sat-
isfactorily dealt with in Durkheim's argument that it is the relative
extent of social integration among Protestants, Catholics, and Jews
that is responsible for their suicide rates.

An alternative hypothesis in terms of "moral casuistry" can be stated
as follows: The potential suicide, whether Catholic, Protestant, or
Jew, feels the necessity of killing himself because of the nature, ordering, and severity of his problems as he sees them. In contemplating suicide, he hopes to achieve essentially two ends, if possible: (1) to rid
himself of the unbearable burden his life's circumstances have placed
on him and (2) to renew his hope for a better lot in the hereafter. It
needs further to be noted that whereas religious prohibitions are not
ultimately binding in preventing suicide, the prospect that one will be
rid of his current set of problems and achieve a better life in the hereafter is binding and serves to encourage suicide. To the extent that
the potential suicide is able, as we have shown, to resolve the moral
prohibitions of suicide and at the same time convince himself that he
will reap all the benefits of a virtuous Christian dying of natural
causes, Judaism holds less promise for future happiness than Catholicism and Protestantism. The Jew, it is true, can "put an end to it all,"
a prospect that is not unattractive for one who feels that he has suffered so much for so long with the expectation of more to come. It is
not surprising that some Jews do commit suicide. However, the prospect that "when you're dead, you're dead" is hardly as attractive as
living on forever in Heaven, or even Hell, when it is supposed that
Hell promises fewer problems than life or, at the very least, the possibility of fewer problems.

Protestantism and Catholicism have provided for the explicit prohibition of suicide through the vehicle of Heaven and Hell. Durkheim's
mistake was to suppose that the potential suicide both knew and internalized his religious beliefs and that these beliefs were binding. As
previously noted, the potential suicide does not think in this way. As a
result, the position of Catholicism and Protestantism from the perspective of the potential suicide is not to discourage, but to encourage suicide, at least with respect to the relative effects of Judaism. The gist of
this is that religious prohibitions do not prevent suicide; therefore, the
fact that Protestants and Catholics are both explicit in their prohibition of it does not per se affect their rates of suicide. This is as Durkheim supposed, but for completely different reasons. However, what
does encourage suicide in the suicidal person is his ability to convince
himself that he will finally be rid of his present troubles and, at the
same time, be able to establish the prospect for a brighter future in

the hereafter. In this regard, the promise is greater for Protestants and Catholics than for Jews. While this offers an explanation for why Jews have lower rates than Protestants and Catholics, it does not explain why Catholics have lower rates than Protestants. As Durkheim pointed out, Protestants are more rational and individualistic in their interpretation of their religious beliefs than Catholics. This makes it easier for the Protestant than for the Catholic to accomplish the "rationalization" necessary to convince himself that in death he is about to be rid of his present troubles and to embark on a better life (the explicit religious prohibitions notwithstanding). Hence, Protestants have a higher suicide rate than Catholics, who have a higher rate than Jews.

The argument above, while it has the advantage of being empirically based and is more consistent and parsimonious than Durkheim's "lack of social integration" interpretation of suicide rates, is not being advocated by the author as an alternative explanation. Rather, it has been presented to show why sociologists would do well to re-evaluate the wisdom of seeking a better understanding of social phenomena through the interpretation of official rates. The author has briefly outlined in the course of the chapter some of the serious dilemmas one is sure to encounter in applying the etiological approach.[64] An alternative source of data, as well as methodological and theoretical orientation, has been presented by the author in this discussion.

The analysis of suicide notes and case-history material presented here has shown how suicides and suicide attempters were able, by their own accounts, to use religion to construct the moral justification of suicide. This is a radical position to offer in that it has been generally held that the teachings of Protestantism, Catholicism, and Judaism either all work equally well to prevent suicide or, in the case of Durkheim's argument, have little or no influence on suicide prevention. In order to arrive at the formulation above, the author was obliged from the outset to take the accounts of the suicides seriously. Furthermore, in order to evaluate these accounts, it was necessary to place them in the context of the suicide's past and present situation and future expectations as he related them. The author recommends that such procedures be generally applied to the study of all social phenomena. To exclude the individual, his beliefs, motivations, and intentions, from the legitimate concern of sociological inquiry is to exclude the discipline from the means of studying suicide in particular and society in general. Given Durkheim's intentions, I need hardly point out how ironic this would be.

NOTES

1. Émile Durkheim, *Suicide: A Study in Sociology* (New York: The Free Press, 1951), p. 151.
2. Peter Sainsbury, *Suicide in London* (London: Chapman and Hall, 1955).
3. Jack D. Douglas, *The Social Meanings of Suicide* (Princeton: Princeton University Press, 1967); Harvey Sacks, "Sociological Description," *Berkeley Journal of Sociology,* VIII (1963), 1–16.
4. Jerry Jacobs, "A Phenomenological Study of Suicide Notes," *Social Problems,* XV, No. 1 (Summer, 1967), 60–72.
5. Louis I. Dublin, *Suicide: A Sociological and Statistical Study* (New York: Ronald, 1963), p. 101.
6. *Ibid.,* pp. 102–103.
7. Helen Silving, "Suicide and Law," in Edwin S. Shneidman and Norman L. Farberow, eds., *Clues to Suicide* (New York: McGraw-Hill, 1957), p. 80.
8. Durkheim, *op. cit.,* p. 157.
9. Douglas, *op. cit.,* p. 205.
10. Heinrich Zimmer, *Philosophies of India* (New York: Meridian, 1957), p. 167.
11. Silving, *op. cit.,* p. 80.
12. *Ibid.*
13. *Ibid.*
14. Dublin, *op. cit.,* pp. 103–104.
15. David Hume, "Of Suicide," in Alasdair McIntyre, ed., *Hume's Ethical Writings* (New York: Collier, 1965), pp. 305–306.
16. Jerry Jacobs, "Adolescent Suicide Attempts: The Culmination of Progressive Social Isolation," unpublished doctoral dissertation, copyright 1967, p. 47. For a more detailed analysis of these aspects, the reader is referred to these additional works of the author: Joseph D. Teicher and Jerry Jacobs, "Adolescents Who Attempt Suicide: Preliminary Findings," *American Journal of Psychiatry,* CXXII, No. 11 (1966), 1248–1257; Joseph D. Teicher and Jerry Jacobs, "The Physician and the Adolescent Suicide Attempter," *Journal of School Health,* XXXVI, No. 9 (November, 1966), 406–415; Jerry Jacobs and Joseph D. Teicher, "Broken Homes and Social Isolation in Attempted Suicides of Adolescents," *International Journal of Social Psychiatry,* XIII, No. 2 (1967), 139–149.
17. Ludwig Brinswanger, "The Case of Ellen West," in Rollo May *et al.,* eds., *Existence* (New York: Basic Books, 1958), p. 267.
18. One of a set of 112 suicide notes from persons successful in suicide in the Los Angeles area.
19. *Ibid.*

20. *Ibid.* See footnote 18.
21. W. Morgenthaler and Marianne Steinber, "Letzte Aufzeichnungen von Selbstmordern," Beih, Schweiz. *Z. Psychol., Anwend.,* I (1945), 150, contains forty-seven suicide notes of persons committing suicide, Case 34–35, in Bern between 1929 and 1935.
22. "Genuine and Simulated Suicide Notes," in Shneidman and Farberow, *op. cit.,* p. 209.
23. "A Youth Who Was Prematurely Tired," in Ruth Cavan, *Suicide* (Chicago: University of Chicago Press, 1928), p. 243.
24. James Jan-Tausch, *Suicide of Children: 1960–63, New Jersey Public School Students* (Trenton: New Jersey Department of Education), p. 18.
25. "Marion Blake and Her Loves," in Cavan, *op. cit.,* p. 204.
26. D. J. West, *Murder Followed by Suicide* (Cambridge: Harvard University Press, 1966), p. 42.
27. Brinswanger, *op. cit.,* p. 258.
28. "Case Histories of Fifty Adolescent Suicide Attempters Completed during Adolescent Suicide Attempt Project," NIMH Grant #1R11MH0-1432–02, 1964–1967, University of Southern California School of Medicine, Department of Psychiatry. Codirected by the author. Hereafter cited as "Case Histories."
29. *Ibid.*
30. *Ibid.*
31. *Ibid.*
32. *Ibid.*
33. *Ibid.*
34. "Marion Blake and Her Loves," p. 205.
35. See footnote 18.
36. *Ibid.*
37. "Case Histories."
38. "Genuine and Simulated Suicide Notes," pp. 214–215.
39. See footnote 18.
40. "Genuine and Simulated Suicide Notes," p. 213.
41. See footnote 18.
42. Morgenthaler and Steinber, *op. cit.,* Case No. 17.
43. *Ibid.,* Case No. 16.
44. *Ibid.,* Case No. 40.
45. *Ibid.,* p. 1.
46. San Francisco *Chronicle,* October 2, 1967, p. 1.
47. "Case Histories."
48. *Ibid.*
49. Morgenthaler and Steinber, *op. cit.,* Case No. 9.
50. See footnote 18.
51. *Ibid.*
52. "Marion Blake and Her Loves," p. 200.

53. Durkheim, *op. cit.*, p. 51.
54. *Ibid.*, p. 149.
55. *Ibid.*, pp. 148–149.
56. *Ibid.*, p. 44.
57. *Ibid.*
58. *Ibid.*
59. See, for example: Harold Garfinkel, *Studies in Ethnomethodology* (Englewood Cliffs: Prentice-Hall, 1967), pp. 11–18, 76–104; and Robert E. Litman *et al.*, "Investigations of Equivocal Suicides," *Journal of American Medical Association,* CLXXXIV (June 22, 1963), 924–929.
60. Durkheim, *op. cit.*, p. 170.
61. *Ibid.*
62. *Ibid.*, p. 168.
63. *Ibid.*
64. For a more complete discussion of these problems, the reader is referred to works of Garfinkel, *op. cit.*, pp. 18–24; Sacks, *op. cit.*; and Douglas, *op. cit.*, pp. 163–234.

Part II

*Studies in the
Social Construction
of Moral Meanings*

9

The Construction of
Conceptions of Stigma
by Professional Experts

Robert A. Scott

Throughout history, the mentally ill, the crippled, the mentally retarded, the maimed, the poor, and others who were similarly stigmatized as morally inferior have occupied an unenviable status in most
societies of the world. Traditionally, such persons have been viewed
as helpless dependents, incapable of mastering the elementary skills
essential for engaging in productive social and economic activities.
Mingled with these ideas were certain imputations about moral culpability. The mere possession of a stigmatizing condition or attribute
was often viewed as prima facie evidence of God's punishment for
one's sins. Those who were stigmatized usually were not allowed to
mingle freely in the community nor were they ordinarily accorded the
rights and benefits that were extended to average citizens. Many of
these people were placed in asylums, where they were treated in punitive and degrading ways; others were at the mercy of their families or
acquaintances, who were obliged by the community to provide for
them but seldom felt compelled to treat them in the same way that ordinary persons were treated.

In the last hundred years or so in industrialized societies of the
Western world, a notable departure from this traditional pattern has
occurred.[1] Among the enlightened in these societies, the view has
emerged that helplessness and dependency are not inherent in condi-

tions that are stigmatizing, so that many such people are able to engage in productive social and economic activities if given help and training. Moreover, the existence of traits or qualities that stigmatize is no longer explained by recourse to notions of moral culpability; rather, the deficiencies are seen as the product of ordinary genetic, psychological, social, and economic processes that operate in all societies. Along with these changes in the connotations associated with stigma there has been a corresponding shift in the locus of responsibility for the education, rehabilitation, and care of people affiliated with them. This responsibility has been moving from the family to professionally trained people who claim to have a special expertise which uniquely qualifies them to understand and treat the problems associated with stigmatizing conditions.[2] Many of these experts have trained in social work, rehabilitation counseling, work with the deaf, work with the blind, psychiatry and the various mental health professions. Moreover, a majority of them work in specialized helping organizations, most of which have become large, complex bureaucratic structures. These trends toward professionalization and bureaucratization are having an enormous impact both on stigmatized individuals and on the conceptions and reactions that laymen have to them.

For one thing, hopelessness, which has been the traditional fate for these people, is gradually giving way to genuine opportunities for education and employment. Because of these opportunities, the social status of the stigmatized is being transformed from one of economic dependence and social isolation to one of economic self-sufficiency and increasing involvements in the main stream of community life. The Vocational Rehabilitation Administration, for example, which sponsors the largest federal program of rehabilitation for the physically disabled in our country, reports that more than 100,000 people who could not work last year because of a physical handicap have been rehabilitated to work.[3] Moreover, through the efforts of this administration, traditional folk stereotypes about physical disabilities are being challenged and replaced with more humane ideas about the limitations and consequences that disabling conditions have for personality and social functioning. It is clear that life chances for the person who has a physical disability have been dramatically improved by these efforts.

These professional and bureaucratic trends have also affected the socialization of stigmatized persons into the social role of deviant. The claim of expertise in treating problems associated with stigmatizing conditions implies that the claimant possess a specialized body of knowledge which has been acquired through careful professional training and/or years of clinical experiences. As a rule, this knowledge is codified into theories about particular conditions such as mental illness, blindness, deafness, poverty, and so on. These theories contain general assertions about the nature of human behavior, its causes, and how to change it; and specific assertions about the nature of the particular stigmatizing condition in question. Specific assertions describe the experts' beliefs about such things as the causes of the condition, the basic problems and crises which people who have it will experience, the ways in which these problems might be solved, the self-attitudes and patterns of behavior that they should develop if they are to make a successful adjustment to it, and the relationships between the condition and normalcy. In these theories, then, are found the meaning which a stigma has to the expert. They embody a kind of putative identity that the expert has constructed for the person who comes to him for help. This putative identity is manifested as the expert's expectations for the clients' self-attitudes and behavior. Some clients internalize these expectations into their self-concepts; others simply play the part that their counselor expects them to play, if only because they want to matriculate through the program as quickly and effortlessly as possible. In either case, this putative identity contained in an expert's theory about a stigma is a potent factor in the client's socialization into the role of deviant.

More and more the character of stigma in industrialized societies is changed to fit professional experts' conceptions. This chapter is about these theories of stigmata that experts have constructed. In it, I will present illustrations of expert conceptions about stigma and attempt to show how these conceptions reflect aspects of the social, cultural, and economic environments of which the experts are a part. I will try to assess the kind of impact that expert conceptions of stigmata have on the individuals on whom they are imposed, and I will comment on the process by which these meanings are constructed.

There are two terminological clarifications I want to make. First, I use terms like "professional ideologies about stigma," "constructed meanings of stigma," "theories of stigma," and "expert conceptions of stigma" to refer to the experts' beliefs, assumptions, and definitions about conditions that are stigmatizing. The experts whose conceptions interest me are not those who are removed from social control agencies, but the ones who are, so to speak, on the firing line. It is the people who design and administer programs and engage in education, care, and rehabilitation at the clinical level whose conceptions and definitions have the greatest impact for change.

Second, I use the term "stigma" to refer to any physical condition, personality trait, or attribute of behavior which marks an individual as being morally inferior.[4] Throughout I will refer to many forms of stigma, including mental illness, crime, delinquency, poverty, blindness, mental retardation, and alcoholism. It is the fact of moral deviation which is common to all of them—the sense of moral inferiority, culpability, and depravity—that allows me to regard them as comparable phenomena.

Variations in Expert Conceptions of Stigma

It is common knowledge among social scientists that stigmatizing conditions that are formally the same can have different meanings to "natives" or laymen who are from different cultures of the world. A part of the evidence for this generalization is drawn from studies of attitudes toward stigma in different periods of history. Haffter, for example, has traced the attitudes found in European folklore toward handicapped children from the Middle Ages to the late nineteenth century.[5] He reports that at the beginning of the Middle Ages, abnormal children were viewed as potential harbingers of good fortune, but that by the late nineteenth century they were seen as evil creatures who had been punished by a vengeful God. Hes and Wollstein report that the attitudes toward mental illness expressed in ancient Hebrew texts were basically empathetic and optimistic ones.[6] There was little evidence of the ostracism and intolerance of mental illness that are characteristically found in contemporary societies. Similarly, Davis reports that prostitution has not always been as demeaning as it is in the contemporary Western world.[7] In ancient Roman society, certain prostitutes were accorded a special, esteemed status, a fact which is also true for certain classes of prostitutes in contemporary Japanese society.

Other evidence in support of this generalization comes from anthropological studies of contemporary cultures of the world. From the Human Relations Area Files we learn of societies such as Tibet, Burma, and Turkey where the crippled and maimed are cast aside as lesser human beings; and of other societies, such as Korea and Afghanistan, where people with these same conditions are believed to possess unusual, culturally valued abilities for which they are accorded a special and superior status. This basic finding is systematically documented in research by Robert Edgerton on cultural variations in the moral meaning of hermaphroditism.[8] According to Edgerton, in our society such persons are viewed as freaks who are encouraged to assume either a male or a female role. He states, "all concerned, from parents to physicians, are enjoined to discover which of the two natural sexes the intersexed person most appropriately is and then to help the ambiguous, incongruous and upsetting 'it' to become at least a partially acceptable 'him' or 'her.'" [9] In contrast, the Navahos offer the hermaphrodite a high-status position in life. Intersexed persons are believed to be the supernaturally designated custodians of wealth, and any family with an intersexed child born to it has its future wealth and success assured. Special care is taken with such children; they are accorded unusual favoritism; and as they grow up they are treated with respect and reverence. A third meaning of intersexuality is found among the Pokot of East Africa. The genital ambiguity of the hermaphrodite in this culture becomes public knowledge from the moment of the child's birth. He is given no opportunity to "pass" as a male or female; indeed, "it" is forbidden to aspire to fulfill ordinary sex role expectations of any sort. Intersexed persons are, therefore, permitted to remain in the Pokot community, but only as members of a kind of third, inferior sexual status.

These illustrations are quite striking; it is not difficult to understand why the generalizations that they support have become common knowledge to the social scientist so quickly. What is not so apparent in the social science literature on stigma is that there are equally striking differences in the meanings of stigma that are found in experts' theories about them. Perhaps one reason why this fact has not been clearly seen is that these differences in meanings are masked by a common, highly vocal commitment on the part of experts to the basic ideal of assisting those who have such conditions to achieve some semblance of a normal life. It is only when one begins to study how expert theories about stigma are actually implemented that these differences in meanings become apparent. I want to present a number of examples to illustrate this point; I will begin with some from a study of blindness.

The significance of these examples from work for the blind will be more apparent to the reader if he is aware of a basic fact about the condition of blindness. It is that the only restriction which the condition itself imposes on an individual results from the fact that the absence of vision prevents him from relating directly to his distant environment.[10] It therefore follows that people who cannot see will be unable to navigate in unfamiliar environments without mechanical aids or assistance from others. If they are totally blind, they will not have direct access to the printed word, nor can they directly experience such things as distant scenery, paintings, or objects such as buildings, that are too large to be apprehended by touch. One can infer from these facts that blind people will not be able to engage in certain types of activities such as reading ink print, flying airplanes, playing tennis, and so on. There is little else, however, that can be predicted about blind people from the nature of the condition alone. With this fact in mind, I want to begin my discussion of blindness by examining some of the theories about it that have been developed by professional experts in a number of different countries.

In the United States, workers for the blind espouse many different theories about blindness. Most of these theories are cast in psychological terms. In them, the focus is on the impact which blindness is thought to have on personality and psychological adjustment.[11] Many experts believe that the loss of vision is a basic blow to self and personality so that deep shock inevitably follows the onset of this condition. Grief and depression also occur; the former because of the loss of basic skills for coping with everyday life, and the latter because of the resulting disorganization of the total personality. A basic goal of rehabilitation is adjustment to blindness. In most expert theories, a blind person is viewed as adjusted when he has faced and fully accepted the fact that he is blind; only then can he be ready to learn the skills and attitudes that enable him to compensate for the losses he has suffered. The final product of rehabilitation is the birth and evolution of a new self: that of a blind man who accepts his condition, having learned to live with it.

Workers for the blind in other countries have defined the meaning of blindness differently. Leading experts in Sweden, for example, regard blindness as little more than the loss of one sense modality. These workers say, "Blindness does not mean that their [blind persons'] other senses are blunted, that their personality has been blotted out or that the structure of the abilities that the individual has been equipped with has undergone a change." [12] Rather, "Blindness is a technical handicap. It can be compensated by the mastery of new techniques and by the use of technical aids." [13] It is recognized that learning to use technical aids correctly implies an acceptance of blindness; however, the "real way back to a normal life [requires the] acquisition of a new technique . . . and the use of technical aids." [14] Great reliance is placed on the development and mastery of technical equipment such as travel guides, special devices for the home and for personal grooming, reading devices, and the like. Rehabilitation is viewed as a process of "learning how to use techniques and technical aids most effectively, and, where necessary, of developing new devices and techniques to aid the particular needs of specific individuals." [15]

The psychiatric counseling, clinical therapy, and adjustment training that are a standard part of most rehabilitation programs for the blind in America are played down or omitted in virtually all Swedish programs.

Professional ideologies about blindness among leading workers for the blind in England are cast in terms of "mood states." These workers feel that the blind are especially vulnerable to the doldrums; they are constantly in danger of becoming depressed and filled with despair about their plight. One of the chief goals of work with the blind is to buoy their spirits. To this end, rehabilitation centers have been established to which many blind people return for a few weeks each year. These centers are usually found in surroundings near the sea. There is a distinctive air of cheerfulness about them which is particularly noticeable when staff members interact with clients. Music is everywhere, and much of the day is spent in diversionary social and recreational activities. Training in mechanical aids such as Braille or the "white cane" is undertaken primarily because it provides the worker with opportunities to "cheer up" his client. In some countries, such as our own and Sweden, the ability to be independent in mobility and other activities of everyday life is a quality which many experts feel a blind man should have. In England, however, many of the blind to whom their leading experts point with the greatest pride and admiration are unable to walk about at all unless they are guided by someone who can see. The meaning of blindness which these workers for the blind in England have constructed centers around good-naturedness and cheerfulness in the face of adversity.

In Italy, and to a lesser extent France, provisions for the blind have been traditionally linked with the Catholic Church. In these countries, some expert meanings of blindness have been formulated in theological terms. According to these theories, blindness is regarded as a kind of spiritual or religious problem, carrying with it the imputation either that those who are blind have had a serious "falling out" with God, or, alternatively, that the blind are a special "chosen" group who are able to enjoy spiritual experiences ordinarily denied to those who can see. The experts who embrace the former meaning think of rehabilitation as a process of prayer and meditation aimed at achieving a new communion with God; those who advocate the latter meaning seek to cultivate and deepen the blind person's special spirituality.

These conceptions of blindness are the ones espoused by some leading workers for the blind in each country. They should not be interpreted as full statements of the "English" or "American" or "Swedish" view of blindness. Indeed, the disagreements among workers for the

blind in some of these countries are so great that it would be misleading to suppose that there is a single conception of this disability. The
point of the examples is to draw our attention to the fact that professional experts may impute different meanings to stigmatizing conditions which are formally the same. We see these differences especially
from a cross-cultural perspective; but, once sensitized to them, we can
begin to make finer discriminations in the meanings of stigma among
experts who are from the same culture. I can illustrate this point with
some examples from work for the blind in America.

I have stated that psychological adjustment is a major theme in
many practice theories of blindness in work for the blind in America.
There are, however, substantial differences among workers for the
blind in different kinds of rehabilitation centers regarding the kinds of
behavior patterns that constitute evidence of adjustment. For example,
some agencies that are sponsored by the Catholic Church emphasize
the discarding of an old self that is no longer living ("the sighted
self") and the rebirth of a new one ("the blind self").[16] Other agencies, which are sponsored predominantly by Jewish philanthropies,
conceive of adjustment in psychoanalytic terms; they draw heavily on
the services of psychoanalysts, psychiatrists, psychiatric social workers,
and clinical psychologists. Rehabilitation is organized around group
and individual therapy sessions, and the agency itself often tries to
create a total therapeutic environment. Still other agencies, which are
predominantly Protestant-supported, see adjustment in terms of work.
Work is said to have therapeutic value in its own right; employment is
the prime indicator of successful adjustment; and preparation for
work is an important focus of rehabilitation activities.

Another illustration of differences of meaning is found in the actual
operations of rehabilitation centers. All rehabilitation centers and related agencies for the blind in the United States are committed to the
goal of helping blind people to become independent and self-sufficient. At the concrete, operational level, there are some important differences of interpretation of this principle. Some centers interpret this
goal to mean that many disabled people have the capacity to function
independently in the everyday life of the community. To this end,
they provide a variety of services aimed at giving the disabled person
the skills that enable him to do this. Other agencies take the view that
the level of independence and self-sufficiency possible for most disabled people is very slight. It is unrealistic to expect the average client
to go back into the community and to live on his own. In turn, one is
limited as to how much he can hope to accomplish in the way of
training the client for independence; the safest course is to alter the

social and physical environment of the center itself in order to accommodate it to him. In centers which take this approach, the independence and self-sufficiency are achieved by lowering demands to a minimal level, by performing for the individual many of the elementary tasks of everyday life, and by contriving and simplifying the physical environment in other ways.[17] These two approaches to rehabilitation signify differing assumptions about the impact that blindness has on individuals and their capacity to recover from it, which in turn implies that workers for the blind are attaching different meanings to this condition.

The case of blindness is not a unique one; there are equally wide variations in the meanings that experts have constructed for other stigmata as well. Mental illness is a good example. In their study of two mental hospitals in Chicago, Strauss and his colleagues found that there were three different practice theories of mental illness: the psychotherapeutic, the somatotherapeutic, and the sociotherapeutic.[18] According to these investigators, the psychotherapeutic theory of mental disorders is cast entirely in psychological terms. Their etiology lies in psychological processes, and "the impact of intrapsychic systems by either internal or external psychological trauma constitutes the necessary and sufficient condition for the development of mental illness." [19] Treatment involves specific forms of psychotherapy for specific types of illnesses. According to the somatotherapeutic ideology, mental illness involves "malfunctioning of the central nervous system, whether it results from physiological, neurophysiological, biochemical, or physical-chemical dysfunctions." [20] Genetic processes are prominently featured in this ideology; they are seen as "interacting with biological systems to produce aberrations or propensities toward mental abnormality." [21] Therapy is individualized and tends to involve drugs, shock treatment, surgical operations on the brain, and similar medical procedures. The sociotherapeutic ideology of mental illness proceeds from the assumption that the mind is a *tabula rasa* on which mental illness is imprinted. Social factors are clearly preemptive, including early deprivation (in social terms) or later processes in which the external environment impinges stressfully on the organism." [22] The treatment that is utilized by advocates of this ideology is nonspecific; the basic notion is to mobilize a large number of therapeutic resources in a setting that is conducive to recovery and rehabilitation.

Other examples of differences in the meanings of stigma that experts have constructed come from a recent study of alcoholism, delinquency, and crime in the Soviet Union.[23] The Soviet views about these forms of deviance have been constructed from two basic "givens." The first is a belief in the inherent rightness of the socialist state, and the second a belief in the perfectibility of human behavior. Several things are said to follow from these assumptions. One is that crime, delinquency, and drunkenness are not inevitable, as "bourgeois" theories of deviance would imply. In fact, according to the Soviet view, there will be no deviance when the socialist state evolves into its final form. Another implication is that the causes of deviance cannot be found in hereditary and biological factors because these factors are not responsive to social manipulation. Since the social environment can be manipulated, it is in nurture rather than nature that the origins of deviance are sought. These assumptions outline the frame of reference in which Soviet experts have constructed meanings for these three types of deviance.

An obvious question that arises is why deviance occurs in the socialist state if it is not an inevitable by-product of the organization of the society itself. According to the Soviet view, crime, delinquency, and alcoholism are alien survivals (*Perezhitki Proshlogo*) of presocialist society. Alcoholism and drunkenness persist because of

religious traditions in the countryside which support the celebration of numerous religious holidays with heavy drinking, and, in urban areas, workers' traditions which see drinking as one of the manly arts. The latter are viewed as reflections of the brutalized life of the industrial proletariat before the revolution, necessitating some escape from misery. The "lag" in workers' consciousness explains their presence today.[24]

Crime and delinquency are linked to two aspects of capitalism.

First, the existence of a capitalist world outside the USSR, which through propaganda and subversion diverts morally unstable citizens from correct conduct, and second, the existence of vestiges or survivals of capitalism in men's minds and behavior. The latter can only exist due to the backwardness of social consciousness relative to the objective conditions of life in socialist society. It is for this reason that transformations of behavior patterns do not immediately follow radical changes in economic and social organization.[25]

Delinquency, crime, and drunkenness persist in the socialist state for two reasons. The first is that man's consciousness changes more slowly than the social structure changes; the second is "institutional malfunctioning," or the failure of core institutions of Soviet society to socialize the individual adequately. Part of the blame for these forms of deviance lies with institutions such as the family, the school, the factory, and youth organizations for failing to be as effective and efficient as they must be for the true socialist state to be realized. For example, experts on delinquency believe that

> in the failure of particular institutions to perform socialization and control functions adequately, there arise first, direct causes of delinquency, such as improper parental socialization, and secondly, conditions under which these causes may operate more effectively, such as teachers' and managers' indifference to the fate of problems of youth. The causes and conditions combine to produce delinquency.[26]

Crime is a product of institutional malfunctioning as well. The schools, youth organizations, the family, the factory, the courts, the militia, are all failing to perform as expected. According to Connor, three varieties of failure emerge as major factors in crime causation:

> Failure of socialization explains why the consciousness and morality of all Soviet citizens are not up to the level of the new Soviet man. Failure of organizations explains why situations arise in which unstable persons are presented with the impetus which thrusts them toward crime. Failure of control explains why, given an unstable person and a criminal motivation, counterforces do not suffice to prevent the criminal act itself.[27]

It is apparent that many of the institutions that Western experts have identified as responsible for crime and delinquency are cited by Soviet experts as well. Parents, teachers, work groups, and youth groups are all held culpable for these problems. There is, however, disagreement between Soviet and Western experts on two basic points. Among Western experts, urbanization is viewed as a critical factor in explaining crime and delinquency.[28] The Soviets reject this view completely. As Connor notes,

> Soviet urbanization since the revolution is seen as a "positive" influence, in that it has opened up cultural opportunities for former peasant classes, increased the political consciousness of the masses, and generally freed man from the most retrograde influences of traditional rural life. While urbanization under capitalism is characterized by exploitation and misery, as well as great increases in crime and delinquency, under socialism the process yields progressive results.[29]

Second, many Western experts would agree that all societies produce deviance in the sense that social problems are inevitable "spin-offs" of a society's core structures and values. Soviet experts regard this as true of capitalism, but not of socialist states. The explanation for deviance

in the Soviet Union is to be found in the infrastructures of the socialist state and not in the patterns of institutional arrangements of the society.

In spite of the belief that social deviance is a survival of a corrupt
ing capitalist system, the delinquent, the criminal, and the drunkard
are nevertheless held accountable for their actions. According to Connor, Soviet experts believe

> "Shortcomings in moral upbringing" may explain instances of deviant be-
> havior, but they do not excuse the deviant. There is a rough-and-ready
> logic in the Soviet view which dictates that excusing the deviant's be-
> havior only makes it more unlikely that he will reject such behavior.
> Thus, citizens are warned against interpreting the "socialist humanism"
> of Soviet justice as "all-forgiveness," and advised to treat deviants with
> intolerance and condemnation.[30]

While the explanations for these forms of deviant behavior contain
elements that are peculiarly Soviet, most of the preventive and corrective measures which they employ are much less distinctive. Connor reports:

> By and large, these [preventive and corrective measures] are much like
> the measures adopted in other modern societies to deal with deviants,
> and are beset by the same problems. Criminals and delinquents pass
> through a process involving police apprehension, a court trial, and a sen-
> tencing to correctional institutions. Alcoholics encounter essentially the
> same assortment of custodial, medical, and social measures in the USSR
> as in Western societies. Whatever innovations Soviet scholars have made
> in explaining criminal behavior, emphasis on the rehabilitation, rather
> than punishment, of the criminal is generally in line with modern penol-
> ogy. The problems and obstacles to such rehabilitation in Soviet correc-
> tional institutions resemble those encountered elsewhere.[31]

There is, however, one major difference between Soviet and Western methods of social control. In the Western world, most efforts at rehabilitation and correction are focused on the individual who is deviant; in the Soviet Union there is a rather strong insistence on public
involvement in these processes. This approach has been most fully developed in the area of alcoholism. The responsibility of those who are
close to the alcoholic to prevent his excessive drinking by exerting
pressures on him is continually reaffirmed as a core theme of the anti-
alcoholic campaign. Connor cites the case of the Minsk Motor Plant as
one example of the sort of activity that is involved in these campaigns
to mobilize the *Kollektiv*. The management of this plant was forced to

hire many workers whose training and other personal credentials would have meant their rejection in times of less acute labor shortages. Many of them were drunkards, and their excessive drinking bouts were disruptive for production schedules. The management decided that efforts should be made to re-educate them. Fellow workers were appointed to be the guardians of hard-core offenders and were asked to accompany them everywhere. Various shaming techniques were adopted, such as criticizing the drunkard by name in the factory newspaper, displaying his picture in public showcases with descriptions of his offenses, and so on. The most recalcitrant of them were subjected to the "workers' circle," a kind of triallike assembly at which the defendant is made publicly accountable for his offenses. These efforts were not limited just to shaming; attempts were also made to protect the offender and his family and to bring him back into the collective. Thus, fellow workers saw to it that an offender's wages went directly to his wife, and every attempt was made to express public approval when the offender's behavior began to change in desired ways.

These efforts by the Soviets to mobilize and involve the *Kollektiv* in prevention and correction measures are by no means fully institutionalized; still, they represent a departure from the American social control practices.

The American experience with these forms of deviance is more difficult to characterize. There is not just one group of experts such as there is in Soviet society; instead, there are different groups, including social welfare practitioners, academic social scientists, legislators, informed laymen, organizations of deviants, law enforcement officials, and so on. The conceptions of deviance constructed by these various groups often differ and even conflict; which ones prevail depends on the outcomes of ongoing political struggles among these groups for control of resources. This picture is further complicated by the fact that our society is not administered and guided by a monolithic administrative structure and doctrine as the Soviet Union is. As a result, few groups can ever capture control of all the resources of a system; as a rule, even the most powerful ones control only a minority of them. One implication of this fact is that the most powerful groups of experts will succeed in imposing their meanings of deviance on only a part of the system, but not on all of it.[32]

In spite of the difficulties of characterizing the American scene, some qualified statements can be made about the approaches to prevention and correction that are used by our social control agencies. One generalization is that the primary focus of most efforts is on the individual deviant himself. By and large, he is held personally responsible for his own behavior, and he is expected to change it in accord with the ongoing system. Frequently, he is removed from the community and put in a special institution in order to be properly rehabilitated. The methods of rehabilitation, such as the various forms of therapy and counseling, are directed toward helping him to gain a greater insight into himself, thereby enabling him to solve his own problems. By their actions, then, our social control agencies treat the individual who is deviant as though he is the cause of his own problems and as though the solutions to these problems lie in the manipulation of intrapsychic forces.[33]

There are two corollaries to this generalization. One is that, by and large, "normals" are not involved in organized efforts at rehabilitation. That they might be is suggested by some recent social science research on deviant behavior. This research indicates that the origins of such behavior lie not only in the personality and early socialization of the deviant but in the reactions that normals have to him as well.[34] This growing body of research on labeling indicates that corrective measures are not likely to succeed if they are aimed only at the personality of the deviant, but do not attempt to modify the reactions that others have toward him. A second corollary is that corrective efforts are distinctly individualistic. They are aimed at modifying individuals and not at modifying the structure of the society itself. That the social structure may induce deviant behavior is suggested by sociological research which shows that such behavior is an inevitable outcome of the institutional arrangements for allocating means to culturally valued ends.[35] This research suggests that one way to reduce crime might be to modify our current system so that the groups that are currently denied access to legitimate means for achieving wealth would be given fair and genuine opportunities to use them. It is clear that the ethics of individualism and personal responsibility for one's actions are pervasive in the social control structure and in the conceptions of stigma that American experts have constructed.

These examples indicate that there are important differences in the meanings which experts have constructed for stigmatizing conditions which are formally the same. Moreover, even a superficial analysis of these examples indicates that these meanings do not vary randomly; they seem to be related to such things as core cultural values, the experts' professional training, and the institutional settings in which they are practiced. A satisfactory understanding and explanation of the theories of stigma that experts construct will not be possible until we have explicitly spelled out what these relationships are. I want to take a step in this direction by identifying some of these relationships.

Some Determinants of Conceptions of Stigma
That Experts Construct

One of the connotations associated with the notion of a professional ideology is that the conceptions of stigma embodied in them are empirically true, or at least truer than the conceptions which laymen hold. The claim of expertise implies that the claimant has a comprehensive understanding of the nature of stigma and its impact on human behavior—an understanding firmly rooted in scientific knowledge. The illustrative materials from the preceding section suggest that this connotation is partially inaccurate if only because the meaning of a stigma to different experts is often quite different and in some cases even contradictory. Moreover, only a small amount of empirical research has been done on most types of stigma, and only a part of it filters down to the clinical experts whose constructed meanings have the greatest impact on people with stigmatizing conditions.[36] Finally, one of the virtues of a comparative approach to this subject (or any one, for that matter) is that it heightens our ability to see that what may appear to be statements of fact from our perspective are in reality expressions of core values that are woven into the basic assumptive world of our culture. These considerations suggest that the conceptions of stigma contained in professional ideologies are only partly determined by empirical knowledge derived from direct experiences with and scientific studies of stigmatized people. Their content is also determined by, and reflects, certain social, cultural, and political forces in the environments in which experts are immersed and on which they depend for economic support. I will identify what some of these forces are and try to show how they are reflected in the conceptions of stigma that experts construct.

There are four sets of forces that I want to consider. They relate to aspects of experts' cultures, the professions in which they are trained, the organizations for which they work, and the clientele on whom their meanings are being imposed. These particular sets of forces do not exhaust the range of factors that affect the experts' conceptions of stigma.

CULTURAL VALUES

Expert conceptions of stigma reflect prevailing cultural values, attitudes, and beliefs. In a sense, this is inevitable. Experts must use the "native tongue" in order to communicate their constructed meanings to laymen, and the modes of expression that a language affords are grounded in the core values of a culture. Moreover, it is laymen who usually grant legitimacy to experts' claims to special knowledge about stigma; any constructed meanings that are dissonant with lay values, beliefs, and attitudes will probably be rejected as nonsensical. Thus, whatever its other merits may be, a purely mechanical conception of a physical handicap is not likely to "make sense" to people who live in a culture in which religious values are the central ones, just as a religious conception of disability will probably be rejected as old-fashioned in a materialistic culture such as our own. This point is simple enough. However, the connections between expert conceptions of stigma and core values, beliefs, and attitudes of a culture go much deeper than this.

Financial resources are the lifeblood of any organized intervention program. Without money a program simply cannot operate. In all industrialized societies that support such programs these resources are controlled by laymen, a fact that has enormous ramifications for the kind and amount of intervention experts can ever hope to initiate. Their core beliefs, values, and attitudes have a tremendously important bearing on this matter. For one thing, there are certain categories of the stigmatized in all societies who are regarded as undeserving because their past or present actions, or even their personal characteristics, violate some major cultural value. Examples of this point are abundant in our own society. In America, it has been very difficult to generate wide congressional or lay support for rehabilitation programs for the disabled who cannot or will not work. Moreover, the very complexion of our welfare system suggests that it is also difficult to generate much enthusiasm for programs that make cash payments to individuals and families when those payments are based on need and not on deservedness. Or, as a final example, a major goal of the rehabilitation movement in this country has been to remake the disabled person's personality as a prerequisite for acceptance into the community, as though his disability makes him somehow contaminated and therefore unacceptable to ordinary people. These examples suggest that the disabled groups a program can help, and the nature of the help they can hope to receive, are partly dictated by the values that are common to real or prospective benefactors.

There is another way in which cultural values bear on the question of support for intervention programs and therefore bear indirectly on the meanings of stigma that experts construct. It is recognized by many people that effective rehabilitation programs must deal with more than just the stigmatized person; they must also involve the groups of normals whose attitudes and reactions to the stigmatized person control that person's participation in the community. This implies that collective action may be necessary to achieve the objectives of full rehabilitation. However, cultural values may operate to limit the possibilities of collective actions. As Zald notes, "If cultural traditions place a strong emphasis on individual responsibility and action, then collective solutions are likely to be resisted. On the other hand, a group can have values which stress the importance of collective actions as a general rule and, consequently, welfare problems, too, will call forth a collective response." [37] An excellent example of this point is provided by Vogt and O'Dea in their study of two communities in the southwestern United States.[38] One community is predominantly Mormon and the other Texan. In the Mormon community there is a strong belief in community co-operation, whereas in the Texan community there is an equally strong belief in the responsibility of the individual for his own welfare. The authors state that in the Mormon community "the expectations are such that one must show his fellows or at least convince himself that he has good cause for not committing his time and resources to community efforts while in [the 'Texan' community] co-operative actions take place only after certainty has been reached that the claims of other individuals upon men's time and resources are legitimate." [39] The authors show how these different value orientations result in different collective responses to similar problems that are presented to both communities.

Some of the core beliefs and values in our culture are grounded in the assumption that man can control nature and his own fate. However, these are societies in which more fatalistic views prevail; in them, the responsibility for man's fate is thought to reside in external forces of nature that are beyond his control. Where such beliefs prevail, there is much less possibility for mobilizing collective actions than in societies which believe in man's capacity to master nature. Such a view prevailed among the ruling elite of England during much of the nineteenth century. Steven Marcus, in an essay on British responses to the Irish famine of the 1840's, shows how these beliefs, which were firmly grounded in Malthusian theory, worked to prevent the British government from taking collective action to save the Irish from starvation.[40] The famine was viewed by many members of the

British elite as "the will of God"; they encouraged Catholic priests to make this clear to the hungry since, as the treasury official in charge of all Irish relief programs said, "It is hard upon the poor people that they should be deprived of knowing that they are suffering from an affliction of God's providence." [41] In fact, as Marcus shows, means were available for alleviating both the famine and the plague, but they were not used. The Malthusian doctrine that famine was "the last, the most dreadful resource of nature" was the justification for the British inactivity. Marcus concludes that the difference between what might have been done and what actually was done "is in considerable measure a result of ideology, of thought which is socially determined yet unconscious of its determinants." [42] The laissez-faire economic theory had a decisive influence on the responses of the ruling elite of England to the Irish famine. Marcus writes:

> The ideas which combine to make this theory, such as the sacred rights of property, complete liberty of enterprise, the laws of the market and of supply and demand, and of government non-intervention in the economic sphere—were held with fanatical, religious intensity by the largest majority of British politicians and authorities. Any plan for the relief of the Irish was preconditioned by the requirement that private enterprise was in no way to be interfered with.[43]

Marcus illustrates once again the basic principle of sociology that a society's core values are deeply rooted in its economic system; they reflect the system, and they change in response to changes in it. The core values of societies with one type of economic system will therefore be different from core values of societies with a different type of system. In view of the fact that experts' conceptions of stigma reflect a society's core values, we are led to expect that the meanings of stigma that experts construct will systematically vary according to the form of the society's economic system. While there is no conclusive evidence on this point, it is interesting to note that expert conceptions of stigma in societies that have a capitalistic system tend to stress individual responsibility, whereas expert meanings of stigma in societies which have a socialistic economic system tend to stress collective responsibility. Clearly, this is a question that deserves serious and extensive study.

I have stated that laymen's values have an important impact on the construction of expert meanings of stigma in societies in which laymen control the purse strings that are the lifeblood of programs in which these meanings are put into practice. Where this is true, lay

values define the boundaries within which the expert is forced to operate as he constructs his own special meanings of stigma. There is still
another, more direct way in which laymen exert an impact on the
meanings of deviance that experts construct. This impact can be described as follows. The existence of stigma poses at least two sets of
problems: one is for the person to whom the stigma belongs, and the
other is for the community in which that person lives. For each set of
problems, there are corresponding needs. For stigmatized persons, the
problems and the needs revolve around such things as social acceptance, a desire to become invisible in the same way that normal people
are invisible, and a wish for others to interact with them on terms
other than those based on stigma.[44] The problems which stigma poses
for the community are different ones, and the corresponding needs
may not coincide with the ones which the victim has. Stigma threat-
ens the community and presents it with unpleasant problems it would
rather not confront or think about. Old people, poor people, people
who are blind or crippled, and those who are crazy make us uneasy;
they threaten our sense of mastery of nature, and they are disruptive
of routines of daily life. A community's needs relating to stigmata may
be to hide them from public view, or at least to dress them up in a
way that makes them more palatable to laymen or at least less offensive to them. In writing about mental hospitals, Goffman has stated
the point as follows: "Part of the official mandate of the public mental
hospital is to protect the community from the dangers and nuisances
of certain kinds of misconduct." [45] Orlans has described public mental
institutions as "American death camps." [46] He writes, "The aged, insane paupers of the American asylum are surely the most pitiful members of American society; but no one will give them more than pity,
and they also evoke feelings of abhorrence and fear. Asylums are institutions which have been created to remove this sight from our
eyes." [47] Such institutions, then, are places to which the unwanted of
the community can be sent and where they can be "taken care of."

We can see these community needs regarding stigma reflected in
the conceptions of stigma that experts have constructed. For example,
in our society, these conceptions focus attention primarily on the individual to whom the stigma belongs. He is treated as though he is in
some way responsible for having acquired his condition, as though the
solutions to his problems are in his own control. This almost exclusive
emphasis on treating the victims of stigma without involving members
of the community reflects a conception of such conditions that is more
attuned to the community's needs than it is to the needs of those who
are afflicted. Or again, in the last section I described two different ap-

proaches to rehabilitating the blind. One was a restorative approach, aimed at teaching the client the kinds of skills required to function independently in everyday life; the other was a custodial approach aimed at creating a special, protected environment in an organization which specifically catered to the client's disability. Blind people who have been clients in agencies following the restorative approach are often able to move back into the community and function independently in it; those who are the clients of agencies adopting the custodial approach are often only able to function in the environment which the agency has created. Indeed, in many cases they come to depend on it quite heavily. There is reflected in the restorative approach to rehabilitation a conception of blindness which is more attuned to the needs and problems of the blind person; on the other hand, the custodial approach is more attuned to the desires of the community for the stigmatized person. It is significant that there are so few rehabilitation centers in America that follow the restorative approach and that those which do are often in serious fiscal difficulty. Custodial agencies, on the other hand, have endured for many years and in most cases are fiscally sound.

The organized intervention programs that experts manage, therefore, have two different constituencies whose "needs" are not only different but may actually be contradictory. As a rule, the constituency consisting of people in the community is a much more powerful one than the constituency consisting of stigmatized people. The reasons for this are that laymen, and not clients, control an institution's financial resources, so that lay control and power are built directly into the fabric of the program.

In summary, the meanings of stigma that experts construct are deeply influenced by values, attitudes, and beliefs that are central to the society. These values affect the expert in several ways: they are a part of the language he uses to express his meanings; they are an integral part of the assumptive world of the culture against which the meanings of his conceptions of stigma are judged; and they are critical elements in decisions concerning the willingness of laymen to give financial support for programs.

PROFESSIONALIZATION AND THE CONSTRUCTION OF
EXPERT MEANINGS OF STIGMA

The development of organized intervention programs for the stigmatized has been accompanied by the emergence of various professions which claim special expertise with the problems that people with stigma have. The processes of professionalizing that began some years ago have had, and continue to have, an important impact on the meanings of stigma that experts have constructed. The most obvious impact is related to the way in which university- and college-based training programs have developed. One of the core problems confronting training programs has been that of gaining enough legitimacy in the academic community and in the world of practice to permit persons trained in them to make their claims to expertise viable. One of the ways this has been done is by borrowing the concepts, procedures, and approaches that have already been proven and accepted in other, more established professions. Most training programs have therefore adopted concepts and theories from the fields of clinical psychology, psychiatry, psychoanalysis, sociology, and anthropology. While most of these emerging professions have drawn ideas from all these fields, there are substantial differences among them regarding the relative emphasis given to these various perspectives. Some training programs rely very heavily on the core concepts of psychoanalysis; others take their approaches from Rogerian and learning psychology; and there are a few others which have drawn primarily from the field of sociology. These differences in training are reflected in the ideologies which are held by practicing professionals. Strauss and his colleagues, for example, found that "social workers and psychologists took upon themselves the role of ideology bearers, proselytizing and working with other team members specifically in sociotherapeutic ideas and practices. Psychiatrists were either consistently psychotherapeutic in their styles of practice or somatic in their utilization of hospital resources." [48] They conclude, "There is patterning of ideology by profession. Although accommodations are made to institutional conditions, professional differences in ideological position do seem to persist." [49]

There is another way in which the process of professionalization has had its impact on the construction of expert meanings of stigma. In the various fields of practice such as mental health, work for the blind, or work for the deaf, there is not just one profession or group of experts; there are many. It is generally assumed that if any effort at helping the physically disabled or mentally ill is to be truly effective, it must involve the skills and the knowledge of professional educators, clinical psychologists, social workers, physicians, rehabilitation counselors, lawyers, professional administrators, psychiatrists, and so on. It is also generally assumed that one's own particular profession ought to play the central role, with other professions subordinated to it. Conflicts and disputes about this point inevitably arise wherever questions are raised about the distribution of financial resources, the allocation of time with clients to various professionals, the kinds of new staff members to hire, the assignment of physical space, and other related policy decisions. Strauss and his colleagues found that the various professionals that work in mental hospitals must continually attempt to "stake out claims in treatment process" [50] and then protect these claims against infringement from other disciplines. In these conflicts, it is rare for any one profession ever to gain full control over all resources. As a result, the meaning of a stigma such as mental illness that is contained in the ideology of a single profession is seldom put into practice in its entirety. The meanings that are practiced are "hybrids" that emerge out of these negotiations among the professionals who are involved in treating the mentally ill.

There is one final point I want to make about professional ideologies. It is that the process of professionalization is not complete in any of these fields. All of them include many people whose expertise is acquired through experience alone and not through formal training of any kind. The opportunity structure and the career patterns open to the expert who has been professionally trained are quite different from those available to personnel whose expertise has been acquired only through practical experience. The essential difference between them is that the expertise of the former is usually generic in character, whereas the expertise of the latter is highly specific. A person who has been trained in a college-based program learns a set of generic skills and approaches to practice as well as the techniques for tailoring them to different circumstances and problems. This generic approach affords the trained professional a tremendous amount of flexibility in pursuing a career. If he is unhappy with the practice of one agency, he can easily move to another; and if he becomes disenchanted in working with the problems of one group of stigmatized people, his skills and training give him the option of transferring into another field. Moreover, one of the most important elements in his career is his colleagues, whose esteem and praise are at the core of his professional self-image.

In contrast to this, the situation of the individual who has not had any professional training is quite different. Typically, such persons have entered helping organizations at low-level jobs, often as clerical workers, secretaries, or administrative assistants. Over time, they are able to gain practical experience with one or a few of the methods and techniques that go into rehabilitation. For example, some learn how to read and record in Braille; others become proficient in the use of particular types of audiometric equipment; and still others learn how to teach the disabled to use particular kinds of prosthetic devices.

The expertise which is thus acquired is limited in two ways. One is that it is technique-specific. By this I mean that the person may know how to teach a blind man to use a "white cane," but in all likelihood he will not know much about the more general problem of physical mobility. The other limitation is that his expertise is often organization-specific. Until recently, and even today, there has been little uniformity in the techniques used by organizations that specialize in helping people with the same type of stigma. For example, most blindness agencies teach their clients mobility, but the methods that are used are quite different, particularly if the mobility expert has gained his expertise through practical experience rather than through generic professional training. This dual limitation—that acquired expertise tends to be technique-specific and organization-specific—has enormous ramifications for the career lines of the experts involved. For one thing, if a program were to change so that the specific technique that the expert has mastered were to be abolished, it would be difficult for him to move on to other activities that are only related in a generic way. As a result, the person whose expertise is acquired is often resistant to any change that might diminish the significance of his specific skills. For another thing, he does not have the same freedom that trained people have to move from one organization to another. His status, income, and influence usually depend on the continued existence of the specific organization in which they have been built. He will therefore tend to resist any policy that jeopardizes "his" organization. The implication of this for the meanings of stigma that are constructed are that untrained experts will evolve meanings that give primary emphasis to specific techniques and will guarantee the survival of the organization for which they work. An example of this point is found in the distinction between custodial agencies and agencies that attempt to restore blind people to the community. In work for the blind, professionally trained experts have been the most vocal advocates of the restorative approach, while persons whose expertise is acquired have been the most vocal advocates of the custodial approach. It is particularly significant that organizations following the restorative approach encounter the greatest fiscal risks and those following the custodial approach seem to enjoy the greatest economic security.

BUREAUCRATIC PROCESSES AND THE CONTENT OF EXPERT MEANINGS OF STIGMA

Most intervention programs of services for people with stigmatizing conditions are housed in bureaucratic structures, many of which are large and complex. These bureaucratic structures and the processes to which they give rise are reflected in the content of expert ideologies about stigma in several ways. For example, the services that are provided in the context of bureaucratic structures must often be programed and routinized. The individual client as the unit of rehabilitation is often replaced by collectivities such as the class, the ward, or the therapy group. Moreover, the same efficiency and formalization that enable the expert to implement certain kinds of service programs to large numbers of people may also become constraining in the sense that they preclude him from engaging in major innovations. Even the physical plant which a bureaucracy requires may impose serious constraints on the kinds of programs and services that are possible and realistic to carry out.[51] Numerous other examples of this point could be given. However, rather than try to develop a comprehensive list of them, I want to select one in particular and explain it in some detail. The example I have selected is the phenomenon of official or "legal" definitions of conditions that are stigmatizing.

When organized intervention programs first began, informal criteria were used in deciding whether or not an impaired person was eligible for an organization's services. As a rule, the early organizations focused their primary efforts on extreme and obvious cases of disability; because these organizations were local and often private, it was an easy thing to make exceptions in order to help people whose needs were great, but whose impairments may not have been extreme. As the state and federal governments began to support these service programs, the problem of whom to consider blind or deaf or mentally retarded or mentally ill became a serious one. It was no longer possible to decide about eligibility for such services as cash payments, comprehensive rehabilitation, or special tax benefits on an ad hoc or common-sense basis. Uniform guidelines had to be developed for deciding who among the hard of hearing was deaf, or who among those with seeing problems was blind, or who among the intellectually impaired was retarded, and so on. These bureaucratic problems gave rise to the construction of "legal" or "administrative" definitions for various kinds of stigmatizing conditions.

In constructing these definitions there was an important factor that had to be taken into account. Conditions such as total blindness, total deafness, or severe retardation are rare ones in our population. It is difficult to justify national or state programs for people with these impairments when the programs are limited only to those who are the most severely impaired. Moreover, such programs can hope to expand only so long as the populations in need are large ones. It seemed desirable to offer services not only to those who were totally impaired but to the severely impaired as well. These considerations had to be taken into account in constructing legal definitions of stigmatizing conditions. The essential question was, how far toward "normal" should one go? In order to answer, it was necessary to develop highly technical definitions of impairment. The legal definition of deafness that was adopted specified the precise level of decibel discrimination that an individual had to be unable to make before he would be considered deaf. The definition of mental retardation adopted by the American Association of Mental Deficiency defined that condition as "intellectual functioning which originates during the development period and is associated with impairment in adaptive behavior." [52] In practice, a mental retardate may be classified in one of five different levels, the criterion being his test score on standardized measures of intelligence. Legal blindness was defined as "Central visual acuity of 20/200 or less in the better eye with correcting lenses; or central visual acuity of more than 20/200 if there is a field defect in which the peripheral field has contracted to such an extent that the widest diameter of visual field subtends an angle distance no greater than 20 degrees." [53]

One feature of these definitions is that there is not a direct correspondence between them and the ones that a layman would use in labeling others as physically or mentally impaired. In order to determine if an individual who has a severe problem seeing is "legally blind," it is necessary to give him a careful, clinically controlled test of visual acuity. This test requires not only an exact determination of maximum levels of vision discrimination; it also requires that his discrimination levels be ascertained after he has been fitted with glasses that correct his vision to its best possible level. Even so, disagreements about "best corrected vision" are common among people who are experts at measuring visual acuity. Another feature is that the closer one is to the point where the experts' demarcation lines are drawn between normalcy and impairment as it is legally defined, the less correspondence there is likely to be between expert definitions of these conditions as stigmas and the lay person's subjective experiences and reactions to them. This point is extremely important for the following reason. The distribution of visual acuity, intelligence, hearing acuity, and related conditions in the general population all approximate the normal or bell-shaped curve. Thus, the number of people who are totally blind, totally deaf, or severely retarded is quite small, and these numbers increase as we move away from the extremes and toward the normal. The legal definition which demarcates the line between the "legally" impaired and the normal creates a population of impaired people, the largest segment of which falls exactly at or very close to this arbitrary demarcation line. A majority of people who are therefore "legally" blind are, in fact, seeing people with visual acuity of exactly 20/200. Similarly, a majority of those who are mentally retarded according to the current "legal" definition are either borderline or mildly retarded. As one expert on this subject has observed, "Most people who are defined as mentally retarded are not profoundly, severely, or even moderately retarded. Quite the contrary, fully 85% of all mental retardates are only mildly retarded." [54]

It was bureaucratic necessity that led to the creation of legal definitions of impairments. However, once they were constructed, they became sacred and were reified. The "legally deaf" were perceived as deaf, the "legally blind" as blind, and the "legally retarded" as retarded. There often resulted some major discrepancies between the definitions that experts imposed on a person who was impaired and that person's own subjective reactions to his condition. According to the definition used by the expert, a person with a tenth of normal vision is blind; from the perspective of the client, however, a blind man is someone who cannot see. It is difficult for him to understand why experts believe he is "denying reality" when he is looking his counselor squarely in the eye. As for the expert, he has been specially trained to give professional help to impaired people. He cannot use his expertise if those who are sent to him for assistance do not regard themselves as being impaired. Given this fact, it is not surprising that the doctrine has emerged among experts that truly effective rehabilitation and adjustment can occur only after the client has squarely faced and accepted the "fact" that he is, indeed, impaired.

In the case of legal definitions of conditions that are stigmatizing, then, we have an example of the impact that bureaucratic structures have on conceptions of stigma that experts construct.

CLIENTELE

A final factor affecting experts' conceptions of stigmatizing conditions is the people whom the expert is attempting to educate, care for, and rehabilitate. This factor can be described in the following way. The organizations in which experts work have many different constituents to whom they must respond. Among them are clients, benefactors, the general community, various professional groups, and the like. As we have seen in the section on cultural values, the problems which a stigma poses for clients and the ones which it poses for an organization's other constituents are often quite different and even contradictory. The issue is whether or not the client has the same "muscle" with experts as other constituents of an organization have; is he able to force experts to take his needs, wishes, and desires as seriously as they must the needs, wishes, and desires of these other constituents? The answer that has been given to this question by several leading students of social welfare is that he does not. This answer is based on several different facts about clients.

For one thing, most clients do not buy the services they receive. This is in part because most of them cannot afford to and in part because many agencies prohibit them from doing so. The consequence of this, according to Zald, is that "the agency personnel may be less intent on satisfying the client and meeting his needs." [55] For another thing, the general societal status of a person with stigma is very low. "Clients in welfare organizations," writes Zald, "are often not full participants in the society; they frequently come to the agency as supplicants without full rights or means. Not only are they legally without full rights but, psychologically, they are not full participants; they are the downtrodden and the vanquished." [56] Social welfare organizations have a greater legal control over clients than most other organizations have; they are authorized to act on the client's behalf in many areas of his personal life over which ordinary citizens retain full control. A client's access to the resources of the community as well as the degree of his participation in it are largely governed by the agency. Genuine alternatives for the client are essentially nonexistent; the client is free to leave an agency and go to another one, but the chances are very great that he will encounter these same problems of powerlessness and overcontrol wherever he goes. This situation and its consequences were summarized in a comprehensive report on deprivation issued by the National Institute of Child Health and Human Development. That report states that "welfare and other recipients of community agencies are not only afflicted by a sense of powerlessness but also are afflicted by a sense that they have no choice but to adopt stances of abject passivity in order to survive." [57]

The implications of these facts are as follows. Most important policy decisions that have to be made affect the interests of every one of the agency's constituents. Those who make these decisions cannot afford to ignore the interests of benefactors, professional groups, or the community at large, if they are to remain in business. They can, however, ignore the clients' interests without seriously jeopardizing either the fiscal integrity or the social reputation that the agency enjoys. This fact suggests in turn that experts have a considerable amount of freedom to define and conceptualize stigmatizing conditions. By this, I mean that they are free to emphasize any one of a great many themes in the life experiences of the stigmatized in order to tailor the conception of stigma to the political and economic realities confronting experts and helping organizations. We have seen that experts in different cultures and even in the same culture have defined the real problems of stigma in different ways that are sometimes even contradictory. The freedom to do this is afforded the expert because his client is basically powerless to resist it. It is important to recognize that one reason why this can be done is that the experts' definitions can become real simply by creating a general consensus and conviction that they are real. The problem of blindness can be defined in a great many ways, any one of which has the potential to become in reality the real problem of blindness simply by persuading others that it is so.[58]

There are only a few cases in which clients have been able to become a truly powerful constituent of an organization. One such case is in services for the blind in Sweden. There, blind people organized themselves and literally took over the major blindness organizations. In fact, bylaws were passed which specifically provided that no seeing person could hold executive office in any blindness organization. All people who are detected as blind are invited to join, and for those who do, the organization acts as the intermediary between the individual blind person and all public programs. It is interesting to note that professional ideologies about blindness in Sweden are distinctly different from the ones that prevail in countries in which services for the blind are in the hands of seeing people. In Sweden, notions about psychological adjustment, total rehabilitation, "accepting one's disability," and so on are largely absent or played down. Most of the financial resources available for services to blind people go either to them in the form of direct financial aid or to research institutes who are commissioned to develop specific pieces of mechanical hardware that the blind themselves have asked for. This mechanical orientation is, no doubt, partly cultural. What is distinctive about the Swedish program is the absence of an ideology that requires the blind person to undergo intensive personality restructuring or basic changes in self. One reason for this may be that the experts who construct special meanings of blindness are clients themselves.

The Effects of Professional Ideologies on the Stigmatized

I have implied that the construction of meanings of stigma by professional experts is a comparatively recent historical development. Previously, the meanings which stigma had were rooted in certain core cultural and religious values and were embodied in traditional stereotypes of the mentally ill, the poor, the deaf, the blind, the crippled, and so on. These traditional stereotypes are by no means dead; indeed, they remain dominant forces, particularly in the informal day-to-day interactions between stigmatized and normal people in the community.[59] In one sense, then, traditional stereotypes represent competing meanings of stigma from those that experts construct. An important question concerns the comparative significance of these expert and competing meanings both for determining the behavior and attitudes of stigmatized people and for societal conceptions of stigma considered more broadly.

One way to gauge the impact that expert meanings of stigma are having on the stigmatized of a society is to examine the extent of development of the organized intervention programs in which these meanings are constructed and enforced. The data relating to this topic suggest that a clear demarcation can be made between highly industrialized nations (especially those in the Western world) and preindustrial and developing nations. In all but the most highly industrialized societies, organized intervention efforts for the stigmatized have been developing only on a small scale, and in some societies these efforts are virtually nonexistent.[60] There are only a few developing countries that have any national program, and even they receive only modest financial backing from the government. Private efforts in these nations are incomplete and uneven. While there are agencies for some stigmatized groups, for others there are none, and even the private agencies that do exist often cater to only selected types of stigmatized people such as children and adults who can work.[61] In preindustrial and developing nations, then, expert meanings probably have little impact on the traditional conceptions of stigma that prevail.

In highly industrialized societies, however, organized intervention programs are legion; viewed in their entirety, they make up intricate and complex systems of services for the stigmatized of each nation. The scope of this bureaucratization and professionalization of such services can be illustrated with some data from our own country. In

America, there are several thousand private organizations that specialize in the problems of physical and psychiatric disabilities, poverty, and the like; moreover, many of the nearly 100,000 voluntary health and welfare organizations, and some of the nearly 300,000 churches, also provide or support services for such people.[62] In the public sector, such organized intervention programs have become elaborate bureaucratic structures. The Vocational Rehabilitation Administration alone spends nearly $400,000,000 annually in order to rehabilitate the physically disabled for work.[63] Moreover, recent legislation (HR 16819) includes plans to increase this amount to about 1 billion dollars in 1971 and to 1.2 billion dollars in 1972. In addition to this program, the National Institute of Health, the National Institute of Mental Health, the Veterans Administration, and several other federal agencies also sponsor multimillion-dollar programs from which people who have physical or psychiatric stigma can obtain help and assistance with their problems. Added to and often co-ordinated with these federal programs are the elaborate networks of services sponsored by state, county, and local municipal governments. This same basic pattern of proliferation of organizations for educating, rehabilitating, and caring for the stigmatized is also found in other highly industrialized nations such as England, Sweden, Norway, Denmark, Holland, Canada, and Russia and to a lesser extent in France, Italy, and Spain. In these societies, especially the ones in which this movement toward bureaucratization and professionalization of responsibility for the stigmatized has been most rigid, expert meanings are beginning to pose a genuine challenge to the older, more traditional folk conceptions and stereotypes of stigma. At the same time, it is important to recognize the limits of this challenge. There is no existing delivery system of services anywhere that has succeeded in reaching the entire population of stigmatized people in a society, and there is some evidence that even the most elaborate of these systems probably reaches only a minority of all those who qualify or need services.[64] Moreover, the public education function, which is aimed at changing traditional attitudes of laymen toward stigma, is one of the least developed of all activities that helping organizations sponsor. By and large, public education campaigns involve little more than occasional advertising of the organization and its programs; very few of these campaigns make genuine efforts either to disabuse the layman of traditional conceptions about stigma or to clarify the nature of his complicity in contributing to the problems of stigmatized people.

The data suggest, then, that expert meanings have little significance in preindustrial and developing nations, that in most highly industrialized nations they are posing a genuine challenge to traditional ideas about stigma, and that in a few countries they are actually emerging as dominant conceptions among laymen and experts alike.

A second gauge of the significance of professional ideologies about stigma is their impact on self-attitudes and behavior of stigmatized people on whom they are practiced. Although there is some dispute about the exact nature of the effects practice theories have on an organization's clientele, the data of three different studies all agree that these effects are profound. From their research on mental hospitals, Strauss *et al.* conclude that "ideology makes a difference in the organization of treatment, in what is done to and for patients and in the accompanying division of labor." [65] They find that professional ideologies affect such aspects of a patient's "life chances" as the kind of treatments he gets, the frequency and direction of institutional transfers, and the times of discharge. Moreover, they note that "if they [the patients] stay long enough they may enter into the ideological discourse of the professional staff, using psychiatric language to evaluate themselves and others." [66] I have come to a similar conclusion about the impact that agencies and organizations for the blind have on their clients. I found that

> when those who have been screened into blindness agencies enter them, they may not be able to see at all or they may have serious difficulties with their vision. When they have been rehabilitated, they are all blind men. They have learned the attitudes and behavior patterns that professional blindness workers believe blind people should have. In the intensive face-to-face relationships between blindness workers and clients that make up the rehabilitation process, the blind person is rewarded for adopting a view of himself that is consistent with his rehabilitators' view of him and punished for clinging to other self-conceptions. He is told that he is "insightful" when he comes to describe his problems as his rehabilitators view them, and he is said to be "blocking" or "resistant" when he does not. Indeed, passage through the blindness system is determined in part by his willingness to adopt the experts' view about self.[67]

I have concluded that "gradually, over time, the behavior of blind men comes to correspond with the assumptions and beliefs that blindness workers hold about blindness." [68]

Goffman has also stressed the impact that professional ideologies have on patients in mental hospitals, although the nature of that impact which he describes is somewhat different than the ones found in other studies. He states:

Mental patients can find themselves in a special bind. To get out of the hospital, or to ease their life within it, they must show acceptance of the place accorded them, and the place accorded them is to support the occupational role of those who appear to force this bargain. This self-alienating moral servitude, which perhaps helps to account for some inmates becoming mentally confused, is achieved by involving the great tradition of the expert servicing relation, especially its medical variety. Mental patients can find themselves crushed by the weight of a service ideal that eases life for the rest of us.[69]

These studies indicate that experts' practice theories have profound effects on the self-attitudes and behaviors of clients and inmates of institutions. Unfortunately, we do not know how enduring these effects are. There is presumptive evidence that they may be short-lived. This evidence lies in the findings of all three of the studies I have cited which show that patients and clients are strongly inclined toward "making out" in the system by going along with their counselors. The implication is that when they are released, these patterns of behavior that they have deliberately or subconsciously feigned may disappear.

The Process of Constructing Expert Meanings

There is a final point I want to discuss: it relates to the process by which experts go about constructing meanings of stigma. There is less known about this topic than about any of the other ones I have covered here. What I have to say about it will therefore be quite brief and based more on anecdotal evidence and impressions than on hard data.

From available materials and cases, it appears that few existing expert meanings of stigma were explicitly and consciously formulated. Experts may have tried to lay out these meanings in advance of beginning to work, but few such preconceived meanings have survived. They are modified, distorted, and stretched as efforts are made to mobilize financial and man-power resources and to deal with the daily problems of running a welfare agency. Only periodically do experts stand back to take a hard look at such things as the consequences of their actions or to attempt to codify the rationale for their activities and to construct explanations for them. It is important to see that when these meanings are codified, the process of doing so is one in retrospect. Meanings evolve which describe, explain, and justify what exists; but what exists has often come into being for reasons that are not entirely related to the problems of stigma. Norton Long has described this process at the community level. He writes, "Much of what occurs seems to just happen with accidental trends becoming cumulative over time and producing results intended by nobody. A great deal of the communities' activities consist of undirected cooperation of particular social structures, each seeking particular goals and in doing so, meshing with others." [70] This statement applies as aptly to the internal dynamics of the social welfare agency as it does to the dynamics of the local community. It is probably impossible for the expert to map out in advance all the implications of a proposed policy, or even to understand how such things as client problems, needs, and interests are modified, stretched, or changed by each successive decision. It suggests that expert meanings are not constructed in advance and by the ordinary rules of logic and scientific reasoning; rather, they evolve, often unconsciously as the expert "muddles through" the day-to-day problems of running a welfare organization.[71] This in turn implies that one can only speak of "constructed" meanings of stigma in the sense that they are genuinely man-made and do not inhere in nature or in the stigmatizing conditions to which they are applied.

NOTES

NOTE: Before I began to write this chapter, I assumed that I would be able to cover this topic adequately in a single essay of moderate length. As I began, I soon discovered that this was a mistaken assumption. The materials on experts' theories about stigma and the issues that surround these theories are far more numerous and complicated than I suspected. In fact, I now believe that a full-length book would be required to do complete justice. The resulting chapter is, so to speak, midway between what I imagined before I actually began and what I now believe must be done to treat the subject in a scholarly way. In a sense, then, this chapter is a progress report of my thinking on this topic to date. As such, it is uneven: some topics are dealt with in detail, while other equally important ones are dispensed with in a brief and superficial way; there are issues which require a good deal more explanation; and, occasionally, assumptions are made that are too simple. However, I believe that the central thesis is a valid one, which will not be altered appreciably when these problems and limitations have finally been ironed out. I wish to thank Suzanne Keller Hubert, Victor Marshall, Anthony Harris, and Arnold Shore for their reactions to earlier drafts and their suggestions.

1. *Rehabilitation of the Disabled in Fifty-one Countries* (Washington: U.S. Department of Health, Education, and Welfare, Vocational Rehabilitation Administration, 1964).

2. Harold L. Wilensky and Charles N. Lebeaux, *Industrial Society and Social Welfare* (New York: Russell Sage Foundation, 1958), Part I.

3. *Indicators* (Washington: Department of Health, Education, and Welfare, 1968).

4. Erving Goffman, *Stigma: Notes on the Management of Spoiled Identity* (Englewood Cliffs: Prentice-Hall, 1963), p. 3.

5. Carl Haffter, "The Changeling: History and Psychodynamics of Attitudes to Handicapped Children in European Folklore," *Journal of the History of the Behavioral Sciences* (1968), pp. 55–61.

6. Josef P. Hes and Shlomoh Wollstein, "The Attitude of the Ancient Jewish Sources to Mental Patients," *Israel Annals of Psychia ry and Related Disciplines* (1964), pp. 103–116.

7. Kingsley Davis, "Sexual Behavior," in Robert K. Merton and Robert A. Nisbet, eds., *Contemporary Social Problems* (New York: Harcourt, Brace, and World, 1966), pp. 322–372.

8. Robert B. Edgerton, "Pokot Intersexuality: An East African Example of the Resolution of Sexual Incongruity," *American Anthropologist*, LXVI (1964), 1288–1298.

9. *Ibid.*, p. 1290.

10. From a conversation with Professor Roelf G. Boiten, Laboratorium Voor Werkuigkundige Meet-en, Regeltechniek, Technische, Hogeschool, Delft, The Netherlands.

11. See H. Robert Blank, "Psychoanalysis and Blindness," *Psychoanalytic Quarterly*, XXVI, No. 1 (1957), 1–24; Thomas J. Carroll, *Blindness: What It Is, What It Does, and How to Live with It* (Boston: Little, Brown, 1961); Louis A. Cholden, *A Psychiatrist Works with Blindness* (New York: American Foundation for the Blind, 1958); Louis A. Cholden, "Some Psychiatric Problems in the Rehabilitation of the Blind," *Bulletin of the Menninger Clinic*, XVIII, No. 3 (1954), 107–112.

12. Seved Erikson, "We Are Sure to Manage," mimeographed, p. 1.

13. *Ibid.*

14. *Ibid.*, p. 2.

15. From an interview with Mr. Charles Hedkvist, Director, De Blindas Forening, Stockholm, Sweden.

16. Carroll, *op. cit.*, pp. 11–13.

17. Robert A. Scott, *The Making of Blind Men* (New York: Russell Sage Foundation, 1969), pp. 80–89.

18. Anselm L. Strauss *et al.*, *Psychiatric Ideologies and Institutions* (New York: the Free Press, 1964), pp. 54–56.

19. *Ibid.*, p. 56.

20. *Ibid.*

21. *Ibid.*

22. *Ibid.*

23. Walter D. Connor, "Deviance, Control and Social Policy in the USSR,"

doctoral dissertation, Department of Sociology, Princeton University, April, 1969.

24. *Ibid.*, p. 51.
25. *Ibid.*, p. 165.
26. *Ibid.*, p. 67.
27. *Ibid.*, p. 174.
28. See Albert K. Cohen, *Deviance and Control* (Englewood Cliffs: Prentice-Hall, 1966), Chapters 4, 5, 6, 7.
29. Connor, *op. cit.*, p. 73.
30. *Ibid.*, p. 219.
31. *Ibid.*, pp. 218–219.
32. Norton E. Long, "The Local Community as an Ecology of Games," *American Journal of Sociology*, LXIV, No. 3 (November, 1958), 251–261.
33. Erving Goffman, *Asylums* (Garden City: Doubleday, 1961), pp. 356–357.
34. See, for example, Howard S. Becker, *Outsiders: Studies in the Sociology of Deviance* (New York: The Free Press, 1963); John Kitsuse, "Societal Reactions to Deviant Behavior: Problems of Theory and Method," *Social Problems*, IX (1961); Edwin Lemert, *Social Pathology* (New York: McGraw-Hill, 1951).
35. Robert K. Merton, "Social Structure and Anomie," in Merton, *Social Theory and Social Structure* (New York: The Free Press, 1957), pp. 131–160.
36. Roger G. Barker *et al.*, *Adjustment to Physical Handicap and Illness: A Survey of the Social Psychology of Physique and Disability* (New York: Social Science Research Council, 1953).
37. Mayer N. Zald, *Social Welfare Institutions: A Sociological Reader* (New York: Wiley, 1965), p. 141.
38. Evon A. Vogt and Thomas F. O'Dea, "A Comparative Study of the Roles of Values in Social Action in Two Southwestern Communities," *American Sociological Review*, XVIII (1953), 645–654.
39. *Ibid.*, p. 648.
40. Steven Marcus, "Hunger and Ideology," *Commentary* (November, 1963), pp. 389–393.
41. *Ibid.*, p. 390.
42. *Ibid.*, p. 392.
43. *Ibid.*
44. Goffman, *Stigma*, p. 7.
45. Goffman, *Asylums*, p. 352.
46. Harold Orlans, "An American Death Camp," *Politics* (Summer, 1948), pp. 162–167, 205.
47. *Ibid.*, p. 167.
48. Strauss *et al.*, *op. cit.*, p. 362.

49. *Ibid.,* p. 363.
50. *Ibid.,* p. 368.
51. *Ibid.,* pp. 45–50.
52. Robert B. Edgerton, *The Cloak of Competence* (Berkeley: University of California Press, 1967), p. 3.
53. *Facts and Figures about Blindness* (New York: American Foundation for the Blind, 1967).
54. Edgerton, *Cloak of Competence,* p. 5.
55. Zald, *op. cit.,* p. 555.
56. *Ibid.*
57. *Perspectives on Human Deprivation: Biological, Psychological and Sociological* (Washington: U.S. Department of Health, Education, and Welfare, Public Health Service—National Institutes of Health, The National Institute of Child Health and Human Development, 1968), p. 233.
58. In this sense social welfare organizations have a much greater degree of flexibility than organizations that manufacture material goods. Material goods in a manufacturing firm are the most critical "constituent" by virtue of the fact that they either sell and make money or do not. This condition cannot be changed, nor can it ever be ignored. Companies are forced to be more responsive to profit and loss than to any other consideration. The "material goods" in a social welfare organization are its clients. However, "profits" and "losses" or the definitions and the relativization of basic goals for the client are matters that are determined by social consensus; and one can alter this consensus by persuasion alone.
59. Barker *et al., op. cit.*
60. *Rehabilitation of the Disabled in Fifty-one Countries, op. cit.*
61. *Ibid.,* pp. 9, 20, 22, 39, 53, for example.
62. *Voluntary Health and Welfare Agencies in the United States* (New York: Schoolmaster's Press, 1961), p. 9.
63. *Annual Report,* Vocational Rehabilitation Administration, 1968.
64. Scott, *op. cit.,* pp. 69–70; Samuel M. Miller, Pamela Roby, and Alwine A. de Vos van Steenwijk, "Social Policy and the Excluded Man: The Prevalence of Creaming," mimeographed, June, 1968.
65. Strauss *et al., op. cit.,* p. 361.
66. *Ibid.,* p. 373.
67. Scott, *op. cit.,* p. 119.
68. *Ibid.*
69. Goffman, *Asylums,* p. 386.
70. Long, *op. cit.,* p. 252.
71. Charles E. Lindbloom, "The Science of 'Muddling Through,'" *Public Administration Review* (Spring, 1959).

10

Normlessness in Management

Paul Campanis

Years ago Karl Mannheim compared the advancement of corporation managers' careers to climbing a ladder. The managers ascended through promotions, and when they attained each position they were given a prescribed set of privileges and duties as well as definite roles to play. This predictability maintained the organization's equilibrium. In the present era of rapidly expanding corporations, managers must adjust to changes and instabilities in areas that formerly remained relatively stable. Careers today are more like ill-defined, hazardous mazes than ladders. Managers run the course with no hint of what the next turn will reveal, while they try to cope with moral dilemmas, conflicting interpersonal relationships, and general uncertainty.

This chapter explores aspects of corporation managers' jobs from the viewpoint that an accurate portrayal must include discussion of both the organization and the meanings its managers attribute to their situations in the organization. It is also a study of ambiguous moral definitions in a climate of unremitting change. The aim is to suggest complexity, rather than to delve deeply into any one area, and to show the layers of moral confusion which often lie behind what is described as role conflict.

The material for the study is based on long-lasting relationships with the managers of various manufacturing and service areas of large and prosperous corporations which are subjected to abrupt changes when processes are modified or new products are introduced. The data and ideas in the study are distilled from tapes and notes of management-development and other meetings of executives and from long, confidential interviews with company employees of all levels.

For purposes of this chapter, a projection has been made of a composite corporation which has been dubbed *Expansionetics*. On the average, the number of men above the level of supervisor and below that of vice-president from 1958 to 1968 in Expansionetics ranged from three hundred to seven hundred. Some companies have no women managers; others, only one or two.

Since work and success are still important values in this society, research must go beyond the identification of simplified models of people—in this case, corporation managers—playing roles. To understand how managers choose to act, an examination must be conducted of the beliefs and ideologies in the company and of its changes in policies, personnel, products, and environment. At the same time, managers themselves require individual study to record how they change as their careers progress. The gamut of behavior that can be observed is limited in practice to acceptable behavior, but the variety of feelings and motives within this range will be shown to be great.

The bureaucratic system effectively controls the manager who has experienced some years of corporate life before ascending to his high position. He is a grand socializer rather than a Grand Inquisitor. He exercises a brokerage function between the top officers of the company and all those whom he manages. By being a middle man, a purveyor of ideas, customs, habits, history, policy, and lore, he keeps the system running. In general, managers are morally reliable. It is the system of beliefs that is in flux. Confusion in an organization that changes rapidly makes it hard to decide what is normal and right, whether the organization is a manufacturing plant, a university, a medical center, or a government agency.

An approach that sees more of a man's web of reactions and feelings than a narrowly conceived study of role lends credibility to the conclusion that exhaustion from fighting moral ambiguities often afflicts managers. Moral fog blunts their discriminating and energy-sustaining powers. This occurs at around age fifty, when a manager is in the stage of life that is somewhat unkindly referred to as executive menopause, but the symptoms appear years earlier.

To add to the confusion caused by rapid expansion of a corporation, the new philosophy of leveling with others, instead of using the corrosive diplomacy of masking feelings, meanings, and motives, also changes the relationship that managers have with company members. There is, for example, the popular cult of the training or T-group, a secular movement with many variations, whose adherents react as to a new religion. Cult leaders refer to members as disciples, and they encourage their followers (company employees) to say what they feel and what they mean in private dealings and group meetings—to "tell it like it is." This trend is a distinct break with traditional business practice, and managers strive to cope with its resultant unpredictable behavior while maintaining rationality and discipline.[1]

A description of the social atmosphere at Expansionetics will provide a backdrop for viewing managers in action. It should dispel any notion that the corporate manager is a skeptic or that he is a rigid role-player, despite the fact that he is an exemplar in the corporation and one who does not like to break rules. By looking at managers in more fully variegated circumstances as they attempt to discern the implications of their decisions, a greater understanding of their often cynical, querulous posture may be gained. And by studying ambiguous moral definitions in the corporate climate of change, the reader may feel a certain sympathy for the manager who says he is never sure he is right. The truth is, however, that in making a decision the manager validates its morality. Any specific moral construction he ascribes to the meaning of an act is plausible to all participants.

Management Philosophies

The Two Ethics

The management philosophies of Expansionetics are exercises in contradictions. "The Boss," as the president of the company is called, sincerely believes that people are improvable, industrious, and basically good. He advocates a democratic personnel policy which his managers refer to as the "softie approach," or the human-relations ethic, and he expounds this philosophy regularly in his well-meant social messages to employees. However, the realities of meeting production schedules and quotas, of retooling for new products and processes, and of maintaining an effective work force amid constant change are not always consistent with the Boss's humanistic policies. Many managers believe that a tough-minded approach is the only way to get things done. This authoritarian personnel policy is called the production ethic. The two philosophies naturally conflict, but they are also subject to modification as Expansionetics continues to grow and change.

The principal concerns at Expansionetics are products and people. A satisfying and worth-while job for every man is the goal stated by the Boss and by the policy manual. Just as interpretations of the Bible vary, so individual interpretations of the formal statements of company policy vary in content and intensity. Managers are categorized according to the seriousness with which they espouse the Boss's social messages, but the enthusiasm a manager shows for either the human-relations or the production ethic may depend on what he thinks others, especially his vice-presidents, want to hear. Privately, he often expresses other attitudes, and on bad days when he is displeased with his job or his associates, he may air still different views.

The managers who practice the human-relations philosophy spend time helping subordinates learn new skills and building harmonious work forces. They are careful not to hurt other people's feelings when it is necessary to criticize or to make suggestions. But the exciting new products and processes that make the company enormously successful demand sacrifice on the part of many. Those who devote their undivided attention to reaching quotas in production and to developing the fine new products generally prefer the tough-minded approach. They worry about meeting schedules, about workers' getting to the time clock too early at punch-out time. Overtime costs are a source of worry for them, too. These managers complain that "people just don't work as hard as they used to."

AN ECOLOGY OF MORAL ATTITUDES

Managers and staffers in what company members call "people functions" feel obliged to adopt the human-relations ethic. An education manager in charge of basic reading and math programs for workers tells of having to sell the plans for his next year's programs to a senior vice-president who chided him because in presenting the plans the education manager had backed down too easily to the vice-president's criticisms and demands for economy. "You're supposed to argue on behalf of the worker and not to give in and accept refusals for your programs," the vice-president said.

Personnel, vocational and personal counseling, education, training, and management-development groups are among those who have championed the human-relations ethic. Production managers, machine shop managers, maintenance managers, and top management emphasize production and profit interests. Some groups mix the policies and use whichever suits their current purposes.

For example, groups in research and development (R and D) support the human-relations ethic because managers lead highly paid scientists, engineers, and technicians to goals that are often vague and distant, related to the perfecting of a process or developing a new one, or to creating a new experimental product. Production is not defined in terms of pieces completed per hour; it is an accumulation of ideas and strategies that are often tried, only to be abandoned for others as the work progresses. Professionals and their subprofessional assistants simply insist on democratic treatment and a pleasant environment, or they withhold, mask, or slow the flow of ideas and supportive help needed to master a problem. In this area a joint concern for people and production exists. In production departments, however, the major emphasis still falls on coaxing maximum yield from the machines and from workers who tend their sometimes temperamental mechanical charges. Pressures of production and research occasionally make it impossible for employees to attend classes to improve their knowledge or skill, even though the Boss has stressed the virtues of weekly in-plant education for everyone.

The Old and the Young

The older managers often read up on new theories, try them out, and then become uncertain and go back to their old, familiar ways. But they realize they are missing something, and they may try again to put into practice the human-relations ethic. Each failure or discouraging problem merely augments their basic mistrust of coddling workers. Younger men usually adopt the human-relations approach wherever they work in the company, even in production departments where demanding schedules and repetitive work allow little latitude for developing subordinates' talents or for treating them especially well.

Regardless of their ages, managers vary their degree of zeal as the winds of change blow. If a vice-president shows interest in T-groups or some other training device, managers quickly become interested. So, too, with the larger issues in the community, managers become involved in an activity they perceive to be important. With their careers in a fluid state and subject to influence of the higher-ups, the managers play with new roles, adjusting their energy loads to meet exigencies and trends.

One manager says, "You never know what's coming next here. It's always changing, and you can never be sure you're right." Another likened the situation to a "commitment of the month," the way Howard Johnson's features a flavor of the month. The social reality is about that uncertain at Expansionetics. This constant realignment of priorities seems to cause company managers to crystallize only partially their views of themselves. One is reminded more of adolescents than the type of adults that psychologists used to posit as being well adjusted and fully mature. But Expansionetics itself is far from being crystallized. Nothing has settled into a permanent form because the company is always fluid, moving, expanding, changing.

SOME OF THE PROBLEMS

Which ethic is better? Who's right: the humanists or the driving production types? How would you measure the merits of one approach over the other by the available criteria of cost and profits?

Managers and subordinates spend hours arguing these issues. Some say that Expansionetics' success stems from its philosophy toward people. Data show this to be at least partly the case as it relates to hourly paid members early in their careers who gratefully support the company which has "cared enough" to give them training and better jobs. Others chalk all the "education stuff" off as propaganda, a clever ruse to pacify the natives. And then there are others who thank their lucky stars that there are still enough really tough-minded people around to counteract the softies' impractical ways. Thus the controversy between the beliefs continues, and there seems to be no solid base which managers can use to decide once and for all the better policy to follow.

When business is slow. When top management emphasizes cost controls over pay raises and purchases of new equipment, the two philosophies are sorely tested, because managers have to make do with whatever they have, even though the work loads have increased. Usually the first six months of the year, when business is slow, are a time for belt tightening. This is true in many business firms dependent on heavy consumption by consumers in the summer months through Christmas. This past year, the austerity or "poverty" program, as it is called, has continued through midyear and will go into next year. Managers say they do not know why, exactly, except that it has to do with keeping the profit figure high in order to maintain a hefty selling price for the stock on the New York exchange. Dissatisfaction in the managers' departments increases under these circumstances. The measures taken to alleviate discontent are the same for both types of belief holders: they apologize to their subordinates and promise to improve conditions as soon as the freeze on raises and increases lifts.

The die-hards. At Expansionetics the humanitarians are winning, but the sounds of disagreement are still heard. A key vice-president says that human relations is all nonsense, a sissyish, namby-pamby way to treat people. He thinks that management should firmly control and forcefully direct people. "If you give them an inch, they'll take a mile." Corporate colonialism is still his answer, with subordinates kept in "their places" following orders and keeping their mouths shut and their feelings to themselves. The most vocal proponent is a sales manager, a vice-president who can say such things and get away with it because he deals largely with the world outside the company. Other managers who share such sentiments cannot express them because they are accountable to subordinates with whom they are in daily contact. Men who have left Expansionetics have dared to voice such unpopular opinions. One former manager called Expansionetics "Fairyland" and yearned for the good old days when army discipline and order were also part of the workplace. There are still companies practicing autocratic policies, but they are growing scarce. This die-hard manager may have settled in such a place, but more probably he has had to change his attitude in dealing with his workers.

Routine problems. There are, of course, the usual routine problems which face any executive. For example, a manager often has to make the difficult decision of whether to move a weak man out of a difficult job or to try to rehabilitate him. The problems may be routine, but the decisions the managers make will no longer be based on routine philosophy. The decisions will reflect the managers' attitudes toward either the human-relations or the production ethic.

Problems caused by change. Recently, a group of technicians complained about washing glassware and asked the management to buy a large dishwasher to do this job, which they deemed beneath their new status. These men, many of them at least, had been doing dirty jobs on machines only a few years before and had been upgraded through in-plant education and training. What is fair? What is right? What is a good day's work? When the nature of the work itself changes dramatically with the introduction of new products and methods, the bargain between employer and employee is also subject to change. It is another area for the manager to worry about and to try to straighten out, and often it is an entirely new area completely without precedent.

THE TURNOVER RATE

Expansionetics offers security, benefits, and a good salary amid a pleasant and lively community setting, which probably accounts for its low turnover rate. Employees respond to the Boss's social messages. They call themselves "company members" instead of "workers" or "employees," and they think about what the president has to say and search for his "real" meanings.

Both unskilled and skilled, both professionals and paraprofessionals, plan to stay at Expansionetics with most of their working years ahead of them. Managers are almost all local men, with the exception of a few manager-scientists. They are not itinerant professionals or cosmopolitans who will move on in a year or two. The "company members" settle comfortably in the surrounding community and expect to live there a lifetime. Further, the average age of company members is in the low to middle thirties—quite a young company when compared to the average age of many companies, which is nearer the mid-forties.

SOME EFFECTS OF AUTOMATION

The Boss talked a few years ago of people who would play a machine and control it as a pianist does a piano. Instead of being tied to a machine, pulling finished products off every few seconds, the technicians now stroll around monitoring huge automatic machines that run by themselves. It takes far less time to become a technician than it does to become a concert pianist, but the piano remains the same, whereas the technician may find that his monster of a machine is to be replaced with a newer, even larger and more complicated machine which he must learn to control.

The new technology has raised the expectations of those who used to do menial jobs. Technicians who work in production as well as technicians who assist scientists take courses and counseling to improve their corporate lots. This is a direct result of the human-relations philosophy and one of its best features. As more production areas automate, unskilled workers and semiskilled workers upgrade to become technicians around machines, and the new corporate philosophy at Expansionetics amplifies and thrives on their freed existence. Managers have begun to see these technicians, who may be new arrivals from other company areas, in a different light. These are men who work with their heads, not with their hands, and they must be treated differently. Members who have taken courses on company time demand that the human-relations philosophy be applied to them; they no longer remain silent. And management accedes, slowly but surely.

Honesty in Interpersonal Relations

The new approach to interpersonal relations which is often called "leveling" amounts to telling people "like it is." This unvarnished frankness reduces social distances, but it also creates a new set of problems as interpersonal communication reaches a new dimension.

Feedback. The shift from sweat labor to mind labor, caused largely by new machine technology, finds most managers at Expansionetics just as concerned with how their associates think and feel as with how well the job is done. Unfortunately, the average manager has no sure way of knowing how to act toward others on the job to promote the desired atmosphere of mutual respect and understanding. He may never have read books on interpersonal relations, etiquette, sociology, or social psychology; or he may not be up to date on the newest scientific findings as they relate to his work. This man probably speaks to more than fifty people each day, and most of the time he can only assume that he is acting in rough accord with the way other managers act simply because he hears nothing to the contrary. As he goes along, he learns from his mistakes and from a wide variety of acts which have neutral results. One of his most frequent remarks is: "You don't know how you're doing here or what other people think of you."

PROBLEMS

The vindictive receiver. Younger managers often become inspired by the idea of getting close to their people, becoming involved with their problems, and helping them develop by leveling with them on their good and bad traits. If the subordinate who is the receiver of this personal feedback is not a believer in this new truth-telling approach, or if his feelings have been hurt, or even if he believes, but wants to harm the manager, he has been provided with enough ammunition for becoming a troublemaker. The vindictive receiver may complain to his peers and superiors. He may see to it that the young manager's good intentions are completely misinterpreted and labeled inconsiderate, tactless, abusive, or anything else he chooses. By thus enlisting sympathy, the receiver can make the manager a scapegoat.

Private versus business areas. There is danger of invading privacy when a manager tells a worker of his faults, and this embarrassment of a subordinate could become a form of tyranny. On the other hand, to improve a fellow member's technical and interpersonal skills requires that the manager speak frankly, chancing violation of some norms. Other private areas that should be separated from business are those that have anything to do with the home, religion, or politics. One manager related how hard it was for him to resist the temptation to give advice on domestic problems. He met a subordinate's wife and decided that the wife's domineering ways were making a wreck of a potentially capable employee.

Self-revelations of the manager. Managers, especially those who attend sensitivity training groups, may reveal some of their own short-comings, weaknesses, and insecurities by way of example when leveling with a subordinate. Such behavior can prove risky, especially if the employee does not react in the expected manner. Furthermore, attempts to show liberal amounts of humane concern by managers may be suspect by wary employees, or such attempts may lower the manager in the employee's esteem. Some managers tell it like it is by giving vent to their feelings and swearing, showing affection, concern, or anger. Women are quick to take offense at a manager's swearing even mildly or placing his hand on their shoulders.

The Pendulum Effect

One manager cited O'Neill's play *The Iceman Cometh* as a reason for not getting mixed up with people's problems. In the play, dead-end drunks momentarily take hope and confidence when an optimist enters the bar, but the effort is too great and perhaps not worth while.

The managers who show evidence of the pendulum effect, deep involvement followed by a kind of emotional exhaustion and avoidance of involvement, make one wonder if such committed men are better off than the neutral men who do not go around making problems to solve. Harm may be perpetrated by the person who says what he sees and who leads a crusade to change what he sees. Attempts to help a person by telling him he does not work hard enough, that he lacks much of any drive, may be enough to start a storm. This is particularly true if the manager has not made a correct judgment of the subordinate's strength to withstand such criticism in the right spirit.

Group Behavior

The behavior of groups is just as problematic. For example, "Should you and do you talk in your group about an absent member of the group or about some other person in management?" Usually, the answer is Yes, but within reason and not in a damaging fashion. Some people insist that such talk must be relayed to the absent member at the earliest possible moment, so that he will know what people said about him.

Some questions are more important and more difficult to answer. If a manager builds solid feelings among subordinates in his group, they tend to see boundaries firmly established, with outsiders as adversaries. Certain key training administrators lament that Expansionetics does not really have groups in the sense that members are close to one another. A loose affiliation that happens to report to the manager in question exists instead. One is reminded of the homeroom in a high school as a base with most of the important events occurring outside it. Many men are individual career holders who operate at the peer level, co-ordinating and scheduling with members of other departments singly and in group meetings. Experiences in primary groups are replaced by consultative relationships which are formed to solve pressing technical problems. A closely knit group, although comfortable for its members, tends to confuse those in adjacent departments, making them both envious and angry. With no group at all to fall back on, they build resentment toward the others in the close group. Managers today try to form cohesive groups in preference to loose affiliations.

Much more tolerance of individual actions in groups is apparent in recent years. Managers who had met to explore ways of improving their human relations took a test which included the question: "What would you do about a member in a meeting you were conducting who blew his stack unaccountably?" Before their discussions began, the answer invariably was to shut up the violator, then reprimand him privately. After the group sensitivity training meetings, which went on for several months, these managers changed their minds and said that they would hear the man out in the meeting instead of trying to silence him.

This example lends support to the idea that people self-consciously become willing to take chances if they believe in the power of honesty in interpersonal relations. The old neutral posture is often abandoned, for a time at least, and interesting interpersonal behavior is displayed by individual company members as well as by groups. Of course, moral issues, responsibilities, and imperatives become much more complicated and variegated in the new atmosphere.

Many company members insist that business space in the corporation ought to be neutral, impersonal, and bland. Expressions of emotion and affect, they say, disrupt the orderly process of "business as usual." Like it or not, the concept of the "whole man" has finally arrived in organizational psychology, and one result is that the human potential is in the process of being expanded at Expansionetics.

In Flux

Change at Expansionetics is sudden and drastic. So much is going on that the imagination goggles at the scope of it all. At IBM in its early days, the story is that the president was apt to evict unsatisfactory managers hastily, piling up the contents of their offices outside the building in a not-so-subtle hint that the man was through. This does not happen at Expansionetics, nor at the now sedate IBM. Instead, new products, offices, walls, partitions, cafeterias, rest rooms, parking lots, and doors appear as if by magic. Men get lost in buildings they knew well until the week end before, when something happened to change the scene.

INTELLIGENCE SHARING

Secretaries complain, "No one ever tells me what's going on." It is not at all unusual for a secretary to be informed by movers that her desk and chair and other office furnishings are to be moved—perhaps to the next office, to another floor in the same building, or to another building entirely. A busy boss has forgotten to "tell the girl" that they were moving again or that other changes in plans were to be made.

Managers have much the same problems, and they must use both intellect and personality to glean advance information. They need to have information about mundane affairs as well as the more interesting gossip and rumor. However, to get, they must give, and a symbiosis of data passing or intelligence sharing must be operative at all times if a manager is to live successfully. A manager never hears enough, because so much information is needed to keep abreast of the constantly changing system.

PROTECTIVE SECRECY

The company maintains stringent policies of secrecy to protect the monopolies it enjoys on its various products. Professionals new to the organization are carefully sheltered for six months from sensitive areas where they might learn too much too soon. It is assumed that after a trial period they will be loyal and not give away trade secrets. Even long-term members often know relatively little about the intricacies of some products as whole working units. Instead, they become more or less expert in one aspect, say, a particular area of R and D or some special manufacturing machine in production.

Specialization and protective secrecy also apply to groups working in concert on special programs. A favorite game is guessing what the latest secret project is. Groups have names such as *Badger, Tiger,* and *Cardinal.* The project being developed by any one of these groups might easily mushroom into a multimillion-dollar division within a year. In one case, a set of secrets held by a small working group called by an animal's name became a manufacturing organization employing seven hundred men. Comparison between preliterate societies and corporations using totemic names to bind members by sentiment is tempting.

MANAGEMENT BY CRISIS

Managers actually go to the annual stockholders' meetings to find out for certain about the next year's products, processes, and plans. For years the Boss has mobilized the system by telling stockholders that a new product would be introduced within the next six-month period. As the Boss makes his electrifying announcements to the stockholders, the managers visualize the consequences: hard work, new building complexes, promotions, new machines, new processes, new products, and a mobilization of redirected energies throughout the company. At such times the managers quake, because they realize the enormous demands on their time and energies that will be called for.

Leaks occur before word gets out to the public, to be sure, but top management is chary of passing information about future plans on to the managerial cadre, perhaps because it would quickly filter through to the ranks. Top management is so remote from managers that few loyalties exist up the line. Secrets from above are not kept, and managers experience little guilt over sharing revelations.

Expansionetics has been known to advertise and take advance orders on products not fully tested in the field and not perfected a few months before they were scheduled for delivery to dealers. Miraculously, deadlines were met, even though some products had to be recalled and adjusted.

This is management by crisis, and its suddenness and precipitate consequences add to uncertainties with which managers must cope. A student of organization and corporate management is often in awe that the system works at all, that the various, loosely affiliated suzerainties can get together to accomplish anything—especially with a deadline to be met.

MANAGERS REACT

Job assignments are flexible. If a product or process goes haywire, managers drop daily personnel and scheduling issues to attend what are often frenetic and lengthy meetings to correct the sensitive balance of factors causing the trouble. Engineers, scientists, and managers talk to one another to pool knowledge on solutions. Most often, since products and processes are unique to this company, men get the answers from one another rather than from books or formulas.

Changes in the work week under these circumstances compete with demands of the manager's own group—a group which is usually growing in number and becoming more complex in its relations with other groups. When a problem with a new product is solved, professionals and subprofessionals must be hired to tool up and manufacture. New company members take up a manager's attention as he attends to their training and supervises their joint activities.

These tactics work through the superhuman efforts of managers, but after some years of management by crises, managers tire of fighting annual battles and fires of one sort or another. They become burned out, used up, overworked objects in fights against deadlines. No dignified mechanism exists for them to leave the scene or to rest much between bouts. Rotation into less hazardous staff positions and sabbaticals would help, but the company probably couldn't spare them.

The threat of reorganization is constant. A manager must always be subject to reassignment. He tries to anticipate and second-guess what may be coming so that he can meet contingencies with some plan in mind. He wonders who the new boss will be that may come in over him, if he stays on his current job; or he worries about the superior he will meet, if he is transferred to a new position in another division. Since the company grows almost constantly, a redistribution of existing managers and the addition of new managers go on all the time. A new superior may be an irritant for a number of reasons. He may fill the top job the manager saw himself getting. Many top positions of late have been filled from the "outside." Also, the new man may have a different philosophy of management, or he may have an inordinate amount of brashness and opportunism.

Each major reorganization and related appointment at the top level in the company require the manager to do a pocket reassessment of his position. That may occur a number of times each year.

WHAT OF THE FUTURE?

The charismatic president. Charisma, the special charm and grace a dynamic man brings to an office, often affects the success of an organization more than any other factor. This has certainly been the case at Expansionetics. But even the Boss is mortal, and positioning among his potential successors has started. The No. 2 man, first under the Boss, retires in a year or so. Whoever moves into his place may have claims on the presidency which the other top executives do not enjoy. The Boss is in his fifties and the major stockholder with a fifth of the outstanding common stock, and it is possible that he might step down and out. It is also possible that he may step up and out to serve in a ceremonial capacity on the board of directors. At present he is said to make or approve every key decision regarding policies as well as promotions and hiring.

The Boss is a national figure on presidential committees in Washington, and he has raised his office to heights that an enterprising vice-president or official of some other company would envy. A new occupant of the top post in the company might affect managers' jobs, but it is impossible to foresee just how, without knowing who the lucky man is to be. Then, too, it is impossible to predict what the effect of loss of the president and his stimulating, charismatic personality would be to the company.

If the next president of Expansionetics is an engineer or a scientist, he will probably continue the current policy that emphasizes innovative technology and manufacture of products that result from secret formulas. A production executive as president might turn most of the company's energies to manufacturing goods, letting R and D slide. So, too, the sales executive would stress selling large quantities of products. He might reduce expenditures for development of new products and concentrate on low-cost, mass-produced items that require little sophistication at the manufacturing end of the business. It is a rare man, such as the present company president, who can operate in more than one direction and be a man of great vision at the same time. Thus the managers ponder their future and wonder what will become of Expansionetics if and when the Boss leaves.

What is best for the company. Behind the current growth and change are rationales that top management makes in its daily practice. Managers who carry out policies have strong opinions about what Expansionetics should do, depending on the way they feel the company should move. For example, should the company manufacture in-house the hardware that uses an expendable consumer item on which the company makes huge profits? Managers differ greatly in their answers to this question.

Some production managers, despite the high labor costs in the area where Expansionetics is located, say that they could make the hardware more economically than it is made in the distant state where the bulk is manufactured now. This is because the immense engineering capability at Expansionetics could be turned to designing automated lines. Other managers disagree. They think that constantly changing and improving the hardware would rule out the economies of automation which are effected only with a standardized product. The more scholarly R and D managers question the manufacturing emphasis, opting for the scientific and engineering direction. They would have much of the manufacturing done by small outside contractors, and the idea making and the developing of products would then engage more of the total energy of the company.

Automation. "People-people" in personnel and education, though unimportant in key decision making, oppose mass production of hardware because it creates more dull jobs except when lines are largely automated. With changes of significant magnitude in some of the products coming every six months or so, much automated facilities seem unlikely. Current production managers favor hiring semiskilled operators for them to supervise as a viable alternative to the automated ideas for production.

The radicals. Some years ago a few radicals seriously proposed holding back the growth of the company intentionally in order to ensure the high quality of life in the plant. Their conviction was that a small company was a better place for members to make a good product. They argued that the topsy-turvy growth which mass markets dictated led to great pressures and strains on individuals that should be avoided at all costs. Such ideas were quickly discarded by officials, who most likely were appalled by the un-American notion of retarding growth for any reason whatever. The only institutions that seem to stay small are wealthy colleges and hospitals which may do so by choice, while companies and government agencies that cannot mobilize the necessary energy and capital do so by necessity. But even though the managers are sure that the radicals will never have their way, the fact remains that no manager is certain what the directions of major policy at Expansionetics will be. It is safe to say that there are many who cannot state what the policies in effect at present are, although they busy themselves trying to piece together workable ideas in order to cope with corporate realities.

Unionization. For purposes of this study, let us set aside the corporate composite which has been dubbed Expansionetics and examine the effect of change and growth at one of the companies. This company is not unionized, and the power structures prevailing there fear unions. In such circumstances the mixture of skilled and semiskilled members matters to a significant degree over the long run. A corporation with a high level of technology and skilled work forces operates largely on voluntary effort, even on sheer enthusiasm from the career holders themselves, and not on the inspiration of the "Try-harder" signs on the bulletin boards. If a high percentage of professionals and subprofessionals (technicians and white collar) continue to join the company, it is probable that unions will stand less of a chance of entry than if many hands are hired for the production lines. In recent years the subprofessional or paraprofessional levels have increased in number and variety, while less skilled machine workers have not grown in number very much. Should the manufacturing emphasis carry the day, in the event of a policy change for some reason like a change in top management, the union issue would become more dominant. Supporters of R and D hold this view, because they think that technicians would be less likely to unionize than factory hands. Companies which do not favor unionization try to keep their members contented by means of bonus plans, profit-sharing plans, fringe benefits; and they are careful to maintain a wage scale that is competitive by community standards.

The Search for Meaning at Work

Before attaining the position of manager at Expansionetics, each man had a typical bureaucratic career. All of them were either line supervisors, research scientists, engineers, or staff men in personnel. Moving from the core activity in which they received practical experience to the position in management, they now pause for a little introspection and redefine their central life interests.

"Where Should I Go from Here?"

Moral crisis. Most of the men are glad to move up to positions as managers, because this change brings higher status and raises in pay. However, they are now in mid-career, and a moral crisis sets in which is easily recognized by the symptomatic queries: What now? Where should I go from here? Am I doing right by the company? by the community? by my family? Is this really what I want from life?

Plateauing. When managers think about themselves in mid-career, the meaning of reaching a plateau hits them with full impact. They look ahead and see more of the same—too many meetings, too many crises, too many uncertainties about the company's direction—with increased responsibilities, and all this weighs on them. For years they kept sleek in order to run the big race, and now they wonder how long they wish to keep running. Some loss of energy is apparent, but few managers leave Expansionetics, because they have invested too much of their past lives in the company. So it becomes a matter of settling in and formulating a rationale for their daily lives. "Plateauing" has always happened to the other guy, and now it has happened to them. As they face this fact and contemplate their next twenty years of life at work, their often vaguely conceived plans for existence take on intense moral overtones, and they give more thought to a constructive life away from work as well as to using their skills to do a better job for Expansionetics.

Hazards. In the managers' jobs, the hazards are many. Men fail to keep up, or they make mistakes and are shunted aside. Perhaps they are judged not to have what it takes to make a good manager. So they wonder whether continuing at Expansionetics is what they should do.

Staff or line jobs. No single path or pipe line exists that would help managers know where to move next in their careers. They may put their hat in the ring ("bid" is the term used in several companies) for any job that comes up at the level of middle management. They compare their progress with that of other men of their own age or degree of education or years of seniority in the corporation, but the directions their careers may take are almost too numerous to permit a wise choice. One great distinction is between staff and line jobs. Staff refers to advisory jobs with few subordinates to direct apart from those in their own staff area, and line refers to active managerial jobs where orders are given by the manager and carried through by his subordinates. Managers go back to staff jobs, but the general belief seems to be that such moves are demotions, rather than promotions to an advisory capacity. The men who return to staff jobs are looked on as managers who have found the pressures of work too great to handle. Although a dual ladder is said to exist, few believe that the staff specialist has much standing or that he can reach the pay levels the line manager may expect to attain. Within the line positions, men hope to land in departments that will "take off" and grow. But it is hard to predict which departments and divisions will go, because everything depends on what products sell best, and for that the ultimate judge is the consumer.

Dreams. Workers dream of retirement, a small business, a promotion, even though their chances are slim. Managers also dream. One wants to be a ski buff; another, to go into a small lumbering business that his brother runs; a third, to work with his hands as a carpenter; a fourth, to become production manager of a small manufacturing company that may be a comer. But the majority of the managers feel a vague longing to do something more constructive and worthy in the years to come.

THE DRIVE TO DO GOOD

Moral aspects in careers and questions of proper disbursal of personal energy develop importance in a society where there are numerous alternatives. The drive to do good and to be good is strong and central, but progress is halting.

Having reached the position of manager, a goal which they have long sought, the next phase or goal of their careers must be set up. The first goal was mostly for the managers' own personal gain; the next one must transcend the self and include some constructive good for mankind. Concerned with getting some greater sense of reward than pay and security, managers desire to be useful to others while they exercise their talents to the full.

These issues are intimately personal and private. They are seldom discussed with others, although managers who seek to formulate moral ends toward which to direct their lives occasionally voice these thoughts to listeners who are trusted. This information would be hard to capture in a questionnaire.

A VARIETY OF TYPES AND CHOICES

Managers ask what their lives mean. They wonder whether the initiative they squander on behalf of Expansionetics contributes anything at all to the general good of mankind. Some of these managers have been able to accumulate a small nest egg, which they can use as insurance in case a new venture does not yield the hoped-for results. Others have built up retirement funds which they can spend to get themselves started over again in a new, more public-spirited or more soul-satisfying pursuit. A few of these managers have put their humanitarian ideas into action by taking leaves of absence to work for the government and the Peace Corps. The public service and teaching professions draw the interest of more and more men.

Most managers have children of college or high-school age and have to keep making good pay, which precludes indulging in acting-out dreams. They think that perhaps issues in their personal careers can be solved when financial pressures of this sort lessen. But even those with young children talk about their careers as involving sacrifices which do not allow them to follow their inclinations. They dream of the goals, perhaps, but they are hamstrung by financial troubles and responsibilities.

Some managers are overwhelmed by too many setbacks on the job and turn away from the company to outside interests. Tired from overwork in the atmosphere of management by crisis at Expansionetics or discouraged by frustrations on the job, managers often channel their energies into church work, community service, Boy Scout or other activities for young people, or causes like civil rights. Losing interest and rejecting their careers, they may substitute something entirely unrelated and make it the central focus of their lives. They may choose a neutral interest—a hobby, like gardening, or a closer relationship with their families. This type of manager may have mentally withdrawn from the struggle entirely and merely be "waiting it out," as one manager said in reference to his plans for the years which remained before he would become eligible for retirement.

Then there are the drifters, the uninvolved managers who seem to be interested in nothing in particular. They content themselves with a combination of television, travel, and easy living. When they work, they work well enough; and when they relax, they relax completely. They differ from the kind of managers who appear to be nearly pure hedonists, concerned only with making more money and advancing faster and farther than others, so that they can support habits of their leisure life.

A few managers, especially in scientific and engineering fields, see themselves as professionals and not as locals. Their commitment is to the field, to adding knowledge. The important events in their work lives are contributions to their professions. In the process they realize that they add some prestige to the name of Expansionetics. The majority are local in their interests and seldom have close associations with their counterparts in other corporations or in the universities.

An interesting aspect of this search for meaning at work is that a number of managers would like to start or to return to graduate school and study more about a particular science, or explore a field new to them like psychology, sociology, archaeology, botany. Few follow through and realize this ambition, however. The (usually invalid) excuse most often given is that they cannot afford the time or the money to go back to school. This may be because it would be a form of self-indulgence, and the managers as a whole want to live what they consider useful, constructive, meaningful lives, with the service-to-others orientation dominant.

MORAL ENERGY

Moral questioning about the proper use of energy in daily life goes on as managers search for useful, central life interests. Moral energy is expended in being a good boss, in treating subordinates fairly and seeing to it that they develop on the job. From some place they have learned to expect much from life, but since they cannot achieve what they really want, they pour their energies into helping others at work.

The manager who cannot change the world order, or perhaps who regrets he cannot leave his mark on history, can at least feel good because he has helped a supervisor under him see some aspect of his behavior that holds him back. For example, one man who was shy and reticent in his dealings with peers received coaching which had dramatic results. The manager felt a great glowing sense of worth and accomplishment in seeing his pupil do so well.

If this kind of moral energy is not used up on the job, perhaps the manager saves it for nonwork activities in the family and community. It would be interesting to study whether the committed manager exhausts his store of energy at work, or whether he is just as enthusiastic about involving himself with people and causes on his own time. Informal findings at Expansionetics suggest that some managers seem to have a finite supply of energy which, if used up at work, does not regenerate in life away from the job. At other times in these same men's lives, they seem to be capable of infinite concern with moral actions, especially social improvements, with do-good actions in the community. Levels of moral energy probably vary in the same person and may rise more readily when stimulated by the enthusiasm and satisfaction the men derive from doing good. To determine relevant factors would require close knowledge of a manager over a long period of time.

THE EFFECT ON SUBORDINATES

Frequently, when managers shift from job to nonwork commitment, the new, nonwork area of life begins to assume greater importance than the work life. The loss of energy and the shift in emphasis are not lost on the manager's subordinates, and the effect on them is noticeable. When subordinates discover that their manager does not care much, a spirit of defeat quickly pervades the department.

Redirected interest can be interpreted in several ways. One reason for this letdown, or lessening of interest in work, may be that work itself is simply decreasing in importance, and the manager is a victim of the trend. Also, repeated frustrations and crises just wear men out quickly, and such managerial jobs have a short life of maximum efficiency for any occupant. Like a combat pilot who is washed up at an early age, the manager, too, has survived in a hazardous occupation. The latter interpretation may be closer to the truth. Managers start out by being hooked on the belief that work is central to life, but they abandon this belief when frustrations pile up. Their jobs do not provide the moral satisfaction they crave.

Perhaps the younger subordinates reflect the thinking and attitudes of their managers. But it is also possible that the younger men are bringing a different viewpoint with them. They do not expend as much moral energy in making a living as they use in enjoying their lives away from the job. How will these new men react when they reach the plateau? It is interesting to speculate that the transition may be easier for them.

Coping

Wars, city ills, the rights and obligations of institutions and individuals, raise serious questions for many in society. The world is superabundantly ambiguous when it comes to understanding why what is happening is happening. Such ambiguities are magnified by the blurring of the right and wrong of issues in organizations. To know how to survive successfully can be difficult both for managers in mid-career and for neophytes just entering a profession or subprofession. Related to a sense of career crisis is the effect of marketing the personality and the consequences of running the race to earn and use up more goodies than the other fellow.

RULES AND RULE MAKING

Norm-writing, norm-erasing, and norm-confounding are common today at Expansionetics and in other institutions—governmental, medical, and educational as well. No one knows who is right for all time, nor for today and tomorrow. At Expansionetics one important question is: How should you act toward hourly employees? These employees are workers; in short, labor which should be treated with force and active direction, say some. Others say No, they are latent professionals, subprofessionals at least, who merit dignified treatment and benefits in keeping with their new station in postindustrial society. Rules for dealing with this new by-product of automation, this army of nonproduction workers (or whatever they are to be called), simply have not been written, and if some rules had been written, no one would read them.

Rule making on a formal basis is not in fashion in a society feeling its way like a blind man in an unfamiliar setting. Rules in the making are tentative and are applied gingerly, the test being the extent to which they are disruptive. The good rule turns out to be the one which works for the moment, but it is abandoned as soon as events suggest a need for change. This process throws off old conceptions because it operates backward. A testing is required to see if a rule applies; and the results determine whether it will qualify as a rule or whether those affected will criticize it as an autocratic ruse.

For example, a rule in one plant set a fifteen-minute limit on coffee breaks. Some workers took more time; others, less. Individual supervisors had to decide what to do about stragglers coming back to their work stations after the allocated time period. In this instance, the reactions of the workers determined how this rule fared. They approved it, so the fifteen-minute rule worked well enough.

Formal rules are stretched all the time in matters of tardiness, poor performance, and absence from work. Constant offenders over a period of time suffer reprimands eventually. Firm rules are few and not of much interest to students of such matters. Although stealing, drinking, and lewd behavior seldom occur, such acts bring immediate dismissal.

Organizations need to be seen as experimenting and groping in their attempts to right themselves, to regain their precarious balance. Imagine children's erector sets at many places in the organization. Only now the pieces are values, assorted views of what should be done, what needs to be avoided, and the like. Values are played with as youngsters play with erector sets, first testing this combination, then quickly changing the configuration to see if it will work better, or simply because of a whim or another set of images in their minds. In sum, Madison Avenue's "Run it up the flagpole and see if it flutters" seems to hold. Such is the case at Expansionetics, where the art of managing in a changing, growing company requires a willingness to treat most issues and their possible solutions as problematic and tentative.

A Dearth of Occupational Heroes

Management is not an art, particularly; it is a hard science, or so business schools, textbooks, and magazines such as *Business Week* and *Fortune* imply. The dominant traits are intellect, reason, and a cool, calculating, decision-making mechanism in the manager's brain. Input leads to output, and all this can be measured and stated in logical formulas. Obviously, management is a far more intricate, complicated process. After changes in products and policy have been announced to delighted stockholders, it remains for the managers to transform the brilliant new plans into workable, practical detail and action that produce the desired results. In a fast-growing, fast-changing, human system, intertwining variables defy most logical formulas for managerial action. More often, coping and muddling through are the rules.

One of the problems managers face is a dearth of occupational heroes. Management is not a gallant, clean business from which heroes emerge riding white steeds. The champion who muddles through to success can hardly expect to be extolled like Joan of Arc, Florence Nightingale, or Paul Bunyan. Who can be said to do right or best, when it is impossible to define *right* and *best* in this business?

Sages of the future writing for business publications may be accurately defining *management* in a system that has few or no people in it. On the other hand, the "cool-as-a-cucumber" model of the manager playing a rational role may apply to a negative utopia where people are simply vegetables, desensitized and neutralized completely.

He Specializes in People

The nonrational, downright irrational—in short, the human—aspects of the job force a human response from the manager. He acts as a moral choosing man, not as a walking slide rule applying mathematical formulas. Moral acumen tells him which stance to assume at any particular time. If his moral sensibilities are blunted, if his moral mechanism is tilted, or if he becomes apathetic and retreats to taking only defensive steps, he will probably suffer more than if he had made a technical mistake in a meeting. The division of labor is such that he specializes in people and human processes, while the technical specialists under him and around him handle everything else to do with products and processes.

Foremen are a dying breed. Managers are moral brokers, as middlemen have always been, but it used to be the foremen who were in the middle, between top management and workers. At Expansionetics, foremen are a dying breed because with automation there are fewer unskilled people to supervise and because it has entered the managerial mentality that it takes supervisors with a college education (preferably trained in engineering) to lead subordinates, both the unskilled and the increasing numbers of subprofessionals.

Managers have definitely abandoned core activities for which they received training in high school and college. As managers, they find that ambiguities regarding what constitutes good management are rife. Never having studied much in the art of leadership, they grope around looking for formulas that will ease their daily lives. Not that books would yield much information to ease the plights of their existence, but at least they might contain a few useful terms which could be applied to some of the events befalling them.

Moral Choices

Perhaps a single moral system is needed for a time of change in a particular business institution. These data suggest that because a bewildering array of sometimes competing moral postures provide the only pinions for action, such a system is not likely to evolve.

What, then, is it to be for managers? Apathy and confusion? A deep concern for interpersonal trust and close groups or temporary, barely felt contact in groups? Lone individuals, searching to validate ambitions in careers? No single answer emerges. This study of managerial morality suggests that a tough hide and a great tolerance for ambiguity are among the chief requisites in the corporate managerial career. The term "coping" seems most on the mark to explain the way managers solve their dilemmas. All that the business schools might have to do in the future to train neophytes in business would be to teach Coping 100, 200, and 300.

Choices from among the various alternatives are required every day. Managers find themselves faced with problems whose solutions never seemed apparent before and which have to be solved with no basis for decision making. Managers, uncertain about how best to proceed in an environment of change and growth in their organization, are constantly faced with such problems. Even after attempts at resolution are made, it is not clear to them which attempts worked because the amount of accurate feedback is negligible. And if the attempt which did work is clear, there is no guarantee that a similar attempt would work in a changing environment. If top management does not complain, the manager assumes he is doing well enough. But managers have more than two publics to satisfy, and the need to choose which public to serve and how to do it most effectively does not ease the manager's lot. He must not anger or unduly disturb peers and professionals who work for him. Hourly paid members care greatly about pay, so he must also keep some attention focused on their wants.

MANAGERS GO IT ALONE

Managers do not speak with one voice. They have no association or union to champion their causes. They have freedom to act among their publics. As more or less free agents within the broad scope of their jobs, they are subject to excesses, oversights, and mistakes in personnel and other matters. Yet, because of an ingrained sense of "keeping a stiff upper lip" and a need to "sink or swim" in their careers, they seldom meet in concert with other managers to discuss problems connected with their jobs.

A few abortive attempts to bring in experts from the local, world-renowned business schools were abandoned because they led to somewhat explosive meetings where managers vented their considerable anger and resentment openly against top management and the Boss. Managers knew they were saying too much, and they feared word might get back. It also seemed that the behavioral scientists from the schools were unable to offer many truly constructive suggestions.

When managers try to work out moral formulas, they have no models because top management is out of view, because other managers are physically and sentimentally distant from one another, and because no agency exists to praise or to enforce moral stances. Sentimental distance is also partly the result of their having been trained to value struggling alone in careers; beds they make, and beds they have, therefore, to lie on. Managers make the company what it is; yet these indispensable men have no one to protect them, to speak for them, or even to reward them. They go it alone.

To whom or what is a manager responsible? It should be clear that answers range from one client as a possible referent to another. The temptation is to suggest that, basically, they feel responsible to no one or no thing. What is witnessed is a disbursal or allocation of considerable moral energy needed to keep afloat, making it nearly impossible to come out clearly for or against one position or another. One of the appeals of the media, television especially, and of sports in particular, is the certainty men must have in their lives. Games have a finite beginning and end. Too, leisure activities of a physical nature provide this. A life is a balance of known and comfortable events and the unknown. In return for the machine that does everything by itself, managers have bought a loosening of managerial controls, making their work lives on one hand more varied and on the other more confusing and defeating.

MANAGERS AND THEIR CAREERS

Merit and pay raises. Company members, hourly and salaried, receive merit raises which are supposedly based on high performance. In fact, hourly paid members get periodic raises based largely on seniority. This is important to mention because managers now wield minimal influence over pay checks, and thus they have lost the rights they delegated to themselves before unions or employees' grievance committees became powerful. Managers themselves receive raises in pay by roughly the same scheme. If nothing disastrous has happened in their tour of duty, they get periodic increases for service. Thus, the written policy of Expansionetics of paying for merit and performance notwithstanding, pay is based mostly on length of service. This adds to the troubles of managers, because it is another area of uncertainty: that of measuring one's own and others' performance.

A ceiling to managers' careers. Managers are expected to supervise groups that create products and innovations in a dependable, predictable fashion. Striving to bring honor to themselves by their own brilliance and diligence may be passé. They are paid about the same as others of like seniority and will probably never become vice-presidents.

As if dimly aware of this ceiling to their careers and the futility of lone striving, managers have in many cases turned to deal with subordinates and peers in a new manner. If the old kind of power is irrelevant—namely, having more responsibility and more people working under one—new possibilities arise. Managers might more willingly transfer to staff work, which would tax their moral senses less. A movement is afoot to make a dual-ladder system a reality. This would involve technical people's making as much pay as managers for their contributions to Expansionetics. At present managers make a bit more than the specialists. Some managers may be anachronisms competing when there is no race left or when no one knows where the starting line is, or the finish line, either. What remains for other managers could be a mental withdrawal or resignation to interests in leisure and mild concern with experimenting with new human-relations theories on the job.

Pure and total interest in leisure seems unlikely for these men who have moved high in a striving system that emphasizes sustained effort and devotion to work and to the company. They might leave Expansionetics to work with young people, to improve cities, but they would lose the security of a guaranteed, high-pay, and liberal retirement plan at a time when college expenses for their children mount. So most of them will stick it out at Expansionetics, but now they begin to see possibilities for testing out new ideas that might make work more meaningful and exciting as a result of the training in human relations they are undergoing.

The direction of broadened concerns. The study of careers has often been seen narrowly as concerned with jobs, or in the case of women, with producing and caring for children. My main concern has been with managers' beliefs and frustrations as they move in the direction of broadened concerns with the entire life plan, including their jobs. Admittedly, the data are suggestive rather than complete, but a more inclusive project would be prohibitively time-consuming. A model of what is probably happening in managers' careers goes as follows: Work is full of ambiguity and conflict. This leads to immobility of the spirit and a deadening of desire to advance further and to change the system in one direction or another. One option is to fulfill life at leisure; the other, to search and find more immediately satisfying pastures where service may be rendered the society, such as teaching, the Peace Corps, and civil rights.

It should be apparent that managers at Expansionetics do not react automatically and salivate like the good little conditioned dogs of the psychologist when the bells ring. The automaton is not yet here as a model for a career. In a plural, conflict-laden system, it is hard to program a man as an automaton. Nor are men soulless and faceless, as some novels indicate; at least, at Expansionetics they are not. A plausible explanation is that they are modern searchers for right and light, for meaning, just like the rest of us. Hooked to the system they are. Underneath, however, they churn.

Perhaps Marcuse is right in *One-Dimensional Man* in his indictment of modern man as a lifeless reactor to life today.[2] On the level of acts, these man are dull, but their intents, hopes, and fears are a fascinating, potentially life-giving source of energy. The problem is to free more of that energy without destroying both man and institution in the society as it is now constituted.

Who Are the Clients?

The old-time general practitioner trudging through the snow to reach an ailing patient knew exactly who his client was. And the entrepreneur knew who his clients were, too. He may have worked for himself and his dependents, or perhaps some of his family or friends worked with him as his business partners. His efforts had a close relationship to the results of his actions. If he made a certain product or created a service, he marketed it himself, and he saw and felt the dollars it earned.

Today's organization man experiences confusion when he attempts to define his clients. The manager visualizes himself as working with and for an audience which is the beneficiary of his daily labors. This audience or client may be a person, an organization, or a set of groups. In a time when industrial organizations have become more public in ownership and stance or image toward the world, referents multiply and overlap in the minds of many managers. Today's institutional man rarely touches the customer's dollars and seldom makes or markets anything. As a member of another of the emerging professions, he gets too few cues to feel certain of his true mission in the organization and in life.

SOME OF THE CLIENTS

Of course, there are a few managers who have never thought much about referents besides themselves and their careers. One type of manager is purely instrumental, embarrassingly so, and his mission can be labeled *selfish*. Self-interest or concern with the career is dominant. In private he will say his driving motive is to make as much money and to advance to as high a level as possible. A variant type, and a type which is far more common, displays a sophisticated approach with other clients also playing significant roles. He says that he wants to serve the company, his building, and his direct subordinates.

Some managers claim that developing their immediate subordinates is a major objective. By training their people to be able to market themselves, the manager as a sponsor puts out a kind of product from which he can derive psychic benefit and possibly advancement for himself. He trains his successors, hoping to enhance his own career in the process. Other managers may see peers as clients, but they compete with one another and hold back information. Then there are the managers who revere an officer of the company and those few who are great admirers of the company president, but such referents as clients are distant and do not provide enough propelling power to sustain a continued pitch of activity in their lives. The top officers themselves are not paternalistic. Because of their unwillingness to involve themselves in the day-to-day activities of the departments under their jurisdiction, they avoid the cults of personality which tend to develop around them.

The people closest to the man's daily work life are those who work in his department, building, or project. He feels loyal to them and views them as clients whose approbation he values greatly. Managers in production, R and D, machine maintenance, and personnel services cite as clients those whom they service. In addition, they express loyalty and commitment to the enterprise as a whole, to Expansionetics. Occasionally they see the profession as a client referring either to the profession of management or to their specialty from college days— chemistry, physics, engineering, and accounting. Since they are locals, by and large, any specialty gained in an earlier period of schooling is couched in terms that relate to the specific technology and systems at Expansionetics. Some attend professional meetings for scientists and for managers, but few are very active in professional organizations. Service to the communities in which the plants are located or to the communities in which they live is sometimes mentioned. (This type seldom lives in the community where he works.) A few feel an obligation to uplift and serve the hourly paid members of the corporation, especially those who work in their own departments and division. Such concerns are with raising the levels of education or seeing that they do not overextend themselves or get bilked in unwise purchases.

CLUSTERS AND SHIFTS

Loyalties toward clients cluster. A manager who labors for the organization desires to please either an officer or the president. He works hard for his people and often musters considerable energy to get along well with his peers and their subordinates.

Managers shift referents as their careers progress. An earlier devotion to science or engineering is superseded by an interest in management when the person leaves the core activity for which he was hired to become a manager. Not only is it difficult to know whom to serve in the career, but changes in status in the career also affect the man's feelings and commitments. When the company was smaller, it was more common to hear them talk affectionately about their organization. As growth has expanded the organizational size in the last five years, managers express their regret that it is "just another big company now," not the comfortable old place where everyone knew everyone else. These uncertainties regarding the client exacerbate the other ills described earlier and compound attitudes of managerial drift and strain.

DISTANT CLIENTS

Distant clients are potential referents, but they are seldom mentioned in managers' discussions. They see pictures of the board of directors in the annual report, but probably have not met them—especially the New York financiers and those company officers in the legal, general administration, and financial control areas. The stockholders are never mentioned as clients. This finding casts doubts on saccharine statements about corporations serving the owners of the enterprise. Once in a while customers' interests are championed by the production managers or the R and D managers who worry about putting out quality products for them to enjoy in their leisure activities. The dealers who buy the products from the company to sell to the consumers have never been referred to by the managers.

Another kind of referent might be a political party, region, or country, but executives never cite these. Communist executives refer to the quotas and goals of the party. Executives in other countries at various stages of development may refer to the state as a greater goal. Interestingly, only a few managers refer to the college or graduate school in which they were primed. Allegiance to the school seems weak, except for the few who view the local business schools as important molding forces in their past lives and mild stimulants in their current lives.

Why They Do Not Deviate

Observers would have trouble picking up the layers of meaning behind a managerial utterance in a natural setting, say, a meeting or a casual discussion. A student of management would have difficulty trying to pin down what constitutes a moral act without detailed knowledge of the larger organization of the company, the departments and building that the manager works in, the kinds of relationship he has with peers and subordinates, the point he has reached in his career and the way he feels about it.

THE TANGLED CHAIN OF MEANINGS

A manager has said in a meeting with subordinates, "I'm going to fight [the division manager and the vice-president] on this. It's hurting us too much to have to put out twice the work with no addition in force. My people aren't going to be subjected to his kind of pressure." This remark is illustrative of the tangled chain of meanings. First, this is a statement of right and wrong, good and evil, good guy and bad guy. The manager may be about to fight because he feels he has nothing to lose; he may be shamming and really not mean to take any action whatever; or he may be unwilling to risk anything, if he has prospects of a promotion. His threat most likely ends in some mewling gripes to fellow managers.

If the manager stated his case baldly to the vice-president, thus fulfilling his promise to his subordinates, the vice-president might reply with a sigh, "I don't make the decisions," and go on to say that the Boss, a few key vice-presidents, and New York financiers were responsible. Thus the manager's fighting stance is neutralized; it loses its meaning because it is an irrelevant piece of gesturing before men who almost invariably know nothing will come of their superior's ranting. The angry manager has assured his own ultimate disarming. An event of this description reaches the ears of other managers in closely related areas, usually in the same building. The others think, "Poor Tom has gone soft in his old age. He doesn't realize this is a tough league."

Such responses are typical. The point is that the student of such matters must unravel meanings in managerial speech. It is fallacious to say the manager is violating norms. What can be safely called managerial rhetoric is not right or wrong in terms of the system. It is either appropriate or not, but the inappropriate statement cited above is within the range of various people who are able to understand its threatening tone. In an absolute sense the charge can be leveled that the manager is wrong because he lied about fighting for a cause and turned down a good scrap. In this case, norms are to be determined individually by the various actors, reactors, and observers. The trouble is that private opinions vary, and nothing gets crystallized that necessarily will hold the next time under similar circumstances.

MANAGERS ARE NORMLESS

Managers are not paid to develop new moral codes, but to make the existing slippery ones work. They are not initiators of norms themselves, but reactors to them. The pure model of the middleman applies: he buys anything from anyone and in turn sells it to any buyer who will pay the price. A spirit of not belonging to oneself is found here, making it hard to live by the motto "To thine own self be true," because the self is irrelevant. In short, managers are normless in carrying out their official duties as mainsprings, key cogs, and kingpins of the system.

Why don't managers deviate more? As has been documented, it is hard to know what to deviate from. Understanding the changes and gyrations in the company and department takes up energy and time, leaving a man worn out. Not enough energy remains for carrying out deviant acts. Aging is undoubtedly important. The middle-aged manager is a scarred and scared veteran biding his time. Also, a weeding out has occurred. The middle-of-the-roaders stay, exemplars of normal behavior and drives—whatever *normal* means to each of these men. A renegade might be obnoxious, dress or talk inappropriately, act disrespectfully toward sacred symbols like the Boss or toward the policies of the company. In his private life he could be a drunkard, a wastrel, a thief, but this would lead to public censure if revealed. Another area of possible excess is the overinterpretation and subsequent overadherence to policy. (This is what a saint does; he carries to excess a virtue such as belief in total chastity or vows of poverty or penance.) Not one of the managers now at Expansionetics whose work lives have been studied is a renegade. Not one deviates from the middle course. Admittedly, these managers could be discreet, they could be accomplished liars or actors, but that seems entirely out of character.

No strong professional association or in-plant ties with peers exist. Managers are not members of an association which sets rules, limits entry to the field, or sets standards of performance. The ethic of the lone career-striver still exists, and in these circumstances a man is vulnerable, whereas he would be less so in a self-protecting grouping. Plural forces exert influence on a larger scale in sales, manufacturing, R and D, and personnel. Thus, no company criterion exists for how *the* Expansionetics manager should act. No firm or known bases for promotion and raises are found from which the manager could deviate. Some combination of good luck, Ivy League schooling, nice personality, pleasing appearance, youthfulness, seniority, sponsorship, willingness to accede, residence in prestigious communities, family background, leisure activities, interest in the product and its technology, ambition and ability at self-publicity, reputation among peers, and waspishness (being white, Anglo-Saxon, and Protestant) probably operates as a key factor, but it is impossible to choose a combination that will guarantee success.

Summarizing the reasons why managers do not deviate: norms are so vague that deviance has no clear meaning. No models exist for them to emulate. Constant change plays an important part. The two polarized ethics—the production and human-relations ethics—are acceptable at this point in industry and allow for latitude in the nature of relationships. Managers, confused and uneasy, become immobilized; they are "playing it cool" and "not rocking the boat." In short, managers at Expansionetics are coping.

Conclusion

The bureaucracy is sluggish until a crisis arises. When an organization grows fast, flounders, or otherwise changes abruptly and drastically, its members extemporize their corporate governances. Each crisis mobilizes and focuses the organization's energies and programs its next set of trial directives and decisions. Under these conditions the manager is indispensable. He is also somewhat of a hero, but a modern hero, confused and frustrated by situations having no firm precedent. He fleshes out the tenuously existing moral climate and somehow keeps things going in a steady state. In spite of this, many managers lack a thorough understanding of how and why organizations function or of how the system might and should work. Neither the manager's academic training nor his experience in a core activity at Expansionetics helps him as he copes with the contingencies and the moral ambiguities of crisis.

Sociologists in general have visualized roles, statuses, hierarchies, in more fixed positions than now exist in proliferating corporations like Expansionetics. Situational rationality is one thing one day and another the next. The word "rational" does not apply; words such as "temporary," "ameliorative," and "fluidity within the organization" are more appropriate. The tendency of the literature is to promote the myths of rational organization by depicting the manager as a kind of moral computer choosing from among rational decisions to reach known goals, but this is not the case in the present climate of situational solutions.

In studying current organizational realities, it becomes evident that growth is ungovernable because it responds to the market. Expansionetics makes dependable products known and used by satisfied consumers for years, and it reinforces its good image with new products which create their own ripples of excitement and demand. Success chances are loaded in favor of managers, however overburdened they may be by the demands of changes and growth. Managers do not control the ultimate success of the company, and they cannot fail badly; but the fact remains that unmitigated growth precipitates material benefits at a cost of considerable human sacrifice. Corporations provide "due process" for workers, but seldom for managers. And managers do not govern. They have extremely limited power. That managers are normless, nearly powerless, and without due process is a truth rarely mentioned in sociological literature and little recognized in the organizational structure. Planning concentrates on manipulating machinery and funds to meet future exigencies, while the human aspect is neglected. Thus the executive is caught in the spiral he helps to create.

The workplace is throbbing with life and a new attitude made possible by changes brought about by automation—changes that force leisured members of the organization to look at one another and to consider the moral aspects of what they are doing with and to their fellow workers. This concern for others is a paradox because lone career-striving isolates each manager and makes conjoint activity wellnigh impossible. T-groups and sensitivity training sessions represent early attempts of the corporate structures to deal with the antihuman consequences of their technical decisions, but such efforts raised anxieties to a point which made the meetings abortive. A semblance of collective reasoning is beginning to operate in large organizations, nevertheless. Even though T-groups have not helped much, they may have yielded a certain residual plus effect in catering to the human affiliative drive by encouraging participation and increasing acceptance of more humanistic ethics. It is not the solution to the problem of the normlessness of management, but it is a step forward. Constructive grouping is one way to combat some of the anonymity and aimlessness which plague managers. Organizations, perhaps for the first time since the Industrial Revolution, are thinking in a self-conscious manner.

NOTES

NOTE: Extensive editorial consultation, collaboration, and clarification of ideas came from Genevieve E. Cormack. Sheila C. Campanis edited early drafts. Everett Cherrington Hughes helped the author to ask the questions raised and discussed in this chapter.

1. See the detailed treatment of the T-group ethic in Alexander David Blumenstiel, "An Ethos of Intimacy: Constructing and Using a Situational Morality," Chapter 14 in this volume.
2. Herbert Marcuse, *One-Dimensional Man* (Boston: Beacon Press, 1964).

11

The Problematics of Respectability

Donald W. Ball

> Sociologists are the professional custodians of what little scientific knowledge we possess that is conversant with personal relations. But from them we have, as yet, little to learn, for they are in general little aware of the problem of . . . the affairs of everyday life.[1]

> People considered them very respectable . . . because they never had any adventures or did anything unexpected; you could tell what [one] would say on any question without the bother of asking him.[2]

Given the character of what passes for typical sociological concern —such as crime and delinquency, stratification, ethnic relations, and so forth—the generic topic of respectability might seem, at least on surface consideration, to be more than somewhat cavalier, capricious, trivial, even gratuitous. We suggest and shall attempt to demonstrate, however, that the social meanings of respectability and its various cognates of unrespectability, disreputability, and the like are worthy of serious sociological attention as important concepts for the understanding of human conduct.

Thus, for instance, a recent monograph on the social organization of dying and death[3] ethnographically describes the relationship between the caliber and amount of care and attention given patients arriving at hospital emergency rooms and their appearance as it provides the

ER staff with an index of the new arrival's perceived-to-be *respectability*. It follows, not surprisingly, that perceived-to-be alcoholics, for instance, are among the class of persons deemed by the staff to lack respectability and therefore morally unworthy of maximum life-saving efforts. A similar fate also awaits persons designated by the staff as members of other derogated social categories, such as would-be suicides, narcotics addicts, prostitutes, vagrants, and the like. This ethnographic account is fully in accord with the conventional folklore (and its factual basis) concerning persons refused immediately necessary hospital admittance because of their other than respectable appearance. Such popular tales usually build, of course, to a crescendo with the death of the central character.

What is important to our purposes, however, is not the dramatic nature of these hospital-centered events, but that rather than being trivial or unimportant, *respectability may become a life-and-death matter* for particular actors implicated in social episodes; [4] and even if more typically it is of less momentous import, it is still a major aspect in the management of the practical but problematic affairs of everyday/anyday life.

Respectability is not, though, only a matter of individual or personal concern; it also becomes a matter of collective import, calling forth the attention and involvement of pluralities and groups of persons along with those patterned social entities subsumed under the rubrics of organization and establishment. Thus, a central goal for the United States Negro middle class has been provided (at least until very recently) by their orientation toward the symbols and trappings of respectability as defined and manifested by their white-class counterparts. For the "Black Bourgeoisie" [5] the quest for the grail of respectability became almost a social movement as members worked full time at the jobs of "playing seriously" at the game of "society" and managing respectable appearances.

Additionally, whether by design or accident, the ordinarily publicly notorious Hell's Angels motorcycle gang in California found itself doing collective respectability work when temporarily catapulted toward an unlikely and unwanted accorded-status-as-respectable by United States supporters of the war in Vietnam; this when they attacked a peace march near the Berkeley-Oakland city line in the fall of 1965.[6] And finally, in the world of work, attempts by occupations to upgrade themselves (as by claims of professionalism) may be interpreted as collective movements oriented toward a desire for the accordance of respectability by clients, customers, and members of other occupational categories.[7]

Further, that respectability is a useful concept for organizing, interpreting, and understanding some of the more traditional substantive sociological concerns should not blind us to the importance and prevalence of respectability seeking in everyday/any-day life. These practical management efforts are to be found among the daily activities of all persons going about the day-to-day social business of interacting with other human beings: the problematic job of performers displaying themselves as worthy and deserving of respectful recognition (1) in order to maximize their presentations of self, and thus (2) to enhance the concomitant instrumental rewards associated with favorable accorded or assigned identities and the attainment of goals dependent on self-presentation and its acceptance, and (3) perhaps most basically, because to be defined as respectable by one's audiences is to be considered as a regular or normal human being; that is, as a member of that category of persons perceived as morally acceptable, as other than evil, and so on.

Thus, a newspaper account (in the writer's files) of a recent wedding in a typical Los Angeles suburb describes the ceremony, the bride's white "A-line frock, Empire style," and the roster of the wedding party, which includes the names of the unmarried misses attending the bride; and as the best man—the groom's older brother, a draftee at a nearby boot camp. Omitted from the report, though, are the educational biographies of the bride and groom, information routinely carried by the paper in which the story was published. Now, it might be asked: what kinds of brides are more likely (in an inferred, but probabilistic sense) to be marrying a groom so young that his older brother is a recent army inductee; to wear a dress cut so as to fit loosely about the waist and abdomen; to lack the middle-class-appropriate published educational biography (as does also the groom), such as high-school attendance and/or graduation; and to have only unmarrieds, to wit, misses, as her attendants?

The most likely answer we would submit, and one verified by admittedly informal and unsystematic inquiry, is an already pregnant teenager; but one who is, or whose parents are, oriented toward conventional middle-class canons of respectability concerning weddings, conceptions, and their normatively defined temporal priorities. To be married in a church is, *ceteris paribus,* to be worthy of respect; and it is to the appearance of *ceteris paribus* that such strategies as pregnancy-hiding A-line and Empire-dress styles are addressed by reputation-conscious suburbanites; no less than are other gambits by the officially unworthy of respect (that is, those formally or legally so defined, as criminals or the mentally ill).

I. Perspective

We argue, as suggested in the foregoing, that respectability is a central concern of actors in the problematic dramas of mundane life. Furthermore, it seems that historically this has particularly been the case since the nineteenth century, when what Harold Nicholson has called "the cult of respectability" developed, concomitant with the rise of the middle class and their special version of bourgeois morality.[8] And although the quest for respectability is perhaps not as frenzied as it was in the Victorian era—for instance, when censors were concerned to bowdlerize Shakespeare and even Robinson Crusoe [9] and the entire sociocultural milieu was organized around respectability-centered norms and values [10]—it is still a major focus in day-to-day, practical affairs and should, perforce, also be one for students bent on a sociological analysis of such conduct. However, though a fundamental form of orientation for lay sociologists,[11] respectability is not, perhaps unsurprisingly, in the indices of most sociological treatises, even in the introductory textbooks which are, after all, heavily laden with "slice of (the student's everyday/any-day) life" examples and illustrations pertinent to his or her experience.

Thus, the study of respectability is an example of the study of the unstudied; that is, what has been called "front-line sociology." [12] Consequently, any and all observations, analyses, and remarks concerning this area of social reality must be taken as especially tentative and exploratory, there being little in the way of existing data or theory, at least of an "official, certified," sociologically orthodox kind on which to draw. However, roughly following Simmel, we shall treat respectability as a form, by which is meant a grammar: concern with the generalized social elements constituting it, rather than specific instances or contents of its occurrence—a tendency to focus on abstractions rather than particular cases.[13]

II. Toward a Sociological Conception of Respectability

It will be apparent to the reader that as yet there has been no attempt at specification or definition of the meaning of respectability; merely examples relying on common-sense consensus regarding a hopefully mutually understood referent as concerns what respectability is all about.

Now, one strategy for attempting to arrive at a sociologically ac-

ceptable definition of respectability is the one which is perhaps so obvious that its technique is frequently ignored by sociologists: simply
going to a good dictionary. This approach may be justified sociologically on at least three counts.

First of all, words are social facts; their conventional meanings are
understandings attributed to others; that is, assumed to be shared.
Their meanings are thus Durkheimian social facts having "the note-
worthy property of existing outside of the individual consciousness." [14] Thus, words and their meanings fall directly in the province
of traditional and central sociological concerns.

Second, as Edward Rose has demonstrated in an undeservedly neglected paper,[15] dictionaries, as collections of words and their definitions, are compilations of *natural sociologies,* albeit originally nonprofessional conceptual categories and schemes, but eminently suitable
and powerful, however, for sociological expression and, furthermore,
forming the basis for by far the vast majority of concepts in current
professional sociological usage. Thus, although respectability might be
a newcomer as a sociological construct, it would hardly be novel in
terms of its antecedents. On the contrary, it may be argued that it is
the occasional neologism, such as syntality and plurel, which are alien
to the sociological conceptual tradition, since most of our intellectual
baggage has been drawn from the pre-existent stock of natural sociologies found in dictionaries and in everyday conversations.

Last, but no less importantly, the reason for and existence of any sociological reality is to aid in the systematic description and understanding of *social reality* as this is produced and apprehended by the
actors constituting and constituted by the dramas of everyday/any-
day life. For such actors, their experienced social reality may be
thought of as a set of language-determined categories, a set of social
meanings [16] which may be visualized spatially as a collection of pi-
geonholes arranged in rows and columns so as to form a grid. Into
cells formed by this grid are "plugged" actors' social experiences, thus,
by assignment, becoming *socially meaningful realities* of perception
and experience and forming over time a background reservoir for future use in according and ratifying meaning and reality for the ex-
periential reality of the social world.

Now, the sociologist also has a grid: one which is used to order the
sociological reality of social reality. However, to the extent that the
language-determined categories of the sociologist's reality are syntheti-
cally created out of theoretically or methodologically inspired operational activities,[17] rather than based on the social phenomena of the
mundane world, they are likely at best to distort and at worst to mis-

interpret completely the meaningful reality of this mundane world. In other words, unless it is rooted in the everyday language of actors' meanings and experiences, sociological reality will cross-cut rather than be congruent with social reality.[18] To return to the analogy of the grid, the sociological one will run the danger of being tilted (an unknown number of degrees) in such a way that its cells will include varied proportions of adjacent but therefore *heterogeneous categories* drawn from the grid of mundane social reality.[19]

In other words, to the extent that our conceptual schemes are artificially rather than naturally based, we run the constant risk of trying to explain apples and oranges, as it were, in the same breath. Obviously, at some level of abstraction apples and oranges will belong to the same language category of order (fruit, flora, and so forth), but such a discovery cannot be made by imposition or fiat; it must come from an understanding of the phenomena under study; that is, it must arise from data rather than dictate. The same sequence must hold for a sociological examination of respectability; such an effort must start with the mundane world and its consensual categories of social facts, respectability and its lack, and their corollaries among them. And one such source, as Rose has shown, is the dictionary. Although dictionaries present ideal or "correct" meanings rather than those actually in vogue at a particular time in space, there is no a priori reason for assuming that the discrepancy is either large or systematic; and furthermore, such definitions are constructed by lexicographers out of the stuff of social reality rather than imposed as a sociological version. Thus, short of a sampling of meanings extracted via interviews and content analysis (and, of course, subject to their usual sources of distortion), a dictionary seems to provide the best starting place for deriving a sociologically appropriate definition of respectability and its correlatives.

The Oxford English Dictionary (1931, pp. 535–536) defines *respectable*, when referring to persons, as "worthy of respect, deserving to be respected by reason of moral excellence," and *respectability* as "the state, quality, or condition of being respectable in point of character or social standing." Other dictionaries give similar meanings, stressing the moral nature of the terms: being respectable is to appear morally or socially worthy, that is, deserving of deference; [20] and respectability is, then, *the perceived appearance, the imputed state, quality, or condition of being* assumed-to-be morally or socially worthy and deserving of deference. As to be expected, these lexical definitions are quite consistent with our own common-sense, taken-for-granted knowledge of these terms (as members of the culture); and

they thus provide a basis for constructing a sociological definition
which attempts to avoid doing violence to the language and meaning
of the everyday/any-day social world—that is, a sociological reality
more consistent with social reality.

But before going on to that task it would be well to give some consideration to a key element of respectability; specifically, the social
meaning of moral worth. And here we may turn to the writings of
Harold Garfinkel and his sociological investigations of the lay sociologies, the social realities constructed and used by members to make
some practical sense of their experienced social worlds.[21] It is to this
work, albeit with a nod also to Durkheim, that we look for an understanding of the meaning of *moral* as an evaluative dimension in mundane or secular contexts.

In a series of studies Garfinkel has demonstrated ethnomethod-
ologically that for members, *moral* as social reality *equals normal;* to
be perceived-to-be-normal means appearing to be conventionally situated or placed in the-natural-order-of-persons-taken-for-granted, to be
socially located in the "of course" environment of nonreflective every-
day/any-day life.[22] Thus, to be accorded such placement is to be
deemed normal, and this location is a moral one: normal = moral, and
therefore to be respectable one must appear to be normal, must be received as such, confirmed as such (for example, through deferential or
respectful responses from others), and thereby socially demonstrate
one's moral worth. It is in a sense close to this that some sociologists
conceive of society itself as a moral order—that is, as a set of normally, and thus morally, ordered locations of positions and roles realized in symbolic communication—although traditional sociological
reality has usually stressed the more explicit and obligatory rather
than the implicit and taken-for-granted exchanges of mutual understanding in social realities.

At this point we are now ready to suggest a more sociologically useful definition of *respectable* and *respectability,* one which is based on
(1) dictionary statements as they may be considered descriptions of
the members' social reality, (2) Garfinkel's studies of these social realities and (3) a conception of social conduct common to symbolic inter-
actionists, dramaturgical analysts, some rule theorists, and most nonex-
perimentally oriented students of face-to-face encounters. For sociological concerns herein, then, we shall consider *respectable* to mean:
to be a person (1) perceived-to-be normal, thus possessing moral
worth, (2) the appearance of which is thereby accorded through deferential displays, that is, signs of person-appreciation from others, (3)
in socially situated encounters. Thus, being respectable interdepend-

ently involves conceptions of and perceptions of the appearance of normality, leading to the accordance of moral worth, along with deferential displays of ratification, by other socially located actors.[23] Therefore, we should note that if we know who is respectable or otherwise, we thereby know what is considered normal or otherwise.

CONNATES OF RESPECTABILITY

It should be clear by now that the phenomenon of respectability involves two basic elements: (1) actors and audiences, those whose performances may or may not be deemed morally worthy and those who make such evaluations; and (2) the conception and perception of such worth and, by extension, the "knowledge," the belief in the accuracy or "rightness" of these judgments. Further, although we have not to this point been explicit on the matter, assignments and accordance of respectability can obviously be made concerning self as well as vis-à-vis others; that is what we mean when we speak of *self-respect*.

By now manipulating the two dimensions of actor and audience and presence or absence (actually degree) of knowledge or belief, we are in a position to generate some conceptions which are closely related to respectability. Such a strategy yields a set of refinements not always recognized by lay analysts, but useful for the further light they shed on the core term of respectability; as discussed below the mundane world most often makes use of a binary model, involving only the mutually exclusive categories of respectable/not respectable.

First of all, the denial of the assignment of moral worth—that is, the imputation that a person is *disrespectable*—will be associated with revulsion and disgust in the case of the audience, and frequently anxiety and/or outraged righteousness on the part of persons so denied moral worth, provided that such withholding is actually defined by the perceived-to-be-lacking-respectable-appearance as inaccurate, unfair, unjust, wrong, or the like; that is, that he is in fact morally worthy and deserving of deferential person-appreciation gestures by virtue of truly being part of the natural-world-of-persons-taken-for-granted. We are speaking, here, of cases where actors and their audiences are in genuine disagreement regarding the accordance of moral worth, and thus respectability. It is important to note that the open, overt expression of indignation in such situations is one of the major management strategies by which disrespectables, whether individuals or collectivities, may attempt to counter their morally unworthy designations and thus become respectables.

We may contrast such disrespectables with *unrespectables;* that is, those to whom the denial of respectability by their audience represents an accepted-as-accurate response to their genuine lack of respectability. This obtains in situations where there is consensus between the viewer and the viewed concerning a true lack of moral worth. Such is the case, for instance, for those stigma-bearing persons who accept the collective meanings of "normals" concerning their condition.[24]

However, to the extent that appearing respectable is a prerequisite to certain lines of action—those of the confidence man, for instance [25] —as well as being rewarding in and of themselves in a more general, expressive sense, we may expect such façades, even while not subscribed to by the performer, to be artfully feigned; in this sense being respectable may be an instrumental goal to be actively sought and pursued. In cases where apparent respectability shields actual, if known by the audience, lack of respectability (for example, the self-defined confidence man again), we may wish to use the term "disreputable" to emphasize its qualitative social difference as compared to situations where the denial of moral worth is made by the audience monitoring the performance, whether accurate or not; here the knowledge of lack of respectability is held by the actor rather than those before whom he performs.[26] Clearly, to the extent that all of us are, from time to time, less deserving of morally based deference than we appear or wish to appear to others, we all disreputably dupe our audiences on occasion; sometimes intentionally, as when we hide our harmful goals from the objects of such action (the unctuous sincerity of the used-car salesman comes to mind); sometimes accidentally, as when we do not contradict those who take us to be of higher social or moral rank than is actually the case. In these latter situations, of course, it is often more cruel to illuminate than to continue to deceive, more kind to con than to cue, since such efforts to adjust situational definitions call into question the "normal" judgmental processes of the audience and therefore their own respectability.

Further, we should take note of the fact that under certain conditions actors who define themselves as actually worthy will *instrumentally* pretend to their audience a lack of respectability, a *feigned unrespectable* appearance. Such a pretense seems to be the case for some (an unknown proportion) of the male hairdressers taken to be homosexuals who are actually sexual normals, staging an act quite functional, given the microecological structure of their occupational tasks and performances. It is a characteristic of hairdressing—the barbering of males, too, which interestingly does not evidence many overt homosexuals or stereotyped allegations about them—that the practitioner and patron are in close physical, bodily copresence; that they are spatially intimate. In the heterosexual situation of the male hairdresser and his female patron such a bodily juxtaposition is potentially sexually threatening and tension-generating. By socially withdrawing— that is, by presenting himself as other than sexually normal, as not physically attracted to women—the hairdresser taken to be homosexual minimizes the potentially disruptive, strain-provoking, sexually threatening aspects of the spatially intimate male-female, practitioner-patron dyad. He thus feigns unrespectability, misinforming his audience for instrumental purposes. More mundanely, by the way, we sometimes call the *expressive-oriented* feigning of unrespectability by the prosaic label of *slumming.*

Finally, there are those transitory social situations where considerations of respectability are not relevant and if at all so, very minimal, superficial, automatic, and reflexive. These are to be found in those comings together of social actors who are and are likely to remain relative strangers to one another; for example, at bus stops, airline terminals, and other sites involving behavior in public places.[27] In such instances, we might perhaps be pardoned for speaking of *irrespectables* in these residual situations.

	Perception or Belief	
Categories [28]	*Actor*	*Audience*
Respectable	Yes	Yes
Disrespectable	Yes	No
Unrespectable	No	No
Disreputable	No	Yes
Feigned Unrespectable	Yes, but . . .	No
Irrespectable	Perhaps, but unimportant	Perhaps, but unimportant

In summary, then, when we consider the generic categories of respectability and its cognates, we are dealing with presentations; with appearances and their acceptance; with perceived-to-be or claimed-to-be normality and concomitant moral worth and its ratification or rejection through deferential, person-appreciating actions and/or the withholding of such gestures. And although our definitions have been phrased in terms of individual persons and their audiences, the conceptions are not limited to this level but are also relevant to aggregates, establishments, and organizations. Thus, it may be useful from time to time to make a distinction between *propriety,* or respectability at the individual level, and *legitimacy,* its analogue at the collective level; persons may appear proper while larger-scale social units are perceived to be legitimate.

III. Respectability and Social Interaction

Although in discussion we may speak "as if" respectability (or its allied concepts) were a characteristic, a characterological attribute, most fundamentally it is actually *a relational category* (compare Goffman on stigma [29]). It is an inherent limitation of our language of discourse that we are led to speak of aspects of social relationships, like power and intimacy, as though they were static, personal traits. However, we should not be confused on this matter: respectability emerges and has meaning only as an element in social relationships. It always involves a presenter and an audience: one to display, and one to be displayed to; and without each of these, the phenomena of respectability cannot exist.[30]

It should also be made clear that when we speak of respectability, we are not referring simply to some residual category of perceived-to-be abnormality, lack of moral worth, deviance, or the like. For as has been at least suggested above, it is a basic property of respectability that it is actively sought in social transactions, just as the appearance of its antitheses (such as disrespectability and unrespectability) is actively avoided—in the case of disreputability, successfully so. However, just as there are variations in the degrees of deviance (as conventionally defined) and associated penalties, so too there are degrees of respectability or a lack thereof, along with associated consequences. The relationship between deviance and respectability is much like that of cognac and brandy: as all cognac is brandy, but not all brandy is cognac; so, too, all deviance is other than respectable, but not all that is other than respectable is deviant.

Now, if respectability is a relational category, a dyadic product, its existence or maintenance frequently requires what Goffman has called *teamwork.*[31] In other words, respectable appearances involve co-operation and co-ordination, a joint endeavor by both actor and audience. And in many cases, the participants will mutually help one another to maintain a respectable pose, thus facilitating both personal considerations and the interactional flow. By "normalizing" the identities of the participants, each is able to treat the other in a conventionalized perspective—a routinized frame of reference which also helps to sustain favorable definitions of self as well as predictability concerning others.

For instance, in an illegal abortion clinic (more fully reported on elsewhere [32]), it was found that patrons and staff both co-operated with one another to sustain a definition of the situation as a respectable one. Patrons consistently treated the staff as though they were properly credentialed medical personnel and in return were dealt with as though they were persons seeking and receiving conventional medical care and treatment. Such teamwork acted to maximize the predictability and thus the smoothness of the establishment's activities and at the same time provided the most favorable definitions of self possible for the persons so involved: as patients rather than patrons and as medical practitioners instead of criminal conspirators. Thus, the participants successfully managed appearances of propriety and the establishment, more generally, its legitimacy.

Similarly, Skolnick reports that police in the community he studied designate their stool pigeons as "special employees." [33] Such respectability-enhancing labels for these informants helps to blunt the besmirched moral character which otherwise attends them, as it also does, at least by implication, for those who would deal with them, their police patrons. Thus, both police and their informants work together in sustaining a co-operative evasion, a mutual feigning of moral worth.

Additional evidence of the co-ordinated, dyadic nature of respectability creation and maintenance comes from an unpublished study by Fasken.[34] It has been noted by several sociological observers that the occupational position of the pharmacist is problematic, fraught with strain due to the inherent ambiguity and conflict generated by his simultaneously held professional and commercial responsibilities.[35] He is at one and the same time a respected, highly educated dispenser of specialized skill and knowledge and a merchant, an entrepreneur frequently purveying cosmetics, stationery, toys, and the like—often in greater dollar volume than the drugs and pharmaceuticals on which his professional training centered. Now, in many instances, similar cases of such potential strains are handled by segregation: either spatial, as in the separation of home and place of work, or temporal, seen in the nine-to-five workday, or both,[36] the problematic being controlled and eliminated through complete avoidance of any overlap of the possibly conflicting spheres. For the pharmacist, actual segregation of his potentially disparate tasks is impossible; both the respectable professional involvements and the comparatively demeaning commercial transactions take place within the same time-space context of the drugstore, frequently with the same audience members privy to both aspects of the pharmacist's role as he moves from one to another in response to their variegated medical and merchandise demands.

Fasken has found that a common device used by pharmacists to ease this occupation-based dilemma is a dais (along with a partition some four to six feet high) to achieve symbolic spatial separation. In keeping with the greater respect and prestige it enjoys, the pharmacist mounts a platform raised approximately a foot up from the store's main floor when practicing the professional, the normal, medical elements of his role, thus elevating himself above the plane of the relatively degrading world of merchandising which takes place below. By placing himself spatially above the plane which would ordinarily obtain between himself and his customer-client, the pharmacist symbolically asserts the deference due him as regards his respectable, his regular, moral, professional task. Repeated observation indicates a simultaneous change of mien by the pharmacist toward greater propriety paralleling his spatial alteration along the vertical. And in doing this respectable space work the pharmacist is tacitly aided and abetted by his patrons, who by not invading the sacred space of the dais deferentially support him in his claims to professional respectability. The successful presentation of any such claims depends on teamwork, no less for the legal world of pharmacists than the twilight one of stool pigeon or the illegal one of criminal abortion. Thus, presenter or claimant and audience form an interacting team, mutually assisting one another in the projection and ratification of respectability; that is, respectable appearances.

PROBLEMATICAL ASPECTS

It follows, then, that because respectability requires the co-operation and co-ordination of teamwork, it is always problematic for socially situated actors. That is, it is never, except in a crude, probabilistic sense, a given; it is never completely structurally determined (remember the cautionary moral of the little boy in the story of "The Emperor's New Clothes"). And as a related consequence, given the multiplicity of potential audiences and their varied definitions and standards of what constitutes normality, moral worth, and respectability, it is impossible to appear respectable at all times to all men. Like deviance, respectability is always situated and therefore always subject to the varied and changing properties and demands of differentiated social encounters.

Therefore, it makes little theoretical sense to think of respectability and its cognates as always involving a particular communication content. Respectability (*et al.*) is as much a function of its reception as its inception. It is a truism of daily interaction that the intent of a given communication does not equal or even necessarily resemble its ultimate reception by the audience. To conceive of respectability only in terms of its initiation and management by performing actors is to oversimplify and even distort empirical reality, to ignore the emergent nature of human conduct and the crucial role of audiences in the construction of social encounters and episodes.[37]

Thus, appearances which will generate the accordance of respectability in one situation may be precisely those which lead to assignments of a lack of respectability in another. It is for this reason that managing the appearance of respectability is always problematic; and it is therefore like women's work—never done.

Basically, the respectability problem involves the presentation of proper demeanor so as to be worthy of and to receive the deference from others due us by virtue of our membership in human society.[38] Such deference is necessary in order that we may be assigned the minimal status needed for the successful pursuit of goals in social situations, as well as the creation and upkeeping of definitions of self as a morally worthy person; that is, one who is normal, who upholds social order and is deserving of the order-maintaining and sustaining gestures of worth-acknowledgment from other like-minded persons in society. Thus, respectability becomes central to social order itself, one of the major threads in the fabric of social integration.

At a more mundane and basic level, though, respectable appearances are a necessary prerequisite to merely staying out of "trouble." [39] A major function of law and law enforcement agencies is the proclamation, promulgation, and upkeep of public morality; that is to say, to do society's respectability work. To come under such agents' scrutiny and active jurisdiction is to be, at least potentially, in "trouble"; that is, implicated in the bureaucratic machinery of morality maintainers. Thus, observers of the uses and application of police discretionary powers have commented on the utilization of respectable appearances and the lack thereof as a diagnostic tool for such social control agents; for instance, Skolnick reports on the police's cognitive polarization of the population into respectables and criminals [40] and the mutual exclusiveness of these categories. Those lacking the appearance of respectability automatically fall into the latter, morally unworthy cell of the dichotomy; they are assigned, by virtue of their appearance, criminal status; and the burden of disproving this categorization is, of course, their problem—that is, convincingly demonstrating their actual respectability. What makes such situations even more problematic for persons so stigmatized is that the definitions of what constitutes respectable appearances are constantly shifting and ever changing. That the relationship between such definitions and their enforcement is highly class-bound need hardly be pointed out to students of crime, delinquency, mental illness, and the like.

But at the same time, we should also note that care must always be taken not to appear "too respectable," lest we be accused of paying too much attention to appearances and too little to practical affairs; in a word, overconcern with the appearance of normality will be deemed abnormal and unnatural and sufficient reason for withholding or withdrawing imputations of respectability. Thus, there is social danger in being too well spoken, too correct in our dress, demeanor, and so on. It is even thus that the parvenu and the *nouveau riche* give themselves away to the audiences whom they wish most to impress with their apparent respectability.[41]

This is not, however, merely to equate the quest for respectability with the simple *conformity-approval* models of persons in interaction posited by Zetterberg and others,[42] but rather to suggest that respectability, as well as being an expressively rewarding aspect of definition of self, is also an instrumental means toward other ends and interactional goals. To say, with Zetterberg,[43] for instance, that the maximization of self-image is the basic motivation of actors in social encounters is not necessarily to say that it is therefore an end in and of itself, or that such attempted appearances are basically superordinate to or incongruent with other norms, values, or purposes.

Furthermore, because normality and moral worth are varied in the success of their display and the degree of their accordance by the audience, they are a dimension of *social differentiation,* a basis for hierarchical sorting and invidious ranking like the economic factors of class or the life-style variables of prestige or status. In fact, though it is not always made explicit, respectability in one of its forms or another is a major element in the processes of *status claims and placements* studied by students of social stratification, both as a determinant of hierarchical positions and as a consequence of such placements; and it may become a central defining parameter of such strata as in the frequently reported lower middle-class pervasive concern with respectability.[44] As Douglas has pointed out (in a personal communication), respectability seems to provide the link between the person-centered criterion of morality and the collective ranking dimension of prestige or status; rank and respectability symbolize or "stand for" each other, as do moral worth and respectability, thus providing a transitional device for the problematic tasks of presentation and assignments.

Now, beyond the important general, everyday/any-day concern for respectability and respectable appearances, these are particularly problematic for persons (1) who find themselves in situations and settings typically denied respectability (such as pornographic film screenings, homosexual bars, and the like), where their discovered presence would undermine otherwise accepted claims of normality, moral worth, and so on, and (2) who find themselves in situations where they have no sanctioned right on the basis of their actual repertoire of socially relevant characteristics (as a pregnant bride at a church wedding) and are thus, in reality, socially ineligible for the role they are claiming and playing. The one involves respectable persons and situations which are otherwise, and the other respectable situations and otherwise persons. Paradigmatically, the discussion in this section can be illustrated as follows:

	Situation	
Person	*Respectable*	*Otherwise*
Respectable	Conventional	Problematic-I
Otherwise	Problematic-II	Unconventional

The first cell, *Conventional*, refers to the normal encounters of everyday/any-day life, the transactions of the mundane world. While these are problematic, too, the degree is relatively low, and the source is not structural, but based on the presentational abilities of the actor and the cognitive capabilities and activities of the audience.[45]

The cells labeled *Problematic*, on the other hand, do involve structurally based discrepancies. The first, *Problematic-I* (upper right cell), attends perceived-to-be-ordinarily-abnormal situations and requires presentations of actual propriety, attempts by the actor to separate or distance himself from the contaminating environment, an effort to communicate that "the real me" has nothing to do with this setting. The other, *Problematic-II* (lower left cell), involves abnormal people in normal situations and generates concealments of actual improprieties. A particularly dramatic example of both of these types of relationships and their concerns is to be found mixed and combined in the problematic existence of persons who are intersexed, whose whole life may be devoted to the concealment of one set of characteristics and the presentation of another. Thus, prior to surgery for the removal of male genitalia, one such person reports the efforts necessary to conceal these anatomical contradictions to the female identity being presented to audiences, especially when at the beach or while with an amorous male bent on petting below the waist (*Problematic-II*).[46] On the other hand, Agnes, the case in point, defined himself/herself as a female long before the operation, or even prior to adopting the dress and other presentational strategies of the female role—that is, while still being socially defined by others as a male—and thus was thrust into situations incongruent, to Agnes at least, with the internalized female sex role definition (*Problematic-I*).

Much less bizarre than the case of Agnes, the writings of Stephen Potter,[47] though satirical at one level of meaning, can be read at another as a set of manuals delineating respectability display tactics in various problematic encounters of both types, particularly the second, *Problematic-II*. Gamesmanship, one-upmanship, lifemanship, and so forth are all strategies for maximizing one's own appearance of respectability, often by minimizing that of the other.[48] Where Potter shines particularly is in his accounts of how this may be done by those whose claims to respectability are most marginal or tenuous.

Finally, the *Unconventional* cell points to those cases traditionally subsumed in the study of deviant behavior. The premier case is, of course, crime, where criminal persons and their situated criminal activities intersect; more generally, where both persons and their role-related activities are deemed other than respectable.

There is yet another analytic sense in which we may consider respectability as problematic: in what has been called *game framework*. The analogue between games, particularly board and card games, and everyday/any-day interaction has been made by a number of social scientists.[49] While the various formulations of the game analogue differ from one another in greater or lesser degree, they all seem to share several elements in common: (1) *interdependence of outcomes*, such that any player's pay-offs or losses are contingent on the actions of other players; (2) *monitoring* of the actions of self and others, due to outcome-interdependence; (3) *rules*, a situated set of normative prescriptions and proscriptions by which the game proceeds or alternatively, in their breach, breaks down; and (4) *imperfect knowledge* for the players of each other's intensions, motives, perceptions, game plans and strategies, and so on. Additionally, it has been suggested by some (Goffman, Leary) that (5) games have *style criteria* by which players' performances can be judged irrespective of win-lose outcomes. Thus, each player in attempting to pursue his goals must take the norms of the game into account, both the rules and those which provide stylistic evaluative dimensions, along with the actions and perceived or imputed inner states of consciousness of his opponents, about which he has only imperfect knowledge, especially as they may be deliberately concealed or misrepresented (as with bluffing in poker).

As regards respectability, all these characteristics are both relevant and, like games in general, problematic. Respectability itself is an interdependent outcome: presentations are for nil unless they are accepted by the audience. Because of this, actors constantly monitor their own displays and the receptions they receive and must be ready to alter their presentations accordingly. And, of course, both actor and audience are within the context of both game rules and style criteria in making their assessments. But perhaps most important vis-à-vis respectability is the aspect of imperfect knowledge, affecting both performers and those before whom they perform.

Because of this, actors can never be sure during the course of an encounter whether or not they are being accorded respectability-based deference or merely being paid lip service; while ultimate outcomes may serve to validate respectability, these are after the fact and provide no clues during the performance itself for the actor as regards the success or failure of any particular line of respectability presentation, and thus the necessity of change or maintenance of display strategies. In other words, although the performer may think or feel that he is apparently respectable, he can never know at the time that this is actually the case in the eyes of the audience or whether they are being polite, avoiding a scene, and so on. Thus, for the actor imperfect knowledge always makes his appearance of respectability problematic.

Similarly for the audience: since they have imperfect knowledge of the actor's motives, intentions, and so forth—that is, the sincerity of his display—their situation, too, is problematic and subject to exploitation as well as confirmation by the outcomes of the transaction. For them, no less than the actor, respectability has the constituents of a game. Put another way, the game framework underlines the ever-present possibility of players' subjecting one another to a put-on.

THE IMPOSITION OF RESPECTABILITY

It should be emphasized that respectability is not only managed and presented by actors—directed from within, as it were—but also externally imposed by audiences, not necessarily at the behest or even willingness of the actor receiving such assignments. Thus, the appearance of respectability is not only staged by actors who either share definitions, values, and the like with their audience, or alternatively hope to exploit them; but respectability is also thrust upon them; for instance, by audiences with different cognitive and valuational systems than those of the actors performing before them, but who hope to remake such actors, to change them toward conformity with their own perspectives. Hence, Eskimos reporting for enrollment in federally operated boarding schools in the Northwest Territories of Canada find themselves fumigated and deloused, showered, barbered, and deprived of their native clothing by white school officials who then garb the boys in blazers and flannel slacks and the girls in blouses and jumpers à la traditional preparatory school in the white, middle-class, urban-suburban worlds of main-stream North American culture.[50] They thereby impose on the Eskimo students the standards of respectable appearances of their own; that is, the school officials' reference groups. This suggests that respectability is problematic not only in terms of presentations and concealments of appearances by actors but also in terms of its being thrust, willing or no, upon such actors by their "well-meaning" audiences.[51] The Job Corps programs for women provide an example of imposition on more receptive and willing-to-change persons; girls were described by one knowledgeable reporter trained as anthropologist as "coming full circle from a nadir of disorganization and sometimes debauchery to a promised land of respectability and good reputation." [52] In a different context one can look at the practice of some church-related colleges of bestowing honorary doctorates on the administrators of sister institutions drawn from the clergy, thus giving them the instant academic respectability of the title "doctor." Again, to recapitulate, respectability involves the appearance of normality and thus moral worth and the right to and receipt of deferential consideration; it is not the residual of deviance, but, on the contrary, is actively sought and vied for in interactional encounters; it is, therefore, not an attribute, but a relational category, and because of this involves the concept of teamwork. Furthermore, it is always problematic; in its presentation, in its outcomes, gamelike; and finally, not only managed, but also imposed.

IV. The Rhetoric of Respectability

Though from a sociological perspective respectability (or its lack) is a rational category, from that of the members of the everyday/anyday world this is not the case. From the members' viewpoint it is a person-centered phenomenon, whether regarding self or others; it is a characteristic, in the original moral, root sense of the word. People in the mundane world either are taken to be respectable or are not.

And although neither of these common-sense categories is irreversible, the latter—the lack of respectability—is particularly resistant to change or alteration, once the assignment has been made. Thus, for instance, persons released from prison after serving their term are not free men again, but rather they are ex-convicts, with the taint of prior lacks lingering on to structure presents and futures for those so labeled.

Since members are either respectable or not, this characteristic's perceived presence or absence becomes a crucial concern, both for identifying others and for presenting selves.[53] Just as respectable appearances are used to measure others, similarly we use our own appearances to impress others, so that hopefully we may (1) instrumentally maximize the pursuit of our goals and (2) expressively procure favorable responses from others in the process of defining and maintaining self. We are thus under constant constraint to present appearances indicative of good character, especially since the lay interpretation uses an either/or model. Respectability is therefore central in the interactional activities of identification and control of others as well as the construction and upkeep of one's self.

And since it is a matter of appearances, respectability is, in the way that Simmel used this term, a form of communication, having a particular set of structural characteristics, irrespective of the particular symbolic contents involved. It is to such matters that we now turn: respectability as a rhetoric, as a patterned communicative strategy or tactic, having a regular dimensional structure within which specific meanings or contents are manipulated by social actors in search of respectable appearances.[54]

As suggested above, the rhetoric of respectability is dimensionally structured: these dimensions minimally being the two continua of *truth-falsity* and *presenting-concealing;* we shall consider these essentially separately, although their intimate relationship mitigates against completely maintaining this course, even in the pure, theoretical case.

As it always is, in all situations and circumstances, the matter of truth is a complicated thing. In the present context we are not referring simply to information subject to conventional scientific test as to its validity or invalidity but to information which is subject rather to *social criteria of validity,* and these are two in number: (1) *conviction* of the actor, and (2) *acceptance,* that is belief, by the audience.

Conviction by the actor refers to his definition of his presentations as they relate to some perceived-by-him-as-actually-the-case state of affairs or condition. Thus, it may range from the complete to the totally lacking and may coincide with or contradict scientific criteria of validity which may or may not be relevant to the situation, the participants, and the problems at hand. A person who genuinely believes that he is six feet tall is likely to accept the confirmation or disconfirmation of this conviction which may be scientifically provided by precise linear measurement tools and their application; while on the other hand, a paranoid sincerely taking the role of Napoleon is little likely to be swayed by any contradictory historical data which would deny his claim to Napoleonic status.

In a like manner, audiences may accept or assume appearances which are capable of scientific refutation, even in the face of such contradictory evidence—particularly when such evidence flies in the face of the "of course" or "everyone knows" criteria of social reality and its folklore; consider, for instance, the public stereotypes regarding "laziness" and persons on relief, Negro intelligence, and the rehabilitation prospects of persons criminally convicted. Similarly, they may also reject appearances capable of scientific confirmation, as well the examples in the immediately preceding sentence suggest, too.

Thus, conviction does not necessarily imply acceptance, nor acceptance conviction, but neither does one automatically cancel the other one out; the relationship, like social conduct more generally, is problematic for the participants, subject to the structural constraints of membership categories and socialization experiences, the situational contingencies of social actions and their meaning located in specific contexts, and the goals—both short- and long-run—held by the actors implicated in the encounter. Conviction of moral worth and audience-acceptance generates respectability; lack of conviction and/or acceptance produces the varied types of respectability-lack discussed earlier; that is, unrespectability, disrespectability, disreputability, and the rest.

Where socially validated truth leads to a consideration of both actor and audience, as a rhetorical device, invalidity or falsity is linked, however, to the presenter only. This is not to say that audiences may not discern and ignore or alternatively protest elements of untruth in a performance (the varied responses to professional wrestling come to mind), but rather to suggest a special sociological locus of concern regarding deliberate misrepresentation by actors as it is related to the management of respectable appearances, especially as regards the phenomena studied under the rubric of deviance.

Falsity refers to a presentation concerning which the performing actor is phenomenally convinced that some other state of affairs is actually the case; that is, it is deliberate misrepresentation on his part—more specifically, for our concerns, of his normality, moral worth, and deserving of the deferential appreciation of accorded respectability. It thus involves activities of prevaricating, conning, deceiving, and the like; and as truth, falsity, too, qua rhetorical tactic is closely related to presenting and concealment of information and appearance.

If we combine these two variables dichotomously (ignoring, as we have done in this discussion, their actually continuous nature), we find that there are four theoretical combinations: present-truth, conceal-truth, present-falsity, and conceal-falsity. However, from the standpoint of the actor's rhetoric, only the first three are empirically relevant: we can present the truth (or what would be accepted and taken to be the truth); we can conceal the truth (or what would be accepted and taken to be the truth); and we can present falsity (or what would be rejected and considered to be false by the audience if aware of contradictory evidence). However, it obviously makes little sense to conceal falsity (as we are using these terms), except to conceal that it, the content, is falsity; but again, at the level of form this is a special case of presenting falsity in order to conceal truth.

Thus, in managing respectable appearances there are three basic strategies of manipulating information: (1) the presentation of virtues; and (2) the concealment of vices; along with (3) the creation of appearances of virtue where other circumstances actually obtain. And within the concerns herein, it is concealment, along with falsity—that is, the presentation of the otherwise—which seems of most saliency to the problematics of respectability, although we should not be blind to the alternative strategy of manufacturing new truths for presentation; that is, attempts to promote redefinition so as to obviate the need for concealment and falsity. Such is the activity, for instance, of the Mattachine Society, the Daughters of Bilitis, and other "special pleading" organizations representing homosexuals before government and public.[55] Neither should we ignore the fact that even those actors bearing membership in the most despised social categories are able to marshal a high proportion of normal or respectable-appearing attributes and activities for truthful presentation: except for those labeled mentally ill, for instance, they obey the "residual rules" of the culture, the everyday etiquette of normality described by Scheff.[56] Thus, Simon and Gagnon describe lesbians as conventional, even "stodgy" in all but their sex-partner gender preferences.[57]

However, if respectability is always problematic, still it is particularly so for those situations and the persons situated in them who are traditionally subsumed by sociologists under the category of deviance and by laymen under the labels of illegal, immoral, illicit, evil, bad, wrong, dirty, sinful, and all the rest. It is here that the activities of concealment and falsity appear most dramatically and here that they are linked to the highest stakes (contrast the consequences of "white lies" and incriminating testimony in a felony trial): not only definitions of self, but more instrumentally, the ability to carry out chosen lines of action—for example, criminal activities and other forms of "social pathology" and the continued freedom of being "outside" of the confinements of jail, prison, and other total institutional environments.[58]

These acts of concealment and falsity may further be subdivided by degree into those of *hiding, denial,* and *lying,* these being the simpler and more complex versions, respectively, of the same underlying tactic.[59]

Hiding the simplest form of concealment, involves keeping appearances detrimental to imputations of respectability out of the perceptual field of relevant audiences. Thus, it means the keeping of dangerous information completely out of the potential awareness of threatening others; in short, keeping secrets. Such matters may range from the extremes of having committed a homicide and disposed of the corpse à la gangland practice of taking victims "for a ride" to the mundane shielding of underwear on clotheslines by placing them between larger neutral articles such as sheets and towels.[60]

The fact that so much of human existence takes place within and behind walls in North American society makes many hiding activities relatively easy.[61] Thus a variety of sexual activities defined as illegal by statute, but with a high degree of actual occurrence, almost never result in arrests, prosecutions, or convictions because of the fact that irrespective of any other characteristics, most sexual acts take place indoors, the norms of privacy further helping to shield both the conventional and the bizarre in sexual practices since such personal pursuits are surrounded by rules of disattention that are generally subscribed to. Further, the body and its surrounding clothing present additional hiding places for the concealment of information implying other than respectable appearances: for example, the addict who shoots under the tongue to shield the visibility of needle marks; the concealed weapon in the pocket, the anally or vaginally cached contraband of the smuggler; these are only a few of the possibilities offered and utilized by the body and its raiment for such purposes.

However, not all hiding activities involve spatially based techniques and visual barriers. Just as information is rooted in an ecological context, so, too, it has a temporal location; thus eventful pasts, such as biographical data, are a major kind of hidden information, along with prior motives for current actions and the future goals of such activities. Pregnant brides attempt to hide the physical evidence of their past indiscretions via the manipulation of the fullness and waistline placement of wedding gowns; and when ultimately faced with the temporal dissonance of length of their marriage, typical nine-month durations between conception and delivery, and date of birth of their offspring, they resort to the more complex strategy of lying (discussed below).

Similarly, former inmates of custodial institutions are under special pressure to conceal this kind of eventful biographical information, particularly if they choose not to return to old surroundings upon release, but to go elsewhere and try for a "fresh start." And finally confidence men, perhaps the paradigmatic case of the problematics of respectability and criminal activity, must ever hide both actual prior motives and desired futures from their chosen victims if their operations are to be successful.

It is only when hiding fails that the arts of denial and lying must be invoked to maintain concealment, when spatially and/or temporally situated evidence which contradicts respectable impressions is discovered or potentially discoverable by the audience. When *denial* is the chosen mechanism, the attempt is made simply to convince the audience that they are mistaken, have a false impression, did not accurately perceive what they thought they did, and so forth. In other words, the attempt is made to brazen it out. This approach will be most successful, of course, when the betraying information is most ambiguous and easily subject to being overlooked, disattended, and/or given alternative interpretations and meanings. Thus, the little boy caught with his hand in the cookie jar is probably unable successfully to carry off the strategy of denial, while his colleague with what appears to be a mouthful of quickly swallowed cookie dough is; the one is caught red-handed, while the other is only potentially, and thus deniably, shame-faced.

Now, a more complex form of concealment and falsity of a lack of respectability involves *lying;* by this we mean efforts at concealment through the use of presented information controverted by actual, empirically based (*if* discerned) appearances—and known to do so by the performer; truths are hidden and untruths are communicated so as to create or maintain taken-to-be respectable performances. Thus, lying is the point at which falsity presentation and concealment intersect each other. And like any other form of communication, it is facilitated or impeded by certain structural characteristics; perhaps the most important one in the case of lying being the probabilities of the availability of contradicting evidence, such as its visibility, accessibility, and so on.

Thus, lying is likely to be especially prevalent and associated with forms of communication which minimize the number and kind of stimulus signals apprehendable by the audience, such as letters and the telephone, though it is by no means limited to these cases. Boiler-room stock swindlers, to note a cardinal instance, are able to use the restricted informational characteristics of the telephone to pretend that they are what they are not—to give the impression that they are legal, conventional stock salesmen, with the attendant respectability attached to such offices—in order to foist on their telephonic clients or victims, who are unable to monitor the setting visually, the bogus stock issues which are their special stock in trade.[62]

A more marginal example is provided by a southern California research foundation. Its literature, mailed to the home, proclaims its lofty goals in the area of medical research: to examine neurological pathologies originating in the spinal cord. To this end it solicits the recipients to volunteer for free X-rays to aid the foundation in building up a sample of various and assorted cases. Persons offering themselves as participants in a medical research project calling the telephone number listed in the brochure, however, find that it is not the number of an autonomous research operation, but that of a doctor's office instead. Should they make an appointment to be X-rayed and go to the doctor's office, they find the doctor is not an automatically respectable one of medicine, a physician, but rather a doctor of chiropractic, a marginal practitioner of questionable respectability or propriety.

Finally, an interesting case of "visual" lying is provided by William Rose in a personal communication. It is the practice of some of the larger brothels in Mexico to utilize a male employee, whose task it is to loiter around the lobby or waiting room of the establishment dressed in a police uniform, drinking and talking to other employees. His presented visual appearance along with his jovial, intimate relationship toward the staff is meant to convey to prospective clients that there is no problem concerning the illicit establishment and the police. He is, naturally, not a bona fide policeman, but a live prop, employed in helping the establishment to manage appearances.

Lying is, of course, the last refuge of those deemed to lack respectability and called upon to account for such lackings; thus, the final claim of prematurity or earlier secret marriage when the pregnant bride's baby arrives too soon. But at the same time it is also one of the ways in which performers lose respectability; that is, when they lie unsuccessfully and by such action forfeit prior claims earlier successfully ratified concerning their respectability, even their whole biographies.

It is thus a two-edged sword: one which can aid in concealment and the presentation of falsity but at the same time can betray respectability claims if it is discovered. And because trust is such a central, though usually unstated, element in social transactions,[63] the discovery of lying frequently generates stronger reactions of hostility and respectability-withdrawal than would the otherwise singular discovery of the information the lie was originally presented to conceal.

Thus, perjury is one of the most heavily penalized of all nonviolent crimes. The detection of lying rips at the very bases of social understandings and mutual activity: the tendency, even the practical need, to trust our interactional partners; and it is for this reason that it is the most risky and heavily penalized form of concealment.

To summarize briefly, hiding involves simply concealment; denial involves concealment of the discovered via bravado; and lying involves hiding of information along with the presentation of other falsified information.[64]

Although we have been focusing for the most part on those endeavors and situations traditionally defined in sociology as deviant, we must, of course, recognize that the kinds of tactics outlined above are not at all restricted to such settings but are an integral part of everyday/any-day life and the actions in it. We might, for instance, turn to the etiquette books for the contents of conventional rhetorics of respectability and to memoirs of the Middle Ages, the Renaissance, and Victorian England for historical accounts. Baldassare Castiglione's *The Book of the Courtier,* for example, is nothing so much as a manual for respectable appearance management in the sixteenth century of Machiavelli, and similar works have done the same job for other periods and settings, such as *Lord Chesterfield's Letters*—and perhaps most recently and most successfully and profitably (for the authors), the self-improvement literature epitomized by advice of Dale Carnegie.[65]

As respectability is not separable or empirically isolatable only to deviants or only to normals, similarly the strategy of concealment is not separable, except analytically, from that of presentation. Thus, when we look to the social world for examples of respectability-management, they will not be limited to one technique or another, but will use any and all which are either necessary or available; the worthy will be presented with one hand while the unworthy is hidden behind the back with the other. Courtship, as a general social mechanism as described by Burke and by Duncan, may be the perfect case of respectability presentation, but the compleat suitor does not limit himself to the proffering of a gentle countenance and gracious speech and manners.[66] He also attempts to conceal bad breath with mouthwash and the odor of perspiration with deodorant, and he hides creature releases such as flatulence and belching as best he can; while at the same time the object of his attentions may gird or falsely pad her torso, artificially color her hair, cosmetically alter her facial appearance, and so on.[67] For females in particular, their art and artifice at such grooming tasks are one of the key signs of their being "respectable" girls or otherwise.

Similarly, the "good neighbors" in a middle-class suburban community observed by the writer simultaneously presented and concealed by getting their front yards landscaped long before turning their attention to the back. Thus, they aided the neighborhood in its collective visual presentation of legitimate suburban gentility and one another in the mutual assurance that theirs was a "nice place to live," even if the properly presented front yards were contradicted by the hidden back yards—which were equally as wild as those in front were splendid.[68]

In many ways this quest for the appearance of floral, suburban respectability became more than a little like the ethnographically well-described potlatch,[69] with display becoming an end, and a costly one, too, in and of itself; for as the participants in the potlatch risked bankruptcy (or its barter equivalent), so also did those suburbanites too zealous about their yards.[70]

It seems quite clear that for these self-defined suburban, "most normal" Americans, respectability, as exemplified by front yards, is a very precarious thing; and this is, of course, a central fact about respectability: to reiterate, *respectability is always problematic.* And this holds whether the analytic or practical interest is in its rhetoric along with the (at best) only partially determinant character of social meanings, or in the varied consequences of acceptance or denial of respectability on situated lines of action, or in the relationship between appearances which are respectable or otherwise and selves and identities of actors in social encounters.

At least briefly we should note, too, that whether the situation involves house yards or yeggs, courtship or confidence men, respectability has a vocabulary as well as a rhetoric. However, where the rhetoric structures the general case, vocabularies, although consensual and collective, are more specific and situated.[71] While admittedly there are general vocabularies of respectability such as the "residual rules" which comprise an etiquette of normality,[72] most situations and set-

tings involve a more precise and limited set of symbols and presentations, in the extreme becoming ritually specified and dramatically codified.

Examples of the latter range from the formality of the etiquettes of
diplomatic encounters and the military [73] to the set of cues which
serve to label characters for their viewers in daytime television serials
as respectable or otherwise, a vocabulary which is basically constant
from program to program and network to network. These signs are especially useful in establishing new characters, whose lines of later dramatic action serve to validate the early cues; it is thus that they are
learned by viewers (and may be discovered by analysts) as art imi-
tates life and viewing substitutes vicariously as parainteraction for
more direct contacts and learning experiences.[74]

The magnitude of the audience watching such programs suggests
that the vocabulary of respectability manifest in the "soaps" is one
shared by a sizable proportion of persons, particularly women, at least
concerning their expectations concerning middle-class settings, which
are central to these programs. Although these dramatic cues are right
out of the white hat–good guy/black hat–bad guy tradition of the
western, they are considerably more complex, subtle, and capable of
nuance. Substantively they include, à la mundane life, the social
meanings attached to clothing and hair style; drinking, both quantity
and type of drink consumed; smoking; attitudes toward children; for
women characters, dedication to cleaning and cooking; extent of contact with family members; number and kinds of friends; and occupational status—in short, a set of cues not limited to television drama,
but coincident with many of the criteria in frequent use in the natural
world, at least that segment dedicated to definitions of respectability
derived from conventional Protestant-Puritanical morality.

V. Respectability and the Self

Roughly following Stone and Goffman, we can make the following
distinctions: *impressions* are definitions communicated or presented
by the actor, about himself, his *self*, to his audiences; in the process of
monitoring actors' impressions and performances audiences make assessments and judgments which are communicated to the actor as responses to his imputed self, that is, his *identity* as assigned by those on-
lookers; both received identity and presented self are experienced by
the actor, and they may or may not coincide—this is always
problematic.[75] This experienced combination of presented self and

imputed identity, whether involving confirmation and ratification or refusal and denial, may be called the *social self* (the combination of gesture and response in Mead's social psychology called the "me" [76]); finally, the enduring aspects of this experienced relationship between presented self and received identity we may call *character*. Directly bearing on respectability and/or its lack is the relationship between types of appearances and the selves and identities thus derived, along with their implications for more basic character. Since respectability and its cognates refer to basic matters of normality and moral worth and their interactional consequences, they are fundamental to phenomenal intrapersonal considerations as well as cognitive and evaluative matters.

Now, without the deferential appreciation, which by definition is part and parcel of respectable relationships, selves cannot be experienced as completely worthy or deserving, no matter what the presented appearances or internal definitions and evaluations. The common-sense conception of *self-respect* (compare with Coopersmith [77]) bears directly on what we are getting at here with its folk conceptualization of the close link between a person's actions and their definitions of self, especially as these are evaluative rather than merely descriptive. The unique sociological contribution to this everyday/any-day viewpoint is, of course, sociology's emphasis on the social meanings of the response of the audience: their assignments of identity to the actor as a basic constituent element in the construction of self, and over time, if internalized—that is, taken over even in the absence of a monitoring audience—of character, too.

We thus return to the concept of the imposition of respectability; as noted above, respectability involves not only an impression, managed or otherwise, which is communicated by the actor but also the assignments which may be imposed by others, with both intended and unintended consequences. The Eskimo students processed in accordance with a model of education not from the Far North, but from urban, middle-class North America are a case in point.

In the process of imposing their versions of respectable identities and appearances, the school officials are involved in creating new selves for these Eskimo children, many of whom come to the residential school from family and home settings not far different from those portrayed forty years ago by Robert Flaherty in his classic documentary film *Nanook of the North*. In the forced environments of the total institution of the boarding school, new imputed selves gradually become stable attributes of the children as their internalization ultimately creates radical characterological alteration in the direction of the identities desired and fostered by the school, its policies, and its officials. Ultimately, of course, even if only for a visit, the Eskimo children return to their traditional homes and families; and it is then that the question of respectability becomes particularly problematic.

Once exposed to the socialization experience of the residential school, no longer are either the children or their parents and other un-schooled kin normal to one another; no longer does either group appear to belong to those categories of persons deserving of person-appreciation because of their moral worth. North Americanized native children and their kin stare back and forth at one another across a cultural void; the children identifying their families with the meanings associated with a no-longer-respectable historical past, while the parents throw up their hands in despair at the generational gap which they don't really understand. Each one becomes to the other a disrespectable. Government hopes for their own definition of native progress and improvement—to wit, modernization—among the northern peoples founders on an unintended familial disorganization founded on loss of respectability in generational relationships, a dissonance between appearances, identities, and imputed selves, and ultimately of basic characters.

Although it is respectability which may be imposed, it is more often its lack which is the aim of such assignment efforts, especially when made by official agencies. The ceremonies of courts in particular have been interpreted as degradation rites, a collective respectability-removing ceremony in which the community or its agents successfully impose definitions of abnormality and moral unworth on their victims, thus destroying their potential claims to future deferential treatment.[78] And it is a fact that later efforts to reimpose respectability are frequently not nearly so efficient or thorough. The vocational training programs in prisons, for example, which are supposed to transmit to convicts a respectable and marketable skill on release, often do no more than equip them with a technology-based trained incapacity for normal, respectable employment in an automating economy. Thus, like many of the physically handicapped, such individuals frequently find themselves unable to find employment other than in workshops and occupational settings where the low wages which can be paid to those lacking respectability offset the gains otherwise accruing through up-to-date technology and production practices; the process of identity-assignment and therefore social self-construction begun with original degradation combines with vocational training policy and the exigencies of the man-power market place to generate a more permanent nonrespectable character, a less worthy self at any moment.

The problematics of imposition can also be seen as regards the *victims,* rather than (more obviously) the perpetrators, of certain crimes, such as rape and child molestation. Here the process of becoming a victim involves actions and experiences which may lead to a questioning of whether or not one continues to be considered normal and morally worthy, of respectable self or character. The question of victim-precipitation has received most attention from professional sociologists as regards homicide,[79] but probably much more from the lay sociologists in the mundane world as concerns sexual assault.

However, we may not assume that all imposed identities or personalities are nonrespectable and that they always have negative consequences for the actor's experiencing of himself or pursuit of his goals. The imposition of respectability may be an excuse, a justification for slips, errors, blunders, and inconsistencies in action which otherwise contradict this assigned respectability. In effect, actors may be able to count on the generalization of either their respectability or its lack to other areas of endeavor, not directly and specifically linked to the basic source of their respectability or lack thereof, thereby to provide their audiences with explanations, interpretations, and meanings for otherwise apparently dissonant actions.

An extreme example of this phenomenon vis-à-vis the generalization of respectability is provided by a cautionary tale current among some of the publishers' representatives who show their lists at academic and professional meetings.[80] It is a belief among them, and some of them claim to have witnessed it, that nuns are particularly prone to steal books from their exhibitions, secreting the purloined volumes in the folds of their habits. What makes this case interesting for our purposes, however, is not that nuns may pilfer, but the reaction of the representatives to this problem (whether giving accounts of their own experiences or retelling those of others). The typical, if not universal, response to the question as to what was done when these book-stealing actions were detected was nothing at all, followed by an explanation of justification to the effect that one simply couldn't do anything because, after all, they were nuns. In other words, their status as respectables was so well established that it constituted virtually a "license to steal"; so firmly established were their claims to moral worth and deference that even in the case of dramatic contradiction, they would not be withdrawn or denied. It is precisely this kind of phenomenon that abets the commission—and, if subsequently discovered, the reluctance to prosecute—of other, less unique kinds of white-collar crime. An analogous situation has been reported by Roth concerning the status of hospital personnel and the wearing of protective clothing around tubercular patients.[81] Those least likely to adopt such cautionary measures were physicians; their status allowed them to "be above" such considerations; then in perfect descending order of status or respectability and ascending order of frequency were professional nurses, practical nurses, aids, and finally, the lowly student nurses, most likely of all to follow the hospital's rules of caution.

VI. Respectability and Moral Entrepreneurs

We should not be blind to those who go about the business of manufacturing the definitions of deviant or reprehensible conduct and thereby respectable and otherwise selves, identities, and characters. The role of moral entrepreneurs has received a good deal of academic sociological attention in late years.[82] This concern, naturally, has usually been as regards the areas examined by students of deviance and has in some ways converted the questions concerning who is deviant and why into the political query of who has the power to propose such moral categories in the first place and furthermore to get such definitions accepted, or institutionalized into public policy.

What has been less emphasized is the fact that such entrepreneurs are also at least implicitly (and often explicitly) generating the labels of what kinds of activities are respectable, normal, morally worthy, to be appreciated, and so on. Definitions of the bizarre, the evil, wrong, or whatever are also statements about the moral meanings which are the conceptions of the good, the pure, the virtuous, the respectable. We—that is, sociologists—have started asking questions about how deviant labels come about and are successfully applied; when we do so we are also at least indirectly considering the other side of the coin: the characteristics of normality which are current in societies and social systems; who or what groups, in other words, by their moral-definitional activities, and their subsequent promotion of these meanings, determine who and what is normal and to be accorded respect. It is out of such stuff that normal selves and identities and characters are built, no less so than those that are deemed deviant or unworthy of respect. The boundary-maintaining activities of a system—whether personal or social—to use a functional approach, require normal, worthy, moral, deference-deserving activities and actors for their continual marking and reiteration no less than they do the dramati-

cally different, the despised and less worthy; that is, the actors and activities constituting the materials of the traditional studies of deviance [83]—in a word, certain types of nonrespectables.

In general we can ask about moral entrepreneurs the same questions that were raised regarding the rhetoric of respectability: What is
being presented? What is being concealed? What part of the presentation is truth? What part falsity? More globally, we can ask why they
are engaged in such activities in the first place? Whether they love
vice less or virtue more? Scheler, at least, would suggest a high probability that such entrepreneurs love virtue not so much as they secretly
covet those vices which they publicly inveigh against; the theory of
ressentiment seems particularly suited for an interpretation of moral
entrepreneurial activities as the respectable version of morality preoccupation and obsession, even while such pastimes are actually based
on a repressed, covert lust for that which cannot be attained, either
because of external constraints or phenomenally experienced inner
controls.[84]

Such promulgating activities almost guarantee the promulgator the
accordance and experience of respectability. For who better to appear
normal and thus morally worthy than those who are involved in the
very definition or enforcement of such moral meanings? If anything, it
is perhaps small wonder that fewer persons are not engaged in such
potentially self- and character-enhancing concerns. Possibly, it is an
awareness of the terrible vulnerability that we all have to such entrepreneurs and their power to make and confer labels which leads most
of us to desist charitably from such pursuits. Furthermore, in a differentiated society such as that of North America there are surely some
allies for any such endeavor; but perhaps it is this very pluralism that
militates in most cases against allies of sufficient number and force
for successful attempts at this kind of rule making and/or enforcing
power.[85]

However, it is precisely such entrepreneurial considerations that
lead to the development of the special-pleading organizations which
speak for the unworthy and downtrodden to the respectable normals
of the public and its political policy-making bodies. And here we see
an interesting case of lay sociological analysis preceding in time that
by those supposedly trained to do so. It is precisely because a naïve
version of labeling theory was recognized by laymen long before it
was discovered by academic professionals that such entrepreneurial
activities, actors, and organizations exist to be studied by sociologists
in the first place; they have been doing respectability work for a long
time, at least since the development of publicly responsive govern-

ment. That this is the case again underscores the necessity for sociological reality to root itself in the social reality of the phenomena it
studies, rather than imposing its conceptual scheme from above, a
priori.

For moral entrepreneurship is just one instance of a more general
type of basic, fundamental social process long recognized in folklore
and proverb: that of *making virtues out of vices*; that is, converting
into respectability that which is not accorded this status—an ideological version of cutting one's losses by redefining them as gains.[86] Such
is the process involved, for example, among the economically impover-
ished believers in those religious sects which emphasize this-world suffering and deprivation as the price to be paid for afterworld
salvation.[87] A lack of respectability by current secular standards is
converted into a respectable cost for future spiritual pay-offs, and thus
a potential vice is given the moral meaning of virtue.

VII. Respectability, Social Conduct, and Sociological Analysis

As the various chapters in this volume indicate and the illustrations
in this chapter suggest, respectability is everyone's problem all the
time. Although the concept tends to bring to mind middle-class prim-
ness and propriety, this is far from its only locus; [88] though definitions
and criteria may vary from one subculture to another, from social category to social category, respectability or the attribution of normality
and thus moral worth and its recognition seems for Everyman a necessary precondition to ordinary social conduct, to the pursuit of goals
and the favorable experiencing of self.

But even though the respectability norm, the injunction to appear
normal and worthy to others, is pervasive, it is usually unstated; thus,
it is a background expectancy, a residual rule of the culture (or
cultures).[89] It is a characteristic of this type of expectancy or rule
that it frequently becomes visible only when punitive sanctioning orientations and activities by offended audiences come into play; then
we first notice or infer back to the norm; it is through this explicit reaction that the implicit to which is reacted becomes evident.

Now, if we look at the consequences of lacking the appearance of
respectability, we find that the penalties run the full range from mild
to severe: from (1) symbolic degradation of self, identity, and character (verbal abuse, sneers, the "cut direct," and other mechanisms of informal interpersonal control) through (2) limits on social participation
such as prohibitions on entrance and exclusion from various member-

ship categories (occupations, voluntary organizations, residential areas, and so on), to the ultimate of (3) removal from the community: either temporary as a prison term or permanent as capital punishment; for a definite time, again a prison term, or indefinitely as in the cases of commitment to mental hospitals and the banishment of political exile such as frequently is utilized by unstable political regimes.[90]

Put proverbially, our argument concerning respectability is that there is a kind of *put your best foot forward* norm which obtains in social life generally.[91] If our focus is on the mundane everyday/any-day world, basically we are led to consider the consensual symbols of respectability, the way they are manipulated, and their consistency or variation in socially differentiated situations and settings.

However, we should also note a tacit implication of this rule, too, and that is this: if actors are under normative pressure to put their best foot forward, they are also constrained to hide or conceal their worst foot. And it is here that the sociology of deviance is most likely to become interested in respectability, when strategies of avoiding the disclosure of damaging information come into play; yet it would be a mistake to assume that only actors typically defined or definable as deviant need become practitioners of such tactics, for, indeed, it is a much more general phenomenon; and the more pluralistic the society, the more heterogeneous the audiences and the greater the frequency that such arts will be utilized by the performers in everyday/any-day life.

Thus, we would argue that the sociological study of deviance should embrace all actors and actions which are considered other-than-respectable—either by the powerful in society or any bounded group in it. This broadens the field of deviance well beyond its traditional concerns with the "criminal" and the "pathological"; but if we build our constructs on actors' meanings and categories we are likely to find that there is no qualitative disjunction, only quantitative differences. Put another way, as part of *social reality* respectability and its cognates subsume the distinction between deviance and mundane normality which is typically maintained in *sociological reality*.

Just as the sociological concept of careers is useful in helping to make sense out of both occupational and nonoccupational phenomena (families, deviant actors and their activities, and so on),[92] so, too, we contend, does respectability, with its allied concepts of respectability seeking, rhetorical forms, vocabularies, and the like, have a similar broad utility. For if, as we have argued, respectability is central to social conduct, as a sociological concept it provides at least sensitization, if not explanatory power as well, as an interpretive framework for the analysis of social life.[93]

Finally, and at the risk of committing a sociological heresy, it can be suggested that if we (all scientists, not just sociologists) knew more, we might be able to make some meaningful analogies between respectability and the display behavior of animals. It has been demonstrated that display behavior is an important mechanism in the establishment and maintenance of social order among certain infrahuman species;[94] among persons a similar function as regards the *moral order* seems to be served by appearances of respectability, each of which serves to reassert and reaffirm definitions of and a dedication to social meanings of normality and thereby morality. This is certainly not to suggest that the quest for respectability is biologically determined, but in terms of functions, there is continuity between this human form of display and its infrahuman counterparts. Similarly, we might look to the mutual grooming activities of dyads in some species as an analogue to the respectability teamwork of humans, although the complexities of grooming may be even more manifold, especially in terms of causes, than the human case, these involving tactile stimulation, dominance hierarchies, and sexual approach, among others. Still, such possible parallels are probably worthy of consideration rather than the short shrift they usually get from the antibiologists of the sociological orthodoxy. For (and this is perhaps the major point of this excursion into ethology) it is not respectable among most sociologists, it is not a normal practice of the field, to remind anyone of the biological substructure on which social conduct rests;[95] not Darwin but Durkheim is to be invoked when seeking respectable intellectual antecedents. Yet it was Darwin rather than Durkheim who investigated communication—the very basic currency of truly social transactions—and provided one of the lasting, classic explications of nonverbal communication, a major mode of managing and conveying the appearance of respectability.[96]

Still, this is not to imply that Durkheim is irrelevant to our purposes. He contributed what, even after more than half a century, is the basic discussion of the relationship between the sacred and feelings of respect.[97] Goffman, in several works, has considerably broadened the Durkheimian insight by demonstrating the sacred nature of interpersonal contacts in routine secular life: that moral communication is part and parcel of both verbal and nonverbal or overt and covert conversations. And one theme of this symbolic exchange is the interpersonal category of respectability, a concept which brings into focus two of contemporary sociology's basic perspectives: Goffman's concern with the strategies and devices of impression-management and labeling theory's emphasis on societal or audience reactions.[98] Hopefully, respectability provides a conceptual vehicle to bridge and integrate these two perspectives; furthermore, it is also hoped that this necessarily tentative and discursive beginning, as well as the other chapters in this volume, may make a small substantive start in this unifying direction.

NOTES

1. L. J. Henderson, "Physician and Patient as a Social System," *New England Journal of Medicine*, CCXII (May 2, 1935), 819.
2. J. R. R. Tolkien, *The Hobbit* (London: George Allen and Unwin, 1937), pp. 1–2.
3. David Sudnow, *Passing On* (Englewood Cliffs: Prentice-Hall, 1967).
4. Similar consequences concerning level of medical treatment and the appearance of respectability are also reported in a paper on ambulance services and the handling of their clients, and examples involving less drastic outcomes could be multiplied *ad infinitum;* Dorothy J. Douglas, Julius A. Roth, and Katherine Atkins, "Occupational and Therapeutic Contingencies of Ambulance Services in Metropolitan Areas," Davis: dittoed, 1967.
5. E. Franklin Frazier, *Black Bourgeoisie* (New York: The Free Press, 1957).
6. Hunter S. Thompson, *Hell's Angels* (New York: Ballantine, 1967).
7. See Everett C. Hughes, *Men and Their Work* (New York: The Free Press, 1958).
8. Harold Nicholson, *Good Behaviour* (London: Constable and Company, 1955).
9. *Ibid.*, pp. 240–241.
10. Peter T. Cominos, "Late-Victorian Sexual Respectability and the Social System," *International Journal of Social History*, VIII (1963), 18–48, 217–250.
11. Consider, for instance, the observations of janitors concerning their tenants reported by Ray Gold, "Janitors versus Tenants: A Status-Income Dilemma," *American Journal of Sociology*, LVII (March, 1952), 486–493, and "In the Basement—The Apartment Building Janitor," in Peter L. Berger, ed., *The Human Shape of Work* (New York: Macmillan, 1964), pp. 1–49—or, alternatively, the sales volume of and the contents in the etiquette books of Emily Post, Amy Vanderbilt, *inter alias.*
12. Peter K. Manning, "Problems in Interpreting Interview Data," *Sociology and Social Research*, LI (April, 1967), 12.

13. Kurt H. Wolff, ed., *The Sociology of George Simmel* (New York: The Free Press, 1950), pp. 21–23, 40–43. Much of our discussion, both above and to follow, is based on observation and examination of the everyday/any-day world; a world in which we—that is, students of social life—no less than our subjects, are participants. We should not, however, let the emphasis of the conventionally defined as scientific (for example, the quantitative), guaranteed replicability and so on, blind us to our own participant-observer role in the society in which we live as well as do our sociology (Severyn T. Bruyn, *The Human Perspective in Sociology* [Englewood Cliffs: Prentice-Hall, 1966]). As formal students of society, we are, in a sense, by virtue of our training —that is, the sensitizing sociological framework for the categorizing and classifying of the observations of experience it provides—in an analogous position to an especially skilled and knowledgeable key informant for the anthropologist in the field; albeit, reporting to ourselves rather than another party. For a similar argument, see David M. Schneider, *American Kinship: A Cultural Account* (Englewood Cliffs: Prentice-Hall, 1968), pp. 8–14. Still, the strictures regarding objectivity, disinterest, and detachment do not seem any more impossible just because the "another party" (that is, another scientist) is missing. Indeed, the distorting biases inherent in retelling are reduced by one power.

Thus, in our examination of respectability we are searching for various levels or conceptions of reality (including those of the actors and audiences in the mundane world); such a search involves what Garfinkel calls "the-socially-sanctioned-facts-of-life-in-society-that-any-bona-fide-member-of-the-society-knows" (Harold Garfinkel, *Studies in Ethnomethodology* [Englewood Cliffs: Prentice-Hall, 1967] p. 76). And such facts should be no less inaccessible to us because we are members of that society under study; on the contrary, by training and perhaps inclination we are likely to possess a good deal of knowledge about them and/or where to look.

14. Émile Durkheim, *Rules of Sociological Method* (Chicago: University of Chicago Press, 1938), p. 2.

15. Edward Rose, "The English Record of a Natural Sociology," *American Sociological Review*, XXV (April, 1960), 193–208.

16. Jack D. Douglas, *The Social Meanings of Suicide* (Princeton: Princeton University Press, 1967), pp. 234–253.

17. See Aaron V. Cicourel, *Method and Measurement in Sociology* (New York: The Free Press, 1964).

18. It should be clear that although this position is close to that of Alfred Schutz (*Collected Papers, Vol. I: The Problem of Social Reality* [The Hague: Nijhoff, 1962] and *Collected Papers, Vol. II: Studies in Social Theory* [The Hague: Nijhoff, 1964]), it does not necessarily imply a strict Husserlian-phenomenological standpoint; it does, however, imply

the need for sociologists to develop "typifications of typifications" as second-order concepts derived from the primary-order constructs of everyday/any-day life.

19. Visually, this may be represented by holding two ice-cube trays one in front of the other and tilting one so that its axis is at a different angle than that of the other; the incongruence thus produced symbolizes the argument above.

20. See Erving Goffman, "The Nature of Deference and Demeanor," *American Anthropologist,* LVIII (June, 1956), 473–502.

21. Also see Fritz Heider, *The Psychology of Interpersonal Relations* (New York: Wiley, 1958).

22. Garfinkel, *op. cit* and *passim.*

23. Compare Goffman, *The Presentation of Self in Everyday Life* (Edinburgh: University of Edinburgh, Social Sciences Research Centre, 1956).

24. These may be abominations of the body, such as physical deformities; blemishes of character (like criminal conviction), or tribal stigmata, for instance, membership in despised minorities or other popularly denigrated aggregates and collectivities (see Goffman, *Stigma* [Englewood Cliffs: Prentice-Hall, 1963]); or situated and given meaning by the context and activities of the occasion.

25. David Maurer, *The Big Con* (Indianapolis: Bobbs-Merrill, 1940).

26. Thus, call girls have historically represented themselves to nonclients, even while communicating their actual vocation to clients, as decorators, models, and so on. Somewhat analogously, street walkers have sometimes used the walking of a dog as both a respectability prop to one audience and an invitation to business to another, more knowledgeable audience. Also, see the fronts used by houses of prostitution in Hong Kong as well as other cities: dancing schools, massage parlors, and the like (Michael G. Whisson, *Under the Rug: The Drug Problem in Hong Kong* [Hong Kong: privately printed, 1965], pp. 60–61.)

27. Erving Goffman, *Behavior in Public Places* (New York: The Free Press, 1963), pp. 33–79.

28. It follows from this for the active cases: *respectability* is the successfully presented state, condition, of being perceived to be respectable (the Hell's Angels gang, temporarily); *disrespectability,* the denial of such appreciation-accord when felt deserved or due by the presenter (*The Black Bourgeoisie*); *unrespectability,* a congruence between actor and audience as regards the denial of respectable appearances (The Hell's Angels Gang, usually); *disreputability,* an accorded respectability not justified by the actual facts of his or her true situation or purpose (the pregnant bride); *feigned unrespectability,* a manipulated case of true normality being denied by the actor for specific reasons (male "homosexual" hairdressers); and *irrespectability,* situations where the

categories above are simply not very important (behavior in public places).

29. Goffman, *Stigma*, p. 3.

30. Again, we must remember that the mechanism of internal dialogue allows for *intra*personal manifestations of such a relationship.

31. Goffman, *The Presentation of Self*, pp. 47–65.

32. Donald W. Ball, "An Abortion Clinic Ethnography," *Social Problems*, XIV (Winter, 1967), 293–301.

33. Jerome H. Skolnick, *Justice without Trial* (New York: Wiley, 1966), p. 130.

34. Joan Fasken, "Pharmacists and the Presentation of Self," unpublished manuscript, 1963.

35. Walter I. Wardell, "Limited, Marginal and Quasi-Practitioners," in Howard Freeman, Sol Levine, and Leo G. Reeder, eds., *Handbook of Medical Sociology* (Englewood Cliffs: Prentice-Hall, 1963), pp. 213–240; Thelma Herman McCormack, "The Druggist's Dilemma: Problems of a Marginal Occupation," *American Journal of Sociology*, LXI (January, 1956), 308–315; Richard Quinney, "Occupational Structure and Criminal Behavior: Prescription Violation by Retail Pharmacists," *Social Problems*, XI (Fall, 1963), 179–185; Norman K. Denzin, "Incomplete Professionalization: The Case of Pharmacy," *Social Forces*, XLVI (March, 1968), 375–381.

36. Harry C. Bredemeier and Richard M. Stephenson, *The Analysis of Social Systems* (New York: Holt, Rinehart and Winston, 1962), pp. 148–150.

37. This paragraph draws from a similar argument I have made concerning sarcasm in "Sarcasm as Sociation: The Rhetoric of Interaction," *Canadian Review of Sociology and Anthropology*, II (November, 1965), 194.

38. See Goffman, "The Nature of Deference and Demeanor," *op. cit.*

39. Walter B. Miller, "Lower Class Culture as a Generating Milieu of Gang Delinquency," *Journal of Social Issues*, XIV (Summer, 1958), 5–19.

40. Irving Piliavan and Scott Briar, "Police Encounters with Juveniles," *American Journal of Sociology*, LXX (September, 1964), 206–214.

41. Thorstein Veblen, *The Theory of the Leisure Class* (New York: Macmillan, 1899); more generally, see Peter M. Blau, "A Theory of Social Integration," *American Journal of Sociology*, LXV (May, 1960), 545–556, and *Exchange and Power in Social Life* (New York: Wiley, 1964), pp. 33–59; Edward E. Jones, *Ingratiation: A Social Psychological Analysis* (New York: Appleton-Century-Crofts, 1964).

42. See Judith Blake and Kingsley Davis, "Norms, Values, and Sanctions," in Robert E. L. Faris, ed., *Handbook of Modern Sociology* (Chicago: Rand, McNally, 1964), p. 479.

43. Hans L. Zetterberg, "Compliant Actions," *Acta Sociologica*, II (1957),

189, and "On Motivation," in Joseph Berger, Morris Zelditch, Jr., and Bo Anderson, eds., *Sociological Theories in Progress* (New York: Houghton Mifflin, 1966), I, 124–141.

44. Joseph A. Kahl, *The American Class Structure* (New York: Holt, Rinehart and Winston, 1957), pp. 202–205; Arthur J. Vidich and Joseph Bensman, *Small Town in Mass Society* (Garden City, N.Y.: Doubleday Anchor, 1960), pp. 49–50, 64.

45. Goffman, *The Presentation of Self.*

46. Garfinkel, *op. cit.*, pp. 116–185, 285–288.

47. Stephen Potter, *Gamesmanship* (New York: Holt, 1948); *Lifemanship* (New York: Holt, Rinehart and Winston, 1951); *One-upmanship* (New York: Holt, Rinehart and Winston, 1952); *Supermanship* (New York: Random House, 1959); *Anti-Woo* (New York: McGraw-Hill, 1965).

48. Donald W. Ball, "Stephen Potter as Interaction Theorist," paper presented to the West Coast Conference for Small Group Research, Long Beach, 1965.

49. Among others, Marvin B. Scott and Stanford M. Lyman, "Paranoia, Homosexuality, and Game Theory," *Journal of Health and Social Behavior,* IX (September, 1968), 179–187; Peter K. Manning, "Sociology as a Game of Games" (Lansing: 1967, mimeographed); Harold Garfinkel, "A Conception of, and Experiments with, 'Trust' as a Condition of Stable Concerted Actions," in O. J. Harvey, ed., *Motivation and Social Interaction* (New York: Ronald, 1963), pp. 187–238; Timothy Leary, "How to Change Behavior," in Warren G. Bennis *et al.*, eds., *Interpersonal Dynamics* (Homewood: Dorsey, 1964), pp. 498–512; Erving Goffman, *Encounters* (Indianapolis: Bobbs-Merrill, 1961), pp. 17–81.

50. This section is based on a personal communication by an ethnographer who wishes to remain anonymous.

51. This distinction between presentation and imposition suggests the modification of an additional column to our earlier cognate paradigm, should one wish an exhaustive typology based on social reality.

52. Carolyn See, "Job Corps: Faith, Hope, and Poverty," *West Times* (Los Angeles), July 16, 1967, pp. 25–29.

53. That such binary coding or polarization is not limited to normals vis-à-vis conventionally defined deviants is suggested by the concept of oppositional subcultures.

54. Also see Ball, "Sarcasm as Sociation." However, some parenthetical caveats are in order: for although we shall deal with this rhetoric from the viewpoint of the individual performer, the empirical case is always infinitely more complicated and problematic because the audience is not, as is permissible in the analytic case, simply a given; rather it is part of a team who may co-operate or conspire against, understand or misunderstand, accept or reject, help or hinder, those who perform be-

fore them. Additionally, although we are discussing respectability at the individual level (of propriety and impropriety), it should be remembered that there is the larger-unit level analogue of legitimacy and illegitimacy and that furthermore, empirical cases may be mixed, involving both levels simultaneously, as the relationship between particular persons and the organizations and establishments in which they may be located—the convict and the total institution of the prison being a case in point. See Gresham M. Sykes, *The Society of Captives* (Princeton: Princeton University Press, 1958).

55. Ned Polsky, *Hustlers, Beats, and Others* (Chicago: Aldine, 1967), pp. 13–40.

56. Thomas Scheff, *Being Mentally Ill: A Sociological Theory* (Chicago: Aldine, 1966).

57. William Simon and John Gagnon, "Femininity in the Lesbian Community," *Social Problems*, XV (Fall, 1967), 219.

58. This latter freedom is actually basic to both choice of action and definitions of self, as Goffman has shown in a very fundamental way in *Asylums* (Garden City: Doubleday Anchor, 1961), pp. 3–124.

59. Additionally, we must remember that these activities take place vis-à-vis specific audiences; the opiate addict, for instance, is concerned to conceal his habit from the conventional world, especially those who do its morality work such as the police, but he has no similar reluctance as regards "the man" who supplies him with drugs. Similarly, confidence men conceal their lack of respectability completely from the legal authorities, while at the same time displaying a certain amount of non-respectability to their marks whose final victimization relies on their being taken in as "partners" in endeavors of questionable legality, such as the fixing of horse races and off-track betting establishments (Maurer, *op. cit.*).

60. Ronald G. Klietsch, "Clothesline Patterns and Covert Behavior," *Journal of Marriage and the Family*, XXVII, February 9, 1965), 78–80. More generally on secrecy, see Wolff, *op. cit.*, pp. 307–376; Stanford M. Lyman, "Chinese Secret Societies in the Occident: Notes and Suggestions for Research in the Sociology of Secrecy," *Canadian Review of Sociology and Anthropology*, I (May, 1964), 87–89.

61. Goffman, *The Presentation of Self*, p. 66.

62. Donald W. Ball, "Toward a Sociology of Telephones and Telephoners," in Marcello Truzzi, ed., *Sociology and Everyday Life* (Englewood Cliffs: Prentice-Hall, 1968), pp. 59–75; Frank Gibney, *The Operators* (New York: Harper, 1960).

63. Garfinkel, "A Conception of, and Experiments with, Trust."

64. For completeness we should mention one other form of concealment, but one about which little is known, either by trained sociologists or by laymen: the arts of *misdirection* and *conjuring* (Truzzi, personal communication). The hows of such activities are little publicized or under-

stood outside of a small coterie—magicians, merchandisers of the occult
such as those who conduct séances, and others—but they or their
analogues are to be found among the technical skills of a few less marginal, although more specifically respectability-lacking, occupations such
as pickpockets and card sharps. The basic technique here is to present
information or activity of a sufficiently engrossing nature that the performer is able to carry on other affairs unnoticed. Thus, a line of chat-
ter may sufficiently divert the mark's attention to let the manipulations
of the shell game continue; the pickpocket's stall or confederate may
jostle so that a pocket can be picked by another (David Maurer, *Whiz
Mob* [New Haven: College and University Press, 1964]); the smooth
dexterity of the dealer off the top may distract others and thus mask
the cards coming from the bottom of the deck. Unfortunately, we know
all too little about the workings of this form of disrespectability-conceal-
ment at this time, either in terms of its technical structure or the situations that encourage its occurrence.

65. Don Martindale, *American Society* (Princeton: Van Nostrand, 1960),
pp. 72–77.

66. Kenneth Burke, *A Grammar of Motives and a Rhetoric of Motives* (in
one volume) (New York: Meridian, 1962), pp. 745–747, 791–792;
Hugh Dalziel Duncan, *Communication and Social Order* (Totawa:
Bedminster Press, 1962), and "The Study of Society: An Outline of
System of Sociology Based on the Proposition That How We Communicate Determines How We Relate as Human Beings" (Carbondale: mimeographed, 1964), and "The Symbolic Act" (Carbondale: mimeographed, n.d.); and *Symbols in Society* (New York: Oxford University Press, 1968).

67. Goffman, *The Presentation of Self*.

68. Compare *ibid.*, pp. 66–88, on front and back regions and the meanings
attached to them.

69. Among others, see Phillip Drucker, *Cultures of the North Pacific Coast*
(San Francisco; Chandler, 1965), pp. 55–65 *et passim*.

70. It is in this context perhaps at least worth mentioning that in many of
the new, instant suburban communities one of the first commercial establishments after the supermarket and the hardware store catering to
the home handyman and gardener is the private finance company; it is
there to loan money to persons mortgaged beyond the point of eligibility for bank loans and thus help them keep up their respectable appearances. Without such lending agencies many front yards would be
unlandscaped, a fact which can be ill concealed, and back yards for
children to play in might, as they sometimes do, never get done.

71. Examples range from the phrase prevalent in the United States South
which describes families vis-à-vis their dwellings as "too proud to white-
wash and too poor to paint" cross-culturally to the British blue-collar
worker's white celluloid collar for special occasions.

72. Scheff, *op. cit.*
73. Morris Janowitz, *The Professional Soldier: A Social and Political Portrait* (Glencoe: The Free Press, 1960), pp. 196–212.
74. Donald Horton and Richard Wohl, "Mass Communication and Para-Social Interaction," *Psychiatry*, XIX (August, 1956), 215–229.
75. Gregory Stone, "Appearance and the Self," in Arnold M. Rose, ed., *Human Behavior and Social Processes* (Boston: Houghton Mifflin, 1962), pp. 85–118; Goffman, *The Presentation of Self*, pp. 1–9.
76. George Herbert Mead, *Mind, Self, and Society* (Chicago: University of Chicago Press, 1934).
77. Stanley Coopersmith, *The Antecedents of Self-esteem* (San Francisco: W. H. Freeman, 1967).
78. Kai T. Erikson, "Notes on the Sociology of Deviance," in Howard S. Becker, ed., *The Other Side* (New York: The Free Press, 1964), pp. 9–21; Harold Garfinkel, "Conditions of Successful Degradation Ceremonies," *American Journal of Sociology*, LXI (March, 1956), 420–424.
79. See several of the papers in Marvin Wolfgang, ed., *Studies in Homicide* (New York: Harper and Row, 1967).
80. Again, I must respect an informant's desire for anonymity.
81. Julius A. Roth, "Ritual and Magic in the Control of Contagion," *American Sociological Review*, XXII (June, 1957), 310–314.
82. Howard S. Becker, *Outsiders* (New York: The Free Press, 1963), pp. 15–18, 147–163; Jack D. Douglas, "The General Theoretical Implications of the Sociology of Deviance," in John C. McKinney and Edward A. Tiryakian, eds., *Theoretical Sociology: Perspectives and Developments* (New York: Appleton-Century-Crofts, forthcoming).
83. Compare with Erikson, *op. cit.*
84. Max Scheler, *Ressentiment* (New York: The Free Press, 1961); see also Sven Ranulf, *Moral Indignation and Middle Class Psychology* (New York: Schocken, 1964); Albert K. Cohen, "The Sociology of the Deviant Act: Anomie Theory and Beyond," *American Sociological Review*, XXX (February, 1965), 6–7.
85. The point regarding pluralism is discussed by Douglas, in "The General Theoretical Implications of the Sociology of Deviance"; also (in the same place) see his stimulating conceptualization of "moral provocateurs."
86. See, for instance, on techniques of neutralization, Gresham M. Sykes and David Matza, "Techniques of Neutralization: A Theory of Delinquency," *American Sociological Review*, XXII (December, 1957), 664–670; also Ball, "An Abortion Clinic Ethnography."
87. H. Richard Neibuhr, *The Social Sources of Denominationalism* (New York: Holt, 1929).
88. See Daniel Bell, "Crime as an American Way of Life," *Antioch Review*, XIII (Summer, 1953), 131–154, on crime and respectability.

89. See Garfinkel, "A Conception of, and Experiments with 'Trust' " and *Studies in Ethnomethodology;* also Scheff, *Being Mentally Ill.*
90. See Peter L. Berger, *Invitation to Sociology: A Humanistic Perspective* (Garden City, N.Y.: Doubleday Anchor, 1963), pp. 63–78; Joseph R. Gusfield, "Moral Passage: The Symbolic Process in Public Designations of Deviance," *Social Problems,* XV (Fall, 1967), 175–188.
91. Not only generally, from situation to situation, but also temporally from birth to death. The cradle-to-grave nature of the quest for respectability is suggested by the rites of baptism, to give the child "a decent name," through to desire of survivors to give the deceased "a Christian burial." Though culturally bound, there are many non-Christian analogies to these practices and their associated meanings.
92. Hughes, *op. cit.*
93. Although considerations of space preclude extended comment—indeed, each is worthy of a monograph in and of itself—the following several areas suggest the utility of the concept of respectability for the sociological analysis of a variety of disparate phenomena (it is not, however, assumed that respectability is the only relevant consideration in these examples).

    Higher Education: The trickling down of publishing norms from universities to colleges; the pressures to expand junior colleges into four-year institutions; the use of professorial ranks in these two-year institutions; faculty demands for the secularization of church-related colleges; the increase in liberal arts courses in military academies; nomenclature and changes in names, such as from teacher's college to state college, from college to university, from department of speech to department of communications, from junior college to community or city college; the "applied sciences," like police science, domestic science, and so forth. Nevitt Sanford, ed., *The American College* (New York: Wiley, 1962); Burton R. Clark, *The Open-Door College* (New York: McGraw-Hill, 1960) and "The 'Cooling-out' Function in Higher Education," *American Journal of Sociology,* LXV (May, 1960), 569–577; Irving Louis Horowitz, "Mainliners and Marginals: The Human Shape of Sociological Theory" in Llewellyn Gross, ed., *Sociological Theory: Inquiries and Paradigms* (New York: Harper and Row, 1967), pp. 358–383.

    Emergent Nations: The construction of fully integrated steel mills, irrespective of the natural availability of raw materials for steel making; the paper establishment of graduate-degree-granting universities; the purchase of often obsolete jet fighters.

    Dress: The removal of labels from expensive clothes, to be resewn into other garments; the white celluloid collars of British blue-collar workers; the copying of Paris designs by the Seventh Avenue garment manufacturers; the legal rules surrounding transvestitism (see also, Stone, *op. cit.;* Mary Shaw Ryan, *Clothing: A Study in Human Behavior*

(New York: Holt, Rinehart, and Winston, 1966); Mary Ellen Roach and Joan Bubolz Eicher, eds., *Dress, Adornment, and the Social Order* (New York: Wiley, 1965).

Professionalization: The quest for professional status; the ecological hiding of "dirty work" by both professionals and service workers; the formulation of ethical codes by trade associates. (Hughes, *op. cit.;* Howard Vollmer and Donald L. Mills eds. *Professionalization* [Englewood Cliffs: Prentice-Hall, 1966]).

Small Group Research: Orne's demonstration of the operation of demand factors and the attempt by subjects to figure out the experimental goals so that they may be "good" subjects and help validate the hypothesis being tested (Martin T. Orne, "On the Social Psychology of the Psychological Experiment: with Particular Reference to Demand Characteristics and Their Implications," *American Psychologist,* XVII [November, 1962], 776–783; also see Robert Rosenthal, *Experimenter Effects in Behavioral Research* [New York: Appleton-Century-Crofts, 1966]; Theodore M. Mills, "A sleeper variable in small groups research," *Pacific Sociological Review,* V [Spring, 1962], 21–28; Kurt W. Back, Thomas C. Hood, and Mary L. Brehm, "The subject role in small group experiments," *Social Forces,* XLIII [December, 1964], 181–187).

That the list above could be proliferated almost indefinitely goes without saying; it merely serves to demonstrate the relevance of responsibility to a diverse and heterogeneous set of areas of sociological inquiry.

94. This literature is far too extensive to cite, but among others: Charles H. Southwick and Ronald W. Ward, "Aggressive Display in the Paradise Fish, *Macropodus opercularis L,*" *Turtox News,* XLVI (February, 1968), 57–62; S. A. Barnett, *A Study in Behaviour: Principle of Ethology and Behavioural Physiology, Displayed Mainly in the Rat* (London: Methuen, 1963); Edward A. Armstrong, *Bird Display and Behavior,* 2nd ed. (New York: Dover, 1965); Konrad Lorenz, *On Aggression* (London: Methuen, 1966).

95. Richard L. Means, "Sociology, Biology, and the Analysis of Social Problems," *Social Problems,* XV (Fall, 1967), 200–212.

96. Charles Darwin, *The Expression of the Emotions in Man and Animals* (London: John Murray, 1872).

97. Émile Durkheim, *The Elementary Forms of Religious Life* (London: George Allen and Unwin, 1915).

98. Edwin M. Lemert, *Social Pathology* (New York: McGraw-Hill, 1951), and *Human Deviance, Social Problems, and Social Control* (Englewood Cliffs: Prentice-Hall, 1967); Becker, *Outsiders;* John I. Kitsuse, "Societal Reaction to Deviant Behavior: Problems of Theory and Method," in Becker, *The Other Side,* pp. 87–102.

Part III

Studies in the Social Construction of Situated Moral Meanings

12

The Nudist Management of Respectability: Strategy for, and Consequences of, the Construction of a Situated Morality

Martin S. Weinberg

In our society the public exposure of human sexual organs is proscribed; at the same time, an organized group exists who breach this moral rule. They call themselves "social nudists."

A number of questions are commonly asked about these people. For example, how can they see their behavior as morally appropriate? Have they constructed their own morality? If so, what characterizes this morality and what are its consequences? [1]

This chapter will attempt to answer these questions through a study of interpersonal processes—those that are used as strategies for carrying out interaction in nudist camps, and those that result from the situated moral order that these strategies effect. I will examine the work of constructing and maintaining moral meanings in nudist camps, the moral contests and territoriality of emotions that develop, and how nudists meet the problem of maintaining respectability in clothed society. The data come from three sources: two successive summers of participant observation in nudist camps; 101 interviews with nudists in the Chicago area; and 617 mailed questionnaires completed by nudists located throughout the United States and Canada.[2]

The Construction of Situated Moral Meanings: Moral Appearances in the Nudist Camp

The basis for the construction of a situated morality in the nudist camp is provided by the official interpretations that camps maintain regarding the moral meanings of public heterosexual nudity. These are (1) that nudity and sexuality are unrelated, (2) that there is nothing shameful about exposing the human body, (3) that the abandonment of clothes leads to a feeling of freedom and natural pleasure, and (4) that nude activities, especially the entire body's exposure to the sun, lead to a feeling of physical, mental, and spiritual well-being.

This official perspective is sustained in nudist camps to an extraordinary degree, illustrating the extent to which adult socialization can affect long-maintained moral meanings (viz., with regard to the first two declarations of the nudist perspective, which will be our primary concern since these are its "deviant" aspects). The relationship that is assumed in the outside society to exist between nudity and sexuality, and the subsequent emphasis on covering sexual organs make the nudist perspective a specifically situated morality. The results of my field work, interview, and questionnaire research will be used to show that nudists routinely use a special system of rules to create, sustain, and enforce this situated morality. I will then look at how this situated morality creates for nudists a bifurcation in moral worlds and what the consequences are of their subscription to these cross-situational multiple realities.

STRATEGY FOR, AND CONSTRUCTION OF, A SITUATED MORALITY

One element in the strategy used by the nudist camp to anesthetize nude-sex appresentation [3] is a system of organizational precautions in the requisites for initial admission to a nudist camp. Most camps, for example, do not allow unmarried individuals, especially single men; or they allow only a small quota of singles. Camps that do allow single males may charge up to 35 per cent higher rates for a single's membership than is charged for an entire family. This is intended to discourage singles. (Since the cost is still relatively low in comparison with other resorts, this measure is not very effective. It seems to do little more than create resentment among the singles, and by giving formal organizational backing to the definition that singles are not especially desirable, it may be related to the segregation of single and married members evident in nudist camps.)

An abundance of single men is constituted by most members as threatening the moral construction of nudism that the organization maintains. Singles at the camp are suspected to be there for purposes other than the nudist way of life. Such a construction of intentions calls into question any denied appresentation of nudity and sexuality.

Certification by the camp owner is another requirement for admittance on camp grounds. This requirement is sometimes complemented by the necessity of three letters of recommendation regarding the character of the applicant. This helps preclude the admittance of social types who present signs constituted by nudists as a threat to the situated moral meanings sustained in camp.

> [The camp owner] invited us over to see if we were *desirable* people. Then after we did this, he invited us to camp on probation; then they voted us into camp. [Q: Could you tell me what you mean by desirable people?] Well, not people who are inclined to drink, or people who go there for a peep show. Then they don't want you there. They feel you out in conversation. They want people for mental and physical health reasons.
>
> Whom to admit [is the biggest problem of the camp]. [Q] [4] Because the world is so full of people whose attitudes on nudity are hopelessly warped. [Q: Has this always been the biggest problem in camp?] Yes. Every time anybody comes, a decision has to be made. [Q] . . . The lady sitting at the gate decides about admittance. The director decides on membership.

A limit is sometimes set on the number of trial visits that may be made to camp; that is, visits made without membership in some camp or intercamp organization. In addition, a limit is usually set on the length of time one is allowed to remain clothed. This strategy helps to mark guests whose sincere acceptance of the situated morality is suspect.

Norms regarding patterns of interpersonal behavior are the second element of the strategy to maintain the organization's system of moral meanings. These norms are as follows:

No staring. This rule controls overt signs of overinvolvement. In the words of a publisher of a nudist magazine, "They all look up to the heavens and never look below." Such maintained inattention is most exaggerated among women, who show no recognition that the male body is unclothed. Women also recount how they expect men to look at them when they are nude, only to find that no one communicates any awareness when they finally do get up the courage to undress. As one woman states: "I got so mad because my husband wanted me to undress in front of other men that I just pulled my clothes right off thinking everyone would look at me." She was amazed (and appeared somewhat disappointed) when no one did.

The following statement illustrates the constraints that result:

[Q: Have you ever observed or heard about anyone staring at someone's body while at camp?] I've heard stories, particularly about men that stare. Since I heard these stories, I tried not to, and even done away with my sunglasses after someone said, half-joking, that I hide behind sunglasses to stare. Toward the end of the summer I stopped wearing sunglasses. And you know what, it was a child who told me this.

[Q: Would you stare . . . ?] Probably not, cause you can get in trouble and get thrown out. If I thought I could stare unobserved I might. They might not throw you out, but it wouldn't do you any good. [Q] The girl might tell others and they might not want to talk to me. . . . [Q] They disapprove by not talking to you, ignoring you, etc.

[Someone who stares] wouldn't belong there. [Q] If he does that he is just going to camp to see the opposite sex. [Q] He is just coming to stare. [Q] You go there to swim and relax.

I try very hard to look at them from the jaw up—even more than you would normally.[5]

No sex talk. Sex talk, or telling "dirty jokes," is uncommon in camp. The owner of a large camp in the Midwest stated: "It is usually expected that members of a nudist camp will not talk about sex, politics, or religion." Or as one single male explained: "It is taboo to make sexual remarks here." During my field work, it was rare to hear "sexual" joking such as one hears at most other types of resort. Interview respondents who mentioned that they had talked about sex qualified this by explaining that such talk was restricted to close friends, was of a "scientific nature," or, if a joke, was of a "cute sort."

Asked what they would think of someone who breached this rule, respondents indicated that such behavior would cast doubt on the situated morality of the nudist camp:

One would expect to hear less of that at camp than at other places. [Q: Why is that?] Because you expect that the members are screened in their *attitude for nudism*—and this isn't one who prefers sexual jokes.

I've never heard anyone swear or tell a dirty joke out there.

No. Not at camp. You're not supposed to. You bend over backwards not to.

They probably don't belong there. They're there to see what they can find to observe. [Q: What do you mean?] Well, their mind isn't on being a nudist, but to see so and so nude.

No body contact. Although the extent to which this is enforced varies among camps, there is at least some degree of informal enforcement in every camp. Nudists mention how they are particularly careful not to brush against anyone or have any body contact, because of how it might be interpreted. The following quotations illustrate the interpersonal precautions that are taken:

I stay clear of the opposite sex. They're so sensitive, they imagine things.

People don't get too close to you. Even when they talk. They sit close to you, but they don't get close enough to touch you.

We have a minimum of contact. There are more restrictions [at a nudist camp]. [Q] Just a feeling I had. I would openly show my affection more readily some place else.

One respondent defined this taboo as simply common-sense knowledge:

Suppose one had a desire to knock one off or feel his wife: modesty or a sense of protocol prohibits you from doing this.

And when asked to conceptualize a breach of this rule, typical of the responses was:

They are in the wrong place. [Q: How is that?] That's not part of nudism. [Q: Could you tell me some more about that?] I think they are there for some sort of sex thrill. They are certainly not there to enjoy the sun.

If any photographs are taken for publication in a nudist magazine, the subjects are also usually allowed to have only limited body contact. One female nudist explained: "We don't want anyone to think we're immoral." Outsiders' interpretations of nude body contact are made in the framework of a constructed morality that would cast doubt on the characteristics set forth as the nudist way of life.

A correlate of the body contact taboo is a prohibition of dancing in the nude. Nudists cite this as a separate rule. This rule is often talked about by members in a way that indicates organizational strain— where the rule itself makes evident that a strategy is in operation to sustain their situated morality. The following remark notes this: "This reflects a contradiction in our beliefs. But it's self-protection. One incident and we'd be closed."

No alchoholic beverages in American camps. This rule guards against breakdowns in inhibition that could lead to "aggressive-erotic" signs. Even respondents who admitted that they had "snuck a beer" before going to bed went on to say that they fully favor the rule.

Yes. We have [drunk at camp]. We keep a can of beer in the refrigerator since we're out of the main area. We're not young people or carousers. . . . I still most generally approve of it as a camp rule and would disapprove of anyone going to extremes. [Q] For common-sense reasons. People who overindulge lose their inhibitions and there is no denying that the atmosphere of a nudist camp makes one bend over backwards to keep people who are so inclined from going beyond the bounds of propriety.

Anyone who drinks in camp is jeopardizing their membership and they shouldn't. Anyone who drinks in camp could get reckless. [Q: How is that?] Well, when guys and girls drink they're a lot bolder—they might get fresh with someone else's girl. That's why it isn't permitted, I guess.

Rules regarding photography. Photography in a nudist camp is organizationally controlled. Unless the person is an official photographer (that is, photographing for nudist magazines), the photographer's moral perspective is sometimes suspect. One photographer's remark that led to his being so typed was, "Do you think you could open your legs a little more?"

Aside from a general restriction on the use of cameras, when cameras are allowed, it is expected that no pictures will be taken without the subject's permission. Members especially tend to blame the misuse of cameras on single men. As one nudist said: "You always see the singles poppin' around out of nowhere snappin' pictures." In general, control is maintained, and any infractions that exist are not blatant or obvious. Any overindulgence in taking photographs communicates an overinvolvement in the nude state of the subjects and casts doubt on the denied connection between nudity and sexuality.

Photographers dressed only in cameras and light exposure meters. I don't like them. I think they only go out for pictures. Their motives should be questioned.

The official photographers taking pictures for nudist magazines recognize the signs that strain the situated morality that characterizes nudist camps. The following comment was made by an official photographer: "I never let a girl look straight at the camera. It looks too suggestive. I always have her look off to the side."

A nudist model showed the writer a pin-up magazine to point out how a model could make a nude picture "sexy"—through the use of various stagings, props, and expressions—and in contrast, how the nudist model eliminates these techniques to make her pictures "natural." Although it may be questionable that a nudist model completely eliminates a sexual perspective for the nonnudist, the respondent discussed how a model attempts to do this.

> It depends on the way you look. Your eyes and your smile can make you look sexy. The way they're looking at you. Here, she's on a bed. It wouldn't be sexy if she were on a beach with kids running around. They always have some clothes on too. See how she's "looking" sexy? Like an "oh dear!" look. A different look can change the whole picture.
>
> Now here's a decent pose. . . . Outdoors makes it "nature." Here she's giving you "the eye," or is undressing. It's cheesecake. It depends on the expression on her face. Having nature behind it makes it better. Don't smile like "come on honey!" It's that look and the lace thing she has on. . . . Like when you half-close your eyes, like "oh baby," a Marilyn Monroe look. Art is when you don't look like you're hiding it halfway.

The element of trust plays a particularly strong role in socializing women to the nudist perspective. Consider this in the following statements made by another model for nudist magazines. She and her husband had been indoctrinated in the nudist way of life by friends. At the time of the interview, however, the couple had not yet been to camp, although they had posed indoors for nudist magazines.

> [Three months ago, before I was married] I never knew a man had any pubic hairs. I was shocked when I was married. . . . I wouldn't think of getting undressed in front of my husband. I wouldn't make love with a light on, or in the daytime.

After she had been married for three months, she posed for national nudist magazines:

> None of the pictures are sexually seductive. [Q] The pose, the look; you can have a pose that's completely nothing, till you get a look that's not too hard to do. [Q: How do you do that?] I've never tried. By putting on a certain air about a person; a picture that couldn't be submitted to a nudist magazine—using [the nudist photographer's] language. . . . [Q:

Will your parents see your pictures in the magazine?] Possibly. I don't really care. . . . My mother might take it all right. But they've been married twenty years and she's never seen my dad undressed.[6]

No accentuation of the body. Accentuation of the body is suspect as being incongruent with the situated morality of the camp. Thus, a woman who had shaved her pubic area was labeled "disgusting" by other members. There was a similar reaction to women who blatantly sat in an "unladylike" manner.

> I'd think she was inviting remarks. [Q] I don't know. It seems strange to think of it. It's strange you ask it. Out there, they're not unconscious about their posture. Most women there are very circumspect even though in the nude.
> For a girl [sitting with your legs open] is just not feminine or ladylike. The hair doesn't always cover it. [Q] Men get away with so many things. But, it would look dirty for a girl; like she was waiting for something. When I'm in a secluded area I've spread my legs to sun, but I kept an eye open and if anyone came I'd close my legs and sit up a little. It's just not ladylike.
> You can lay on your back or side, or with your knees under your chin. But not with your legs spread apart. It would look to other people like you're there for other reasons. [Q: What other reasons?] . . . To stare and get an eyeful. . . . Not to enjoy the sun and people.

No unnatural attempts at covering the body. "Unnatural attempts" at concealment are ridiculed since they call into question the element of the situated morality that there is no shame in exposing any area of the human body. If such behavior occurs early in one's nudist career, it is usually responded to with more compassion, as a situation where the person has not yet assimilated the new morality.

It is the decoding of the behavior, however, rather than the behavior per se, that determines the way in which the concealment is considered.

> If they're cold or sunburned, it's understandable. If it's because they don't agree with the philosophy, they don't belong there.
> I would feel their motives for becoming nudists were not well founded. That they were not true nudists, not idealistic enough.

Communal toilets. Communal toilets are also sometimes part of the strategy to sustain the special moral reality of the nudist camp. Not all camps have communal toilets, but the large camp where I did most of my field work did have such a facility, which was marked, "Little

Girls Room and Little Boys Too." Although the stalls had three-quar-ter-length doors, this combined facility still helped to provide an ele-ment of consistency; that is, if you are not ashamed of any part of your body or any of its natural functions, men and women do not need separate toilets. Thus, even the physical ecology of the nudist camp was designed with respect to the strategy for sustaining situated moral meanings. For some, however, communal toilets were going too far:

> I think they should be separated. For myself it's all right. But there are varied opinions; and for the satisfaction of all, I think they should sepa-rate them. There are niceties of life we often like to maintain, and for some people this is embarrassing. . . . [Q] You know, in a bowel move-ment it always isn't silent.

Moral Contests in the Nudist Camp

In the nudist camp, nudity becomes subjectively, as well as objec-tively, routinized. Its attention-provoking quality therefore recedes; nudity becomes a taken-for-granted state of affairs. This is indicated in the responses received to interview questions regarding staring: "While at camp, have you ever stared at anyone's body? Do you think you would stare at anyone's body?" The responses indicate that nudity of the opposite sex is generally not relevant to invoking one's atten-tion.

> Nudists don't care what bodies are like. They're out there for them-selves. It's a matter-of-fact thing. After awhile you feel like you're sitting with a full suit of clothes on.
>
> To nudists the body becomes so matter-of-fact, whether clothed or un-clothed, when you make it an undue point of interest it becomes an ab-normal thing.
>
> [Q: What would you think of someone staring?] I would feel bad and let down. [Q] I have it set up on a high standard. I have never seen it happen. . . . [Q] Because it's not done there. It's above that; you don't stare. . . . If I saw it happen, I'd be startled. There's no inclination to do that. Why would they?
>
> There are two types—male and female. I couldn't see why they were staring. I wouldn't understand it.

The interview question directs nudists to a frame of possibilities in which routine nudity is taken for granted, and what is relevant to staring is only that which is *unique* for the respondent, that which is not part of his storehouse of taken-for-granteds.[7]

[Q: Do you think you would ever stare at someone's body while at camp?] No. I don't like that. I think it's silly. You aren't going to gain anything. What people are is not their fault; if they are deformed.

I might catch myself staring if they were handicapped. But I might hurt their feelings if I stared.

If I wanted to look at someone, it is usually because something is wrong with them. And then it would embarrass them.

[Q: While at camp have you ever stared at someone's body?] Yes. [Q] A little girl. She has a birthmark on her back, at the base of her spine.

It was this man [who I stared at] who was born with a deformity. His body was very crooked . . . deformed at birth. . . . I didn't make fun of him. It just interested me.

I don't think it would be very nice, very polite. [Q] I can't see anything to stare at, whether it's a scar or anything else. [Q] It just isn't done.

There was a red-haired man. He had red pubic hair. I had never seen this before. . . . He didn't see me. If anyone did, I would turn the other way.

I've looked, but not stared. I'm careful about that, because you could get in bad about that. [Q] Get thrown out by the owner. I was curious when I once had a perfect view of a girl's sex organs, because her legs were spread when she was sitting on a chair. I sat in the chair across from her in perfect view of her organs. [Q] For about ten or fifteen minutes. [Q] Nobody noticed. [Q] It's not often you get that opportunity.[8]

Well, once I was staring at a pregnant woman. It was the first time I ever saw this. I was curious, her stomach stretched, the shape. . . . I also have stared at extremely obese people, cripples. All this is due to curiosity, just a novel sight. [Q] . . . I was discreet. [Q] I didn't look at them when their eyes were fixed in a direction so they could tell I was.

[Q: How would you feel if you were alone in a secluded area of camp sunning yourself, and then noticed that other nudists were staring at your body?] I would think I had some mud on me. [Q] . . . I would just ask them why they were staring at me. Probably I was getting sunburn and they wanted to tell me to turn over, or maybe I had a speck of mud on me. [Q] These are the only two reasons I can think of why they were staring.

The arousal of one's attention by nudity is usually responded to by others as being *unnatural*. Considering the system of situated meanings, staring is unnatural, especially after a period of grace in which to adjust to the new meanings.

If he did it when he was first there, I'd figure he's normal. If he kept it up I'd stay away from him, or suggest to the owner that he be thrown out. [Q] At first it's a new experience, so he might be staring. [Q] He wouldn't know how to react to it. [Q] The first time seeing nudes of the opposite sex. [Q] I'd think if he kept staring, that he's thinking of something, like grabbing someone, running to the bushes and raping them. [Q] Maybe he's mentally unbalanced.

He just sat there watching the women. You can forgive it the first time, because of curiosity. But not every weekend. [Q] The owner asked him to leave.

These women made comments on some men's shapes. They said, "He has a hairy body or ugly bones," or "Boy his wife must like him because he's hung big." That was embarrassing. . . . I thought they were terrible. [Q] Because I realized they were walking around looking. I can't see that.

Organizations and the Constitution of Normality

The rules of an organization *and the reality sustained* are the bases of the order that is routinely used in interpreting behaviors as "unnatural." [9] Construed overinvolvement in nudity is, for example, interpreted by nudists as being unnatural (and not simply immoral). Erotic responses are defined as unnatural, as are behaviors that breach the situated morality.

Erotic reactor:

They let one single in. He acted peculiar. . . . He got up and had a big erection. I didn't know what he'd do at night. He might molest a child or anybody. . . . My husband went and told the owner.

Erotic actor:

I told you about this one on the sundeck with her legs spread. She made no bones about closing up. Maybe it was an error, but I doubt it. It wasn't a normal position. Normally you wouldn't lay like this. It's like standing on your head. She had sufficient time and there were people around.

She sat there with her legs like they were straddling a horse. I don't know how else to describe it. [Q] She was just sitting on the ground. [Q] I think she's a dirty pig. [Q] If you sit that way, everyone don't want to know what she had for breakfast. [Q] It's just the wrong way to sit. You keep your legs together even with clothes on.

> [Q: Do you think it is possible for a person to be modest in a nudist camp?] I think so. [Q] If a person acts natural. . . . An immodest person would be an exhibitionist, and you find them in nudism too. . . . Most people's conduct is all right.

When behaviors are constituted as *unnatural,* attempts at understanding these acts are usually suspended, and a reciprocity of perspectives is called into question (the assumption that if one changed places with the other, one would see the world in the same typical way and that both interpret the world in a similar enough manner for all practical purposes).[10]

> [Q: What would you think of a man who had an erection at camp?] Maybe they can't control themselves. [Q] Better watch out for him. [Q] I would tell the camp director to keep an eye on him. And the children would question that. [Q: What would you tell them?] I'd tell them the man is sick or something.
>
> [Q: What would you think of a Peeping Tom—a nonnudist trespasser?] They should be reported and sent out. [Q] I think they shouldn't be there. They're sick. [Q] Mentally. [Q] Because anyone who wants to look at someone else's body, well is a Peeping Tom, is sick in the first place. He looks at you differently than a normal person would. [Q] With ideas of sex.
>
> [A trespasser] is sick. He probably uses this as a source of sexual stimulation.

Such occurrences call into question the taken-for-granted character of nudity in the nudist camp and the situated morality that is officially set forth.

Inhibiting Breakdowns in the Situated Morality

Organized nudism promulgates a nonsexual perspective toward nudity, and breakdowns in the nonsexual perspective are inhibited by (1) controlling erotic actions and (2) controlling erotic reactions. Nudity is partitioned off from other forms of "immodesty" (such as, verbal immodesty, the communication of erotic overtures). In this way a person can learn more easily to attribute a new meaning to nudity.[11] When behaviors occur that reflect other forms of "immodesty," nudists often fear a voiding of the nonsexual meaning that is now imposed on nudity.

> This woman with a sexy walk would shake her hips and try to arouse the men. . . . [Q] These men went to the camp director to complain

that the woman had purposely tried to arouse them. The camp director told this woman to leave.

Nudists are sensitive to the possibility of a breakdown in their situated morality, and they have, therefore, a low threshold for interpreting acts as "sexual."

Playing badminton, this teenager was hitting the birdie up and down and she said, "What do you think of that?" I said, "Kind of sexy." _____ [the president of the camp] said I shouldn't talk like that, but I was only kidding.

Note the following description of "mauling," what in some camps is referred to as "fondling."

I don't like to see a man and a girl mauling each other in the nude before others. . . . [Q: Did you ever see this at camp?] I saw it once. They got married, but I don't see how he could maul her. . . . [Q: What do you mean by mauling?] Just, well I never saw him put his hands on her breast, but he was running his hands along her arms.

A recognition of this sensitivity to "sexual" signs leads nudists to become aware of the possible communication of certain of their own acts, which are not intended as "sexual" but might be interpreted as such.

Sometimes you're resting and you spread your legs unknowingly. [Q] My husband just told me not to sit that way. [Q] I put my legs together.

Since "immodesty" is defined as an unnatural manner of behavior, such behaviors are easily interpreted as being motivated by dishonorable intent. When the individual is intuited as being in physical control of the behavior and appreciative of the behavior's meaning within the nudist collectivity's scheme of interpretation, sexual intentions are assigned. Referring to a quotation that was presented earlier, one man said that a woman who was sitting with her legs spread may have been doing so unintentionally, "but I doubt it. [Q] It wasn't a normal position. Normally you wouldn't lay like this. It's like standing on your head."

Erotic reactions, as well as erotic actions, are controlled in camp. Even when erotic stimuli come into play, erotic responses may be inhibited.

[Q: While at camp have you ever had an erection?] Yes. It was just when my wife and kids and I were there. When somebody else is around you don't have one, but with my wife there and no others it happened. [Q] There was no body contact. [Q] She was getting undressed and I was watching her. Just a normal reaction for me. [Q] She kind of looked over and laughed, that's all.

When lying on the grass already hiding my penis, I got erotic thoughts. And then one realizes it can't happen here. With fear there isn't much erection.

Yes, once I started to have an erection. Once. [Q] A friend told me how he was invited by some young lady to go to bed. [Q] I started to picture the situation and I felt the erection coming on; so I immediately jumped in the pool. It went away.

I was once in the woods alone and ran into a woman. I felt myself getting excited. A secluded spot in the bushes which was an ideal place for procreation. [Q] Nothing happened, though.

When breaches of the situated morality do occur, the modesty of the other nudists may inhibit any direct sanctioning. The immediate breach may go unsanctioned. The observers may feign inattention or withdraw from the scene. The occurrence is usually communicated, however, via the grapevine, and may rapidly or eventually reach the camp director.

We were shooting a series of pictures and my wife was getting out of her clothes. [The photographer had an erection] but went ahead like nothing was happening. [Q] It was over kind of fast. . . . [Q] Nothing. We tried to avoid the issue. . . . Later we went to see . . . [the camp director] . . . and [the photographer] denied it.

[If a man had an erection] people would probably pretend they didn't see it.

[Q: What do you think of someone this happens to?] They should try to get rid of it fast. It don't look nice. Nudists are prudists. They are more prudish. Because they take their clothes off they are more careful. [Q] They become more prudish than people with clothes. They won't let anything out of the way happen.

As indicated in the remark, "nudists are prudists," nudists may at times become aware of the fragility of their situated moral meanings.

At _____ [camp], this family had a small boy no more than ten years old who had an erection. Mrs. _____ [the owner's wife] saw him and told his parents that they should keep him in check, and tell him what happened to him and to watch himself. This was silly, for such a little kid who didn't know what happened.

DEVIANCE AND SOCIAL PROCESS

There are basic social processes that underlie responses to deviance. Collectivities control thresholds of response to various behaviors, constituting the relevance, meaning, and importance of the behavior. As pointed out previously, erotic overtures or erotic responses are unnatural with respect to the nudist camps' scheme of interpretation. A reciprocity of perspectives, which is normally resupposed in one's associations, is called into question by behaviors that are constituted as unnatural or not understandable.

> We thought this single was all right, until others clued us in that he had brought girls up to camp. [Then we recalled that] he was kind of weird. The way he'd look at you. He had glassy eyes, like he could see through you.[12]

Such a response to deviance in the nudist camp is a result of effective socialization to the new system of moral meanings. The deviant's behavior, on the other hand, can be construed as reflecting an ineffective socialization to the situated meanings.

> I think it's impossible [to have an erection in a nudist camp]. [Q] In a nudist camp you must have some physical contact and a desire to have one.
>
> He isn't thinking like a nudist. [Q] The body is wholesome, not . . . a sex object. He'd have to do that—think of sex.
>
> Sex isn't supposed to be in your mind, as far as the body. He doesn't belong there. [Q] If you go in thinking about sex, naturally it's going to happen. . . . You're not supposed to think about going to bed with anyone, not even your wife.

The citing of deviant cases in this section should not obscure the fact that nudists do effectively manage the official definition of the situation. As with any moral system, however, there are breaches.

The unnaturalness or deviance of a behavior is, as illustrated, routinely determined by relating it to an institutionalized scheme of interpretation that is appropriate to a collectivity of assumed cobelievers: those who work at maintaining a situated moral order. When different schemes of interpretation, however, are applied to a situation and come into conflict—that is, when the finiteness of multiple realities gets questioned by apparent overlap—moral contests are experienced.

In these cases, the occurrences that are "not understandable" in the reality of one collectivity are quite understandable in the reality of another collectivity.[13] Thus, what are "deviant" occurrences in nudist camps probably would be constituted by members of the clothed society as being most natural, rather than being unnatural. The low threshold of nudists to all that is apparently "sexual" is a function of their marginality; the fact that they have not completely suspended the moral meanings of the clothed society is what leads them to constitute so many events as "sexual" in purpose.

Other Consequences of the Construction of a Situated Morality: The Territoriality of Emotions

Participation in, and commitment to, multiple worlds of moral meaning make the relevance of various emotions specific to where an event occurs. Thus, public nudity, which is routinely constituted as asexual in the nudist camp, has a different meaning, even for nudists, in the world of clothed society.

Embarrassment, for example, is more likely to be experienced by nudists when they are viewed in the nude by nonnudists than when they are so viewed by nudists. This is, of course, due to the assumptions that are made by the nudist as to the meaning the nudity has for the different viewers.

It is proposed that embarrassment is a vacillation between role and self, a search for social guidelines, and that in clothed society absence or disruption of clothing may effect such a vacillation. In nudist camps this role-self vacillation does not occur for the following reasons: (1) one's external background is composed of nude persons, and the external audience is not interpreted as being attentive to one's nudity; and (2) the person's own interpretation of nudity has been altered. Thus external and internal bases for embarrassment are neutralized. In the words of some interviewees:

> I would feel out of place [being seen nude] at home because the others are dressed.
> [Outsiders] can't see how anyone can . . . [go to a nudist camp] and not be embarrassed.
> At camp it's expected that someone will see your nude body.
> There's an atmosphere about the place that that's the natural order of the place—for people to be nude. And you can be as nonchalant as in clothed society.

In the nudist camp a person sometimes feels embarrassed, however, when he keeps his clothes on, because attention is then directed to his different state; he "stands out."

> You feel weird wearing clothes in a nudist camp; the same as if one person was nude out in the street with everyone dressed.
>
> First time I go out I say I don't want to take my clothes off, but I say I'd look awful funny walking around with my clothes on.
>
> I felt strange with clothes on. I felt that people were watching me, since I had clothes on.
>
> I had a towel over my shoulder and was walking from the car to the pool. . . . To make a conscious effort of covering yourself with a towel you would draw attention, because you were the one being different. I had the towel over my shoulder, let it fall the way it would, but my husband said it was better to carry it over my arm. It was the first day, a new experience, and you try to be like everybody else. . . . I saw my husband's point about draping it over my arm.

Because of the character of the external background, in the nudist camp embarrassment that occurs because of being nude indicates (1) that the person has not adopted the new interpretation of nudity and evaluates the situation with an internal frame of reference, or (2) that a breakdown in the official definition of the situation due to a *faux pas*, accident, or mistake has discredited the nudist interpretation.

> *An example of internal audience:* [I don't get embarrassed] . . . as long as I don't look at my own body. I just look straight ahead. If I look down at my own body I get embarrassed.
>
> *An example of an accident:* A guy who was a soldier got . . . [an erection] down at the lake. It was the first time he had been to camp. I got embarrassed and turned away.

To socialize people to the moral meanings of any collectivity is most difficult when persons come to the collectivity accompanied by others who strongly symbolize an old scheme of interpretation. Thus, nudist camps that allow single males may insist that they not be accompanied by male friends.[14] Women attending with male friends, or married couples attending together, find it more difficult to adjust. One woman whose embarrassment was "internally" based, and who visited the camp primarily out of a sense of duty to her nudist fiancé, remarked: "We weren't married the first time we went. I think that was my biggest problem; it was him. Just because I knew him as well as I did. Strangers don't bother me as much."

Role problems of identity, poise, or confidence in maintaining identity and poise [15] are minimized with respect to nudity by the moral meanings managed in the nudist camp. Since inattention is maintained, impression management does not become problematic. As one nudist remarked, "We stay mentally clothed."

Outside the nudist camp, the meanings and background of clothed society lead the nudist to use different rules of interpretation. Thus, when nudists were asked how they would feel if a nonnudist saw them walking around nude in their own home, many said they would feel embarrassed. In this situation the person experiences the vacillation from Role to Self; there is an external background of clothed others and a different constitution of the meaning of nudity. Holding one element constant, the external background, nudists were confronted in the interviews and questionnaires with situations at camp where a nonnudist meaning of nudity might be suspect.

[Q: What would you think of someone who concealed their body while at camp?] I wouldn't think they belong at camp. . . . I would know an outsider wasn't a nudist and I would be embarrassed. [Q: Why's that?] I would figure the outsider would be out for what he could see. He would be looking at me the way an outsider would. [Q: How's that?] An outsider doesn't look at you as a nudist. It's like looking at a dirty picture or a dirty book for him.

The following remarks also reveal the assumption that nudity is a different reality for members of the clothed society.

[Q: If seen walking around nude in your home] it's obvious he [the observer] doesn't have the attitude that the people in the nudist camp have. He is obviously a Peeping Tom. We don't want to be stared at by someone who you think is staring at you for lewd purposes.

In the city, they would stare at you like at a burlesque show. The difference [between this and at camp] would be in the attitude of the people staring. . . . Nudity is elevated out there [that is, at camp].

An interesting phenomenon, when fully clothed in a tavern you feel funny walking to the ladies room in front of men. While in a nudist camp there is no embarrassment. The whole atmosphere is conducive to a healthy attitude.

Multiple-meaning structures, illustrated in these remarks, produce the situational variability of emotions. And social emotions other than embarrassment are tied to territories; in nudist camps these emotions are also irrelevant to heterosexual nudity. Since the nudist camp provides its participants with new interpretations of heterosexual nudity, if the old interpretations can be kept out of play, emotions such as shame, guilt, or sexual jealousy lose any relation to heterosexual nudity. In cases where a nudist reported feeling ashamed or guilty about his nudist participation, this feeling was elicited usually when he was away from camp—for instance, in church—where pristine interpretations defined his activities. Like embarrassment, when shame or guilt was elicited in camp, it was because nudity lost its taken-for-granted character due to a breakdown in the official definition of the situation. This happened, for example, when doubt was cast on the meaning or purpose of camp nudity. Some nudists mentioned feeling uncomfortable when others continued to walk around nude during the chilly evening, leading them to suspect that everyone's motivations were not on the "up and up"; and sometimes this led the person to feel ashamed of himself for involvement in something "that was not all that it was made out to be." Sometimes, simply being inside led the person to be aware of his nudity. Just the fact that it was cooler inside directed attention to one's body.

> When I go under a roof . . . I don't think I like it. [Q: Why's that?] Because under a roof I don't feel the same about being nude. [Q: Could you tell me some more about what you mean?] The reason I went is for a suntan. I don't feel you should run around nude all the time. I don't want to lose respect for it; to just strip and run around. . . . Inside, sitting down, you really feel nude.

With regard to sexual jealousy, when respondents were presented in the interview with a hypothetical situation in which someone views their spouse nude outside of camp, some stated that in this situation they would feel jealous. Jealousy (regarding their spouse's seeing and being seen) is irrelevant in a place where one experiences, and assumes that others experience, nudity as a routine, nonaffective phenomenon. Thus, in camp, jealousy also is usually evoked only when the official moral meanings break down. Then the nudity of the spouse or of the other becomes individualized.

> [Q: Could you tell me about some occurrences at camp that have gotten you jealous?] This girl. She was throwing herself on all the men. . . . [Q] She'd do things to try and excite them. She'd twist to the car radio —things you don't do in the nude.
>   [I got jealous] when another nudist paid too much attention to my wife. [Q] Everywhere she went, he went. . . . He kept following her around.

Usually, when the official definition of the situation does break down members assure one another that the person who breached the official definition is "sick." He is labeled a "pig" or a "pervert." Such name calling and status degradation confirm official sentiments; it is the labeled's interpretations and not the collectivities that are deviant. The person is often expelled from camp.

Therefore, if people are effectively socialized to a nonsexual interpretation of nudity and this rule of interpretation is sustained, sexual, moral, and emotional responses that are commonly associated with heterosexual nudity become phenomenally absurd.[16] Because interpretations become tied to "places," the reality sustained in a place determines what elicits an emotion.

Maintaining Respectability:
Management of Appearances in Dealing with Clothed Society

Nudists envision themselves as being labeled deviant by members of the clothed society. They anticipate that if their nudist participation were "known about" they would be socially typed in the following ways: (1) as sexually available or "promiscuous," (2) as "nuts."

Communications of sexual availability result from signs of a lack of sexual reserve put forth by persons who are interpreted to be in physical control of their behavior and appreciative of its meaning. To many outsiders, going to a nudist camp signifies such a lack of sexual reserve. Thus nudists with teenage daughters said that peers would type their daughter as a "whore" if they knew she were a nudist. Other respondents provided the following quotations, which illustrate the "sexual" and "odd ball" labels nudists expect from members of the clothed society.

> Most . . . aren't acquainted with nudism, and get dirty or false ideas about the whole thing. [Q] Usually a man will think "this one you can have easily." [Q] Because, usually men . . . get sexual ideas.
>
> Some people who don't understand might think I'm an undesirable friend because it's misunderstood by most people. . . . Newspapers and other media give people the wrong idea of nudism. I wouldn't want to lose my friends because they have preconceived notions about the movement. [Q] Yes, they think nudism is immoral. . . . They consider the nude body immoral and conclude when nude bodies are together, that immorality is the result. [Q] They think that when nude people are together, that they are promiscuous.

If people knew [you were a nudist], they would look at you kind of funny.

I'd be embarrassed to tell anyone. I'd feel that they were talking about me. [Q] People have funny opinions about nudists. [Q] They think they're odd balls to go around without clothes. [Q] That they can't be quite "all right" to go without clothes.

My mother, she worries about what her friends might think about me, not whether it's right or wrong. She never talks about that. [Q] She is afraid I'll be criticized by her friends.

Nudists anticipate sanctions in both social and economic arenas; social ostracism is anticipated, as well as deleterious consequences for one's occupational career. Fifty-nine per cent of the interviewees mentioned social consequences if their nudist identity were revealed; 22 per cent mentioned economic-occupational consequences. Government employees appear to be especially wary, ever since the case was widely publicized of a post office employee who lost his job because he was a nudist.[17]

[Upon entering camp] when I go down the path to the gate I look behind to see if anyone's behind us. I don't want anyone to know we're going in. . . . The same when leaving. Maybe someone will see us that we know.

Oh yes, especially in the last eight years I don't say anything. The kids go to a parochial school. They wouldn't let them stay if they knew.

When other people hear it in the office of my husband, maybe they wouldn't want him. I don't know. It might be so in America. [Q] My husband heard this from a friend. . . . So we decided it was better not to tell. In Germany the little girls and boys go to the beach without suits, but not here in America.

No. [Q] It might affect my work. [Q] My employer might look unfavorably upon it. [Q] They won't understand. They might think I'm crazy. [Q] I've heard of others losing their jobs because of nudism.

People . . . think you are a dirty guy. It might also hurt me in my work. [Q] That you are real bad. [Q] They think that people only go there for sex, to look at naked women. [Q] If an opportunity for promotion came up they might pass over me because I'm a nudist. [Q] In private life, people might think I'm an odd ball. [Q] People, because of this feeling, might not care to associate with us any more. [Q] The children might be poked fun at by the other children. [Q] Children seem to laugh at people who don't do the average thing.

The anticipation of deviant labels and consequent sanctions leads to a pattern of secrecy. For example, in the camp situation only first

names are used. Knowledge of last names and place of employment
is defined as irrelevant. This fear of being exposed by one's fellow
nudists seems to deny the "one big family" impression that is managed
by the nudist collectivity; but this discrepancy is rationalized by a denial of relevance. If all are members of one big family, last names are
irrelevant forms of identity. Last names are not necessary for interaction in the nudist camp.

Outside of camp, most nudists maintain at least some secrecy regarding their nudist activities. Taking into account the respondent's
years in nudism, three coders rated nudist interviewees in the following gross way: very secret, 36 per cent (22 per cent had never told anyone); somewhat secret, 36 per cent; not very secret 18 per cent; not
at all secret, 10 per cent.[18] Also, when the number of people to whom
nudists had revealed their identity was cross-tabulated by the number
of years they had been nudists, the length of time in nudism did not
explain the variance in the number of outsiders who knew of their
participation.

When the interviewees did reveal their nudist affiliation, in 33 per
cent of the cases this was in response to someone's inquiries regarding
their week end whereabouts. In other words, relatives or friends had
questioned them about where they disappeared to, where they kept
their trailer, and so on. In some other cases, nonnudists had initiated a
general discussion of nudism. And there were instances where nudists
had themselves initiated the discussion of their nudist activities. In
these cases there was usually a process of sounding out:

[Q: Have you ever told anyone about your nudist activities?] No. [Q] I'm
afraid they will think I'm a nut. [Q] I've asked them what they thought
of nudism without telling them I was one. [Q] They think that nudist
camps are sex clubs.
   [Q] Wife swapping, men running around with hard-ons and screwing
all the time.
   I don't want to become a social outcast. [Q] I don't care to have the
tag, "nut." [Q] I have asked people what they thought of nudists. They
think nudists are nuts or sex pots. [Q] Crackpot, that's the best word I
know. . . . I'm a teacher, and I deal with people's children. . . . I'm
worried about my job. It relies on an unquestioned reputation.
   He pretended not to belong and asked if I would be interested (in
visiting a nudist camp). [Q] I said we had (public nudist) beaches in
Germany where you didn't have to wear suits, and we enjoyed it there.
[Q] He said he would find out where a place was and we could go there
together. [Q] We went to _____ (nudist camp) with him. [Q] After
we got to camp he said he had been a member eight or ten years. [Q]

He said he wouldn't tell anybody until they actually went because he was afraid they might say something that would hurt him.

Thus nudists usually told only those from whom they expected a favorable response:

Everyone we talked to reacted favorably. But if we didn't anticipate a favorable reaction we wouldn't have talked with them.

I'm very careful about who I tell. If I thought it would affect our relationship, I wouldn't tell them.

In general, more highly educated persons were to be typified as more accepting of "unconventional" activities. The anticipation of a favorable response usually increased, the higher the educational status of the other.

A higher educated person is more likely to understand, but you wouldn't go tell the postman or grocer. They wouldn't be the type. Like they don't belong to the Elks or Masons. They don't want to find out how the other half lives.

And it was generally considered unwise to tell "persons with sexy attitudes."

My husband told his brother, but he's not interested. He has the wrong idea. . . . He wanted to know what kind of nuts we were. [Q] He has a sexy attitude. We don't care to talk to him. That goes against us because we know better. [Q] His brother doesn't get along with his wife, and he shacks up with others. These are the ideas he has.

When nudists did inform others, the nonnudists were reported to respond often with disbelief. The reactions of outsiders were described as follows:

Disbelief at first. Doubt. When they ask where you go on weekends, I just say, "A nudist park." They say, "Sure." After talking they believe it. [Q] They didn't know they existed. They thought they were beach parties, or fantasies. They didn't know they were run as a business: charters, organization.

Nonnudists, it appears, find it difficult to believe that the suspension of clothing does not lead to a complete breakdown of interaction patterns common to clothed society. They anticipate the usual emotions of embarrassment, jealousy, and so forth. For many, sexual interest and promiscuity seem to be a necessary consequence of a suspension of clothing.

> [They] were surprised that there was swimming, and hiking, and shuffleboard. Some thought nudists just walk around and didn't do anything. Some thought there were sex parties. [Q] They said they always associated nudism with wild orgies. When I gave them a clear picture they were surprised it was so tame.

The rhetoric that the nudist employs in justifying nudism, when he does attempt to give others "a clear picture," includes the following: that nudists are more friendly and sociable than other people (which seems to be a situational truth because of the "minority group feeling" one finds in nudist camps); that there is greater relaxation swimming and sunbathing in the nude, and not having to worry what "resort clothes" one has to buy; and that one experiences a greater "freedom" and enjoyment of the outdoors when nude. In addition, increased physical and mental health for both adults and children are cited as justifications. The nonnudist is also told that one gets quickly accustomed to being nude in the presence of nude members of the opposite sex and that nudity does not generate the sexual feelings that are commonly supposed.

Some nonnudist writers have characterized nudists as using these justifications to proselytize "with a fervor which almost touches on the religious." [19] The present writer, however, did not find any such pattern. Except for a few of the most involved members, anticipations of social typing seemed to limit proselytizing tremendously. Most recruitment was left to the mass media.

It has been shown that nudists are selective in choosing those to whom they reveal their secret, typifying nonnudists by their probable responses. Thus it was found that nudists were more likely to tell those with whom they were in primary interaction. In such instances they were in a better position to suspend very general and anonymous typifications and gamble on the basis of more individualized "personal" typifications.[20] Given that nudists were selective as to those they told, they interpreted nonnudists' responses to this revealed identity to modally be as follows: 21 per cent, positive; 35 per cent, live and let live; 21 per cent, negative. (The remaining 22 per cent of the respondents had never told anyone.) [21] Ten per cent of those who had revealed their nudist participation concluded that their social relationships with the nonnudists were affected negatively.

Because nudists participate in the multiple moral realities of the nudist and clothed worlds, many nudists described themselves as Dr. Jekylls and Mr. Hydes.

[Q: Once you had made up your mind to become a nudist, did you ever have doubts that this was the right decision?] Yes. The reason is whenever you join an organization and accept a label, then you are in a peculiar position of feeling impelled to defend it against any imputations that irresponsible people may bring up. The doubts are still with me. Especially when speaking with other people at camp. When I find they are also concerned. For example one of them teaches. He would like to be an "integrated" person and it irks him to have to keep his nudist membership a secret. And so when I talk to others many of them have this same problem. One doesn't want to live a double life.

The fact that nudists participate in a group that they view as stigmatized, and also the fact that many claim to have found a sense of belonging in nudism, suggest that nudists might be isolates in the larger society. If they were isolated they could more easily participate in such a deviant group, being insulated from social controls.

A comparison of nudist interviewees with a sample of the general population [22] did show nudists to fall substantially below the general population in frequency of informal association.[23] Further, while members of the general population got together most often with relatives, in my sample nudists got together most often with friends.[24] The fact that 34 per cent of the nudist sample got together with relatives less than once a month could reflect a considerable insulation from informal controls, since relatives might provide the greatest pressure in inhibiting participation in such deviant groups.

The degree to which nudists were isolated in the clothed society was found to be related to the length of time they had been nudists. The longer a person had been in nudism, the more likely he was to be isolated. Fifty-four per cent of those who had been nudists for 10 or more years were rated by coders as isolated, 44 per cent of those participating 6–9 years, 38 per cent of those participating 3–5 years, and 22 per cent of those participating 1–2 years. This may be interpreted in different ways. For example, there may be a tendency to become more isolated with continued participation, perhaps to avoid sanctions. (Yet, in regard to formal organizations nudists did not drop out or become less active.) Or, in the past it is likely that nudism was considered even more deviant than it is today, and therefore it might have appealed primarily to more isolated types of people.

Regardless of the correct interpretation, many nudists did find a sense of belonging in nudism, as is indicated in the following quotations: [25]

> People are lonely. It gives them a sense of belonging.
>   Until I started going out [to camp] I never felt like I was part of a crowd. But I do out there. I was surprised. [Q] Well, like I said, I was never part of a crowd. . . . I had friends, but never outstanding. My wife and I were [camp] King and Queen.

While the nudist experience helps to solve this life problem for some, however, it creates this same problem for others. For the latter group, nudism may only ease the problem that it creates; that is, the isolation that results from concealing one's affiliation with a deviant group.[26]

Summary and Conclusion

This chapter has examined how nudists work at maintaining moral appearances, both in nudist camps and in the clothed society. We have discussed some of the consequences of these strategies and of the bridging of multiple moral worlds. As members of the clothed society become more and more liberal in their attitudes toward nudity (or simply more accustomed to it) we would expect that many of these strategies and consequences of nudist camp participation will cease to exist. The result for nudists will be that morality will no longer have this added *multiple* cross-situational structure.

The success that nudists have had in constructing their situational morality within the larger society seems to have started things already in this direction. There are, for example, moral contests going on in the nudist world over the elimination of some of the camp rules that we have discussed. The success that nudists have had in challenging conventional morality is being used by nonnudists also to pave the way for different moral interpretations of other situations. Now that the situated morality of the nudist camp has become increasingly accepted by law and public opinion, "nudism" has, for example, become a rubric used to legitimize girlie magazines. I am here speaking of those magazines which label themselves as nudist magazines and provide a list of nudist camps, but whose models pose seductively in garter belts, stockings, and high heels.

The publicity that has been given nudism, and the tremendous in-

crease in nudity in fashions, in the movies, and in the number of nudist and girlie magazines that are found on the newsstands, have contributed to the impression that there is "a sexual revolution." Members of our society have extrapolated the idea that an underlying pattern of "sexual" permissiveness exists throughout the society.[27] What
might be of interest to social scientists now is the strategies and consequences of these new situated moralities and what feedback, if any,
they may have on the culture of the nudist camp.

NOTES

NOTE: This research was supported in part by a Public Health Service fel-
lowship (No. 7-F1-MH-14, 660-01A BEH) from the National Institute of
Mental Health. I wish to acknowledge my appreciation for this support and
my appreciation to John I. Kitsuse for his guidance and suggestions with
respect to the research.

1. In my previous papers I have dealt with other questions that are commonly asked about nudists. How persons become nudists is discussed
   in my "Becoming a Nudist," *Psychiatry*, XXIX (February, 1966), 15–
   24. A report on the nudist way of life and social structure can be found
   in my article in *Human Organization*, XXVI (Fall, 1967), 91–99.
2. Approximately one hundred camps were represented in the interviews
   and questionnaires. Interviews were conducted in the homes of nudists
   during the off season. Arrangements for the interviews were initially
   made with these nudists during the first summer of participant observation; selection of respondents was limited to those living within a one-
   hundred-mile radius of Chicago. The questionnaires were sent to all
   members of the National Nudist Council. The different techniques of
   data collection provided a test of convergent validation. Cf. Donald T.
   Campbell and Donald W. Fiske, "Convergent and Discriminant Validation by the Multitrait-Multimethod Matrix," *Psychological Bulletin*,
   LVI (March, 1959), 81–105.
3. For a discussion of the essence of appresentation, see Alfred Schutz,
   Collected Papers: The Problem of Social Reality, Maurice Natanson,
   ed. (The Hague: Nijhoff, 1962), I, 287 ff.
4. [Q] is used to signify a neutral probe by the interviewer that follows
   the course of the last reply, such as "Could you tell me some more
   about that?" or "How is that?" or "What do you mean?" Other questions by the interviewer are given in full.
5. The King and Queen contest, which takes place at conventions, allows
   for a patterned evasion of the staring rule. Applicants stand before the
   crowd in front of the royal platform, and applause is used for selection
   of the victors. Photography is also allowed during the contest, and no

one is permitted to enter the contest unless willing to be photographed. The major reason for this is that this is a major camp event, and contest pictures are used in nudist magazines. At the same time, the large number of photographs sometimes taken by lay photographers (that is, not working for the magazines), makes many nudists uncomfortable by calling into question a nonsexual definition of the situation.

6. The writer was amazed at how many young female nudists described a similar pattern of extreme clothing modesty among their parents and in their own married life. Included in this group was another nudist model, who is one of the most photographed of nudist models. Perhaps there are some fruitful data here for cognitive-dissonance psychologists.

7. Cf. Schutz, *op. cit.*, p. 74.

8. For some respondents, the female genitals, because of their hidden character, never became a routinized part of camp nudity; that is, their visible exposure did not lose an attention-provoking quality.

9. Compare Harold Garfinkel, "A Conception of, and Experiments with, 'Trust' as a Condition of Stable Concerted Actions," in O. J. Harvey, ed., *Motivation and Social Interaction* (New York: Ronald, 1963).

10. See: Schutz, *op. cit.*, I, 11, for his definition of reciprocity of perspectives.

11. This corresponds with the findings of learning-theory psychologists.

12. For a study of the process of doublethink, see James L. Wilkins, "Doublethink: A Study of Erasure of the Social Past," unpublished doctoral dissertation, Northwestern University, 1964.

13. Schutz, *op. cit.*, pp. 229 ff.

14. Compare the process of severing past ties that might inhibit socialization as described by Dornbush for the Military Academy: Stanford M. Dornbush, "The Military Academy as an Assimilating Institution," *Social Forces*, XXXVIII (May, 1955). Also see Erving Goffman, "On the Characteristics of Total Institutions," in his *Asylums* (Garden City, N.Y.: Doubleday Anchor, 1961), pp. 1–124.

15. See Edward Gross and Gregory P. Stone, "Embarrassment and the Analysis of Role Requirements," *American Journal of Sociology*, LXX (July, 1964), 1–15.

16. Compare Edmund Husserl, *Ideas: General Introduction to Pure Phenomenology*, trans. by W. R. Boyce Gibson (New York: Collier, 1962), pp. 53–54, 353–354.

17. One federal employee in the interview sample had kept his nudist identity secret for nine years. Then an anonymous letter was received by his state governor, telling of the "immoral nature" of the respondent's weekend activities. After a complete investigation and an appearance before an investigation board, however, the decision was handed down that the employee had done nothing that would require dismissal.

18. Coders were instructed to look at the answers to the specific questions

about secrecy and "whom they had told" and also to take into account how long the respondent had been a nudist (for example, they may have told ten persons; for a nudist of thirty years this would indicate more secrecy than for a first-year nudist). "Very secret" indicated a very active hiding of one's nudist identity. A comparison of different coders' ratings of the same respondent was used as a check on rating reliability. Coding reliability was computed to be .94. All the percentages cited in this section of the chapter are from the interview data.

19. For example, see Lawrence Langner, *The Importance of Wearing Clothes* (New York: Hastings House, 1959), p. 84.

20. See Schutz's description of the character of typifications, *Collected Papers II: Studies in Social Theory*, Arvid Broderson, ed. (The Hague: Nijhoff, 1964), pp. 48 ff.

21. For coding purposes, "positive" was defined as a desire to participate in nudism or to become a nudist. "Live and let live" included those who did not desire participation in nudism, but did not think ill of those who did participate.

22. In this comparison, Axelrod's data on a sample of the general population in the Detroit area were used. See Morris Axelrod, "Urban Structure and Social Participation," *American Sociological Review*, XXI (February, 1956), 13–18.

23. My comparative tables can be found in my "Becoming a Nudist." A limitation in this comparison, however, is that Axelrod collapsed his frequencies of social association of less than once a week into the category of "less often or never."

24. Axelrod finds this greater participation with friends only for members of his sample with high income or high educational or social status.

25. Some nudists also viewed themselves as members of an elite, superior to clothed society because they had suspended the body taboo.

26. For a discussion of information control, see Erving Goffman, *Stigma: Notes on the Management of Spoiled Identity* (Englewood Cliffs: Prentice-Hall, 1963), pp. 41–104.

27. For a discussion of this process of "extrapolation," see Harold Garfinkel, "Commonsense Knowledge of Social Structures: The Documentary Method of Interpretation in Lay and Professional Fact-Finding," in his *Studies in Ethnomethodology* (Englewood Cliffs: Prentice-Hall, 1967), pp. 76–103.

13

The Modern Artist's Asociability: Constructing a Situated Moral Revolution

Ronald J. Silvers

While paintings and sculptures are regarded as having a moral dimension by artists, patrons, art critics, and intellectuals, the moral meaning of art works is open to different interpretations among members of these groups. In this chapter we examine the manner in which modern American artists have defined their paintings and sculptures as tools for constructing and communicating a revolutionary set of morals in contemporary industrial society and the way in which they have developed an asocial role for their mission. We will focus on this role of asociability, reviewing its progressive stages, its terms of reference for other positions in society, and, finally, its relationship to the way in which the artist perceives his self as a creative person. But first we turn to a discussion of the forms of deviance among artists in order to establish the analytical concepts for our study.

Forms of Deviance among Artists

In 1456 the Italian artist Fra Filippo Lippi seduced and eloped with a nun, Sister Lucrezia Buti, and became the father of her illegitimate child. It was not an isolated incident for the friar, as other members of the same convent were known to have visited his quarters. Eventually, Filippo was unburdened of his religious vows; he was removed from his clerical offices and the revenues attached to them. Yet his irreverent behavior in no way diminished his prestige as an outstanding artist. Nor were the merits of his earlier religious works reappraised because of his sacrilegious behavior. Not only did the Pope invoke no sanctions against Filippo as an artist; he was commissioned to produce other religious paintings for the church.

In 1948 American artists contributed to the exhibition, "Advancing American Art," which was to tour the world under the auspices of the U.S. Department of State. The exhibit, displayed in the United States before being sent abroad, contained a heavy emphasis on expressionism, abstractionism, surrealism, and fantasy. Newspapers and art critics campaigned against the exhibit, maintaining that the paintings were alien to American culture. The government ended the tour and ordered the exhibit home in an aura of disgrace. Commenting on the situation, President Truman charged that the works were not art and that the artists were "half-baked, lazy people." [1] The President's remarks identified the kind of immorality involved and provided a justification for the government's actions against the exhibit and its artists.

The absence of sanctions directed against the Italian artist and the invocation of them in the case of the American artists underscore the different forms of deviance represented in these two instances. Fra Filippo's actions conform to the image of the Bohemian artist in the nineteenth and twentieth centuries: one who is thought to be free from moral law because of his creative essence and considered to be in constant conflict with conventional society. [2] Bohemians are pictured as violators of common proscriptions of civil society; they are associated with immoral heterosexual behavior and homosexual activity, with drugs, alcoholism, insanity, and suicide.

Fra Filippo's immorality and the deviance of Bohemians exist in the nonprofessional area of the artist's life; the immoral behavior is conceived as a by-product of the artist's creativity, but it is not considered to be part of, or technically necessary for, creative work. In these cases the artist is often thought to be deviant because of his creative nature, but he is not expected to be creative because he is immoral.

The friar is depicted as alternating between deviance and creativity in such a way that his immoral secular activities were not seen as contaminating the religious content of his creative work. As historians point out, "Few people in the fifteenth and the early sixteenth centuries saw a contradiction between the licentious behavior and the religious works of an artist." [3] If, however, the friar had included obscene images in his paintings, then, as a form of professional deviance, he would have been censured as an artist.

Professional deviance is found in the second case. The artists exhibiting their works in the State Department's "Advancing American Art" were regarded as deviants because they indulged in aesthetic immorality by violating rules concerning the content, style, and handling of subject matter. Thus, the President charged, "There are a great many American artists who still believe that the ability to make things look as they are is the first requisite of a great artist—they do not belong to the so-called modern school. There is no art at all in connection with modernism, in my opinion." [4]

As the President's statement indicates, there are certain expectations about what artists do with their talent; namely, they are to re-create visual subject matter in representative form. The modern painters, failing to do so, either are not artists (according to the standard) or are poor artists; at worst, they are fakes.

This is by no means the only illustration of imputed aesthetic immorality. A few of the better-known cases include:

1. In 1877 the renowned art critic John Ruskin charged James Abbott McNeill Whistler (known for his portrait of his mother) with such impudent and insulting paintings as if to throw a pot of paint in the public's face. Whistler sued for libel and won, receiving a half a cent damages (at the same time he went into bankruptcy because of legal expenses). The public sided with Ruskin, who alleged that a painting should be an exact, detailed, realistic picture of some object, scene, or event. Whistler was considered to be deviant since he worked with the view that his paintings' aesthetic functions were independent of the subject matter.

2. Cubism and other new styles in the Armory Show of 1913 drew reactions in which artists were called degenerate, insane, incompetent, charlatan, and anarchists.

3. In the 1920's and 1930's Dadaists were charged as deviants because they produced ugly and antiart. For example, Duchamp's sculpture (submitted under the pseudonym R. Mutt) was rejected from an art exhibition because it was, in fact, an old urinal.

4. Many of the works of the American sculptor Gaston Lachaise were withheld from exhibition for over thirty-five years because it was thought they might prove offensive and precipitate a scandal. In his sculptures of women he exaggerated the breasts and hips and presented suggestive positions with the female body.

Aesthetic immorality is commonly found in the context of asocial behavior, which is a second type of professional deviance. As a general concept, asocial behavior refers to activities which are the product of an incumbent's judgment to concentrate responsibility exclusively in his own social position. For example, there is the well-known declaration "Art for Art's Sake," [5] which defines the autonomy of art and, concomitantly, the autonomy of the artist's position. It is an expression of deviance in the sense that artists who uphold it dismiss responsibility to others in society by refusing to participate, co-operate, and in other contexts to fulfill a position in the normatively expected way. It may or may not entail the violating of other moral rules, and it may be related to other moral disputes. But it is, at its base, a dissenting definition of the location of responsibility by an occupant of a social position. As the term "social" presupposes an expected, reciprocal dependence of rights and duties between two or more social positions, the concept of asocial behavior indicates the absence of these reciprocal features.

Asocial behavior is the result of a willful break from, and rejection of, former moral meanings given to the activities of a social position and a construction of a new set of meanings which emphasize the independent responsibility of a status. Thus, asociability refers to that situation in which the individual continues to occupy the "same" social position in society, but alters the definition of rights and duties of that status. Those who consider the artist to be asocial, and painters and sculptors who apply this category to themselves, do so in terms of competing sets of expectations: of how the artist is expected to co-operate and participate in society, of the kind of art works he is expected to produce, and finally of how his works are to be regarded in society. When one of these points—his co-operation, his participation, or the meaning and function of his paintings or sculptures—comes to be disputed between artists and others, and when the artist withdraws former meanings of responsibility from other social relationships and exclusively invests moral responsibility in his own position, he is considered to be asocial in his behavior.[6]

The most heated charge of aesthetic immorality in America was directed against abstract expressionism. Beginning in the early 1940's, this art movement developed around the idea that forms were to be based on abstract imagery rather than on common visual subject matter and, further, that the style of presentation should vary with the spontaneous "visual language" of each artist.[7] The public complained that the paintings were meaningless. Many of the forms were unrecognizable, and the manner in which paintings were to be viewed differed drastically from the past. Patrons could no longer rely on a visual reading along horizontal and vertical axes (ordinarily applied to a landscape, still life, or portrait), nor could they use a perspective distinguishing background and foreground. Many of the paintings required a scanning approach so that a series of randomly selected parts of the canvas could be integrated in the mind of the viewer.

In conjunction with the alleged aesthetic immorality of the artist, there developed an extensive construction of asociability. Abstract-expressionist artists constructed a system of beliefs and ideals requiring absolute and exclusive responsibility to nonsocial aesthetic pursuits.

This chapter is devoted to a study of the asociability ethic among abstract-expressionist artists [8] and to the manner in which they constructed their axiomatic posture of social irresponsibility. Before turning to the case material, a methodological framework for the content of this analysis is described.

Artists' Theories of Creativity as Source Material for the Study

1. THE SOCIOLOGICAL SIGNIFICANCE OF ARTISTS' THEORIES OF CREATIVITY

As new paintings and sculptures are points of reference in forming expectations of what artists do and how they are related to others, asociability, as one type of construction of the artist's position, can be located in the meanings given to new artistic works. The methodological strategy of studying the position and social self of the artist is therefore best applied to the meanings given to newly created paintings and sculptures.

We normally assume that it is the nonartist—especially the patron, art critic, and museum curator—who constructs the meaning of art. It is quite true that those outside the artistic profession have an influence on the meanings and value ascribed to paintings and sculptures. But artists also determine the general meanings of their work, chiefly by communicating to others the precepts which they consider to be fundamental in the creation of their works. Artists interpret the meaning and impute values by articulating principles and procedures that govern the production of art items. In this manner they influence the meanings constructed by other members of society. The precepts may be phrased in the most concrete technical terms or in the most abstract theoretical and metaphysical concepts, and, depending on the nature of the audience, the precepts are presented through different modes of communication. Collectively and systematically the methodological precepts of an artist or group of artists endow paintings and sculptures with meaning in terms of an idealization of a creative process. The idealization is, from the artist's standpoint, a theory of creativity. Some such theories have become the central meaning describing a group of art works; that is, a "style" of art. We see evidence of the artist's influence in the identification of art styles over the past hundred years, all of which emphasize the meaning of the creative process itself: impressionism, surrealism, constructivism, and abstract expressionism.

These theories of creativity are rarely restricted to principles and procedures about the construction of aesthetic forms, but usually contain descriptions of the creative and moral substance of the artist's self and statements about what the moral conduct of the artist should be and what types of social relationships he should engage in as well as those he should avoid. Collectively and systematically, prescriptions and proscriptions about the moral conduct of the artist and statements about his moral essence contained in theories of creativity define his position in society and the substantive characteristics of his social self. Descriptions of the artist's moral status touch on role obligations to other positions, the question of the nature and function of his art in society, and the issue of responsibility to specific groups or the entire society. Along these dimensions there is a wide variety of definitions of the status found in different societies and at different points of time. They range from the traditional-religious status of the medieval artist to the contemporary structure of asociability.

Moral descriptions of the artist's social self, in general terms, are contained in the concept of the "creator." It offers a composite picture of a social self which is substantially that of a person who paints pictures or produces sculptural forms. The term "creator" implies a holistic account and, as a quality of a person, the "substantial self." [9] To simplify the terminology we will hereafter refer to the artist's creative substantial self as his "creative self."

2. DOCUMENTARY SOURCES AND METHOD OF ANALYSIS

With this conceptual focus the study of asociability was applied to the analysis of modern artists' writings on creativity. Statements were collected from publications of small-circulation periodicals such as *It Is, Possibilities,* and *Dyn,* well-known ones such as *Art News* and *Magazine of Art,* daily newspapers, museum bulletins and exhibition catalogues, sociological studies of artists which contain direct quotations, and transcripts of artists' meetings. Close to a hundred separate documents written and published, or relating to the period, between the early 1940's and the early 1960's were examined. The collected statements were authored by American artists known as abstract-expressionists, abstract imagists, and action painters; [10] all three types are hereafter referred to as abstract expressionists (or briefly as abstract artists or modern artists).

The artists' statements were examined collectively to discover the specific properties and general dimensions of their meanings of asociability and the creative self. To accomplish this task we used the artists' statements as "external vehicles" of meanings, attempting, first, to discover the separate properties of meaning; second, to ascertain the imputed relationship among the properties so as to obtain a holistic account; and finally, to relate this account to the actions of the artists.[11]

Using this mode of analysis, we inquired into (1) how the meanings of modern art and the creative self were constructed; (2) how asociability was applied to a contest of moral systems; and (3) the relationship between the modern artist's construction of the creative self and asociability. Before dealing with our main research queries, we first turn to a review of the social context in which the moral constructions emerged.

The Social Context of the Modern Artist's Asociability

While various forms of modern abstract art were produced in America in the 1930's, it was not until the early 1940's that the styles acquired a meaning of asociability; the shift in the location of moral responsibility occurred within a decade. Social events in the transition period, as identified by abstract artists, include the curtailment of the WPA Federal Art Works Projects, the exhaustion of radical political movements, and the emigration of European artists to America. Abstract expressionists consider each of these events to have had an important effect on the development of their theory of creativity.

The federal government developed the Art Works Projects in 1935 in order to offset economic hardships created by the depression. Artists were commissioned to paint murals and produce other works for such federal sites as post offices and for schools and hospitals. By the beginning of 1939 the government had commissioned more than a million works of art from about five thousand artists. But on the individual level the projects provided very limited financial support. The importance of the WPA is to be found in the organization it provided and its symbol as a union between artists and the public.

During and prior to the 1930's there was no national, nonpolitical, aesthetically nonpartisan professional organization for artists. It was not until 1947 that artists moved toward professionalization at a national level by organizing the Artists Equity Association. The WPA Federal Art Works program, though promoted by nonartists, thereby became the first organization to provide artists with a basis of national concern, a reference for national identity, and an organizational link to the general public. Consequently, its termination in the early 1940's was a dramatic event for modern artists: they viewed it as a rupture of their relations with the entire society.

The second event that played a part in the emergence of the modern artists' asociability was the exhaustion of political ideological movements. In the 1930's socialist and Communist movements encouraged artists to join them in an effort to reform the economic and political life of America. They invited artists to exhibit their works in publications such as *Liberator, Good Morning,* and *New Masses.* While the publications provided a sense of purpose, they also required a certain style in promoting radical causes: social realism was emphasized as a mode of presenting a visual account of suffering, inequality, and social injustices in America. Artists were asked to communicate the hardships of the factory worker, the unemployed, and the tenant farmer and to portray the corrupt politician in their paintings and graphics.

When the political movements began to fade in the late 1930's and early 1940's, the modern artists started to reject the idea of using their art as a vehicle for the ideological causes of political movements or for any purpose outside art. On the other hand, they retained certain features of the political ideas; in particular, a sense of historicism. This, together with the closure of the WPA, germinated a feeling that a major transition had occurred and that modern artists were at a turning point in their political lives. Looking back critically, an artist comments:

> In the thirties, when many of us were in our thirties or a little older, we
> were doing work imposed upon us by different disciplines, by a certain
> political and economic milieu. Artists who worked on the WPA—and
> that means practically all of them—and who got involved in the Artists'
> Union and communism, were trying to submerge their personalities—al-
> though they didn't use that language. The sense of rebirth came when
> we felt we were really artists and nothing else.[12]

The last major event to influence the rise of asociability was the emigration of a large number of prominent European artists to America. For centuries Europe was regarded as the center of the art world for American patrons and artists. But in the late 1930's noted artists such as Mondriaan, Ernst, Léger, Duchamp, and others relocated in the United States. As internationally known European painters and sculptors arrived in the wake of World War II, they helped to legitimize America, especially New York City, as an international art center. This was a novel experience for American artists, and it contributed to reflection and a redefinition of self:

> It wasn't so much their work, because the European artists came to
> America and continued to do what they had done in Europe. It was
> their way of life that influenced us. You see, they were professional art-
> ists. Most of us were not. We earned our living a dozen different ways.
> They were well-known artists who came here and lived on their success
> —which gave us the idea—we really hadn't thought of it before—that
> one could be an artist and nothing else.[13]

> Then Léger came to America, and X.Y. said everyone stood around with
> bated breath. Léger had this palette, and he picked up a brush, and stuck
> it into red paint and put some on the canvas. They all looked at each
> other and said, "But that's just like us." The same thing happened when
> Max Ernst was here. These men were myths to us as long as they were in
> Paris, and the myths were overpowering. Once they got here, we could
> really take their measure.[14]

The three events were points of concern and attention for artists and became the contextual basis for redefining the image of native American painters and sculptors and their European colleagues. Many of the characteristics of the earlier periods were included in the construction of the new creative self: attention to the global level of societies (WPA Federal Art Works Projects); a sense and philosophy of history (Communist and socialist movements); and an elevation of the importance of aesthetic activities (emigration of European artists).

The Abstract Expressionists' Construction of Asociability and the Creative Self

Modern abstract styles of expressionism, imagism, and action painting attracted attention in America in the early 1940's with the opening of Peggy Guggenheim's gallery, Art of This Century. By 1943 there were increasing signs of a split in ideas of the meaning of art. Various groups joined in the denunciation of the creative work. On the one side, labor groups together with socialist and Communist publications attacked the new artistic style as a betrayal of the working class. On the other side, American Legion organizations and Chamber of Commerce groups denounced the works because of the conspicuous absence of nationalistic themes. The very terms associated with abstract styles began to take on aspects of deviance. One museum changed its name in order to delete the word "modern." [15]

The general thrust toward the definition of abstract painting and sculpture as a form of aesthetic immorality was based on the contention that abstract art was unintelligible. Art works were judged as immoral because they had no meaning according to the established way in which paintings and sculptures were viewed and understood. Perhaps the most succinct statement of this conventional view in American culture (and somewhat consistent with the "alien" perspective of Marxist groups) was presented a hundred years earlier by a special committee of the U.S. Congress. They informed their fellow congressmen that painting and sculpture

> are the handmaidens of history, to record the traits and characteristics of national life, and to convey to after ages, by images presented to the eye, the costumes, arts and civilizations of such periods as the artist may embody upon his canvas or grave upon the marble. . . . Art to be living must be projected from the life of the people . . . must be familiar, must partake of the nature and habits of the people for whom it is intended, and must reflect their life, history, hopes and aspirations.[16]

The traditional meaning of art emphasizes a correspondence between (1) visual forms in paintings and sculptures and (2) social ideals and beliefs, when both are contained in the same historical period. The aim of art was to convert contemporary verbal expressions of the culture into visual forms. In the 1940's moral entrepreneurs on behalf

of the traditional meanings asserted that abstract art lacked symbols
that were American and understandable; therefore, artists were deviant in failing to communicate with the American public and in neg-
lecting to preserve American ideals in visual form. Various nonartist
groups demanded that the collective aspect of society be represented,
either on the level of national themes or with respect to recognizable
segments of American society. But the modern abstract artist refused
to adopt widely acceptable symbols and themes in his work. As a result, the word "unintelligible" became the main charge of aesthetic immorality.

The charge of aesthetic immorality partly developed as a reaction to
the artists' new asocial, deviant position. Abstract expressionists had
already started to construct and apply an immoral role of asociability
—and a related image of the creative self—containing three parts.
The first stage directed them to withdraw their commitment from the
conventional moral system. The second part prompted them to dismiss
their social responsibility to others in society by rejecting the traditional pattern of contributing useful, conventionally meaningful art
works to the cultural life. These two procedures were prerequisites for
the third, and most important, phase: to generate and establish a revolutionary moral system. The three stages are now examined in detail.

WITHDRAWING COMMITMENT FROM THE CONVENTIONAL MORAL SYSTEM

American abstract artists did not contest the label of deviance, nor
did they deny the charge of unintelligibility. In answer to comments
in the *New York Times,* the *New York World Telegram,* and the Communist periodical *Masses and Main Stream,* one abstract painter,
Adolf Gottlieb, argued that the public were intolerant in their refusal
to understand and recognize the new forms. Gottlieb suggested that if
the accusation of being deviant signified that one was reacting against
conventional thought, the charge was a compliment. The deviant is a
justified, honorific title of the nonconformist. It denotes one who inno-
vates, creates, and contributes new experiences in contrast to others
who accept established forms of experience. He wrote, "The true artist
always refuses to conform to any standards other than his own." [17]
From the artist's standpoint, deviance is desirable because it indicates
that the artist is contesting conventional morality. The contest, in turn,
suggests conflicting moral systems, with artists and sympathetic patrons upholding one system and all other members of society maintaining others. As far as the artist is concerned, if patrons find a work

to be unintelligible, it is their fault, not that of the painter who created it. The patron is deficient in his failure to perceive a new reality; that is, his inabilty to transcend the commonplace.

Hence we see that a tactic in contesting civil morality is to deny its unilateral character. Once alternative moral structures are suggested, the stigma of the deviant label is relinquished; the artist removes the negative connotations of immorality by denying the singularity of morals. It is this variety of moral systems and their competition that is constantly emphasized in the construction of the artist's creative self: a fundamental division between himself as a creative artist and all those who do not share his experience; a division founded on a break in time, a sense of duty, and a new mode of artistic technique..

1. The Conception of a Break in History. The construction of this division is based on the notion that there has been a break in history —a break that casts people into groupings in which they belong either to the past and present or to the future. Abstract artists believe that most men are associated with the first grouping, but that the modern painter and sculptor are found in the latter. During a meeting of abstract-expressionist painters, Hare remarked, "An artist is always lonely. The artist is a man who functions beyond or ahead of his society." [18]

The modern artists' idea of a break in time is a key to understanding their new moral position,[19] for they use this temporal category to explain their own estrangement as a creative self. The notion of a break in time is applied to the construction of the creative self in two ways: in a social sense—relating to the way in which the artist finds himself in his social environment—as a "spiritual outsider"; and technically—the way in which he goes about his creative work—the techniques of nonhistory.

2. The Artist as a "Spiritual Outsider." In 1944 Robert Motherwell noted a temporal and social break for the modern artist. He argued that the contest over morality between the abstract artist and others was not simply a breakdown in communication. It was not just the remoteness of modern art, nor was the schism forced upon the artist by others in society. According to Motherwell the modern artist made the choice. This point is also presented in a statement by another abstract expressionist:

> But we chose to start off on a new path. When we began to do non-representational art, we were really undertaking a tremendous adventure. . . . But we were all completely excluded from our society, the society around us, particularly because we were dropping the work whose content was felt to be so important at that time.[20]

Motherwell continued the construction of the creative self by suggesting that the modern artists' choice was one of rejecting almost everything in society and, as a group of outsiders, forming "a kind of spiritual underground." [21] (He uses the term "spiritual" to mean otherworldly or nonmaterial values.) And the abstract artist made this choice, according to Motherwell, because he recognized the spiritual breakdown of the modern world that followed industrialization and the collapse of institutionalized religion and because he observed these conditions leading to a shift of the central values to a material base. Having defined the events of the past and having declared their choice to correct the direction of change, abstract expressionists specify other properties of the creative self. They describe contemporary society as one in which most men are involved in the production and distribution of material goods, and the artist, in turn, as an alien—being neither involved in materialism nor interested in commercial activity. The artist feels that he is no ordinary alien, but rather a spiritual outsider; for as no other institution has replaced religion, art must be directed to the otherworldly sphere, and since he receives no support from others in society, he is alone in his task. In Motherwell's words, the artist "tends to become the last spiritual being in the world." [22]

The sociological significance of the property of being a spiritual outsider in one's creative self is its transformation of the traditional authority of the religious status to the artist, investing the latter with a recognized and commonly accepted mission. The transformation, however, is not simply from one status to another, from clergy to artist, but down to the very core of what the artist perceives himself to be, down to the basic properties of his self.

Modern painters and sculptors believe that becoming a spiritual outsider has its ramifications in the way it sets artists apart from others. As the artist applies his efforts toward nonmaterial pursuits and as he conceives of his station in a different time dimension than members of civil society, he is also caught in the predicament of becoming estranged from others in his own society. In defining the social sphere of the artist's creative self, Motherwell notes, "There is a break in modern times between artists and other men without historical precedent in depth and generality." [23]

From a sociological perspective the social conception of a temporal break provides a historical justification for rejecting conventional morality and for the self-imposed structural estrangement of the artist. It serves as a strategy of removing one's obligation from the accepted moral system in order to construct an alternative one. On the other hand, the term "spiritual outsider" locates the institutional context in which the artist considers his work to be placed.

The social conception of a schism between the artist and others has further consequences. It removes the artist's concern with the day-to-day problems of ordinary men and with the current issues debated by recognized interest groups. According to abstract expressionists, the artist's creative self as a "spiritual outsider" focuses on the task of evaluating the *general* values and reality found in the modern state in order to create new perspectives that are not merely contemporary but timeless: ones that have an "eternal" dimension. This is another example of the modern artist's interest in time. Together with the concern of a temporal break and the desire to be in the future, it suggests that the abstract artist is preoccupied with society as a historical process. Note Motherwell's concentration on history and the necessity of producing timeless art:

> The function of the *modern* artist is by definition the felt expression of modern reality. This implies that reality changes to some degree. This implication is the realization that history is "real," or, to reverse the proposition, that reality has a historical character. . . . It is because reality has a historical character that we feel the need for new art. The past has bequeathed us great works of art; if they were wholly satisfying we should not need new ones. From this past art, we accept what persists qua eternally valuable. . . . By eternal values are meant those which, humanly speaking, persist in reality in any space-time, like those of aesthetic form, or the confronting of death. Not all values are eternal. Some values are historical—if you like, *social,* as when now artists especially value personal liberty because they do not find positive liberties in the concrete character of the modern state. It is the values of our own epoch which we cannot find in past art. This is the origin of our desire for new art. In our case, for modern art.[24]

As the modern artist relates the idea of the world as a historical process to his own identification as a spiritual outsider he assumes a vantage point from which he can subordinate the conventional moral system within a perspective of historicism—within the larger field of a theory of the historical development of societies and changing social values. This denudes the institutional morals of their ultimate and absolute character, since, according to the modern artist's theory of history, the present system is temporally confined to the modern industrial epoch.

This emphasis on producing works that contain a timeless character reintroduces the question of the temporal dimension of the artist's creative self. We have already noted that the artist calls attention to his orientation to the future in contrast to ordinary people who relate to the present or past. The modern abstract artist presses the point further by denying the legacies of history.

3. *The Aesthetic Techniques of Nonhistory.* In a four-part manifesto P. G. Pavia presents a theory of nonhistory. He argues that history has been a burden to the artist and an interference to creative activity. Pavia asserts that the modern artist must embark on a procedure of nonhistory, which is basically a method of spontaneity. The artist achieves spontaneity when he strips away the past and when his consciousness feeds on the transition from one sensation to another. According to Pavia, the modern artist must create in the experience of the present, which he terms "pure experience":

> Associating present sensations with past experience is normal and even necessary in everyday living, but such associations are poisonous in creating art. When the process of association fills the initial intuition with the pastness of dead data-stuff the impact of this intuition is reduced to that of general experience. In abstract art it is absolutely essential that the connecting links be cleared of unnecessary stuffing so that the pristine qualities of primary sensations may be preserved in their full spontaneity. . . .
>
> This is the point: whether we should accept or reject the abridgement that history and its determinism brings to our experience. Abstract art makes this decision clean—like a meat cleaver. The sense of second space itself becomes purer and more exposed only as it rejects the application of causes and effects (history). Non-history welcomes the turns, twists and surprises of spontaneity. Pure experience abolishes and transcends the dialectic of cause and effect. In short, pure experience is a no-cause and no-effect type of comprehension: NON-HISTORY, beyond and unbeholden to history.[25]

The purpose of the technique of nonhistory is to remove habits and memories that provide, in the form of images, meanings for accepted societal beliefs, values, and interaction patterns. Modern abstract artists believe that the influence of history reduces the status of the artist to that of a vehicle for the present moral and value systems. History compels him to abandon the truly creative task of providing new visual realities. As Wolfgang Paalen points out:

> The true value of the artistic image does not depend on its capacity to *represent*, but on its capacity to *prefigure*, i.e., upon its capacity to express potentially a new ordering of things. . . . The artist of the time

can be authentic only when he creates new modes of seeing, only when he is original.[26]

The technique of nonhistory is the modern artists' concerted attempt to establish an asocial approach to painting both by emptying themselves of any images based on their collective human environment and by prescribing creative activity solely in terms of their individual faculties. From a sociological standpoint the technique of non-history is a tool for neutralizing the affective meaning of contemporary conventional morals, values, and reality so that the creatively oriented individual is thus enabled to advance alternative value systems and new images of reality. In this manner, the technique of nonhistory is used both to compartmentalize the conventional moral system and to define the character of the artist's social location.

The Negation of Social Responsibility

The artist's emphasis on his own ego as the source of experience and his exclusive concern with his personal freedom stand in opposition to the expected forms of social responsibility. Being socially responsible, as indicated earlier, would require that the artist make an attempt to translate the physical environment and social relationships, as well as the public events and activities, into aesthetic images.

1. The Desire for Social Irresponsibility. As the construction of the creative self contains negative counterpoints of conventional morality, and as spokesmen for the traditional image define the function of art in terms of relevance to contemporary reality, abstract expressionists express the desire to be irresponsible. They view earlier American artists with contempt, for they judge their predecessors as popularizers who were available to any interest group, especially ones with revolutionary causes. Modern abstract artists feel that past American art has been vulgarized by the socially responsible tendency to apply art to nonartistic ends such as business, education, politics, a war effort, or religion. In rejecting the earlier view they isolate art from all other concerns in society. Art is defined in an absolute, exclusive manner so that creative work is estranged from all other human activity. No statement is more emphatic on this point than Ad Reinhardt's comment:

> Fine art can only be defined as exclusive, negative, absolute, timeless. It is not practical, useful, related, applicable or subservient to anything else. Fine art has its own thought, its own history and tradition, its own

reason, its own discipline. It has its own "integrity" and not someone else's "integration" with something else. . . . "Art is Art, and Life is Life." [27]

And Motherwell adds to this position by noting the character of modern art:

> One of the most striking aspects of abstract art's appearance is her nakedness, an art stripped bare. How many rejections on the part of her artists! Whole worlds—the world of objects, the world of power and propaganda, the world of anecdotes, the world of fetishes and ancestor worship. One might almost legitimately receive the impression that abstract artists don't like anything but the act of painting.[28]

Modern artists construct the meaning of social irresponsibility in two ways: first, in terms of the freedom it allows the creative worker; and second, in its compatability with accountability and individual responsibility.

The idea of freedom in social irresponsibility springs from the belief that the social usefulness of an activity places it under practical, social demands so that what must and must not be done are guided by the interests of the larger social group. On the other hand, useless behavior is free activity, and as artists involve themselves in useless pursuits, they too are free. Estrangement from everyday activities and the public is believed to be an avenue of freedom. John Ferren writes,

> The avant-garde abstract expressionist artist accepted his status as an outsider. He faced the consequences of this status, and curiously derived some benefits from it. . . . Our complete divorce from the official world, from magazines and museums—in a word, our hopelessness gave us the possibility of unknown gestures.[29]

This is one of many statements by abstract expressionists in which the meaning of alienation is recast from the pathological-negative realm to a dimension of desirability. Estrangement is considered to be desirable because it means that the artist is liberated from the constraints, habits, and security of the community. And with the isolation, he feels "transcendental experiences become possible." [30]

Continuing the same mode of reasoning, modern artists believe that in order to be useless and therefore free, they must resist pressures, political groups, or any other sources of commitment that take them outside the aesthetic perspective. A commitment to art means an active resistance to any other group idea that would identify art with nonaesthetic goals. They argue that "the real commitment is *non-commitment* . . . an active resistance of propaganda by not joining." [31]

The other part of the constructed meaning of social irresponsibility is its positive association with the idea of the burden of individual responsibility. Paul Jenkins explains that the artist is personally responsible when he rejects the pressures of others and offers new objects and meanings and when he pursues his own interests; he is "responsible to others by being himself." [32] For abstract expressionists, social irresponsibility signifies a division of interests, commitment, and morality where the individual is solely and completely responsible to his creative activity. The absence of social responsibility, in turn, expands and deepens the problem of being held accountable for one's own actions. This idea is underscored in Clyfford Still's comment, "We are now committed to an unqualified act, not illustrating outworn myths or contemporary alibis. One must accept total responsibility for what he executes. And the measure of his greatness will be in the depth of his insight and his courage in realizing his own vision." [33]

Looking at the general features of the artist's meaning of social irresponsibility, it appears that it has been constructed as a negative parallel of social responsibility: the latter is regarded as a state in which the individual adheres to collective sentiments and, especially, feels accountable to other members of society; in the former, conversely, the painter or sculptor adheres to the restricted, asocial artist position and feels accountable only to himself.

This issue of responsibility and irresponsibility is one of many areas in which the modern artist uses an abstract model of contemporary society as a point of departure in constructing very different—in fact, conflicting—situated meanings of his asocial position and creative self. Yet, paradoxically, abstract expressionists adamantly reject the existing social milieu as a source of new and timeless morals, values, and reality in their social revolution.

2. The Irrelevance of Conventional Society. In the first few decades of the century in Europe and America artists and poets constructed the meaning of their work around the word "Dada." Originally, the term had no substantive denotative quality, but was, instead, a starting point for producing hostile forms of art, or antiart. Dadaism, as an artistic movement, was an attack on middle-class values. These values were the stimuli for producing immoral—negative—art. For example, as the middle class desired public order, the Dadaists attempted to produce disorderly or chaotic art. But abstract expressionists do not attempt to be deviants by reversing the moral code and by abusing existing values. From their viewpoint, society's morals and values are irrelevant to the substance of their art. In fact, social issues—such as minority group persecution, conflict, suppression, wars—are totally un- related to the aesthetic activity of the artist. No matter how spectacu- lar and consequential the social issue may be, the abstract-expression- ist artist dismisses it from his work. For example, Tworkov comments:

> I saw a reference in a periodical to the opinion of a distinguished art his- torian that in other times when the art and civilization of a period de- clined, the facts were hidden from the artists—they had no idea that their art was in decline; but that in our time the artists are not only aware but consciously and actively participate in the destroying process. Is anybody sad? Not me. Neither the threat of atomic destruction nor the promise of a return to vitalistic barbarism nor the various shining fu- tures promised by various Utopias have much substance in my thought.[34]

Unlike the Dadaists, Tworkov does not use moral and political is- sues as a point of departure for producing a new morality; rather, he indicates that modern social problems are outside his artistic interests.

3. *A Cynical Response to Public Acceptance.* With their idea of a temporal-social break with society, their denial of the relevance of conventional morals, and their desire to be socially irresponsible, mod- ern abstract artists expect the public to oppose their art. Indeed, the accusation of "unintelligibility" and other labels of aesthetic immoral- ity are regarded by the artist as evidence of success in presenting new systems of morality, values, and social reality. Conversely, public ac- ceptance of their work—especially in the form of rapid sales of paint- ings and sculptures and quick popularity—is generally received with suspicion. Baziotes remarks, "I have a horror of being easily under- stood." [35] Acceptance means that the public is applying its own mean- ing to the paintings or, far worse, that the artist is producing accept- able work because he has become socially responsible. Baziotes com- ments that if the artist should find himself accepted he would send him

> to the mirror to take a deep examination of himself, to see if the lines of complacency had settled around his mouth, to see if his eyes had lost their passion. And if he were to find all that true, he would smash the mirror and whip himself into despair. A despair that only the madman in the cage can ever know.[36]

Sociologically speaking, the "despair" would follow the acknowledg- ment that the artist's substantial self was the same as that of the ordi- nary member of society and that the artist had changed to the point where he was responsible to others and neglectful of himself. To be ahead of one's time is to be cut off from others in the modern artist's perspective of history, and thus to be accepted by others may mean that one is no longer in the future, but in the present. Acceptance suggests that no temporal or social gulf exists between the artist and others and that there is no ground for distinguishing the artist's creative self—especially as a spiritual outsider—from any substantial self in the population associated with the production of material goods. Easy and quick acceptance is thus a dangerous sign for the abstract-expressionist artist.

4. The Nonwillful Aspects of Aesthetic Creativity. As social responsibility is conceived as a willful contribution to the welfare of the community, abstract expressionists escape conventional responsibility by denying the element of choice in the dynamics of the creative act. Although they hold the dismissal of history and the creation of the self-image of the spiritual outsider as conscious choices, the act of painting or sculpturing is not seen as volitional. John Ferren explains that abstract art is based on a self-imposed "innocence." By this he means that the path to creative work is through the "negation of the will," an attempt to suspend choice or direction. The artist is expected to express an image "automatically" and intuitively rather than work purposefully toward a preconceived form.

The submersion of the will is also evident in the belief that artistic creativity operates with separate agents and a teleological pattern. Abstract expressionists talk about the artistic process as containing an active impetus apart from the painter and sculptor and involving sets of creative stages impelled toward some final end. Michael Goldberg speaks of the painting as "fighting back," [37] and other artists comment on the resistance of the painting. Richard Lippold and Jackson Pollock explain:

It may be that my work, by nature, almost determines its own conclusion; it is not possible to make changes once the thing is quite far along.[38]

When I am *in* my painting, I'm not aware of what I'm doing. It is only after a sort of "get acquainted" period that I see what I have been about. I have no fears about making changes, destroying images, etc., because the painting has a life of its own. I try to let it come through. It is only when I lose contact with the painting that the result is a mess. Otherwise there is pure harmony, an easy give and take, and then the painting comes out well.[39]

These conceptions suggest that the painting is introduced in a neutral field of interest so that neither personality nor group influence can be injected into the forms. With regard to the aims of abstract expressionism, this is a very significant property of the artist's creative self. Since modern abstract artists believe that control may contribute either special idiosyncratic features of the artist or social meanings of his society, they place importance on action, suspension of the will, an automatic approach, and a teleological process as mechanisms for more basic, universal sources from which new and timeless moral and value systems may be drawn. Through these techniques the artist can consider the new morals, values, and reality as possessing an absolute, ultimate quality. The various facets of the creative self functioning together create new morals in an atmosphere removed from a field of human influence, and therefore the completed products are inherently "novel" and "eternal." In this construction the artist's creative self seems to approximate definitions of the substantial self of religious leaders and prophets who are thought to be divinely inspired.

Generating and Establishing a New Moral System

The first two elements of the role of asociability and its parallel properties in the image of the creative self are divesting obligation from the conventional moral system and the negation of social responsibility. Both, as prerequisites, are aimed at the third element, generating and establishing a new moral system. In the first part the artist depicts himself as shedding the established morality, in the second as rejecting his former responsible nature, and in the third as constructing and establishing a new moral system.

As the new moral system is offered in the expectation that it will change the world, artists confront the problem of how to formulate and communicate new ideals. They attempt to locate both the foundation of the new morality and the manner in which it is to be presented to the public. To fulfill the two tasks they inject attributes of what they consider to be the substance of the intellectual and properties of the prophet into their concept of the creative self.

1. The Artist as an Alienated Intellectual. As we mentioned earlier, the adoption of the title "spiritual outsider" expresses the artists' interest in transforming the moral and value system of society. Abstract expressionists wish to extend their work past a simple transcription of nature to the more important tasks of analyzing reality, offering new insights, and presenting new visual experiences. In these pursuits modern artists attempt to incorporate the social characteristics of the intellectual. But the application of an intellectual substance to their own creative self results in certain changes and distinctions in the meaning of such a substance.

Traditionally, intellectuals are considered to be related to some social class. They are regarded as men of ideas who provide a service either for a ruling class, by attempting to protect existing ideals, or for a disenfranchised subordinate class, by offering reformative or revolutionary ideals. Intellectuals are expected to view either type of social class as the focus of their concern; members of the class are considered to be the recipients of their services and to function as a vehicle for the preservation or formation of an ideology which is directed toward the problems of that class.

When modern artists consider the task of generating a new moral system they adopt an intellectual perspective, indicating a concern about their relationshp to social classes. They consider their relationship to economic-social units in general and to the middle class in particular. Motherwell suggests that since the French Revolution there has been an uneasy relationship between the bourgeois and artists. Through the decades and in an atmosphere of tension, artists have chosen to ignore, support, or oppose the middle class. The modern artist adopts the first and last course of action. He also rejects the working class. Motherwell explains:

> The middle-class is decaying, and as a conscious entity the working-class does not exist. . . . The materialism of the middle-class and the inertness of the working-class leave the modern artist without any vital connection to society, save that of *opposition;* and that modern artists have had, from the broadest point, to replace other social values with the strictly aesthetic.[40]

The remaining class, the ruling stratum, is rejected because it is considered to establish itself through the accumulation of private property and because property is judged, in the Marxist sense, as an item which destroys personal freedom. Therefore, as a general view abstract artists believe that all classes are unworthy of their efforts. But this complete rejection presents difficulties in constructing the creative self from what are considered to be the substantive properties of the intellectual. Without a collective to serve as a source of concern or a base on which new morals are constructed, what is to be the point of departure? What is to be the substance of the new morals? In Motherwell's own words, "The artist's problem is with what to *identify himself*"[41] (author's italics).

The answer provided by Motherwell shifts the source of ideals from the collective to the individual level. He suggests that the modern artist establishes new morals for and upon his own self.

> In the spiritual underground the modern artist tends to be reduced to a single subject, his ego. . . . Hence the tendency of modern painters to paint for each other.[42]

Abstract artists deny that this choice is indicative of narcissism. Instead, they suggest that their own personalities are the source of a new ideal of humanism in the industrial setting. Motherwell thinks that art is

> a technique for expressing human feelings, and that to express human feelings is to humanize oneself, and to humanize others. I don't think art can do anything but arouse one's sense of humanity. It is this that constitutes its "purity of heart"; it is moral by nature; it cannot do anything but humanize.[43]

Abstract expressionists present themselves as a new breed of intellectuals who, concerned with humanity, reject service to the ideals of any social stratum and establish new morals from their own egos. These intellectual and socially alienated properties of the creative self are elevated to the point of emulation and often described in the most heroic terms. Jack Tworkov writes,

> Cézanne is the very image of the artist of our time: the alienated intellectual, deeply concerned with meaning, awkward with all those who get along smoothly in life, and especially awkward in fashionable settings, slightly incompetent, and lost beside those whose religion is to get on in the world. He is a person, however, who in his innermost center has a fierce pride and sure conviction about the values of the artist in the world.[44]

2. The Artist as a Prophet. While modern artists assimilate qualities of the intellectual to construct the base from which new morals are generated, they turn to attributes of the prophet to formulate the way in which ideals will be established in the social order. The task of establishing the morals focuses their concern on their power and authority in society. Abstract expressionists recognize the fact that they do not hold positions of authority and that they do not have organizational position or institutional legitimacy to direct the course of morality. Yet they argue that their function is to make the spectator see the world their way—not his way. Ray Parker describes the process by which the new morals are incorporated into the social order:

> The artist's relation to society, and the art world in particular, is a product of his own integrity and of his viewers' learning. His image is validated when it has been learned and is in use. Until that time the motives of the intent painter seem anti-social. His "integrity" means an effort, with an insistence that is nearly moral in intensity, to reject in his work all known images known and accepted by society. At first, the presentation of an image seemingly stripped of meaning and value causes reactions of shock and irritation. Then, as the image comes to be learned and is accepted in its isolation, it begins to unfold in meanings, revealing values and gaining the power to gather to itself ideas previously scattered. The artist's courage is regarded as heroic. A new tradition is established.[45]

Like the prophet, the artist believes that he has a personal mission and that his power is one of a personal gift. For example, the modern artist's claim to a special unique creative essence, dramatized in the technique of nonhistory and the method of suspending the will, injects mystery and a self-definition of charisma which are similar to the religious prophet's declarations of personal revelations. The abstract expressionist's contention that he is the "last spiritual being in the modern world," producing an absolute and timeless morality from a process free of psychic and social influence, is similar to the ancient religious prophets' claim of sole acquaintance with God and that only through faith in their power could the followers find salvation.[46] Abstract expressionists, like the prophets, apply an emotional appeal. They claim that art is a way of finding and inventing objects whose felt qualities satisfy the passions. Ancient prophets and modern artists are also similar in directing their attention to the absolute. The religious prophet uses terms such as "divine law," while the abstract artist applies the words "reality," "truth," "accuracy," and "validity."

There is also a similarity between the artist's denial of an economic interest for his services and the prophet's disregard for compensation. The prophet is distinguished from other religious functionaries by the fact that his activity is unremunerated. Abstract expressionists admit that they receive payment for their art, but they argue that their aim is not commercial, nor are they "professionals." [47]

In contrast to the parallel properties, there is one important difference between the modern artist and the prophet. While the latter attempts to provide a unified view of man and the world in a systematic, coherent fashion, the former advocates continuous development of the new moral system. Abstract expressionists emphasize the activity of the search and value the novel in constructing new ideals, and, as a result, their process cannot be a final one, for if it were, the creative function would be terminated. Indeed, the abstract artist's emphasis on creativity prevents him from ever offering a total, coherent system which is the prophet's legacy. The modern artist's inability to present a unified view of the world is to a large degree prohibited by his antipathy to rationalism and to the general stress on a lack of organization. The creative process is expected to include mistakes, accidents, and spontaneous, unplanned expressions. As a consequence abstract expressionists liken the artist to the gambler "who takes a chance in the hope that something important will be revealed." [48] Perhaps the painting will provide something; perhaps "something might turn up."

As explained earlier, the modern artist's creative self is defined in terms of nonwillful qualities. The painter and sculptor are described as acting innocently, intuitively, automatically. According to these procedures they cannot intentionally co-ordinate, relate, fill in, add to, or complete a set of morals into a holistic pattern. While abstract artists do not consider this general point, they express concern for the same kind of problem as it emerges at the concrete level of the creative act. Many abstract artists find that they cannot tell when the painting or sculpture is finished. Biala, Hare, Sterne, De Kooning, Crippe, and Motherwell comment, in respective order,

> I never know when it is "finished." I only know there comes a time when I have to stop.

> A work is never finished, the energies involved in a particular work are merely transferred at a certain movement to the next work.

> There comes a moment when I can't continue. Then I stop until the next time.

> I refrain from "finishing" it. I paint myself out of the picture, and when I have done that, I either throw it away or keep it.

> A work of art is never really "finished."

> We are involved in "process" and what is a "finished" object is not so certain. [49]

Thus the modern artist admits his inability to determine the terminal state of an art work and indirectly the completeness of the moral statement. Some artists suggest that the meaning is continuous through a number of art works, but they too would concede that the perimeters of the moral statement are undefinable. For all modern artists, the most basic, dynamic creative elements of their substantial self prevent them from completing a moral system.

The Relationship between the Modern Artist's Asociability and the Creative Self

Asociability is a transitional role containing three stages. In the initial phase the individual renounces an institutional moral system in order to invest his commitment in a social position from which he can produce an alternative system. The mid-point in transition lies in the formation of new ideals, and the termination of asociability rests on the presence of a new moral system for society. A commitment to the over-all social structure prevails only when a newly constructed set of morals is available.

Our analysis of abstract expressionists has shown that there is considerable attention placed on the initial and intermediate stages, but that the conditions for terminating the asocial position are denied by the artist's construction of his creative self. The modern artists' original supposition that they could become integrated into society when members of the social order adopt their morality, values, and world view is controverted by their singular theory of creativity and definition of the substantial self, which places an emphasis on the impermanent and novel. In spite of the profuse dialogue, the continual effort to hammer out a creative system, and the elaborate philosophizing, abstract expressionists have failed to hypothesize a creative self that would fulfill the requisites of the asocial position that they chose to adopt. Whereas they previously divested themselves of conventional sociability, in the end, they cannot divest themselves of asociability.

They continued to embrace an asocial role through the late 1950's and early 1960's even though their paintings and sculptures were no longer considered aesthetically immoral; abstract-expressionist works received special honors and wide recognition by museums and patrons. Modern artists also ignored opportunities for structural integration into society. They accepted teaching posts in prominent colleges and universities,[50] received commissions from well-known banks and large industrial corporations, and worked with entertainment enterprises in preparing television and motion picture shows. Paintings began to sell at over $10,000. Yet their construction of the creative self prevented them from defining their new activities and sales as a *moral* acceptance of social responsibility.

It is not surprising, then, that the integration of the American artist came finally with countermovements which rejected abstract expressionism: new styles such as the Happenings, Pop Art, Junk Culture, and Commonly Object Art are based on the idea that the artist must relate to and use the moral and authority system in society. From the perspective of the abstract expressionist, the new approaches are considered to be a renunciation of freedom and thus a loss of the creative self. He must therefore reject the new constructions. Responding to the suggestion of an integrated status for the artist, and applying the ideals of abstract expressionism, the editor of *Art News* writes:

> The Pro artist, when he opts to become a Man of the World, subscribes to worldly racism, he joins the religion of Holy Private Property, he sells out his rights as a man for comforts of tenure in a university, membership in a country-club, cocktails with the boss. The artist as a company-man is reduced to an entertainer.[51]

NOTES

NOTE: Helpful comments on earlier drafts of the chapter were made by Roy Turner and R. S. Ratner.

1. As quoted in Daniel Catton Rich, "Freedom of the Brush," *Atlantic Monthly,* XVIII (February, 1948).
2. Mason Griff, "Alienation and the Artist," unpublished paper. Also, by the same author, "The Commercial Artist: A Study in Changing and Consistent Identities," in Maurice Stein, Arthur J. Vidich, and David Manning White, eds., *Identity and Anxiety* (Glencoe: The Free Press, 1960).
3. Rudolf and Margot Wittkower, *Born under Saturn* (New York: Random House, 1963), p. 157.
4. Rich, *op. cit.*
5. Albert L. Guerard, *Art for Art's Sake* (New York: Schocken, 1936).
6. The removal of social responsibility emphasizes a division of interests between the artist and others in society. This social schism is ordinarily, though mistakenly, interpreted within the concept of alienation. For example, in their social-psychological study, Rosenberg and Fliegel conclude that American abstract-expressionist artists are alienated from the dominant commercial values of their society. (Bernard Rosenberg and Norris Fliegel, *The Vanguard Artist* [Chicago: Quadrangle, 1965], p. 9.) Yet there is a conceptual difference between the phenomenon of

estrangement in their study, which to a large degree rests on artists' declarations of their own alienation, and other sociological research on estrangement. Empirical sociological studies of alienation have been applied to industrial workers, medical patients, prison inmates, and voters. (Robert Blauner, *Alienation and Freedom* [Chicago: University of Chicago Press, 1964]; Melvin Seeman and John W. Evans, "Alienation and Learning in a Hospital Setting," *American Sociological Review,* XXVII [December, 1962]; Melvin Seeman, "Alienation and Social Learning in a Reformatory," *American Journal of Sociology,* LXIX [November, 1963]; Wayne E. Thompson and John Horton, "Political Alienation as a Force in Political Action," *Social Forces,* XXXVIII [March, 1960].) Though focusing on different groups, these studies apply a three-part sequential framework in which alienation, as an intervening variable, is handled as a diffuse social-psychological state of feelings. Using this framework, the sociologist operationalizes the concept of alienation through sets of questions that are designed to tap indices of *feelings* of estrangement—such as powerlessness or normlessness—since the phenomenon is not regarded as fully-developed conscious belief or ideal on the part of the subjects under study. Those who feel alienated are not expected to understand the idea that describes their condition.

When, as found in the Rosenberg and Fliegel study, artists have used ideas of social estrangement to define their experiences and ideals, the sociological concept of alienation is no longer applicable since the phenomenon of alienation is then an ideology rather than a diffuse, unconscious feeling of being separated from others. On the other hand, asociability is a useful concept for an ideology of alienation since it denotes an ideal of one's self and position in society. The construct of the ideology of alienation is subsumed under the generic concept of asociability.

7. Though abstract expressionism spread across the United States through the 1950's, the center of the movement remained in New York City and enjoyed very little organizational structure. The only record of a sustained collective enterprise is a group that began in 1945 with about seven abstract expressionists meeting casually at a cafeteria in New York City. As the group enlarged it began meeting almost daily, shifting the location to bars, homes, and finally a large hall. Eventually it organized as "The Club" with a body of 31 charter members, and by 1952 it enlarged to over 100 artists. The Club's activities centered on exchanging ideas about artistic work and related topics. Philosophers, priests, poets, musicians, mathematicians, dancers, and necromancers were invited to group discussions. Other gatherings were restricted to members. In spite of contacts with nonartists, abstract expressionists never attempted to proselytize their ideas so as to enlist the services of other intellectuals.

The movement also promoted a direct protest in January, 1951, in the form of a denouncement of the Metropolitan Museum of Art jury exhibition of contemporary American art which excluded abstract expressionism. Eighteen artists joined in picketing the Museum.

8. Well-known artists of this group include William De Kooning, Hans Hofmann, Franz Kline, Robert Motherwell, Jackson Pollock, Mark Rothko, Clyfford Still, and Mark Toby.

9. Jack D. Douglas, *The Social Meanings of Suicide* (Princeton: Princeton University Press, 1967), pp. 280–283.

10. The sample of 48 artists and the bibliography was extracted from William Seitz's *American Abstract Expressionists and Imagists* (New York: Guggenheim Museum, 1961).

11. For a more extensive discussion of the methodology and its assumptions, see Douglas, *op. cit.*, Chapters 13–16; and Ronald J. Silvers, "The Logic and Meaning of the Logico-Meaningful Method," *Canadian Review of Sociology and Anthropology*, III (February, 1966), 1–8.

12. Rosenberg and Fliegel, *op. cit.*, pp. 33–34.

13. *Ibid.*, p. 23.

14. *Ibid.*, pp. 23–24.

15. " 'Modern Art' and the American Public," a statement by the Institute of Contemporary Art, formerly The Institute of Modern Art (Boston: February 1, 1948).

16. *U.S. Congress House Reports*, 35th Congress, 2nd Session, No. 198, pp. 1 and 5.

17. Adolph Gottlieb, "Unintelligibility," unpublished mimeographed paper presented on May 5, 1948, at the Museum of Modern Art in New York City.

18. Robert Motherwell and Ad Reinhardt, eds., *Modern Artist in America*, First Series (New York: Wittenborn Schultz, 1951), p. 10.

19. The importance of such a social belief has been pointed out by Mannheim in his remark, "The innermost structure of the mentality of a group can never be as clearly grasped as when we attempt to understand its conception of time in the light of its hopes, yearnings, and purposes." Karl Mannheim, *Ideology and Utopia* (London: Routledge and Kegan Paul, 1960), p. 188.

20. Rosenberg and Fliegel, *op. cit.*, p. 29.

21. Robert Motherwell, "The Modern Painter's World," *Dyn* (November, 1944), p. 10.

22. *Ibid.*, p. 10.

23. *Ibid.*, p. 9.

24. *Ibid.*, pp. 9–10.

25. P. G. Pavia, "The Psychology of Non-History," *It Is* (Winter–Spring, 1959), p. 4; "The Second Space," *It Is* (Autumn, 1959), p. 6. Also see "Excavations in Non-History," *It Is* (Autumn, 1959); Grace Hartigan and William De Kooning, "Is Today's Artist with or against the Past?"

Art News, Vol. LVII (September, 1958); Mark Rothko in *New Americans* (New York: Museum of Modern Art, 1958–1959), p. 68.

26. Wolfgang Paalen, "The New Image," *Dyn* (April–May, 1942), translated by Robert Motherwell. Also see Robert Motherwell, "Painters Objects," *Partisan Review,* Vol. XI (Winter, 1944); statement by Milton Resnick in *It Is* (Spring, 1948).

27. Ad Reinhardt, "Twelve Rules for a New Academy," *Art News,* LVI (May, 1957), 38.

28. Robert Motherwell, "What Abstract Art Means to Me," *Museum of Modern Art Bulletin,* XVIII (Spring, 1951), 12.

29. John Ferren, "Epitaph for an Avant-Garde," *Arts,* XXXIII (November, 1958).

30. Statement by Mark Rothko in *Possibilities 1* (1947/48). Also see statement by Adolph Gottlieb in Selden Rodman, *Conversations with Artists* (New York: Capricorn, 1961), p. 89.

31. Quotation in William Seitz, "Abstract-Expressionist Painting in America," unpublished doctoral dissertation, Princeton University, 1955, p. 391.

32. Paul Jenkins, "An Abstract Phenomenist," *Painter and Sculptor,* I (Winter, 1958/1959), 3.

33. Clyfford Still, "Statement" in Dorothy C. Miller, ed., *15 Americans* (New York: Museum of Modern Art, 1952). Also see "Statement" by James Brooks in *12 Americans* (New York: Museum of Modern Art, 1956).

34. Jack Tworkov, *Tworkov Exhibition* (Chicago: Holland-Goldovsky Gallery, 1960).

35. William Baziotes, "The Artist and His Mirror," *Right Angle,* III (June, 1949), 3. Also see Motherwell and Reinhardt, *op. cit.,* p. 10.

36. Baziotes, "The Artist and His Mirror."

37. Michael Goldberg, "The Canvas Painting or Onwards and Upwards," *It Is* (Spring, 1958), pp. 17–18.

38. Richard Lippold, in Motherwell and Reinhardt, *op. cit.,* p. 11.

39. Jackson Pollock, "Statement" in *Possibilities 1* (1947/48). Similar statements are presented by William Baziotes in the same issue of *Possibilities,* in *15 Americans,* and in "The Creative Process," *Art Digest,* Vol. XXVIII (January, 1954). Also statements by James Brooks in *12 Americans;* Barnett Newman in *The New American Painting* (New York: Museum of Modern Art, 1958/1959); Esteban Vicente, "Statement" in *It Is* (Spring, 1958); and Philip Guston in *12 Americans.*

40. Motherwell, "The Modern Painter's World," pp. 11, 14.

41. *Ibid.,* p. 11.

42. *Ibid.*

43. Quoted in Seitz, "Abstract-Expressionist Painting in America," p. 312.

44. Jack Tworkov, "Four Excerpts from a Journal," *It Is* (Autumn, 1959), pp. 12–13.

45. Ray Parker, "Intent Painting," *It Is* (Autumn, 1958), pp. 8–9.

46. See Max Weber, "The Prophet," in his *Sociology of Religion* (Boston: Beacon, 1963), p. 47.
47. Rosenberg and Fliegel, *op. cit.*, p. 184.
48. Motherwell and Reinhardt, *op. cit.*, p. 15.
49. *Ibid.*, p. 12.
50. In our sample of abstract expressionists we find that 59 per cent (N = 37) held teaching positions in art schools, universities, and colleges sometime during the period 1940 through 1962.
51. Editorial, "The Artist as a Company Man," *Art News*, LXIII (October, 1964), 19.

14

An Ethos of Intimacy: Constructing and Using a Situational Morality

Alexander David Blumenstiel

Should we ask, "What is love?" two perspectives provide answers. For those innocent, idealistic, or romantic by mood, the answer is that the question is meaningless: love is an emotion too mysterious for words. From the other perspective, however, such an answer seems merely adolescently ignorant or, more graciously, naïve. Love, from this perspective, is quite describable. Description is a practical concern; mystery is merely a matter of ignorance. In their weaker moments, it is true, those who invest in this perspective may claim that they are not talking about "love." But, in their stronger, they know very well that that is what they mean.

In this chapter I delineate aspects of a practical consideration of love. This is, thus, a description of an interpretation. I choose to call the subject "intimacy" for a very simple reason. This is the report of an empirical study, and the people involved considered themselves to be intimate; upon occasion they used the word "love" to refer to their relations with one another.

The love described is practical since a strain of pragmatics runs through this intimacy. In short, this description of an ethos of intimacy is a description of a morality of practical intimacy and of the practice of intimacy prescribed by that morality.

The Basics of the Situation: Sensitivity Training
and the T-Group

"Sensitivity training" is a term that describes a variety of contexts. In them attempts are made to utilize interpersonal communication toward the end of improving the interaction skills of participants. The social scientists who conceived of and established sensitivity training—also called laboratory education and laboratory training—intended to apply behavioral science findings toward this end. They felt that such an application would provide an opportunity for persons in responsible positions to improve their responses in interpersonal situations.

There is a strong emphasis on voluntary participation in the events of laboratory training. "The originators of the laboratory were convinced that the ethical commitments implicit in the scientific enterprise are consistent with the ethical commitments explicit in democratic patterns of social management." [1] Emphasis is placed on participants' efforts "in building new groups in which membership becomes important to them because they are groups which they have built."

Essentially, each training laboratory is a one- or two-week program of conferences, lectures, and group sessions. During the course of a laboratory, the development of small groups, called "T-Groups" or "training groups," is considered central. Each T-Group consists of between eight and eleven delegates and one "trainer." The latter is a staff behavioral scientist who usually has completed a program of apprenticeship which qualifies him to train T-Groups. Depending on the design of the particular laboratory, there may be from one to three T-Group meetings daily.

"Group development involves the overcoming of obstacles to valid communication among the members or the development of methods for achieving and testing consensus." [3]

The two training laboratories from which the data for this report were drawn are called, herein, "Woodlands" and "Executive." Woodlands was held at a small western college and consisted of four ongoing separate laboratories, two of which were used. Executive was held at a midwestern resort. [4]

The Ethos of Intimacy

In the T-Group there is a situational definition of intimacy which entails prescriptions for being intimate and a rhetoric of pragmatics to justify so behaving. I offer the term *ethos* as a characterization of intimacy there.

There is a quasi-religious implication to ethos. Intimacy in the laboratory becomes somewhat of a creed for participants. Often in the laboratories I attended I heard persons refer to a "kind of religion." They meant intimacy.

Establishing the Initial Propriety of Intimacy

The propriety of intimacy is established in the T-Group in part by declarations of trainers during initial group sessions. Though trainers may not explicitly state that intimacy is proper, they may declare that participants in a T-Group are supposed to be "open," to be "honest," and to "own up" to their feelings about each other. Delegates often infer, from such declarations, that they are participating in something other than a formal and structured group situation and that there will be some demand for personal revelation.

After delegates have attended their first T-Group session, the word *intimacy* often makes sense in reference to how they expect to relate with one another, whatever their feelings about the value of those expected relations.

Initial declarations about "openness" and the like do not impart to delegates that they are supposed to be intimate with everyone else in the laboratory community.[5] The proper extent of openness outside the T-Group is usually left undeclared.

Initial declarations by staff are only preliminaries. The construction of an ethos and the appearance of a "real intimacy" (defined in its terms) are products of engagement in interactions which initial prescriptions are taken to indicate and in the emergence of more prescriptions, behavior in accordance with which will then be taken to evidence intimacy in the T-Group.

Intimacy and Intimacy in Training

There are, of course, a great variety of relations considered intimate. I do not catalogue them here. They may all be considered intimate [6] by those involved; for instance, marriages are usually distinguished from affairs and friendships from psychiatrics.

Intimacy in sensitivity training can be compared to that in medical situations. In the latter there are external and internal physical observation and contact.[7] Physical contact also occurs in sensitivity training laboratories, but is limited to arm-punching, hugging, and caressing. Observation of nude others is likely both in medical situations and in the dormitory life of a training laboratory. But it has different connotations. To observe another in the nude in a training laboratory does have connotations of intimacy for those concerned, but is not an explicitly usual matter for mutual involvement.

In the laboratory, touching others is an activity often pragmatically justified. One "exercise" used in T-Groups entails hugging other participants. "Nonverbal communication," as it is called, is considered a way to "get at feelings" and to help participants experience a "depth of feeling."

Confidentiality is an expectation of patients and physicians and of participants in T-Groups. For example, when one of the delegates engaged in revealing personal feelings about his life which, he claimed, were "brought to the surface" because of interaction with other members, he lowered his voice. Other group members began to whisper, and they drew their chairs close together, into a huddle. These are the gestures which construct a visible insider-outsider situation. Those on the inside are assumed "confidants" of the one revealing. For them, it is a situation of confidentiality.

The supposed confidentiality of the T-Group may be used to urge revelations. Demands are made of researchers to ensure participants' anonymity. This fact is broadcast to the laboratory community. Trainers announce that the T-Group is a safe situation. Participants mutually assure one another that whatever openness is performed, the materials revealed will "go no further." A situation of "why not" is established.

The Safety of the Remedy

As is medicine, sensitivity training is considered to be remedial. To those participating in it, the rationale for participation is pragmatic. It is not supposed to be an end in itself, but a means toward some kind of "health." I suppose that the end usually taken to justify participation in medical situations is physical health. The end which, it seems to me, is most generally used to justify participation in sensitivity training laboratories is social health.

Also, both in medical contexts and in laboratory training, participants can allude to the role of "professional practitioner" as a structural feature of the occasion. In medicine the role is that of "physician" or "doctor." In sensitivity training it is that of "trainer." Many trainers hold a Ph.D. degree, and often they, too, are considered doctors.

However, in terms of what the practitioners are supposed to do, they are not the same kind of doctors. Situations of medicine and sensitivity training are quite different. Physicians are considered responsible for deciding the dispositions of the bodies of their patients. The possibility of fulfilling that responsibility in any particular case can be estimated by evaluating evidence of the physician's capability. Given his good will, it is a matter of his skill. His remedies can be determined to be more or less effective and, even more important quite often, more or less safe. The certainty that safety is, at least, determinable (the clearest evidence for a known failure is a death attributable to physician malpractice) pervades the medical situation.

Trainers are supposed to train T-Groups and, given their professional certification, are reasonably supposed to be practitioners of sensitivity training. However, they are not supposed practitioners of sensitivity training in the same way that physicians are supposed practitioners of medicine.

Sensitivity training is also called "laboratory education." As with other kinds of education, some of the skills of the educators are said to be the capability to stimulate students to learn. Delegates are told that trainers help create a proper atmosphere, but that the full utilization of the atmosphere is up to them.

The operations productive of ambience are notoriously difficult to determine. And the announced voluntarism of the situation informs delegates that perhaps they should not try too hard to determine other capabilities of trainers: to do so may be taken as an abdication of their own responsibility.

While the trainer is said to be a skilled behavioral analyst, delegates are told that they should try to attain such skills themselves. During T-Groups trainers say they make an effort not to co-opt this learning opportunity. It often seems to delegates that, perhaps, the trainer's obvious reluctance to display skills, often in the face of vociferous demands that he do so, simply taken evidences their absence.

Trainers often admit to confusion about the true nature of their own skills. While they claim that the skills are valuable—else why enjoin delegates to learn them?—when put upon they are usually hard pressed to state explicitly what they really do. There is no reference to formula. Even the textbooks are of little help. One usual answer is, "I'm just another participant." [8] Delegates often take such a statement as an admission of pretense to status, or mysticism, or simple concession to their own success at the same undefinable tricks. A frequent response is, "Then why do we need you?" Trainers usually have no answer—in terms of skills, that is. They do often reply, "I'm a person and in need of help too." This, of course, simply affirms the relevance of the delegates' question.

In other words, the very reality of training skills as the practices of professionals is moot. Delegates cannot refer to evidence of capability to determine the safety of a remedy. In fact, it seems that trainers are not even responsible for the provision of a remedy. Yet, on the other hand, as trainers, they enjoin "openness" and "feedback." They direct delegates to hug each other, to push each other. They enjoin them, in other words, to produce revelations that they can take as intimacies. These revelations, it is claimed, enable learning. But the process of that learning—the remedy—is a debatable reality. Delegates do not know "what is going on." When asked, neither, it seems, do trainers. Since their skills may not exist, the capability of trainers to produce remedies is unknown. And the T-Group, then, can be characterized as a situation in which it is certain that the safety of the remedy is indeterminable.

The Relevance of Reluctance

The propriety of demonstrating hesitation to participate and of admitting reluctance during the course of T-Group participation is a feature of relations in the T-Group.

Were the T-Group considered a situation in which safety was determinable, it would likely not be proper to demonstrate hesitation or reluctance to participate in the revelations enjoined, unless the performance of a particular practitioner warranted such reluctance. Were the trainer's actions recognized as skilled practices, other things being equal, delegates would not be likely to consider fear quite right to admit to. Were it an apparently unsafe situation, the reasonable person would, so it seems to me, not hesitate to leave. In the T-Group, however, it is quite proper for participants to express their fears and yet stay.[9]

Since delegates consider themselves called upon to "reveal," and since revelation is a central feature of T-Group participation, they express reluctance to reveal.

A. "If you say what is the problem of revealing, I tell you I'm a little scared . . ."

B. "There are probably very few things I'd be afraid to reveal."

C. "I lost my confidence in you when you said that there were few things you were afraid of revealing."

B. "Well, I've reconsidered that and there are some things."

D. "I distrusted you when you said that also. B, you are making too big a deal of how afraid you are."

B. "Maybe I'm making too big a deal of how little afraid I am." [10]

In the T-Group, revelation is prescribed as a requisite for change. However, to be afraid to reveal and to admit to that fear are also proper. Indeed, such an admission is a revelation itself.

Another feature of the T-Group provides for the relevance of reluctance. In the T-Group each delegate confronts, as an inherent and definitive feature of training, other delegates. Therefore, each delegate cannot regard himself as the sole possessor of rights to a contractually guaranteed, unconditional ally—that is, the trainer, who, whatever the apparent state of his skills, as at least an ad hoc professional, can still be rightfully professionally involved in the group process. The case for sensitivity training is similar to that stated by Lieberman for psychotherapy:

In individual therapy, the patient is paying for a certain kind of love and attention from the therapist. The situation permits him to believe that the therapist is unconditionally on his side (at least for the moment forsaking all others), and that if he, the patient, abides by the rules set down, the therapist will do certain things to him or with him in such a way that relief will be forthcoming.[11]

In group therapy, many of the terms of such a contract are literally impossible for the therapist to produce. He cannot offer his undivided and total attention to a particular patient, and he is unlikely to express unconditional positive regard at all times. He cannot be on the patient's side totally and uniformly, because the protagonists are not all outside but are right there in the group and share an equal call on the therapist.[12]

[A group] with its competing demands, its shifting alliances, its complex and ever-changing emotional web does not allow the protective guarantees that are available from the therapist in a two-person relationship.[13]

In short, even were the trainer considered professionally skilled and his remedies reasonably safe, he would be at best a contended-for ally.

Given demands to reveal, the delegate, faced as he is with the complexities of alliance, the power struggles—the maintenance of face— that arise in even the most trivial of expressive situations, feels that his reluctance is quite admissible. And, in many cases, it seems reasonable to admit that he is reluctant, if only to justify refusing to be open about something else.

The Rejection of Cool

With reluctance being considered relevant, participants in T-Groups can behave in ways commonly interpreted as symptomatic of immediate unease. They can admit their hesitations, fears, and feelings of mistrust which might seem otherwise best kept to themselves. Given the relevance of reluctance, it is proper for such admissions to be considered merely aspects of the training situation. They are considered "openness."

One of the norms for intimacy is characterized by the term "feedback." According to the laboratory *Reading Book*, distributed to participants at Woodlands, feedback is defined as "a way of helping another person to consider changing his behavior. It is communication to a person (or a group) which gives that person information about how he affects others."[14]

In practice, feedback usually entails telling another participant about the aspects of his behavior which seem to oneself a reasonable basis for not wishing to relate with him; that is, telling him how he is annoying. For example, in one T-Group at Woodlands, a white delegate was told that he was behaving in a condescending manner to a black participant. Other group members told him that, given his condescension, they did not think he was someone with whom they could feel comfortable. This delegate denied that he felt condescending;

subsequently he confronted the other delegate, with much emotion displayed by them both. Thereafter he seemed to adjust his behavior to everyone's satisfaction, with periodic relapses, to be sure.

The accusations, rebuttals, refusals to speak, shouting, tears, anger, pleading, admissions of fear, and so on, during this incident were, of course, entirely proper as openness and feedback.

More generally, given the relevance of reluctance, persons can reveal and be properly urged to reveal their feelings about each other, be these feelings "good," in the sense that they are interpreted as positive evaluations of the person's behavior, or "bad," in the sense that they are interpreted as negative evaluations of that behavior.

During another T-Group session, a trainer remarked that he thought two female delegates were ignoring each other.[15] One of them, he said, did seem rather shy, but she had talked with other members of the group, while she had not had much to say to the other girl. The latter, he remarked, seemed unduly reticent with the former, but quite open with other members. He asked this girl why she had not had much to say to the other. She did not reply.

He then asked if they had spoken outside of the group sessions. They both shook their heads and murmered, "No." He suggested that they then say something to each other. They both shrugged their shoulders, and the more forward of the two asked, "What?" The trainer replied that they should say whatever came to mind. She said that she did not have anything to say. He then suggested that, perhaps, they were somewhat afraid of each other.[16] He asked the more forward of the two if, to her knowledge, she had any particular reason for being afraid of—that is, not speaking with—the other. She said, "No."

The two girls looked at each other and smiled weakly. This seemed to provide the occasion for the "more open" one to say that she might be mistaken but she had received the impression that the other might disapprove of her. The trainer then asked her why she had this impression. She replied that it seemed that whenever she was near the other girl outside of the group, the latter frowned at her and that, given this, she found it hard to speak with her, though she would like to be friends.

The trainer then looked at the first girl—the quiet one—and asked if she did think poorly of the other. She said that she certainly did not, but she was shy and found it hard to talk with people she didn't know. The other girl then said that she had definitely received an impression of hostility. The shy girl then looked down and said nothing.

The trainer suggested that one of them go over to the other and speak quietly with her or touch her. He recommended the latter. Both refused to do it, saying that they did not see the point. The bolder of the two then said that she thought it was a very tense situation and that she did not want it to get "too emotional." The trainer replied, "Well, if you don't do it now you may never get another chance. Anyway, this is the place for it." She then got up and walked over to the other girl, who remained seated. She stood to one side of her and said, "Hi," in a very soft voice. The other looked up and broke into tears. Shortly, they were clutching each other, the one still standing, both weeping.

The point here is that the confrontation took so much urging—such urging, in fact, that here appeared to be a recognizable trainer skill.

The "cool" thing for these girls to have done would be to get up promptly, go to each other, and greet each other without argument, without tears. That would have been a way, in a group situation, to "save face."

However, in the T-Group, one can be reluctant without risking face. Reluctance is proper. Thus, one does not have to be "cool." Cool can be rejected. The following remarks from T-Group sessions are not cool.

> A. "He can't, as a member of the group, tell me . . . tell any of us how to behave. We have to go at our own pace."
> B. "I guess that's well said."

> "It came as a shock; and we were together in the bowling and we were kidding and getting a kick out of it; but as we were sitting around the table I got the feeling, 'These guys are just putting me on.' I don't know you! Isn't that a hell of a thing. I was being natural." (Stated with a broken voice and ended in tears by a forty-five-year-old man.)

> "You don't trust me enough to say what you feel."

> "I could trust you enough with $20 or to drive my car two miles, but I couldn't trust you enough to reveal myself by telling you about myself."

When it is relevant to be reluctant, cool can be rejected as a mode of proper behavior. And one of the injunctions often heard during T-Group sessions was, "Don't put us on. Don't try to be so cool. Say what you feel!" The rejection of cool is an aspect of the ethos of intimacy.

The Irrelevance of Explanatory Biographical Revelation

Frequently trainers claim that "serious psychological problems" are not supposed to be treated in sensitivity training laboratories. They also state that the dynamics of treatment for such problems are not proper practices, that delegates should not demand such treatment, and that neither trainers nor delegates are supposed to practice psychotherapy during the laboratory. They claim that the T-Group is not a psychotherapy group. The focus of T-Group learning is behavioral problems in the "here and now," and the situation in the "here and now" presents the possibilities for improvement. Thus there is a proscription of the disclosure by participants of the kinds of information that they might consider suitable to reveal were they in a psychotherapeutic situation. The biography of sex and psyche is not a relevant learning practice in sensitivity training.

This prohibition enjoined, it is proper for participants to be reluctant to listen to revelations of each other's past psychosexual and other relational troubles. They can be intolerant toward each other's attempts to attribute difficulties in the "here and now" of the T-Group to experiences with "outsiders" in the "past."

While participants are not supposed to consider the help they get to be the kind that resolves serious psychological problems, they do consider the T-Group a "helping situation." In that situation they are supposed to be concerned with the effects of their behavior on each other. Hence, feedback makes sense as a therapeutic principle and an ethotic prescription: feedback, as it is generally defined in the laboratory, requires the emission of "here and now" behaviors which are considered events of the relationships in which participants are involved in the laboratory.

Persons who do begin to describe biographical details in instances where those details explicitly or implicitly are taken as offered explanations for behavior in the laboratory are often accused of wasting time and, just as often, as attempting to obfuscate the real issues. Immediate appearance is the proper substance of relations and the proper consideration of those who are relating in the T-Group.[17]

Regardless of the irrelevance of biography for explanation, such revelations are accepted in the context of documentation. Thus, while participants cannot properly refer to events in their pasts by way of "because," they can by way of "for instance." While biographical explanations are taken as obfuscations, biographical documentations are taken as personal revelations which may help participants get to know each other. In particular, such documentation may substantiate the reality of interaction troubles which have been identified as evident in the T-Group. The following T-Group exchange, I think, exemplifies the latter point.

A. "I do a good job running a business (but there's something missing)."
B. "But you're not accepted as one of the boys."
C. "Why are you respected?"
A. "Honesty and so forth."
C. "Are you accepted (for being yourself) or for running a business?"
A. "An instructor I know referred to me as a mystery man."
D. "Clark Kent."
A. "Why am I a mystery man to you?"
D. "Stereotyping. Perhaps it will change when I get to know you better."
E. "I think you want friendship even if, by God, you got to make him a friend. I don't think you have to force friendship. I don't think you can force it. Last night you said, 'Let's relate to each other in a friendly manner.' I think out of respect for you the group got together last night."
C. "Would you have been offended if no one showed up?"
A. "Would have had negative feelings toward myself."
F. "I think the more we know each other (the faster we'll learn)."

As rhetoric, the irrelevance of biographical explanation has at least two uses in T-Group sessions. Biographical revelation may be considered an evasion and the person so revealing accused of not being "really open." That accusation may be followed by the suggestion that, rather than evade the "real issues," he be "really open" and reveal his "feelings about us in the here and now." Thus, when behavior is not taken as "genuine" intimacy, the prohibition may be incorporated in a rhetoric directed toward the production of behavior which can be so taken. The following discussion in a T-Group session at Executive was resolved in a decision not to reveal biography. In spite of this decision, later biographical documentation was permitted.

A. "I asked you how you felt and you gave me an opinion. It's important to discriminate between these two."
B. "The object for study, the here and now, is what we'll learn from. I suggest that we generate a here and now to provide an optimum of feedback."
C. "I think that you're concerned and anxious about feedback."
A. "I think the sooner we tell (about our personal histories)—now I'm not necessarily proud of what I've done till this time—but if we get to know each other."

B. "Now I think we do much better without this information. Like we're doing now."

D. "Are you saying to anybody you meet, 'You have to give me your background before I'll like you?'"

A. "No, often you get to know a man just from interacting without knowing background. I've met fellows I got to know pretty well until I found out about their background."

Second, the irrelevance of biographical revelation, particularly the exclusion of psychosexual accounts in a situation where the safety of remedies is indeterminable, implies to a psychoanalytically aware, though perhaps naïve, group of participants that there is, at least, some safety by exclusion. They need not, that is, provide materials which, in their minds, could conceivably be used by other participants to do them severe damage. By excluding such revelations from intimacy in the T-Group, the revelations that are prescribed seem to provide a safer intimacy.

The Tone of Tragedy

Simmel maintained that the dyad is "a group that feels itself both endangered and irreplaceable, and thus into the real locus not only of authentic sociological tragedy, but also of sentimentalism and elegiac problems." [18] This, he felt, was so, since "the end of the union has become an organic part of its structure." [19] He felt that persons were more likely to consider larger groups as "realities" apart from particular members and thus as more permanent.

Participants in it consider the immediate sensitivity training laboratory an impermanent structure and usually regard the relationships they form in T-Groups as merely transient. Even if they expect to associate with each other outside the laboratory, they expect their outside relationships to be different. For those involved in a T-Group, "You can't go home again." Acknowledging the transcience of T-Group relations is an "organic part of its structure." [20]

Recognizing, while one is involved in a relationship, that it will end provides for "authentic sociological tragedy." The transcience of relations for participants in a laboratory, the end of which is foreseen, provides a tone of tragedy for its duration. This is particularly so, given the supposition that relationships formed during the laboratory are unique. The laboratory provides a different kind of involvement than do the relationships participants have in the outside world—or so it seems to those involved. This difference is substantiated by frequent discussions about the difficulties of forming the same kind of relationships on the outside. Reference may be made to the difficulties of being really open in other settings.

Interestingly, while the indeterminateness of remedial safety, so I think, provides for the relevance of reluctance and the rejection of cool as forms of openness, that participants consider the laboratory and the T-Group safe in other ways provides a rationale for considering relations in it to be really different. One main supposition is that the laboratory is detached from the outside world and that the boundaries of the laboratory make it a separate situation. What occurs there is considered occurrence apart from the "real reality" of their everyday lives. Further, the supposition is that the laboratory is a confidential situation in the sense that its boundaries are also boundaries of information exchange. Participants can consider themselves free from the effects of their behavior in the laboratory insofar as their everyday lives are concerned. This is similar to the interaction with a stranger that Simmel discusses. The supposed restriction of the relationship provides a freedom from effects which then seems to warrant, to participants, a greater freedom of expression. Whether such expression is "really" freer is beside the point. To those involved, it seems freer. Since the outside world seems larger, geographically, temporally, and relationally, it makes sense for participants in a sensitivity training laboratory to consider the laboratory somewhat singular and their relationships therein somewhat unique.

I have heard elegy in the laboratory: "There is a tragic note to our relationship and we're all going to feel it more in the next two days. It is a lonely life and we're not going to bridge a chasm. You reach out and it fails; you reach out again and sometimes you love. . . . And there are those lovely moments when you reach out and you love."

The tone of tragedy composed of a sense of specialness and the awareness of transcience is a supposition of the ethos of intimacy.

Intensity and Involvement: The Reality of Relating

Laboratory participants claimed that their interpersonal relations there were more intense than many of those they were involved in on the outside. One trainer defined sensitivity as an intensity of perception accompanying involvement with other people. Others said that sensitivity is an intensity of care. In the laboratory, they said, care is demonstrated by openness and feedback since these are acts of help. Persons who did not seem intensely involved in the group process were liable to be called pretty cold fish. They were told that they should loosen up.

One trainer stated that during sensitivity training, people were free to involve themselves with each other with almost the abandon of children. He claimed that by being childlike and creative they could experience a real intensity that is usually missing on the outside. Another trainer told me that only in the training laboratories in which he participated did he feel he was "really living." Everything on the outside seemed flat in comparison, he said. Claiming that he found it very difficult to communicate and to get involved with people in places other than laboratories, it seemed to him that opportunities to participate in sensitivity training provide an escape from this trouble.

Many delegates expressed amazement at the depths of emotion they were experiencing and which they considered displayed by their fellow participants.

Pragmatics support the prescription for intense involvement. (1) The supposition that the T-Group "dies" when they leave and "lives" only in their immediate interaction,[21] and the supposition that learning is a proper motive for participating—both lend sense to the assertion that intense involvement is requisite in an opportunity for learning which exists only in the immediacy of that opportunity, if learning is to occur. (2) The laboratory being considered a unique opportunity, it seems to participants that they should relish their own involvement in an experience not available to them in the outside world. In order to experience joy, it can be proposed to the delegate that it behooves him to become intensely involved in what trainers and other delegates proclaim is a really swinging experience. (3) Since in the laboratory learning is seen as a group project, a participant's failure to involve himself can be taken to reflect his lack of consideration for the others. With the involvement of all group members considered the best means toward the end of learning for all, all delegates can be urged to involve themselves lest they waste each others' time. Participants expressed concern with "not wasting our time" and "not wasting each other's time."

As in everyday life, in laboratory life persons distinguish between behavioral form, content, and style. All are considered empirical phenomena. The most convincing form and content is that performed in the style thought to be most proper.[22] The contents and forms of openness, feedback, reluctance, tragedy, are best performed in the T-Group in the style of intensity. Then one's involvement is convincing.

Trainers sometimes serve as role models for the performance of involvement in an intense style. They thus show delegates how to be convincing. One trainer, in particular, comes to mind. Hands clenched between his knees, head bowed, brows wrinkled, he spoke very slowly, his tone of voice definitely "concerned" when he said, for instance, "I really feel uncomfortable about that." After several sessions, other group members assumed the same position and imitated his tone of voice when giving feedback.

The kinesis of intensity in the laboratory is frowns, hunched shoulders, sweaty palms, nervous fidgeting, squirming in one's seat, tears, stretching, leaning forward, clenching one's fists, and the like. The paralanguage of intensity entails vocal tones of anxiousness, concern, joy, anger, hate, and fear. To be convincing when saying, "That really bothers me," it pays to frown. That is the style. Others can then decide if the speaker is "being flip." Should he "come off" in that way, he can then be told, "I don't think you really care. Maybe you're saying that so that we don't get around to you." Or he can be accused of "not being very involved here. I don't think we're getting anywhere with you." Or, "You're a man without feelings."

Of course, a form may be considered contentless. But even silence can be performed with style. In the T-Group there is a silence which indicates one's involvement and one which indicates one's boredom. The style of silence can evidence intense involvement. One can, that is, be intensely silent.

A participant's style, however, qualifies more than his own behavior. For those interacting, style evidences the quality of their relations. In the T-Group, to be intensely involved is to indicate to other members one's concern for them. In other words, it presents evidence of one's own conception of one's involvement with them. While the pragmatics of sensitivity training provide reasons for intense involvement, once the style is established and performed, participants take it as evidence of their reciprocally intense involvement with each other. Thus, after several T-Group sessions, it is quite common for members to begin to consider themselves as intimates, as friends. During final group sessions tears are not shed over the end of the learning experience so much as over the end of relationships. Love, whatever the pragmatics of its justification, then seems real enough to participants without pragmatics.

But, though intense involvement qualifies relationships (that is, given such style, it seems reasonable for group members to consider themselves to be "really relating"), on the other hand their relationships by definition seem imminently pragmatic. In sensitivity training one can regard a relationship that, on the one hand, seems "real" in the sense that participants' involvement with one another is evidently intense, on the other as merely pragmatic. In the training laboratory all relating can be considered a "part of the learning experience."

Whether such alternate interpretations qualify the reality of whatsoever intimate relations persons may form during everyday life is a question to be answered by additional and, obviously, extensive research.

Suffice it to say that in the ethos of intimacy, the reality of relationships is evidenced by an intensity of involvement and is qualified by a pragmatic interpretation. Really relating, in the sensitivity training laboratory, is considered the best way to learn. But, regardless of however intense is one's involvement, those real relationships remain merely a learning experience.

NOTES

NOTE: I am indebted to George Psathas for his help, in various ways, throughout the course of the research on the basis of which this chapter was written. Professor Psathas, Professor Lee Rainwater, and Ellen Blumenstiel read earlier versions of this material and contributed valuable comments. I have also benefited from discussion with Robert Boguslaw, Richard De Charms, Helen P. Gouldner, Martin Greenberg, William Wallis, and William L. Yancey. The errors are all mine.

1. Kenneth D. Benne, "History of the T-Group in the Laboratory Setting," in Leland P. Bradford, Jack R. Gibb, and Kenneth D. Benne, *T-Group Theory and Laboratory Method* (New York: Wiley, 1964)', p. 86.
2. Kenneth D. Benne, Leland P. Bradford, and Ronald Lippitt, "The Laboratory Method," in *ibid.*, p. 29.
3. W. G. Bennis and H. A. Shepard, "A Theory of Group Development," *Human Relations*, IX (1956), 415.
4. I am grateful to the Midwest Group for Human Resources, Dr. Vladimir Dupre, Executive Secretary, and to Dr. Charles Seashore of the National Training Laboratories for making it possible for me to attend these laboratories for research purposes in the spring and summer of 1966.
5. I found only one case in which a delegate assumed it his duty to "make as many friends here as possible," as he put it. This person in particular seemed somewhat of a boor, given his efforts to do so.
6. As Simmel put it, "Intimacy is not based on the *content* of the relationship." George Simmel, *The Sociology of George Simmel*, trans. by K. Wolff (New York: The Free Press, 1950), p. 127.
7. According to Parsons, this is a context which is "strongly charged with emotional and expressively symbolic significance, and which [is] often

considered peculiarly 'private' to the individual himself or to especially intimate relations with others." Talcott Parsons, *The Social System* (New York: The Free Press, 1951), p. 451.

8. The following, from my field notes, also exemplifies the point:
   Delegate: Have you seen any movement this morning?
   Trainer: Why ask me?
   Delegate: You're the trainer!

9. In medical situations, on the other hand, great effort may be exerted not only to get patients to stay but to calm them into a sense of security. Trainers may not resort to deceptions in order to ensure a sense of security on the part of their delegates and thus in order to inhibit expressions of reluctance. In medical situations—particularly as far as children are often concerned and in cases where equanimity on the part of a patient is by no means certain without it—the phrase, "This won't hurt at all," is, for instance, commonly enough asserted, with more or less success, to be sure. For an excellent example of such an assertion carried to great lengths under conditions of great pain, see Hanna Green, *I Never Promised You a Rose Garden* (New York: Signet, 1964), p. 45. Also see Berton Rouche, *A Man Named Hoffman* (New York: Berkley, 1965), pp. 68–82, for a discussion of the use of placebos in medicine to provide similar assurance for patients whose security is in jeopardy. In contemporary obstetrics, also, it is common to assure the prepartum mother that pain in childbirth, particularly during the first stage of labor, is nothing to fear and should not be taken as a proper motive for demanding total anesthesia (that is, it is not a proper motive for displays of great reluctance).

10. From my field notes.

11. Morton Lieberman, "The Implications of a Total Group Phenomena Analysis for Patients and Therapists," *International Journal of Group Psychotherapy*, XVII, No. 1 (January, 1967), 75.

12. *Ibid.*

13. *Ibid.*

14. National Training Laboratories, *Reading Book, Twentieth Annual Summer Laboratories in Human Relations Training, 1966* (Washington: National Training Laboratories, National Education Association, 1966), p. 65.

15. While, to the uninitiated, this might seem a skilled trainer intervention and thus inferred to be evidence of his professional capabilities, for those involved in a T-Group that the trainer said this is practically incidental. Anyone could have.

16. Here, the trainer, should he wish, could claim some "professional skill" in the situation. He could claim to be "more sensitive to the issues."

17. As another writer observed, "At Bethel there was no exploration of the members' anxiety or its origin and no discussion of other aspects of their lives. Only interpersonal feelings evidenced in the immediate

sessions were subject to comment." Helen E. Durkin, *The Group in Depth* (New York: International Universities Press, 1964), p. 60.

18. Simmel, *op. cit.*, p. 124.

19. *Ibid.*

20. As one trainer put it, and I paraphrase his statement, "Now that we've learned to love, we have to learn to leave those we love."

21. Participants use the terms "live" and "die" in reference to the duration and termination of both T-Groups and entire training laboratories.

22. For those familiar with his works, my debt to Erving Goffman should here be apparent. For those who are not, I recommend in particular *The Presentation of Self in Everyday Life* (Garden City, N.Y.: Doubleday Anchor, 1959); *Stigma* (Englewood Cliffs: Prentice-Hall, 1963); and *Interaction Ritual* (Garden City, N.Y.: Doubleday Anchor, 1967), particularly pp. 5–46 and 113–136, in reference to this point.

Index